Whatever piques our curiosity and holds our interest—useful or not—has cultural or intellectual value. Never sneer at the still, small voice within you that breathes, "So that's where that came from!" Words are tools to be examined for their provenance and honed to meet expression's present needs; if meaning-mining loses its attraction, then what's a metaphor? And the more we poke around in the language, trying the doors, the more avenues are opened for exploration. . . . All too often we lurch through our lives, metaphorically wise and etymologically ignorant, using tropes like dopes, seldom lifting the lid of our daily discourse to examine the history within.

—*William Safire*[1]

FROM LITERAL TO LITERARY

The Essential Reference Book for Biblical Metaphors

JAMES ROWE ADAMS

THE
PILGRIM
PRESS

Cleveland

In association with
The Center for Progressive Christianity

In memory of Charles F. Adams and Charles F. Penniman

The Pilgrim Press
700 Prospect Avenue
Cleveland, OH 44115-1100
thepilgrimpress.com

In association with The Center for Progressive Christianity

Previously published by
Rising Star Press, Bend, Oregon

Printed in the United States of America on acid-free paper with post-consumer fiber

12 11 10 09 08   5 4 3 2 1

Library of Congress Cataloging-in-Publication Data

Adams, James R., 1934-
  From literal to literary : the essential reference book for biblical metaphors / by James Rowe Adams. --
2nd ed.
      p. cm.
  Includes bibliographical references and index.
  ISBN 978-0-8298-1788-1 (alk. paper)
  1. Metaphor in the Bible. 2. Bible--Language, style. I. Title.
  BS537.A33 2008
  220.6'6--dc22
                    2007048002

CONTENTS

INTRODUCTION

All religions are approximately equally
inadequate metaphors for the same reality.
— RABBI NEIL KOMINSKY

Personal commitment to an organized religion in most of the industrialized western world has declined almost to the vanishing point. Church attendance in North America and Ireland appears to be the exception, but both countries show evidence of the general trend toward secularism. At the same time, however, interest in matters loosely labeled "spiritual" may be at an all-time high. Fascination with the mysteries of life and death has drawn people to motion picture theaters to see fantasies such as *Harry Potter* and *Lord of the Rings* while preachers in mainline churches on a Sunday morning look out over rows of empty pews. Too many preachers have ignored the fact that if there is another reality beyond the one people can see, touch, and feel, that realm can be reached most effectively through fantasy, and fantasy's partners—metaphors and extended metaphors such as art, poetry, drama, music, dance, and myth. Like knotholes in a fence around a construction site, metaphors allow the curious to peek into the realm of God.

Some people have problems with metaphors. The poet John Brehm had one of these metaphorically challenged people in a freshman class that was studying Matthew Arnold's classic nineteenth-century poem "Dover Beach," which likens the decline of organized religion to the outgoing tide of the "Sea of Faith."[2] When the student complained that the expression confused her, the teacher gently asked what confused her about it.

"I mean, is it a real sea?" she asked.

"You mean, is it a real body of water that you could point to on a map or visit on vacation?"

"Yes," she said. "Is it a *real* sea?"

Those lines of dialogue are now part of a poem Brehm wrote—a poem that continues with the words he wanted to say, but did not.

"It is a real sea. In fact it flows
right into the Sea of Ignorance,
IN WHICH YOU ARE DROWNING.
Let me throw you a Rope of Salvation
before the Sharks of Desire gobble you up.
Let me hoist you back up onto this Ship of Fools
so that we might continue our search
for the Fountain of Youth. Here take a drink
of this. It's fresh from the River of Forgetfulness."

The poet himself has been a freelance (and no, he doesn't carry a large spear) writer living in Brooklyn, New York.

In my opinion, Christians who can't cope with metaphors have done their best, perhaps unintentionally, to spoil the faith for the rest of us. Part of progressive Christianity's task is to reclaim the classic metaphors for what they are: figures of speech that inspired beautiful narratives. To name a few: Son of God, Resurrection of the Dead, Body of Christ, and Kingdom of Heaven.

Over the years, many people have abandoned Christianity because their teachers and preachers were metaphorically disabled. Once they discover that religious language is primarily figurative by nature, the experience of faith can open up for them. You can be a follower of Jesus without thinking that "heaven" is a place, that a "son" has to be a biological relative, or that "dead" necessarily refers to the condition you're in when the undertaker comes for you.

Most terms used to express religious concepts began life as the names for concrete objects or observable actions. When sages and prophets needed to express abstract concepts, they seized upon familiar words that would give their followers a vivid picture of what they had in mind. For example, both Hebrew- and Greek-speaking teachers used a familiar picture to identify self-destructive behavior. They used a word that meant "the hunter missed what he had aimed for." This metaphorical use of a verb related to hunting in English is translated as "sin."

Some will argue that by the time the many metaphors appeared in the writings that became the Bible, the words could have taken on new connotations. This is the same problem that J. R. R. Tolkien identified in connection with translating Anglo-Saxon poetry into modern English. In his prefatory remarks for an edition of *Beowulf*, he pointed out that the translator often cannot tell if or when a colorful description had become the accepted name for a thing. For example, at some point did "wall roots" become the common name for what we would call "foundations"? Looking back over the centuries in which the various parts of the Bible were written, we cannot tell when a transition from a metaphor to the name for a thing or for a kind of behavior might have taken place. This dictionary stresses the colorful metaphor at the possible expense of a biblical author or editor's intended meaning.

People frequently communicate with colorful language when the meaning of the original metaphor has long been forgotten. Today, people speak of antagonists engaged in a vigorous argument as being "at loggerheads." Although the speaker and the listener may not have the faintest idea of what a loggerhead might be, they understand each other. People may enrich their communication, however, by becoming aware of the vivid pictures that gave rise to their figures of speech. The expression "at loggerheads" takes on new intensity when you realize that a loggerhead was a long pole with an iron ball on one end. Sailors in the nineteenth century heated the iron balls to melt tar, but sometimes they employed the tools to settle arguments. They swung them at each other's legs, trying to inflict severe damage and, if possible, to break bones. Just as the picture of sailors literally at loggerheads can enrich the metaphor for people who come across it, the literal meaning of the original metaphors employed in the Christian tradition can stimulate the imaginations of today's readers. For a reader to get a glimpse of God's realm, it does not matter whether the biblical author or editor knew the origin of a particular metaphor being employed.

A few authors of documents that are regarded as holy scripture let their readers know that they were writing metaphorical language. The author of the Gospel according to John is one of them. Near the beginning of the book (Chapter 3), the author tells a story about a leader of the Jews named Nicodemus who completely missed the point of what Jesus was saying by taking literally Jesus's words about being born anew: "How can anyone be born after having grown old? Can one enter a second time into the mother's womb and be born?" Then, toward the end of the book (Chapter 16), the author again reminds the reader about the nature of this kind of writing by attributing to Jesus the comment, "I have said these things to you in figures of speech."

St. Paul's letters show that he had little interest in taking the Hebrew Scriptures, his Bible, as being either historical or factual. Writing to the community in Corinth about the Exodus events, he said, "These things happened to them to serve as an example, and they were written down to instruct us." (I Corinthians 10:11) The Greek word Paul used for "warning" was *typos.*, which originally meant a blow from a hammer and then a mark left by a blow, hence our word "type." In other words, Paul looked at the ancient stories as marks along the way, trailblazes, that offer guidance on life's journey. Paul revealed in a letter to the Jesus followers in Galatia how he found guidance in such stories. In reviewing the story of Abraham, Sarah, and Hagar, he wrote: "Now this is an allegory." (Galatians 4:24) Paul does not question the historical accuracy of the stories, but at no point does he suggest that anyone could find the meaning of the ancient texts by taking them literally. To be useful in drawing the reader into the realm where ultimate meaning may be glimpsed, scripture must be read as metaphor.

The beauty of returning to the original metaphorical language is that this approach opens up the wisdom of the ancients to twenty-first century readers who may not be of a theist or a supernaturalist persuasion. Thinking people who have been educated in the natural sciences can approach the Bible and Christian tradition without compromising their intellectual integrity. When biblical language is understood primarily as metaphor, the insights of the scriptures are revealed to the skeptic as well as the conventional Christian, to believer and doubter alike.

ACKNOWLEDGMENTS

The two men to whom I have dedicated this book—Charles F. Adams and Charles F. Penniman—instilled in me a curiosity about language that eventually propelled me into assembling this collection of biblical metaphors with their Hebrew and Greek roots.

Charles Adams was my father. A country lawyer, he had a concern for precision in the language used for laws and contracts. Our dinner table conversations often turned to the exact meaning of words. Whenever a disagreement arose, he would suggest that somebody fetch the dictionary. During my childhood, we wore out more than one dictionary as a result of these meal-time discussions.

Charles Penniman was the director of the Educational Center in St. Louis when I first met him in 1962. In supervising my parish work in Christian education, he often reflected on the issues that arose in classes by opening up a Greek word to expose the original image contained in the root. Many of the explications of these key Christian concepts appear in a document the Educational Center published in July 1956: "Things It Should Help Us All to Know." I have drawn heavily from that resource, for which I wrote a detailed commentary in 1980.

In spite of my interest in words and their origins, I might not have worked toward publication if it had not been for Cynthia Shattuck, the editor of Cowley Publications, with whom I had worked on three books. In 1997, shortly after I retired from parish ministry, Cynthia suggested that I produce a dictionary of religious terms for people who have problems with organized religion. I have worked on the project intermittently ever since.

In the final stages of the project, two people have been of invaluable help: Lawrence Wills and Jonathan Wortmann.

Lawrence Wills is a professor of biblical studies at the Episcopal Divinity School in Cambridge, Massachusetts. One of his many scholarly gifts is transliterating ancient languages into English in a way that approximates the original sounds of the words without requiring the use of esoteric markings favored by some of his fellow scholars. This was particularly important for transliterating Hebrew, a process for which no consensus has emerged in the field. Larry also pointed out several places where I had written about a theory that appealed to me as if it were generally accepted by experts when such is not the case. Of course, I have to take responsibility for any errors that remain in the text.

Jonathan Wortmann is the pastor of Pilgrim Congregational Church in Southborough, Massachusetts, and the New England Coordinator for The Center for Progressive Christianity. After seeing early drafts of some entries, Jon came up with the idea that the book might be written in a way that could be useful to conservative and evangelical Christians in addition to the "people who have problems with organized religion." He has been unstinting in volunteering his time to go through the entire manuscript, pointing out the places where I had been needlessly offensive to conventional Christians and where I had been pushing ideas that did not necessarily arise from the metaphor under consideration. If any offensive or tangential remarks remain, I must take the blame for not always accepting Jon's advice.

The only other people who have seen parts of the manuscript in process are the members of my retired clergy colleague group. When it was my turn to make a presentation, I circulated a number of entries for discussion. I have incorporated many of their comments and am grateful for them.

For the first edition, one of the most delightful aspects of assembling the book was the collaboration with the illustrator, Hannah Bonner, whose sensitive and humorous drawings I have long admired. I also must express my appreciation for the patience that Donna Jacobsen, editor of Rising Star Press, exhibited. Donna at all times was an understanding and encouraging collaborator in each edition of this project.

USING THIS BOOK

To make this book as easy to use as possible, I have not included abbreviations or cited passages in the Bible for the reader to look up. To avoid duplication of information, I have placed an asterisk (*), with an explanatory footnote at the bottom of each page, after each word in the text that has its own entry.

I have taken most of the Bible quotations directly from the New Revised Standard Version. In order to clarify the context of some passages, however, I have replaced pronouns with their antecedents. Where other translations appear, I have identified them. Readers who are accustomed to using other versions of the Bible might want to compare passages to see how particular metaphors have been handled.

On page 328, I have included an "Index to the Hebrew and Greek Words" that appear in the text; on page 344, an "Index of Bible Citations" and the entries under which they appear are also provided.

Transliterations—the writing of Hebrew and Greek words with the sounds of the American English alphabet—are at best approximations and do not always make clear how the words originally might have been pronounced or how they are pronounced by speakers of those languages today. Although inexact, in order to facilitate discussion of the ancient words, I have included "Pronouncing Transliterated Hebrew and Greek Words" on page 15.

Readers who want to pursue the subject of the Hebrew and Greek metaphors on their own might make good use of the electronic tool that I have found most helpful: QuickVerse Version 4.0 produced by Parson's Technology. Although many subsequent versions have appeared, Version 4.0 remains unsurpassed for simplicity and efficiency. It is still available for downloading from the Internet. With this version, I kept on the computer monitor in parallel columns the New Revised Standard Version, the King James Version, and Strong's transliteration of the Hebrew and Greek words.[3] At the bottom of the Strong's column, I kept a small window open for Strong's dictionary. Strong's work, now somewhat out of date, follows the word order of the King James Version. When you do a word search in either the King James Version or *Strong's Concordance*, the program highlights the corresponding word in the other, which is why I kept the old translation on the screen along with the modern one. With a computer and a decent Bible program, biblical metaphors is a game that anybody can play.

PRONOUNCING TRANSLITERATED HEBREW AND GREEK WORDS

Each vowel has a particular sound but not always the one that first comes to mind.

a is *ah*, as in "father"
e is *ay*, as in "neighbor," or *eh* as in "end"
i is *ee*, as in "petite"
o is *oh*, as in "hope"
u is *uh*, as in "up"
y is also *uh* for Greek words
y is *ee*, as in "see" for Hebrew words—when it is not a consonant

Combination vowels (diphthongs) have predictable sounds.

au is *aw,* as in "author"
ei is *ih*, as in "sit"
eu is *yoo*, as in "eulogy"
io is *yo*, as in "fiord"
oi is *oy*, as in "boil"

Double vowels are always two separate syllables.

baal is *bah-ahl*
raah is *rah-ah*
eleeo is *ayl-ay-ay-oh*
teleioo is *tayl-ih-oh-oh*

A final *vowel* is never silent.

chay is *chah-ee*
pyle is *puh-lay*
yare is *yah-ray*

Consonants sound as they do in English, but …

g is always hard, as in "get"; never soft, as in "George"

ch in Hebrew words stands for a sound that does not exist in English but occurs in the German *ach* and the Scotts *loch*

A

Abba, *noun*   The word for father in the Aramaic language appears untranslated in the Greek portions of the Bible* and in most English versions. Some people have tried to make a theological statement based on Jesus's use of Abba, which appears similar to a toddler's expression of intimacy with a father, such as dada and papa. By using the term, Jesus is supposed to have broken with Jewish tradition, which required the use of more formal terms in addressing God.* This attempt to show the superiority of Christianity to Judaism is based more on a need to make Christianity unique than on the available evidence:

- The Hebrew Scriptures provide ample evidence that Jews called on God as *ab*, Father.*
- Aramaic had no formal word for father. If Jesus did follow a Jewish custom in calling God "Father" in the Aramaic language, he had to say "Abba."

Although the gospels in many places report that Jesus called God "Father," in only one instance do the gospels relate a story in which he uses Abba, and that was at a moment when no one could have heard him. He was praying alone in the Garden of Gethsemane before his arrest and execution.

> He said, **"Abba,** Father, for you all things are possible; remove this cup from me; yet, not what I want, but what you want." [Mark 14:36]

Elsewhere in the gospels, in words attributed to him, Jesus speaks of God as *Pater*, the formal Greek term for father.

> Look at the birds of the air; they neither sow nor reap nor gather into barns, and yet your heavenly **Father** feeds them. Are you not of more value than they? [Matthew 6:26]

> Jesus said to them, "Why were you searching for me? Did you not know that I must be in my **Father's** house?" [Luke 2:49]

> Philip said to him, "Lord, show us the Father, and we will be satisfied." Jesus said to him, "Have I been with you all this time, Philip, and you still do not know me? Whoever has seen me has seen the Father. How can you say, 'Show us the **Father**'?" [John 14:8-9]

If Jesus ever taught in common Greek, as some suppose he must have done on occasion, he could have referred to God familiarly as *papas*, a word that was in use by children at that time. If Jesus ever called God *papas*, nobody bothered to write it down.

The Christian fondness for Abba may owe more to St. Paul than to Jesus. In two letters, which most people accept as being genuinely from Paul, he includes the term.

> For you did not receive a spirit of slavery to fall back into fear, but you have received a spirit of adoption. When we cry, **"Abba! Father!"** it is that very Spirit bearing witness with our spirit that we are children of God, and if children, then heirs, heirs of God and joint heirs with Christ—if, in fact, we suffer with him so that we may also be glorified with him. [Romans 8:15-17]

> And because you are children, God has sent the Spirit of his Son into our hearts, crying, **"Abba!** Father!"** [Galatians 4:6]

If Jesus prayed in Aramaic, his possible use of Abba indicates nothing more than his following a tradition dating back to the formation of the Hebrew Scriptures, but the metaphor has proved to be useful to succeeding generations. Because of its similarity to words children now use when they are

Marks a word in the text that has its own entry

small and dependent on their fathers, Abba does not carry all of the negative emotional baggage attached to Father. A Father can be remote, stern, demanding, and punitive, but a Dada or a Papa enfolds the child lovingly and protectively in his arms.

Helpful as the Abba metaphor may be, a word of caution is in order: If overused, the term has a way of domesticating or trivializing God. If God becomes too sweet and cuddly, a person might lose the sense of being accountable to God for every decision and every action taken.

abomination, *noun;* **abhorrent, abominable**, *adjectives*   The English concept of abomination is used to translate four Hebrew words, the most common being *to'evah*. The word is used to describe an object, behavior, custom, or cult practice that evokes disgust, hatred, loathing, revulsion, or even nausea. Until the seventeenth century, the aptness of the English translation was more apparent because of the letter "h," which disappeared from abhomination and abhominable. With the old spelling, the words clearly meant away from mankind, inhuman. People throughout history have used such terms to differentiate themselves from other religious groups or cultures and to show their superiority to them. *To'evah* appears in Genesis and Exodus describing the attitude of the Egyptians toward the table manners of the Hebrews.

> Egyptians could not eat with the Hebrews, for that is an **abomination** to the Egyptians.
> [Genesis 43:32]

The Egyptians had the same feeling about the Hebrews' most common occupation, herding sheep.

> All shepherds are **abhorrent** to the Egyptians. [Genesis 46:34]

The Egyptians had similar reactions to the worship practices of the Hebrews.

> And Pharaoh called for Moses and for Aaron, and said, Go ye, sacrifice to your God in the land. And Moses said, It is not meet so to do; for we shall sacrifice the **abomination** of the Egyptians to the LORD our God: lo, shall we sacrifice the **abomination** of the Egyptians before their eyes, and will they not stone us? [Exodus 8:25-26, KING JAMES VERSION]

Just as Genesis shows how the Egyptians wanted to keep themselves distinct from the foreigners in their midst, other books of the Bible illustrate how the Hebrew-speaking people attempted to differentiate themselves from the Canaanites among whom they had settled. They employ *to'evah* to declare the superiority of their culture and religion to the indigenous culture and the fertility cults in Canaan.

> You shall not lie with a male as with a woman; it is an **abomination**. [Leviticus 18:22]

> The images of their gods you shall burn with fire. Do not covet the silver or the gold that is on them and take it for yourself, because you could be ensnared by it; for it is **abhorrent** to the LORD your God. [Deuteronomy 7:25]

> You shall not eat any **abhorrent thing** . . . Yet of those that chew the cud or have the hoof cleft you shall not eat these: the camel, the hare, and the rock badger, because they chew the cud but do not divide the hoof; they are unclean for you. And the pig, because it divides the hoof but does not chew the cud, is unclean for you. You shall not eat their meat, and you shall not touch their carcasses. [Deuteronomy 14:3, 7-8]

Marks a word in the text that has its own entry

> Ahaz walked in the way of the kings of Israel. He even made his son pass through fire, according to the **abominable** practices of the nations whom the LORD drove out before the people of Israel. [II Kings 16:3]

Later books of the Bible go beyond an emphasis on cultural differences and use *to'evah* in describing God's reaction to unethical behavior. For example, in the book of Proverbs, God loathes violence, lying, arrogance, and cheating in business.

> Do not envy the violent and do not choose any of their ways; for the perverse are an **abomination** to the LORD, but the upright are in his confidence. [Proverbs 3:31-32]

> There are six things that the LORD hates, seven that are an **abomination** to him: haughty eyes, a lying tongue, and hands that shed innocent blood, a heart that devises wicked plans, feet that hurry to run to evil, a lying witness who testifies falsely, and one who sows discord in a family. [Proverbs 6:16-19]

> All those who are arrogant are an **abomination** to the LORD; be assured, they will not go unpunished. [Proverbs 16:5]

In more recent times, some Christian groups have chosen to ignore the moral imperatives attached to the abomination metaphor and have focused their attention on cultural differences with some identifiable groups in their midst. In order to show their superiority to gay and lesbian people, they pick and choose among the practices that were abominations for the Hebrews living among the Canaanites. They may see nothing wrong with wearing silver jewelry with Native American symbols or eating pork, but they denounce love-making between homosexuals.* They often ignore the biblical context of the abominations that had to do with ritual purity* rather than with morals. The context of the prohibition of sexual intercourse with cult prostitutes—temple employees of both sexes identified as sodomites* in the King James Version of the Bible—is the Purity Code.

As an attitude of God, abomination started out as a metaphor. The ancient writers did not mean that God literally felt like throwing up. As a metaphor, it can still be useful as long as those who use it remember that whatever they find disgusting can be the result of cultural conditioning. For example, the eating of dogs in China is an abomination for most Americans, while the eating of beef in America is an abomination for the Hindus in India; the drinking of wine in Christian rituals is an abomination to some fundamentalists, while the handling of snakes in fundamentalist worship is an abomination to mainline Protestants and Catholics. Whatever a speaker finds abhorrent tells the listener more about the speaker than about the object of the speaker's disgust.

People using the abomination metaphor would be on safer ground if they limited their use of the term to the moral issues raised in the book of Proverbs. Behavior that oppresses or injures other people is usually abominable.

adam, *noun*   In the Hebrew Scriptures, *adam* has several meanings. *Adam* can be the color red. It can be the name of a mythological character who makes his first appearance in the early chapters of Genesis or the name of a town in Palestine. *Adam* can stand for humanity in general, for people of low degree, or for the male of the human species. No one can determine with any degree of certainty which was the original meaning and which were the derivative metaphors. The puzzle is confounded by the fact that the feminine form of *adam—adamah—*means earth or soil. At any rate, the connections are fairly obvious. Light-skinned people show red blood in their faces when experiencing physical or emotional stress. The dirt of a plowed field can have a reddish color. The ancient storytellers could have chosen the name Adam for their character because the word represented all people. Or the word for human being and the color red could have evolved from the name of the character in the story.

Whether an ancient form or a more recent metaphor, as a color *adam* appears at several places in the Hebrew Scriptures.

> Come now, let us argue it out, says the LORD: though your sins are like scarlet, they shall be like snow; though they are **red** like crimson, they shall become like wool. [Isaiah 1:18]

> Her princes were purer than snow, whiter than milk; their bodies were more **ruddy** than coral, their hair like sapphire. [Lamentations 4:7]

In the King James Version of the Bible, Adam is introduced in the second chapter of Genesis; in the New Revised Standard Version, *adam* does not become a person's name until the fourth chapter.

> **Adam** knew his wife again, and she bore a son and named him Seth, for she said, "God has appointed for me another child instead of Abel, because Cain killed him." [Genesis 4:25]

Before this point in the story, the modern translators preferred to use the generic term, the man, rather than the name Adam. In this case, the translators saw *adam* meaning the male of the human species, but that is an unusual meaning for the word. The word for a male human being is *ish*, as opposed to a woman, *ishah*. Some scholars argue that the point of the story has been obscured by translating *adam* as man. The point is that a sexually undifferentiated human creature was divided into two distinct parts: male and female.

> Then the LORD God said, "It is not good that the **man** should be alone; I will make him a helper as his partner." So out of the ground (*adamah*) the LORD God formed every animal of the field and every bird of the air, and brought them to the **man** to see what he would call them; and whatever the man called every living creature, that was its name. The **man** gave names to all cattle, and to the birds of the air, and to every animal of the field; but for the **man** there was not found a helper as his partner. So the LORD God caused a deep sleep to fall upon the **man**, and he slept; then he took one of his ribs and closed up its place with flesh. And the rib that the LORD God had taken from the man he made into a woman and brought her to the **man**. Then the **man** said, "This at last is bone of my bones and flesh of my flesh; this one shall be called Woman (*ishah*), for out of Man (*ish*) this one was taken." [Genesis 2:18-23]

Nearly always, *adam* appears to mean the whole human race, both male and female. That is the way the word generally has been understood. At the time of the early English translations of the Bible, the word man had not acquired its objectionable connotation of exclusive maleness and was often used where *adam* meant human beings in general. What is true for *adam* is also true for the expanded phrase *ben adam*, which in early versions was nearly always son of man.* To be inclusive, except for their slip with Genesis 2, the translators of the New Revised Standard Version have found various ways to avoid using man for *adam*.

> Then God said, "Let us make **humankind** in our image, according to our likeness; and let them have dominion over the fish of the sea, and over the birds of the air, and over the cattle, and over all the wild animals of the earth, and over every creeping thing that creeps upon the earth." [Genesis 1:26]

Moreover the Glory of Israel will not recant or change his mind; for he is not a **mortal**, that he should change his mind. [I Samuel 15:29]

The God of Israel has spoken, the Rock of Israel has said to me: One who rules over **people** justly, ruling in the fear of God, is like the light of morning, like the sun rising on a cloudless morning, gleaming from the rain on the grassy land. [II Samuel 23:3-4]

Whatever prayer, whatever plea there is from any **individual** or from all your people Israel, all knowing the afflictions of their own hearts so that they stretch out their hands toward this house; then hear in heaven your dwelling place, forgive, act, and render to all whose hearts you know—according to all their ways, for only you know what is in every **human** heart. [I Kings 8:38-39]

And you warned them in order to turn them back to your law. Yet they acted presumptuously and did not obey your commandments, but sinned against your ordinances, by the observance of which a **person** shall live. They turned a stubborn shoulder and stiffened their neck and would not obey. [Nehemiah 9:29]

If I sin, what do I do to you, you watcher of **humanity**? Why have you made me your target? Why have I become a burden to you? [Job 7:20]

If I have concealed my transgressions as **others** do, by hiding my iniquity in my bosom, because I stood in great fear of the multitude, and the contempt of families terrified me, so that I kept silence, and did not go out of doors. [Job 31:33-34]

Then I said, "How long, O Lord?" And he said: "Until cities lie waste without **inhabitant**, and houses without people, and the land is utterly desolate." [Isaiah 6:11]

The LORD of hosts has sworn by himself: Surely I will fill you with **troops** like a swarm of locusts, and they shall raise a shout of victory over you. [Jeremiah 51:14]

I will multiply your **population**, the whole house of Israel, all of it; the towns shall be inhabited and the waste places rebuilt; and I will multiply **human beings** and animals upon you. [Ezekiel 36:10-11]

Often the translators tried to keep the inclusive sense of *adam* by resorting to an impersonal form, "one," or simply a pronoun.

And even this was a small thing in your sight, O God; you have also spoken of your servant's house for a great while to come. You regard me as **someone** of high rank, O LORD God! [I Chronicles 17:17]

O how abundant is your goodness that you have laid up for those who fear you, and accomplished for those who take refuge in you, in the sight of **everyone**! [Psalm 31:19]

Happy are **those** to whom the LORD imputes no iniquity, and in whose spirit there is no deceit. [Psalm 32:2]

The LORD knows **our** thoughts, that they are but an empty breath. [Psalm 94:11]

They are like a breath; their days are like a passing shadow. [Psalm 144:4]

Whoever wanders from the way of understanding will rest in the assembly of the dead. [Proverbs 21:16]

Another technique in translating *adam* in a sexually inclusive manner has been to fold it into the qualifying adjective that accompanies it. *Adam* + an adjective frequently becomes a noun in the book of Proverbs.

> A **scoundrel** and a villain goes around with crooked speech. [Proverbs 6:12]

> When the **wicked** die, their hope perishes, and the expectation of the godless comes to nothing. [Proverbs 11:7]

> A wise child makes a glad father, but the **foolish** despise their mothers. [Proverbs 15:20]

> For a prostitute is a deep pit; an adulteress is a narrow well. She lies in wait like a robber and increases the number of the **faithless**. [Proverbs 23:27-28]

All these negative adjectives attached to *adam* are a reminder that the word was sometimes used by a Hebrew author or editor to identify people of a lower class or of a common sort. This use of *adam* shows up in the English translations.

> Samson said to her, "If they bind me with seven fresh bowstrings that are not dried out, then I shall become weak, and be like **anyone else**." [Judges 16:7]

> They captured their livestock: fifty thousand of their camels, two hundred fifty thousand sheep, two thousand donkeys, and one hundred thousand **captives**. [I Chronicles 5:21]

> The sound of a raucous multitude was around her, with many of the **rabble** brought in drunken from the wilderness. [Ezekiel 23:42]

The only drawback to this system of finding English words to fit the context in which *adam* appears is that the translators have obscured the importance of the metaphor in Hebrew thought. From reading English translations of the Hebrew Scriptures, one would never know that *adam* occurs 580 times.

In the early Christian writings, the Greek *anthropos* appears to be the equivalent of the Hebrew *adam* while *aner* is the equivalent of *ish*. The word *adam* itself appears, however, in a transliterated Greek form in letters of Paul and in letters by Paul's imitators. These examples come from letters that most agree were from Paul himself.

> Yet death exercised dominion from **Adam** to Moses, even over those whose sins were not like the transgression of **Adam**, who is a type of the one who was to come. [Romans 5:14]

> For since death came through a human being (*anthropos*), the resurrection of the dead has also come through a human being (*anthropos*); for as all die in **Adam**, so all will be made alive in Christ. [I Corinthians 15:21-22]

> Thus it is written, "The first man (*anthropos*), **Adam**, became a living being"; the last **Adam** became a life-giving spirit. [I Corinthians 15:45]

Paul appears to use the mythological character from Genesis as a metaphor indicating the whole human race. In choosing *adam* to stand for humanity, Paul was probably aware of the Hebrew connotations suggesting that people are less than they might be. Christ,* however, has become a new sort of *adam*. In becoming one with Christ, people have the opportunity of fulfilling more of their potential.

Marks a word in the text that has its own entry

For some of Jesus's followers, Adam is primarily the name of the first man in history, the progenitor of the whole human race; for others, making Adam an historical figure obscures the rich insights that are conveyed through the *adam* metaphor.

advocate, *noun* and *verb*   In earlier translations of the Bible into English, the Greek word rendered advocate in the New Revised Standard Version came out comforter or counselor. All three choices obscure the original metaphor. The word in question is *parakletos,* derived from the verb *parakaleo—para,* with or alongside of + *kaleo,* to call. *Kaleo* is the same verb that is the basis for the Greek word translated as church.* *Parakaleo* means to call to one's side, while the word for church means to call from or to call out of. The author of the Gospel according to John has Jesus saying that God would send the disciples another *parakletos,* the Holy Spirit, the Spirit of truth.* This seems to mean that they would be able to call the Spirit to their side much as a defendant in a judicial hearing would call on an attorney to plead the case. Some Christian theologians, however, insist that John's gospel implies that the Spirit, like their first *parakletos* Jesus, would do the calling and that the disciples have only to respond.

> I will ask the Father, and he will give you another **Advocate,** to be with you forever. This is the Spirit of truth. [John 14:16-17]

> The **Advocate,** the Holy Spirit, whom the Father will send in my name, will teach you everything, and remind you of all that I have said to you. [John 14:26]

This Greek title *parakletos* has been so important to the followers of Jesus that many of them still refer to the Holy Spirit* as the Paraclete. In calling the Spirit another *parakletos,* however, John implies that Jesus himself functions as a paraclete. The First Epistle of John makes that claim explicit.

> My little children, I am writing these things to you so that you may not sin. But if anyone does sin, we have an **advocate** with the Father, Jesus Christ the righteous. [I John 2:1]

When *parakaleo* appears in the text as a verb, the New Revised Standard Version translates it with a wide variety of English expressions. Each of these words or phrases opens the way to a better understanding of what the early followers of Jesus meant when they insisted that they had found one whom they could call to their side.

> Blessed are those who mourn, for they will be **comforted**. [Matthew 5:4]

> A leper came to him **begging** him, and kneeling he said to him, "If you choose, you can make me clean." [Mark 1:40]

> When they came to Jesus, they **appealed** to him earnestly, saying, "The centurion is worthy of having you do this for him, for he loves our people, and it is he who built our synagogue for us." [Luke 7:4-5]

> "A voice was heard in Ramah, wailing and loud lamentation, Rachel weeping for her children; she refused to be **consoled**, because they are no more." [Matthew 2:18]

> Then he became angry and refused to go in. His father came out and began to **plead** with him. [Luke 15:28]

> Peter testified with many other arguments and **exhorted** them, saying, "Save yourselves from this corrupt generation." [Acts 2:40]

> Philip ran up to the Ethiopian eunuch and heard him reading the prophet Isaiah. He asked, "Do you understand what you are reading?" He replied, "How can I, unless someone guides me?" And he **invited** Philip to get in and sit beside him. [Acts 8:30-31]

> As Paul and Barnabas were going out, the people **urged** them to speak about these things again the next sabbath. [Acts 13:42]

> Paul and Barnabas strengthened the souls of the disciples and **encouraged** them to continue in the faith, saying, "It is through many persecutions that we must enter the kingdom of God." [Acts 14:22]

> For this reason therefore I have **asked to see** you and speak with you, since it is for the sake of the hope of Israel that I am bound with this chain. [Acts 28:20]

> When reviled, we bless; when persecuted, we endure; when slandered, we **speak** kindly. [I Corinthians 4:12-13]

Although this great variety of English translations for *parakaleo* brings out the nuances of this verb, the variations also obscure the importance of this word in the early Christian narrative. The word occurs more than one hundred times in the gospels and epistles. This constant use of the verb suggests that when the writers use the noun *parakletos* in reference to the Holy Spirit* and to Jesus, they are expressing a vital aspect of their faith: they will never again be utterly alone.

The fear of abandonment is basic to human nature. A sensitive adult watching a screaming two-year-old child cling to her mother's knees at the door of a nursery can immediately identify with the child. The child is afraid of being left alone. That fear never goes completely away. Having a spouse or a partner or a buddy can help alleviate the fear to some extent, but it continues to lurk just below the level of consciousness. An intimate relationship can help develop an understanding of what kind of experience most effectively puts the fear to rest. It is not pats on the head or good advice or soothing words. What makes a difference is to know that, when called, the other person will be there—alongside. This is the wisdom of the school master in ancient Israel:

> Two are better than one, because they have a good reward for their toil. For if they fall, one will lift up the other; but woe to one who is alone and falls and does not have another to help. Again, if two lie together, they keep warm; but how can one keep warm alone? [Ecclesiastes 4:9-11]

What happens to someone who has never had a special person? What happens when the spouse or partner or buddy will not or cannot respond? What happens in each case is similar to the experience of the disciples when Jesus was taken away from them and killed. In spite of the fear in each disciple of being left alone, they discovered that when they called out, Jesus was somehow still with them in spirit. Through the ages, other followers of Jesus have had similar experiences of terrible loneliness but not feeling utterly alone. They cannot explain that experience, but some of them have said it was as if Jesus or the Spirit had come to their side.

agnostic, *noun* and *adjective*   The nineteenth-century British naturalist Thomas Henry Huxley[4] coined the word agnostic to describe his religious position. He reported that he had taken the term from *agnostos,* which appears in the Acts of Apostles account of St. Paul's visit to the Areopagus in Athens. *Agnostos* is the negative particle *a,* meaning not or without, plus *gnostos,* the word for known.

Marks a word in the text that has its own entry

> For as I went through the city and looked carefully at the objects of your worship, I found among them an altar with the inscription, "To an **unknown** god." [Acts 17:23]

Huxley wrote, "Most of my colleagues were 'ists' of one sort or another ... so I took thought, and invented what I conceived to be the appropriate title of 'agnostic.'" He rejected the charge of atheism that his critics leveled against him, insisting that spiritual inquiry is a more elevated undertaking than slavish belief or disbelief. He once wrote that "a deep sense of religion is compatible with the entire absence of theology."

Today, people who believe with Huxley in an unknown and unknowable God still use the term agnostic to define themselves. When others refer to themselves as agnostics, they may mean that they are undecided about the claims of any religion, or they may mean that the word God has no meaning for them, but they do not want to identify themselves with the militant atheists, who often seem to be as narrow-minded as religious fundamentalists.

ambassador, *noun*   The word ambassador occurs only four times in the New Revised Standard Version of the Bible, twice in the Hebrew Scriptures, once in a letter to the Corinthians from Paul, and once in letter to the Ephesians claiming to be from Paul but probably written by someone else. In each case, the image of an ambassador that comes to the mind of a contemporary reader in an industrial nation is that of a powerful person, one with proven political connections, who can threaten and intimidate as well as negotiate in the international arena. Martyn Percy, however, has pointed out that the title had different connotations in the ancient world:

> "Typically, a community or person sent an ambassador in circumstances of weakness, dependence or vulnerability. Ambassadors were often dispensable people, who in many cases had to extol a brief that simultaneously made them expendable and integral. Essentially, ambassadors were supplicants—even though often they were people of high standing in the communities from which they came. . . . Paul's choice of the metaphor of ambassador precisely illustrates his understanding of his power—and weakness—as an apostle of Christ. . . . It illustrates that at its heart, his task was to appeal, to supplicate, to beg, and to entreat."[5]

The root for one of the Hebrew words translated as ambassador, *tsiyr*, suggests this weakness and vulnerability: hinge. A hinge can be forced to turn, so hinge became a metaphor not only for an ambassador or envoy but also for pain. Here is a sampling of the various translations of *tsiyr*:

> As a door turns on its **hinges**, so does a lazy person in bed. [Proverbs 26:14]

> Ah, land of whirring wings beyond the rivers of Ethiopia, sending **ambassadors** by the Nile in vessels of papyrus on the waters! Go, you swift messengers, to a nation tall and smooth, to a people feared near and far, a nation mighty and conquering, whose land the rivers divide. [Isaiah 18:1-2, messenger = *malak*, see below]

> You journeyed to Molech with oil, and multiplied your perfumes; you sent your **envoys** far away, and sent down even to Sheol. [Isaiah 57:9]

> The vision of Obadiah. Thus says the Lord GOD concerning Edom: We have heard a report from the LORD, and a **messenger** has been sent among the nations: "Rise up! Let us rise against it for battle!" [Obadiah 1:1]

> Then one in human form touched my lips, and I opened my mouth to speak, and said to the one who stood before me, "My lord, because of the vision such **pains** have come upon me that I retain no strength." [Daniel 10:16]

> Therefore my loins are filled with anguish; **pangs** have seized me, like the **pangs** of a woman in labor; I am bowed down so that I cannot hear, I am dismayed so that I cannot see. [Isaiah 21:3]

The other word translated as ambassador is *malak,* which usually appears in English as messenger or angel.*

> He rebelled against him by sending **ambassadors** to Egypt, in order that they might give him horses and a large army. [Ezekiel 17:15]

The Greek word for ambassador in the early Christian letters is *presbeuo,* which is actually a verb meaning to act as an elder or to be a representative.

> So we are **ambassadors** for Christ, since God is making his appeal through us; we entreat you on behalf of Christ, be reconciled to God. [II Corinthians 5:20]

> Pray also for me, so that when I speak, a message may be given to me to make known with boldness the mystery of the gospel, for which I am an **ambassador** in chains. [Ephesians 6:19-20]

The verb *presbeuo* has the same root as *presbyteros,* which is variously translated as presbyter, elder, or priest.* In its original meaning, *presbyteros* identified an older person who was worthy of respect, but it came to be a title for a member of a governing council in Judaism and in the church. The two meanings—an older person and a person of high standing in a community—suggest that an ambassador was both a person of authority and one who was expendable. A sensible community would not want to choose as their envoy to a powerful adversary an able-bodied young person who might be imprisoned or killed. An old man, no matter how wise, was always dispensable. Paul and the one who wrote in his name presumably used the term *presbeuo* to emphasize the weakness of Paul's position.

amen—see **faith**, **truth**

angel, *noun*   The Hebrew word *malak,* often translated as angel, meant literally a messenger, who could be an ambassador* or envoy. *Malak* frequently appears in English versions of the Bible in those terms.

> Saul sent **messengers** to David's house to keep watch over him, planning to kill him in the morning. David's wife Michal told him, "If you do not save your life tonight, tomorrow you will be killed." [I Samuel 19:11]

> Therefore the protection of Pharaoh shall become your shame, and the shelter in the shadow of Egypt your humiliation. For though his officials are at Zoan and his **envoys** reach Hanes, everyone comes to shame through a people that cannot profit them, that brings neither help nor profit, but shame and disgrace. [Isaiah 30:3-5]

> The king rebelled against the king of Babylon by sending **ambassadors** to Egypt, in order that they might give him horses and a large army. Will he succeed? Can one escape who does such things? Can he break the covenant and yet escape? [Ezekiel 17:15]

When *malak* appeared in a Hebrew story, the word became *angelos* in the Greek translation of the Hebrew Bible. This Greek word also appears in the early Christian writings. Like *malak, angelos* occasionally becomes messenger in English versions.

> This is the one about whom it is written, "See, I am sending my **messenger** ahead of you, who will prepare your way before you." [Matthew 11:10]

> When John's **messengers** had gone, Jesus began to speak to the crowds about John: "What did you go out into the wilderness to look at? A reed shaken by the wind?" [Luke 7:24]

> Jesus sent **messengers** ahead of him. On their way they entered a village of the Samaritans to make ready for him; but they did not receive him, because his face was set toward Jerusalem. [Luke 9:52-53]

When either *malak* or *angelos* appears to be something other than a human being, the English translation is always angel. From the stories, it is possible to glean a sense of what angels could be in popular imagination.

Sometimes an angel was an appearance of God* in human form. These stories characteristically begin with the angel who is later revealed to be God.

> The **angel** of the LORD found her by a spring of water in the wilderness, the spring on the way to Shur. And he said, "Hagar, slave-girl of Sarai, where have you come from and where are you going?" She said, "I am running away from my mistress Sarai." The **angel** of the LORD said to her, "Return to your mistress, and submit to her." . . . So she named the LORD who spoke to her, "You are El-roi"; for she said, "Have I really seen God and remained alive after seeing him?" [Genesis 16:7-9, 13]

> Now the **angel** of the LORD came and sat under the oak at Ophrah, which belonged to Joash the Abiezrite, as his son Gideon was beating out wheat in the wine press, to hide it from the Midianites. The **angel** of the LORD appeared to him and said to him, "The LORD is with you, you mighty warrior." Gideon answered him, "But sir, if the LORD is with us, why then has all this happened to us? And where are all his wonderful deeds that our ancestors recounted to us, saying, 'Did not the LORD bring us up from Egypt?' But now the LORD has cast us off, and given us into the hand of Midian." Then the LORD turned to him and said, "Go in this might of yours and deliver Israel from the hand of Midian; I hereby commission you." [Judges 6:11-14]

In other stories, angels are quite distinct from God, but they live with God in heaven. They can go back and forth between heaven and earth, sometimes bringing messages from God to human beings.

> When they rise from the dead, they neither marry nor are given in marriage, but are like **angels** in heaven. [Mark 12:25]

> Jacob dreamed that there was a ladder set up on the earth, the top of it reaching to heaven; and the **angels** of God were ascending and descending on it. [Genesis 28:12]

> Then the woman came and told her husband, "A man of God came to me, and his appearance was like that of an **angel** of God, most awe-inspiring; I did not ask him where he came from, and he did not tell me his name; but he said to me, 'You shall conceive and bear a son.'" [Judges 13:6-7]

> Now the birth of Jesus the Messiah took place in this way. When his mother Mary had been engaged to Joseph, but before they lived together, she was found to be with child from the Holy

                                  Marks a word in the text that has its own entry

Spirit. Her husband Joseph, being a righteous man and unwilling to expose her to public disgrace, planned to dismiss her quietly. But just when he had resolved to do this, an **angel** of the Lord appeared to him in a dream and said, "Joseph, son of David, do not be afraid to take Mary as your wife, for the child conceived in her is from the Holy Spirit." [Matthew 1:18-20]

Although the angels in the stories frequently look and sound like ordinary human beings, they sometimes appear as dazzling light with voices like thunder.

There the **angel** of the Lᴏʀᴅ appeared to him in a flame of fire out of a bush; he looked, and the bush was blazing, yet it was not consumed. [Exodus 3:2]

In that region there were shepherds living in the fields, keeping watch over their flock by night. Then an **angel** of the Lord stood before them, and the glory of the Lord shone around them, and they were terrified. [Luke 2:8-9]

Jesus said, "Father, glorify your name." Then a voice came from heaven, "I have glorified it, and I will glorify it again." The crowd standing there heard it and said that it was thunder. Others said, "An **angel** has spoken to him." [John 12:28-29]

Angels could serve as guides, both to destinations on earth and to heaven.

I am going to send an **angel** in front of you, to guard you on the way and to bring you to the place that I have prepared. [Exodus 23:20]

The poor man died and was carried away by the **angels** to be with Abraham. [Luke 16:22]

Individuals and communities were thought to have their own special angels. These angels may have been understood not as totally separate beings but as an expression of the essence of the person or the community.

Take care that you do not despise one of these little ones; for, I tell you, in heaven their **angels** continually see the face of my Father in heaven. [Matthew 18:10]

When Peter knocked at the outer gate, a maid named Rhoda came to answer. On recognizing Peter's voice, she was so overjoyed that, instead of opening the gate, she ran in and announced that Peter was standing at the gate. They said to her, "You are out of your mind!" But she insisted that it was so. They said, "It is his **angel**." [Acts 12:13-15]

As for the mystery of the seven stars that you saw in my right hand, and the seven golden lampstands: the seven stars are the **angels** of the seven churches, and the seven lampstands are the seven churches. [Revelation 1:20]

Some of the angels had their own names. Those whose names appear in the Bible as well as those found in other literature became known as archangels. The two who do not appear in the Bible are Raphael and Uriel (see **light**). The only two in the Bible with names are Gabriel (Hebrew *gabar*, strong + *el*, God) and Michael (Hebrew *mika*, like + *el*, God).

When I, Daniel, had seen the vision, I tried to understand it. Then someone appeared standing before me, having the appearance of a man, and I heard a human voice by the Ulai, calling, "Gabriel, help this man understand the vision." [Daniel 8:15-16]

Zechariah said to the **angel**, "How will I know that this is so? For I am an old man, and my wife is getting on in years." The **angel** replied, "I am Gabriel. I stand in the presence of God, and I have been sent to speak to you and to bring you this good news." [Luke 1:18-19]

> I am to tell you what is inscribed in the book of truth. There is no one with me who contends against these princes except Michael, your prince. [Daniel 10:21]

> When the **archangel** Michael contended with the devil and disputed about the body of Moses, he did not dare to bring a condemnation of slander against him, but said, "The Lord rebuke you!" [Jude 1:9]

Not all the angels in the Bible stories are on the side of God. Some of them are pictured as evil spirits in league with Satan.*

> To keep me from being too elated, a thorn was given me in the flesh, a **messenger** of Satan to torment me, to keep me from being too elated. [II Corinthians 12:7]

> God did not spare the **angels** when they sinned, but cast them into hell and committed them to chains of deepest darkness to be kept until the judgment. [II Peter 2:4]

> The great dragon was thrown down, that ancient serpent, who is called the Devil and Satan, the deceiver of the whole world—he was thrown down to the earth, and his **angels** were thrown down with him. [Revelation 12:9]

Some of the fallen angels lust after human females. According to one tradition, they try to snare the women by the hair; to protect themselves, Paul advised women to keep their hair covered.

> When people began to multiply on the face of the ground, and daughters were born to them, the sons of God saw that they were fair; and they took wives for themselves of all that they chose. [Genesis 6:1-2]

> Any woman who prays or prophesies with her head unveiled disgraces her head . . . For this reason a woman ought to have a symbol of authority on her head, because of the **angels**. [I Corinthians 11:5, 10]

People reading this ancient literature have to decide whether to take the angels as real beings or as an imaginative literary device. As metaphors the angels, both the good and bad ones, can lead people into a deeper understanding of their encounters with the mystery of existence. Sometimes a person can have a strange feeling of being guided into new ventures or into new insights, or the opposite—of being drawn into destructive behavior. A person can have an equally strange feeling of being cared for or of being tormented. Talking about such experiences in terms of angels is a way of acknowledging the powerful feelings and the sense of mystery the feelings evoke. If overdone, however, reflecting on experience in terms of angels can lead to a denial of individual responsibility.

apple of the eye, *noun*   According to the Oxford English Dictionary, at least since the ninth century, English-speaking people have referred to the black dot in the middle of the iris at the center of the eye as the apple. Apple was a generic term for many fruits of similar shape, in much the same way that corn was the generic term for many types of edible grain. Apparently people thought that what we now call the pupil was a globular solid, like an apple. From a very early period, the apple of the eye also served as a metaphor identifying the person on whom the eye gazed with pleasure.

At about the time that people in England realized that the black center of the eye was not a solid but an opening, they began using the word pupil, from the Latin *pupilla,* meaning a little girl. (The word pupil indicating a student comes from the same Latin root, *pupillus* in the masculine, which could be used for an orphan who was a minor and consequently a ward.)

The roots of the Latin word for pupil are curiously similar to two of the Hebrew words for the pupil of the eye, *ishown* meaning little man and *bat* meaning daughter. These expressions probably came into the language as a result of people seeing a tiny mirror image of themselves when staring into the eyes of another person. A third Hebrew word for the pupil is *babah*, a hollowed out place. Perhaps the ancient Hebrew-speaking people understood that the pupil was actually an opening in the iris.

All three Hebrew words could be used in the same metaphorical sense as the English expression, apple of the eye.

ishown

The Lord's own portion was his people, Jacob his allotted share. He sustained him in a desert land, in a howling wilderness waste; he shielded him, cared for him, guarded him as the **apple of his eye**. [Deuteronomy 32:9-10]

Guard me as the **apple of the eye**; hide me in the shadow of your wings. [Psalm 17:8]

My child, keep my words and store up my commandments with you; keep my commandments and live, keep my teachings as the **apple of your eye**. [Proverbs 7:1-2]

bat

Their heart cried unto the Lord, O wall of the daughter of Zion, let tears run down like a river day and night: give thyself no rest; let not the **apple of thine eye** cease.
[Lamentations 2:18, KING JAMES VERSION]

babah

For thus said the LORD of hosts (after his glory sent me) regarding the nations that plundered you: Truly, one who touches you touches the **apple of my eye**. [Zechariah 2:8]

Although the metaphor, apple of the eye, is familiar and understood to mean a cherished something or someone, many people have no idea that apple was once the common name for the black spot in the middle of the blue or brown iris. In most instances, pupil would be a more accurate translation of the Hebrew equivalent, but "pupil of the eye" somehow does not work as a metaphor.

apocalypse, *noun*   In the original Greek version, the first word in the last book of the Christian Bible* is *apokalypsis*. Although the word is usually translated into English as Revelation, the book is often known by its Greek name, the Apocalypse.

The **revelation** of Jesus Christ, which God gave him to show his servants what must soon take place; he made it known by sending his angel to his servant John, who testified to the word of God and to the testimony of Jesus Christ, even to all that he saw. [Revelation 1:1-2]

Apokalypsis comes from the verb *apokalypto*, formed from *apo*, off or away from + *kalypto*, to cover, hide, or conceal. In other words, an apocalypse is an uncovering or a revelation. Both the noun and the verb appear frequently in the Christian scriptures.

At that time Jesus said, "I thank you, Father, Lord of heaven and earth, because you have hidden these things from the wise and the intelligent and have **revealed** them to infants."
[Matthew 11:25]

Master, now you are dismissing your servant in peace, according to your word; for my eyes have seen your salvation, which you have prepared in the presence of all peoples, a light for **revelation** to the Gentiles and for glory to your people Israel. [Luke 2:29-32]

Nothing is covered up that will not be **uncovered,** and nothing secret that will not become known. Therefore whatever you have said in the dark will be heard in the light, and what you have whispered behind closed doors will be proclaimed from the housetops. [Luke 12:2-3]

For I am not ashamed of the gospel; it is the power of God for salvation to everyone who has faith, to the Jew first and also to the Greek. For in it the righteousness of God is **revealed** through faith for faith; as it is written, "The one who is righteous will live by faith." [Romans 1:16-17]

As it is written, "What no eye has seen, nor ear heard, nor the human heart conceived, what God has prepared for those who love him"—these things God has **revealed** to us through the Spirit; for the Spirit searches everything, even the depths of God. [I Corinthians 2:9-10]

For I want you to know, brothers and sisters, that the gospel that was proclaimed by me is not of human origin; for I did not receive it from a human source, nor was I taught it, but I received it through a **revelation** of Jesus Christ. [Galatians 1:11-12]

Sometimes the Hebrew word *galah* has a meaning similar to *apokalypto.*

A man of God came to Eli and said to him, "Thus the LORD has said, 'I **revealed** myself to the family of your ancestor in Egypt when they were slaves to the house of Pharaoh.'" [I Samuel 2:27]

For you, O LORD of hosts, the God of Israel, have made this **revelation** to your servant, saying, "I will build you a house"; therefore your servant has found courage to pray this prayer to you. [II Samuel 7:27]

The heavens will **reveal** their iniquity, and the earth will rise up against them. [Job 20:27]

I am going to bring it recovery and healing; I will heal them and **reveal** to them abundance of prosperity and security. [Jeremiah 33:6]

More often, *galah* appears in its original sense of uncovering, stripping , denuding, or disclosing.

Noah, a man of the soil, was the first to plant a vineyard. He drank some of the wine and became drunk, and he lay **uncovered** in his tent. [Genesis 9:20-21]

None of you shall approach anyone near of kin to **uncover** nakedness: I am the LORD. [Leviticus 18:6]

When Boaz had eaten and drunk, and he was in a contented mood, he went to lie down at the end of the heap of grain. Then Ruth came stealthily and **uncovered** his feet, and lay down. [Ruth 3:7]

A gossip **reveals** secrets; therefore do not associate with a babbler. [Proverbs 20:19]

For the LORD comes out from his place to punish the inhabitants of the earth for their iniquity; the earth will **disclose** the blood shed on it, and will no longer cover its slain. [Isaiah 26:21]

Come down and sit in the dust, virgin daughter Babylon! Sit on the ground without a throne, daughter Chaldea! For you shall no more be called tender and delicate. Take the millstones and grind meal, **remove** your veil, strip off your robe, **uncover** your legs, pass through the rivers. Your nakedness shall be **uncovered,** and your shame shall be seen. I will take vengeance, and I will spare no one. [Isaiah 47:1-3]

In the Bible, apocalypse is often a metaphor suggesting the uncovering of a hidden truth.* Apocalypse later became the generic name for a class of literature popular in the centuries just before and after the birth of Jesus. The biblical book Revelation is typical of these apocalyptic writings, which focus on predictions of calamities to take place at the end of time. Only those with proper beliefs and loyalties will be spared the disasters that are to come at any moment. These end-time prophecies have become so popular in North America that widespread destruction itself, not just the prediction of it, has become known as an apocalypse—thus the title of the 1979 film about the war in Viet Nam, "Apocalypse Now."

apocrypha—see **Bible**

apostle, *noun*   The English word apostle comes directly from the Greek *apostolos*, which is the noun formed from the verb *apostello*, which meant to send out or to send away.

Although people familiar with the story of the early followers of Jesus tend to assume that the inner circle of twelve disciples* were always known as apostles, a careful reading of the gospels and of St. Paul's letters reveal that applying this title to the Twelve might have been a rather late development. John's gospel and Paul's letters never refer to the Twelve as apostles. Matthew uses the term only once and Mark just twice. When Matthew and Mark talk about apostles, they do so in a particular context. The disciples were being sent out.

> And he appointed twelve, whom he also named **apostles,** to be with him, and to be **sent out** to proclaim the message. [Mark 3:14]

The author of the gospel attributed to Luke and of the Acts of the Apostles, however, uses the term frequently in reference to the Twelve. One explanation is that by the time Luke and Acts were written, apostle had become a desirable title because St. Paul, who applied the title to himself, had become a dominant figure in the Jesus movement. As far as Paul was concerned, an apostle was someone like himself who had been sent on a mission. He restricts the use of the term to a few of his lesser-known colleagues and to Peter and James, whose task of preaching to the Judeans (Jews*) paralleled his own mission to the Gentiles.

> Greet Andronicus and Junia, my relatives who were in prison with me; they are prominent among the **apostles,** and they were in Christ before I was. [Romans 16:7]
>
> Then after three years I did go up to Jerusalem to visit Cephas and stayed with him fifteen days; but I did not see any other **apostle** except James the Lord's brother. [Galatians 1:18-19]
>
> They saw that I had been entrusted with the gospel for the uncircumcised, just as Peter had been entrusted with the gospel for the circumcised (for he who worked through Peter making him an **apostle** to the circumcised also worked through me in sending me to the Gentiles). [Galatians 2:7-8]

Perhaps Paul had made the title so important that it was conferred back on the founders of the church.

appear—see **vision**

Armageddon, *noun*   The Revelation to John says that the last great battle between the forces of good and evil will take place at *harmageddon*, a Greek name of uncertain origin that appears to be derived from the Hebrew *har*, hills or mountains + *Meggido*, a Canaanite enclave in northern Palestine.

> The sixth angel poured his bowl on the great river Euphrates, and its water was dried up in order to prepare the way for the kings from the east. And I saw three foul spirits like frogs coming from the mouth of the dragon, from the mouth of the beast, and from the mouth of the false prophet. These are demonic spirits, performing signs, who go abroad to the kings of the whole world, to assemble them for battle on the great day of God the Almighty. ("See, I am coming like a thief! Blessed is the one who stays awake and is clothed, not going about naked and exposed to shame.") And they assembled them at the place that in Hebrew is called **Harmagedon**. The seventh angel poured his bowl into the air, and a loud voice came out of the temple, from the throne, saying, "It is done!" And there came flashes of lightning, rumblings, peals of thunder, and a violent earthquake, such as had not occurred since people were upon the earth, so violent was that earthquake. The great city was split into three parts, and the cities of the nations fell. God remembered great Babylon and gave her the wine-cup of the fury of his wrath. And every island fled away, and no mountains were to be found; and huge hailstones, each weighing about a hundred pounds, dropped from heaven on people, until they cursed God for the plague of the hail, so fearful was that plague. [Revelation 16:12-16]

References to Megiddo occur throughout the Hebrew Scriptures. According to tradition, this was an area inhabited by Canaanites whom the Hebrew-speaking people had not conquered. It overlooked the plain where decisive battles were fought. Two kings of Judah died there after losing a battle. Zechariah uses Megiddo as the scene of extreme grief.

> Manasseh did not drive out the inhabitants of Beth-shean and its villages, or Taanach and its villages, or the inhabitants of Dor and its villages, or the inhabitants of Ibleam and its villages, or the inhabitants of **Megiddo** and its villages; but the Canaanites continued to live in that land. [Judges 1:27]

> "Awake, awake, Deborah! Awake, awake, utter a song! Arise, Barak, lead away your captives, O son of Abinoam." Then down marched the remnant of the noble; the people of the LORD marched down for him against the mighty ... The kings came, they fought; then fought the kings of Canaan, at Taanach, by the waters of **Megiddo**; they got no spoils of silver. [Judges 5:12-13, 19]

> When King Ahaziah of Judah saw this, he fled in the direction of Beth-haggan. Jehu pursued him, saying, "Shoot him also!" And they shot him in the chariot at the ascent to Gur, which is by Ibleam. Then he fled to **Megiddo**, and died there. [II Kings 9:27]

> In his days Pharaoh Neco king of Egypt went up to the king of Assyria to the river Euphrates. King Josiah went to meet him; but when Pharaoh Neco met him at **Megiddo**, he killed him. His servants carried him dead in a chariot from **Megiddo**, brought him to Jerusalem, and buried him in his own tomb. [II Kings 23:29-30]

> I will pour out a spirit of compassion and supplication on the house of David and the inhabitants of Jerusalem, so that, when they look on the one whom they have pierced, they shall mourn for him, as one mourns for an only child, and weep bitterly over him, as one weeps over a firstborn. On that day the mourning in Jerusalem will be as great as the mourning for Hadad-rimmon in the plain of **Megiddo**. [Zechariah 12:10-11]

Although no one can say for certain what the author of Revelation had in mind, it seems likely that he imagined that the Roman empire would collapse after a great battle, opening the way for the establishment of God's realm, the kingdom* of heaven. He may well have been influenced by his knowledge of Hebrew Scriptures to invent a name for the scene of the battle.

Some Christians have drawn upon the scene of the battle in Revelation and made Armageddon a key part of their end-of-the-world predictions. For them, it is almost synonymous with the apocalypse.* For others, Armageddon is a metaphor pointing to any clash of cultures resulting in violence and loss of life.

ascend, *verb*; **ascension**, *noun*　　*Anabaino*, the Greek word translated ascend, originally meant to walk upward (*ana*, up + *baino*, to walk). By the time St. Paul employed the term, he could use it in either the original sense of walking uphill or in the metaphorical sense of drawing close to God, whose dwelling place was thought to be above, that is, in heaven.*

> Then after fourteen years I **went up** again to Jerusalem with Barnabas, taking Titus along with me. [Galatians 2:1]

> The righteousness that comes from faith says, "Do not say in your heart, 'Who will **ascend** into heaven?' (that is, to bring Christ down) or 'Who will descend into the abyss?' (that is, to bring Christ up from the dead)." But what does it say? "The word is near you, on your lips and in your heart." [Romans 10:6-8]

All four of the gospels frequently use the word in the original sense of going upward, but John alone uses the *anabaino* metaphor to indicate the perception of the disciples that Jesus developed a particularly intimate relationship to God.

> Jesus said to Mary Magdelene, "Do not hold on to me, because I have not yet **ascended** to the Father. But go to my brothers and say to them, 'I am **ascending** to my Father and your Father, to my God and your God.'" [John 20:17]

A story in the Acts of the Apostles, although it does not include the word *anabaino*, draws a vivid picture of ascension.

> As they were watching, Jesus was lifted up, and a cloud took him out of their sight. While he was going and they were gazing up toward heaven, suddenly two men in white robes stood by them. They said, "Men of Galilee, why do you stand looking up toward heaven? This Jesus, who has been taken up from you into heaven, will come in the same way as you saw him go into heaven." [Acts 1:9-11]

For a small fee, visitors to Jerusalem can enter a mosque and see a rock that supposedly bears the imprint of Jesus's foot, the result of the tremendous heat generated by his ascension. Impressive as the achievement of Jesus's ascension may be for some believers, it pales in significance when compared with that of Mohammed who was accompanied by his favorite horse on his direct, physical ascent to heaven.

Neither Jesus nor Mohammed was the first in tradition to have gone bodily to heaven. That honor belongs to the prophet Elijah. The Hebrew uses the verb *alah*, which like *anabaino* had a variety of uses but generally suggested "going up."

> As Elijah and Elisha continued walking and talking, a chariot of fire and horses of fire separated the two of them, and Elijah **ascended** in a whirlwind into heaven. [II Kings 2:11]

The stories of physical ascent to heaven probably developed from a metaphor commonly employed to indicate moving into the presence of the divine. To many of the ancients, the sky was the dwelling place of the gods. This notion of the gods being in the sky may well have begun with the worship of the sun and the moon and have continued with the evolution of tribal deities who had human characteristics. If the gods lived in the sky, their devotees would hike up to the top of tallest available hill or mountain to get close to them.

> Then Moses **went up** to God; the Lord called to him from the mountain, saying, "Thus you shall say to the house of Jacob, and tell the Israelites." [Exodus 19:3]

> Who shall **ascend** the hill of the Lord? And who shall stand in his holy place? [Psalm 24:3]

Although the ascension metaphor may create problems for people who have difficulty thinking of God living in the sky, it may have useful connotations in reference to Jesus. First, the imagery depicts Jesus in the way that his original disciples experienced him. He was one of those individuals who seemed particularly close to God. Second, the imagery suggests that, after his death, Jesus was no longer limited by time and geography. Through his story and his teaching, he was available to all people in all places at all times. Third, the ascension happening forty days after the death of Jesus can be a constant reminder that grief-stricken people often have to lose more than once a person they loved. After the initial shock of death, grieving usually continues for a month or six weeks, and then the mourners have to let go of their intense attachment to the one who died. Although they will carry the sadness with them always, they have to get on with their lives just as Jesus's disciples had to let Jesus go and get themselves together in order to carry on his work.

atheist, *noun*   The equivalent of the word atheist appears in the Bible in only one place, the Epistle to the Ephesians. The Greek word is *atheos*, formed from the negative particle *a* + *theos*, god.*

> Remember that you were at that time without Christ, being aliens from the commonwealth of Israel, and strangers to the covenants of promise, having no hope and **without God** in the world. [Ephesians 2:12]

In this context, the word may have been simply descriptive, but atheist has often been used as an epithet. In the early centuries of the church, those who worshiped the traditional Greek and Roman gods called Jews and Christians atheists. The Christians described those who worshiped gods other than their own with the same word. Traditionally, believers classify atheists as anyone who does not accept their god or gods.

In today's world, some people are pleased to call themselves atheists. For the most part, those who call themselves atheists are of two sorts. For some, atheism is the simple absence of a god belief, for whatever reason—a position held by many who prefer to call themselves agnostic.* Other atheists militantly deny the existence of God. The former tend to be open and philosophical in their approach to religion; the latter closed and dogmatic.

Militant atheists are not popular with most Christians, but liberal and progressive Christians often choose as their friends and companions those who simply have no god belief.

Marks a word in the text that has its own entry

atone, *verb*; **atonement**, *noun*   The people of ancient Israel identified one purpose of sacrifice* with a metaphor often translated as atonement. The original meaning of this word *kaphar*, and its derivative *kippur*, was to cover.

> Make yourself an ark of cypress wood; make rooms in the ark, and **cover** it inside and out with pitch. [Genesis 6:14]

The object of some sacrifices was to cover over the sins* of the worshipers, that is, the wrongdoing of a person would never go away. The person would remain forever the one who did the deed, but through the ritual of sacrifice the sin would no longer get between the person and God.*

> Also every day you shall offer a bull as a sin offering for **atonement** (*kippur*). Also you shall offer a sin offering for the altar, when you make **atonement** (*kaphar*) for it, and shall anoint it, to consecrate it. [Exodus 29:36]

> You shall bring to the LORD, as your penalty for the sin that you have committed, a female from the flock, a sheep or a goat, as a sin offering; and the priest shall make **atonement** on your behalf for your sin.—*kaphar* [Leviticus 5:6]

> Now, the tenth day of this seventh month is the day of **atonement**; it shall be a holy convocation for you: you shall deny yourselves and present the Lord's offering by fire.—*kippur* [Leviticus 23:27]

The sacrifice was central to the covering over of sin but was only one part of the process. The first step was admission of guilt, and the second was restitution with interest.

> When any of you sin and commit a trespass against the LORD by deceiving a neighbor in a matter of a deposit or a pledge, or by robbery, or if you have defrauded a neighbor, or have found something lost and lied about it—if you swear falsely regarding any of the various things that one may do and sin thereby—when you have sinned and realize your guilt, and would restore what you took by robbery or by fraud or the deposit that was committed to you, or the lost thing that you found, or anything else about which you have sworn falsely, you shall repay the principal amount and shall add one-fifth to it. You shall pay it to its owner when you realize your guilt. And you shall bring to the priest, as your guilt offering to the LORD, a ram without blemish from the flock, or its equivalent, for a guilt offering. The priest shall make **atonement** on your behalf before the LORD, and you shall be forgiven for any of the things that one may do and incur guilt thereby.—*kaphar* [Leviticus 6:2-6]

The centrality of the cover metaphor in Judaism may not always be apparent; the translators have used a variety of English words in addition to atonement when they have come across *kaphar* in the text.

> **Absolve**, O LORD, your people Israel, whom you redeemed; do not let the guilt of innocent blood remain in the midst of your people Israel. Then they will be **absolved** of bloodguilt. [Deuteronomy 21:8]

> Praise, O heavens, his people, worship him, all you gods! For he will avenge the blood of his children, and take vengeance on his adversaries; he will repay those who hate him, and **cleanse** the land for his people. [Deuteronomy 32:43]

> Hezekiah prayed for them, saying, "The good LORD **pardon** all who set their hearts to seek God, the LORD the God of their ancestors, even though not in accordance with the sanctuary's rules of cleanness." [II Chronicles 30:18-19]

> Therefore I (the LORD) swear to the house of Eli that the iniquity of Eli's house shall not be **expiated** by sacrifice or offering forever. [I Samuel 3:14]

> Yet God, being compassionate, **forgave** their iniquity, and did not destroy them; often he restrained his anger, and did not stir up all his wrath. [Psalm 78:38]

> The seraph touched my mouth with it and said: "Now that this has touched your lips, your guilt has departed and your sin is **blotted out**." [Isaiah 6:7]

> And I will make justice the line, and righteousness the plummet; hail will sweep away the refuge of lies, and waters will overwhelm the shelter. Then your covenant with death will be **annulled**, and your agreement with Sheol will not stand. [Isaiah 28:17-18]

> A king's wrath is a messenger of death, and whoever is wise will **appease** it. [Proverbs 16:14]

This last use of *kaphar*, meaning appeasement, does not appear to be the appropriate translation when the subject is the relationship of human beings and God. The idea of sacrifice being for the appeasement or propitiation* of God crept in through the Greek words frequently chosen to translate the word: *hilasterion, hilaskomai,* and *hilasmos.* The three are rooted in *hilaos,* as is *hilaros* meaning cheerful. *Hilaros* is the source of the English word hilarious. The Greek concept of sacrifice for sin may have implied that the purpose was to cheer up an angry God. It is not possible to tell from the context whether the earliest Christian writers had in mind the Hebrew or the Greek concept of atonement when they used the metaphor in considering what the death of Jesus meant to them.

> They are now justified by his grace as a gift, through the redemption that is in Christ Jesus, whom God put forward as a sacrifice of **atonement** by his blood, effective through faith.—*hilasterion* [Romans 3:24-25]

> Therefore Jesus had to become like his brothers and sisters in every respect, so that he might be a merciful and faithful high priest in the service of God, to make a sacrifice of **atonement** for the sins of the people.—*hilaskomai* [Hebrews 2:17]

> My little children, I am writing these things to you so that you may not sin. But if anyone does sin, we have an advocate with the Father, Jesus Christ the righteous; and he is the **atoning** sacrifice for our sins, and not for ours only but also for the sins of the whole world.—*hilasmos* [I John 2:1-2]

Although words translated atone or atonement appear infrequently in the earliest Christian writings, the concept of Jesus taking away sin may have been established near the beginning of the movement. The atonement metaphor seems to lie behind the language Matthew chose to tell the story of Jesus's last meal with his disciples. Whether such language originated with Jesus or with those who later had chosen the atonement metaphor is a matter of dispute. Although John's gospel does not include a story of Jesus instituting a ritual meal for his followers, it does include a similar metaphorical reference at the beginning of the book.

> Then he took a cup, and after giving thanks he gave it to them, saying, "Drink from it, all of you; for this is my blood of the covenant, which is poured out for many for the forgiveness of sins." [Matthew 26:27-28]

> John saw Jesus coming toward him and declared, "Here is the Lamb of God who takes away the sin of the world!" [John 1:29]

In the sixteenth century, the choice of atonement for both the Hebrew and Greek words changed the emphasis of the original metaphors from covering of sin or appeasement to finding unity with God. The earliest phrase "set at one" eventually merged into the single word at + one + ment. For those who find all the images of sacrifice repugnant, the idea of finding unity with God through their experience of Jesus may allow them to use the English atonement metaphor and forget its Hebrew and Greek origins.

Those who have benefitted from understanding the cover metaphor may also remind themselves that if they find help through Jesus in putting aside their sin and making a fresh start, they also have an obligation to acknowledge their faults and to make restitution when possible.

Those who think that God may be angry with them may find some comfort in the metaphor that suggests God does not need to be cheered up. Whatever else Jesus accomplished in his life and death, he convinced his followers that they no longer needed to participate in the sacrifice of animals to put God into a better mood. Through Jesus, his followers discovered that God was already favorably disposed toward them.

authority, *noun*   In the Hebrew Scriptures, a great number of metaphors appear in English as authority:

> Let them gather all the food of these good years that are coming, and lay up grain under the **authority** of Pharaoh for food in the cities, and let them keep it.—*yad*, an open hand. [Genesis 41:35]

> These were the chief officers of King Solomon, two hundred fifty of them, who **exercised authority** over the people.—*radah*, tread down [II Chronicles 8:10]

> Queen Esther daughter of Abihail, along with the Jew Mordecai, gave full written **authority**, confirming this second letter about Purim.—*toqeph*, from root meaning overpower [Esther 9:29]

> When the righteous are in **authority**, the people rejoice; but when the wicked rule, the people groan.—*rabah*, enlarge or increase [Proverbs 29:2]

> All this I observed, applying my mind to all that is done under the sun, while one person **exercises authority** over another to the other's hurt.—*shalat*, dominate [Ecclesiastes 8:9]

> For a child has been born for us, a son given to us; **authority** rests upon his shoulders; and he is named Wonderful Counselor, Mighty God, Everlasting Father, Prince of Peace.—*misrah*, empire [Isaiah 9:6]

> On that day I will call my servant Eliakim son of Hilkiah, and will clothe him with your robe and bind your sash on him. I will commit your **authority** to his hand, and he shall be a father to the inhabitants of Jerusalem and to the house of Judah.—*memshalah*, rule [Isaiah 22:20-21]

Marks a word in the text that has its own entry

In the gospels, the Acts of the Apostles, and the letters of Paul, the Greek word for authority is nearly always *exousia*, formed by *ex,* out of + *ousia*, a form of the verb to be. This suggestive metaphor—from out of one's being—is a reminder of the English words related to authority, such as author, autonomy, and all the other terms that have auto as a prefix. The metaphor clearly points to what impressed those who became followers of Jesus. Jesus's authority came from within himself and was not derived from an institutional source.

> Now when Jesus had finished saying these things, the crowds were astounded at his teaching, for he taught them as one having **authority,** and not as their scribes. [Matthew 7:28-29]

> They were all amazed, and they kept on asking one another, "What is this? A new teaching—with **authority**! He commands even the unclean spirits, and they obey him." [Mark 1:27]

Although the disciples recognized that the authority of Jesus was not derived from an institutional source, they understood that his authority had been granted to him—by God.

> After Jesus had spoken these words, he looked up to heaven and said, "Father, the hour has come; glorify your Son so that the Son may glorify you, since you have given him **authority** over all people, to give eternal life to all whom you have given him." [John 17:1-2]

In the understanding of the early Christians, God was the source of all authority, which God had delegated not only to Jesus but also to those with responsibility for governing society.

> Let every person be subject to the governing **authorities**; for there is no **authority** except from God, and those **authorities** that exist have been instituted by God. [Romans 13:1]

> For the Lord's sake accept the **authority** of every human institution, whether of the emperor as supreme, or of governors, as sent by him to punish those who do wrong and to praise those who do right. [I Peter 2:13-14]

The followers of Jesus understood that they also exercised a derived authority, but theirs was delegated by God through Jesus.

> Then Jesus summoned his twelve disciples and gave them **authority** over unclean spirits, to cast them out, and to cure every disease and every sickness. [Matthew 10:1]

> So I [Paul] write these things while I am away from you, so that when I come, I may not have to be severe in using the **authority** that the Lord has given me for building up and not for tearing down. [II Corinthians 13:10]

The English word authority has two distinct meanings. According to the Oxford English Dictionary, authority exists in two forms of power, which can best be understood by this grid:

authority =	1. Power to enforce obedience: *imposed*	2. Power to influence or inspire: *granted*
in people	Established right and coercive means of control	Weight given to opinions and judgment
in documents	Enforceable rules, laws, and codes of conduct	Source of wisdom and guidance

Marks a word in the text that has its own entry

The Hebrew metaphors and the use made of the Greek metaphor suggest that authority in the church must be of the first type, the power to enforce obedience. However, the Greek metaphor itself—out of being—suggests the possibility that the power to influence or inspire might be the more appropriate form of authority to be exercised by the followers of Jesus.

The authority granted to the early leaders of the church appears to have been of the second type. Paul, for example, could not give orders to Christian communities, even those that he had established. He did not have the means or the right to control any of his fellow Christians. In the surviving letters generally attributed to him, he frequently resorts to the word *parakaleo*, meaning urge or appeal (see **advocate**). For Paul, authority was more a matter of mutual respect than it was the power of one person to control the behavior of another. His view of authority in marriage could be applied to other relationships.

> For the wife does not have **authority** over her own body, but the husband does; likewise the husband does not have **authority** over his own body, but the wife does. [I Corinthians 7:4]

Similarly, Paul understood the authority of the Bible* to be the second sort of power, a source of wisdom and guidance rather than enforceable rules, laws, and codes of conduct. His Bible, the Hebrew Scriptures, provided examples* that he thought were useful for the instruction* of Jesus's followers. He had a dim view of the scriptures as law.*

B

baal—see **God**

baptize, *verb*; **baptism**, *noun*   The root of the Greek words for baptize and baptism is *bapto*, which meant to dip into a fluid. The word in this simple form occurs in the gospels* and in Revelation.

> The rich man called out, "Father Abraham, have mercy on me, and send Lazarus to **dip** the tip of his finger in water and cool my tongue; for I am in agony in these flames." [Luke 16:24]

> Jesus answered, "It is the one to whom I give this piece of bread when I have **dipped** it in the dish." So when he had **dipped** the piece of bread, he gave it to Judas son of Simon Iscariot. [John 13:26]

> The rider on a white horse is clothed in a robe **dipped** in blood, and his name is called The Word of God. [Revelation 19:13]

The verb *baptizo* is an intensive form of *bapto* and originally meant immerse or wash. In non-Christian literature it could also mean plunge, sink, drench, or overwhelm. Three Greek nouns evolved from the verb: *baptisma* (the ritual washing of human beings), *baptismos* (the washing of dishes or people), and *baptistes* (the baptist or the baptizer).

> The Pharisees, and all the Jews, do not eat unless they thoroughly wash their hands, thus observing the tradition of the elders; and they do not eat anything from the market unless they **wash** (*baptizo*) it; and there are also many other traditions that they observe, the **washing** (*baptismos*) of cups, pots, and bronze kettles. [Mark 7:3-4]

> The Pharisee was amazed to see that Jesus did not first **wash** (*baptizo*) before dinner. [Mark 11:38]

> Therefore let us go on toward perfection, leaving behind the basic teaching about Christ, and not laying again the foundation: repentance from dead works and faith toward God, instruction about **baptisms** (*baptismos*), laying on of hands, resurrection of the dead, and eternal judgment. [Hebrews 6:1-2]

References to a man named John called *baptistes* appear in the early Christian writings and in the works of Josephus. The latter may be suspect, however, because the only copies remaining were made by Christians who could have been trying to reinforce the credibility of their accounts. At any rate, by the time of Jesus, Jews* were apparently welcoming Gentile converts through a ritual washing, a *baptisma*. This may have evolved from the ancient forms of washing required under certain circumstances for the purification of those who had become ritually unclean. For example, before they were welcomed back to the community, bathing (Hebrew *rachats*) was required of those who set free the scapegoat* and of those who ate carrion.

> The one who sets the goat free for Azazel shall wash his clothes and **bathe** his body in water, and afterward may come into the camp. [Leviticus 16:26]

> All persons, citizens or aliens, who eat what dies of itself or what has been torn by wild animals, shall wash their clothes, and **bathe** themselves in water, and be unclean until the evening; then they shall be clean. [Leviticus 17:15]

Ritual washing continued as a tradition associated with synagogue worship. Excavated first-century synagogues show clear evidence of spaces outside the entrances for the purification rites that required water. If ritual washing was required to assure purity* for those born into Judaism, of course no less would be required of Gentiles who wished to join them. Although they clearly made a distinction between the *baptisma* of initiation and that of the normal sabbath* routine, the understanding of what was at stake in both instances was much the same.

According to tradition, John insisted that Judeans should consider themselves to be as distant from God as Gentiles. To be counted among God's people, they should repent* and be readmitted to the community as if they were Gentiles, that is, they should be baptized.

> John the baptizer appeared in the wilderness, proclaiming a baptism of repentance for the forgiveness of sins. And people from the whole Judean countryside and all the people of Jerusalem were going out to him, and were **baptized** by him in the river Jordan, confessing their sins. [Mark 1:4-5]

> In those days John the Baptist appeared in the wilderness of Judea, proclaiming, "Repent, for the kingdom of heaven has come near." . . . Then the people of Jerusalem and all Judea were going out to him, and all the region along the Jordan, and they were **baptized** by him in the river Jordan, confessing their sins. But when he saw many Pharisees and Sadducees coming for baptism, he said to them, "You brood of vipers! Who warned you to flee from the wrath to come? Bear fruit worthy of repentance. Do not presume to say to yourselves, 'We have Abraham as our ancestor'; for I tell you, God is able from these stones to raise up children to Abraham. Even now the ax is lying at the root of the trees; every tree therefore that does not bear good fruit is cut down and thrown into the fire." [Matthew 3:1-2, 5-10]

All four gospels imply that Jesus went through the baptism ritual. The Gospel according to John (a different John) does not say so explicitly, but it goes further than the other three in suggesting that Jesus and some of his followers were at one time disciples* of the baptizer. John's gospel alone says that Jesus himself presided at baptisms, but either he later reversed himself or an editor inserted a disclaimer.

> In those days Jesus came from Nazareth of Galilee and was **baptized** by John in the Jordan. [Mark 1:9; see also Matthew 3:13 and Luke 3:21]

> John said, "I myself did not know him; but I came **baptizing** with water for this reason, that he might be revealed to Israel." . . . The next day John again was standing with two of his disciples, and as he watched Jesus walk by, he exclaimed, "Look, here is the Lamb of God!" The two disciples heard him say this, and they followed Jesus. [John 1:31, 35-37]

> After this Jesus and his disciples went into the Judean countryside, and he spent some time there with them and **baptized**. John also was **baptizing** at Aenon near Salim because water was abundant there; and people kept coming and were being **baptized**. [John 3:22-23]

> Now when Jesus learned that the Pharisees had heard, "Jesus is making and **baptizing** more disciples than John"—although it was not Jesus himself but his disciples who **baptized**—he left Judea and started back to Galilee. [John 4:1-3]

Although Jesus's participation in the ritual washing of his followers is a matter of dispute, the use of baptism as a rite of Christian initiation seems to have been well established not long after his death. Paul, the author of the earliest Christian writings that have survived, mentions baptism frequently in his letters.

> Has Christ been divided? Was Paul crucified for you? Or were you **baptized** in the name of Paul? I thank God that I **baptized** none of you except Crispus and Gaius, so that no one can say that you were **baptized** in my name. (I did **baptize** also the household of Stephanas; beyond that, I do not know whether I **baptized** anyone else.) For Christ did not send me to **baptize** but to proclaim the gospel, and not with eloquent wisdom, so that the cross of Christ might not be emptied of its power. [I Corinthians 1:13-17]

> For in the one Spirit we were all **baptized** into one body—Jews or Greeks, slaves or free—and we were all made to drink of one Spirit. [I Corinthians 12:13]

> As many of you as were **baptized** into Christ have clothed yourselves with Christ. There is no longer Jew or Greek, there is no longer slave or free, there is no longer male and female; for all of you are one in Christ Jesus. [Galatians 3:27-28]

Although baptism seems to have been practiced by most communities of Jesus followers in the early days, they held a variety of opinions about how it should be done and what was required of those to be baptized.

One difference of opinion was over in whose name* the baptism should be done.

> And Jesus came and said to them, "All authority in heaven and on earth has been given to me. Go therefore and make disciples of all nations, **baptizing** them in the name of the Father and of the Son and of the Holy Spirit." [Matthew 28:18-19]

> Peter said to them, "Repent, and be **baptized** every one of you in the name of Jesus Christ so that your sins may be forgiven; and you will receive the gift of the Holy Spirit." [Acts 2:38]

Marks a word in the text that has its own entry

Some passages seem to suggest that baptism required belief on the part of the candidate, while other texts tell of whole households, including slaves and children, being baptized without their consent let alone their believing.

> When they believed Philip, who was proclaiming the good news about the kingdom of God and the name of Jesus Christ, they were **baptized**, both men and women. [Acts 8:12]

> The jailer called for lights, and rushing in, he fell down trembling before Paul and Silas. Then he brought them outside and said, "Sirs, what must I do to be saved?" They answered, "Believe on the Lord Jesus, and you will be saved, you and your household." They spoke the word of the Lord to him and to all who were in his house. At the same hour of the night he took them and washed their wounds; then he and his entire family were **baptized** without delay. [Acts 16:29-33]

The baptism language, besides referring to a ritual washing, often appears as a metaphor pointing to an ordeal—perhaps suffering or even death:

> John the baptizer said, "I **baptize** you with water for repentance, but one who is more powerful than I is coming after me; I am not worthy to carry his sandals. He will **baptize** you with the Holy Spirit and fire." [Matthew 3:11]

> Jesus said to them, "You do not know what you are asking. Are you able to drink the cup that I drink, or be baptized with the **baptism** that I am **baptized** with?" They replied, "We are able." Then Jesus said to them, "The cup that I drink you will drink; and with the **baptism** with which I am **baptized**, you will be **baptized**." [Mark 10:38-39]

> Jesus said, "I came to bring fire to the earth, and how I wish it were already kindled! I have a **baptism** with which to be **baptized**, and what stress I am under until it is completed!" [Luke 12:49-50]

> Therefore we have been buried with him by **baptism** into death, so that, just as Christ was raised from the dead by the glory of the Father, so we too might walk in newness of life. [Romans 6:4]

> I do not want you to be unaware, brothers and sisters, that our ancestors were all under the cloud, and all passed through the sea, and all were **baptized** into Moses in the cloud and in the sea. [I Corinthians 10:1-2]

Because in English baptize and baptism refer exclusively to a religious ritual, English speakers may miss some of the nuances of the biblical texts. If today's followers of Jesus talked about washing in the name of Jesus or being plunged into the body of Christ, perhaps the ritual would not seem so detached from ordinary life. Even the clearly metaphorical uses of baptism might take on more power if Christians spoke of being washed by fire* or plunged into death.

Beatitudes—see blessed

Beelzebul—see Satan

behold, *demonstrative particle*   Many people who grew up listening to the King James Version of the Bible find something missing in more recent translations. One of the missing elements is the use of the word behold. According to one computer count, behold occurs 1,326 times in the King James Version and only 21 times in the New Revised Standard Version. In the earlier translation, behold usually stands for the Hebrew *hinneh* or the Greek *idou*. Grammarians call these words demonstrative particles—little words that are not really verbs—although they may have evolved from verbs. In the case of *hinneh* and *idou*, the verbs from which they came meant to look or to see. The little words punctuated the narrative, calling the listeners' attention to what they would hear next.

The translators of the Bible, working under the guidance of King James I of England in the seventeenth century, knew that most people would become acquainted with the scriptures by listening rather than by reading the text themselves.

For the authors and editors of the Hebrew and Greek texts, the challenge had been much the same. What they wrote, most people would have to take in through their ears rather than their eyes. By rarely failing to translate *hinneh* and *idou* with behold, or occasionally lo, the seventeenth-century scholars were more faithful to the cadence of the original text than their modern counterparts, who frequently ignored the little words altogether. In the following examples taken from the New Revised Standard Version, words in standard, bold-faced type simply translate *hinneh* and *idou*, while those in bold italics have been inserted to supply the particles missing from the translation.

Hinneh and *idou* sometimes introduce a new character . . .

> When Gideon arrived, *look*, there was a man telling a dream to his comrade; and he said, "I had a dream, and in it a cake of barley bread tumbled into the camp of Midian, and came to the tent, and struck it so that it fell; it turned upside down, and the tent collapsed."—*hinneh* [Judges 7:13]

> Now *look*, there was a man in Jerusalem whose name was Simeon; this man was righteous and devout, looking forward to the consolation of Israel, and the Holy Spirit rested on him.—*idou* [Luke 2:25]

. . . or a new idea.

> **See**, the day is coming, burning like an oven, when all the arrogant and all evildoers will be stubble; the day that comes shall burn them up, says the LORD of hosts, so that it will leave them neither root nor branch. —*hinneh* [Malachi 4:1]

> Then *look*, someone came to him and said, "Teacher, what good deed must I do to have eternal life?"—*idou* [Matthew 19:16]

The words announce the beginning of a new story.

> Just then, *look*, the servants of David arrived with Joab from a raid, bringing much spoil with them. But Abner was not with David at Hebron, for David had dismissed him, and he had gone away in peace. —*hinneh* [II Samuel 3:22]

> Jesus told them many things in parables, saying: "**Listen**! A sower went out to sow."—*idou* [Matthew 13:3]

They emphasize the importance of what is to follow . . .

> When Aaron and all the Israelites saw Moses, *look*, the skin of his face was shining, and they were afraid to come near him. —*hinneh* [Exodus 34:30]

> They were on the road, going up to Jerusalem, and Jesus was walking ahead of them; they were amazed, and those who followed were afraid. He took the twelve aside again and began to tell them what was to happen to him, saying, "**See**, we are going up to Jerusalem, and the Son of Man will be handed over to the chief priests and the scribes, and they will condemn him to death; then they will hand him over to the Gentiles; they will mock him, and spit upon him, and flog him, and kill him; and after three days he will rise again."—*idou* [Mark 10:32-34]

. . . or call for closer attention.

> Thus says the LORD of hosts, the God of Israel: **Look**, I am now bringing upon this city and upon all its towns all the disaster that I have pronounced against it, because they have stiffened their necks, refusing to hear my words.—*hinneh* [Jeremiah 19:15]

> When John's messengers had gone, Jesus began to speak to the crowds about John: "What did you go out into the wilderness to look at? A reed shaken by the wind? What then did you go out to see? Someone dressed in soft robes? **Look**, those who put on fine clothing and live in luxury are in royal palaces."—*idou* [Luke 7:24-25]

Sometimes the words are used in a way that is similar to the English use of here or there, but without an intransitive verb immediately following and without the attention-getting simplicity.

> Before he had finished speaking, **there was** Rebekah, who was born to Bethuel son of Milcah, the wife of Nahor, Abraham's brother, coming out with her water jar on her shoulder.—*hinneh* [Genesis 24:15]

> So Philip got up and went. Now **there was** an Ethiopian eunuch, a court official of the Candace, queen of the Ethiopians, in charge of her entire treasury. He had come to Jerusalem to worship and was returning home; seated in his chariot, he was reading the prophet Isaiah.—*idou* [Acts 8:27-28]

For public readings of the Bible, people who want to pick up the rhythm and the emphasis of the original Greek and Hebrew texts, but still make the best possible use of recent translations, have an option. They can put the King James Version of the Bible alongside the newer version and, following the examples above, they can insert look or see wherever the King James has a lo or behold.

believe—see faith

Bible, *noun*   The word bible made its way to English from the Greek *biblia* through the French and Latin equivalents. The original Greek word was a neuter plural meaning books, but over the centuries Christians came to use it as if it were a feminine singular meaning The Book. Thinking of the Bible as one book was an unfortunate development that obscured the reality that Protestant editions of the Bible are collections of sixty-six separate pieces.

The Jews have a different way of arranging and counting the portion of the Bible that Christians inherited from them. Catholics have added seven other writings that were once part of the Jewish tradition but later rejected by the rabbis, a collection known as the Apocrypha. Catholics and Protestants, however, agree on the twenty-seven books in the Christian portion of the Bible.

In the early days of Christianity, the revered writings of Judaism were usually referred to as the scriptures, *graphai* in Greek.

> Jesus said to them, "Have you never read in the **scriptures**: 'The stone that the builders rejected has become the cornerstone; this was the Lord's doing, and it is amazing in our eyes'? Therefore I tell you, the kingdom of God will be taken away from you and given to a people that produces the fruits of the kingdom." [Matthew 21:42-43]

When you look through the Christian books of the Bible, you can easily see why Jews have accused Christians of "colonizing" their holy books. Christians have adopted them and used them for their own purposes, sometimes without regard for their original meaning or for their meaning in contemporary Judaism. To compound the insult to the Jews in taking over their scriptures, Christians at an early date began referring to the collection as the old covenant,* or old testament. This may have been originally a term of respect, meaning the ancient and honorable testament. At the same time, however, they began referring to their relationship with God as a new covenant, or new testament, which eventually became the name they used for referring to their sacred writings.

> The minds of the children of Israel were blinded: for until this day remaineth the same veil untaken away in the reading of the **old testament**; which veil is done away in Christ.
> [II Corinthians 3:14, KING JAMES VERSION]

> Not that we are sufficient of ourselves to think any thing as of ourselves; but our sufficiency is of God; Who also hath made us able ministers of the **new testament**; not of the letter, but of the spirit: for the letter killeth, but the spirit giveth life. [II Corinthians 3:5-6, KING JAMES VERSION]

As a way of objecting to the assertion that the Christian arrangement with God has superseded God's covenant with the Jews, Harold Bloom, a professor of humanities at Yale University, suggested that "Jewish critics and readers might speak of their scriptures as the Original Testament, and the Christian work as the Belated Testament." According to Bloom, what the Christians call the New Testament is "a revisionary work that attempts to replace a book, Torah, with a Man, Jesus of Nazareth."[6]

Although Bloom's suggestion has not been widely adopted, progressive Christians have learned to be a bit more respectful. At the risk of offending their more conservative fellow Christians, they now refer to the early portions of their Bible as the Hebrew Scriptures. This designation is not altogether satisfactory because it ignores the fact that part of the writings are in another language, Aramaic, nor is everyone entirely happy with calling the specifically Christian parts of the Bible the Greek Scriptures.

This contemporary disagreement over naming fits well into the tradition of controversy that has always surrounded the Bible. One major source of controversy has always been what books deserve to be included in the collection of sacred writings. As noted above, several texts revered by some authorities in ancient Judaism were ultimately rejected. These writings had appeared in a collection of sacred texts that had been translated into Greek about 150 years before the birth of Jesus. By that time, Hebrew was no longer spoken, and Greek had become the language of government, commerce, and education. Known as the Septuagint (because of the story that 72 scholars in Alexandria took part in the work), the collection was probably translated over a considerable period of time by a large number of scholars in a variety of places. When early Christians quoted the scriptures in their writings, they were using this Greek version of the Hebrew and Aramaic texts, and this was the version that formed the basis of the Latin translations of the Roman Church. Protestants, Catholics, the Eastern Orthodox, and the Jews still do not agree on which books rightly belong in the Bible.

Although now Christians generally agree about which books belong to their part of the Bible, this was not always the case. Well into the fourth century, doubts persisted about the inclusion of Hebrews, Jude, II Peter, II and III John, and Revelation. Other books, which did not make the final list, were considered sacred to some, such as the Epistle of Barnabas and the Shepard of Hermes. In addition to the four gospels that came to be accepted, early in the second century other gospels apparently had their adherents.

One of these, the Gospel of Thomas, was rediscovered in 1945 at a site in upper Egypt. Unlike the other four, Thomas is primarily a selection of teachings attributed to Jesus, many of which are similar to those found in Matthew, Mark, and Luke. Unlike John in particular, Thomas has no emphasis on correct belief. The Jesus Seminar—a group of North American scholars sponsored by the Westar Institute—included Thomas in their translations of the gospels. Their work, published with the title *The Five Gospels*,[7] has found its way into some churches, which now include readings from Thomas at their worship. Perhaps in time, Thomas will become widely accepted as belonging in the Bible, but it is not the only candidate. At least twelve other gospels appeared in the first three centuries of Christianity.

In addition to the ongoing controversies over which books belong in the Bible, Christians also argue about the nature of the books themselves. In the late eighteenth century, the spirit of scientific inquiry began to affect the way some scholars approached the Bible. They applied the same critical methods that scholars in other fields were using to study ancient documents. They noted that certain identifiable types or forms of stories appear in the Bible and in other ancient literature. Some of these stories may have started as explanations for a natural phenomenon and then used for another purpose by a later writer. For example, the earliest version of a flood story was probably a reflection on mortality, while the later Bible version seems more concerned about the gap between human beings and God. Scholars also noted that many of the stories in the Bible do not seem well connected and that some are repeated in slightly different terms.

These observations led to the conclusion that most of the books in the Bible are the work of editors who assembled older material from a variety of sources to deal with issues facing their constituents. The version of the Hebrew Scriptures that we have inherited is largely the work of editors belonging to the priestly caste who were attempting to reconstitute their community following their return from exile about 500 years before the birth of Jesus. The present version of the Greek Scriptures is the work of the orthodox faction of the early Christian movement, the people who wanted to defend the belief that Jesus was God. Finally, scholars recognized that no original manuscripts of books in the Bible still exist. They were dealing with copies of copies of copies. They identified many variations in the texts, most inconsequential, but some having great impact on the meaning.

Using the scientific approach, the scholars of the Bible were participating in the spirit of the age, the age that produced modern geology, astronomy, and physics, as well as Darwin's theory of evolution. Many Christians felt threatened by science, which seemed to dispute the biblical record of creation, and by scholarly criticism, which undermined people's confidence in scripture. To protect their faith, they fought back by making claims for the inerrancy of the Bible, a claim that no one had thought to make before. This antiscientific movement in the church took shape in the late nineteenth century. In the United States, the movement had its intellectual center at Princeton and gained its name—fundamentalism—from publications promoting the fundamentals of religion.

Most progressive Christians embrace the Bible with all its ambiguities and contradictions. The scriptures contain the myths,* legends, and teachings that provide the symbols employed by the followers of Jesus in making sense out of their lives and in developing rituals for life's transitions. They understand that their task is not so much to interpret the Bible but to let the Bible interpret them. Passages of the Bible can function as mirrors held up to life for those who want to see themselves more clearly and to understand their unique responsibilities.

Marks a word in the text that has its own entry

bishop, *noun*   The English word bishop evolved from a Greek word that appears in two of the later epistle, which carry a claim to have been written by Paul but probably were not. The word is *episcopos*, formed from *epi*, on or over + *skopos*, look or watch. It was the title carried by civil servants in the Roman empire who had responsibility for the oversight of various government operations. Apparently, early in the second century, some Christian communities picked up the term as they put behind them the radical principles of St. Paul and began to mirror the Roman society around them. This organizational move away from a loose, collaborative structure was one way they attempted to gain respectability in the eyes of their neighbors.

> The saying is sure: whoever aspires to the office of **bishop** desires a noble task. Now a **bishop** must be above reproach, married only once, temperate, sensible, respectable, hospitable, an apt teacher, not a drunkard, not violent but gentle, not quarrelsome, and not a lover of money. He must manage his own household well, keeping his children submissive and respectful in every way—for if someone does not know how to manage his own household, how can he take care of God's church? He must not be a recent convert, or he may be puffed up with conceit and fall into the condemnation of the devil. Moreover, he must be well thought of by outsiders, so that he may not fall into disgrace and the snare of the devil. [I Timothy 3:1-7]

> For a **bishop**, as God's steward, must be blameless; he must not be arrogant or quick-tempered or addicted to wine or violent or greedy for gain; but he must be hospitable, a lover of goodness, prudent, upright, devout, and self-controlled. He must have a firm grasp of the word that is trustworthy in accordance with the teaching, so that he may be able both to preach with sound doctrine and to refute those who contradict it. [Titus 1:7-9]

As the Roman empire began to crumble, Christian bishops took on more and more of the trappings and authority once associated with government supervisors. In some branches of the divided church, bishops are thought to be essential to the ministry. Many protestant denominations prefer to get along without them, but the function of oversight remains in the hands of people with other titles.

blasphemy, *noun*; **blaspheme**, *verb*   The English words blasphemy and blaspheme come directly from the Greek *blasphemia* and *blasphemeo*, respectively. In Greek, however, the words could be used in relation to human beings as well as to God. They had to do with injuring the reputation of another; in other words, slander and defamation of character.

In the New Revised Standard Version of the Hebrew Scriptures, the words blasphemy and blaspheme occur only once each. The first is a Chaldean word *shalah*, which meant wrong. The second is *naqab*, often translated as curse.*

> Therefore I make a decree: Any people, nation, or language that utters **blasphemy** against the God of Shadrach, Meshach, and Abednego shall be torn limb from limb, and their houses laid in ruins; for there is no other god who is able to deliver in this way. [Daniel 3:29]

> Speak to the people of Israel, saying: Anyone who curses God shall bear the sin. One who **blasphemes** the name of the LORD shall be put to death; the whole congregation shall stone the blasphemer. Aliens as well as citizens, when they **blaspheme** the Name, shall be put to death. [Leviticus 24:15-16]

In the Greek portions of the Bible, when *blasphemia* and *blasphemeo* are used in regard to anything except a direct reference to God, they have been translated with a number of English words, but not blasphemy and blaspheme—even in reference to Jesus.

> For out of the heart come evil intentions, murder, adultery, fornication, theft, false witness, **slander**. [Matthew 15:19]

> Those who passed by **derided** him, shaking their heads and saying, "You who would destroy the temple and build it in three days, save yourself! If you are the Son of God, come down from the cross." [Matthew 27:39-40]

> Now the men who were holding Jesus began to mock him and beat him; they also blindfolded him and kept asking him, "Prophesy! Who is it that struck you?" They kept heaping many other **insults** on him. [Luke 22:63-65]

> They set up false witnesses who said, "This man never stops saying **things** against this holy place and the law; for we have heard him say that this Jesus of Nazareth will destroy this place and will change the customs that Moses handed on to us." [Acts 6:13-14]

> When they opposed and **reviled** him, in protest he shook the dust from his clothes and said to them, "Your blood be on your own heads! I am innocent. From now on I will go to the Gentiles." [Acts 18:6]

> So do not let your good be spoken of as **evil**. [Romans 14:16]

> If I partake with thankfulness, why should I be **denounced** because of that for which I give thanks? [I Corinthians 10:30]

> For people will be lovers of themselves, lovers of money, boasters, arrogant, **abusive**, disobedient to their parents, ungrateful, unholy, . . . [II Timothy 3:2]

> Likewise, tell the older women to be reverent in behavior, not to be slanderers or slaves to drink; they are to teach what is good, so that they may encourage the young women to love their husbands, to love their children, to be self-controlled, chaste, good managers of the household, kind, being submissive to their husbands, so that the word of God may not be **discredited**. [Titus 2:3-5]

> Many will follow their licentious ways, and because of these teachers the way of truth will be **maligned**. [II Peter 2:2]

> The fourth angel poured his bowl on the sun, and it was allowed to scorch them with fire; they were scorched by the fierce heat, but they **cursed** the name of God, who had authority over these plagues, and they did not repent and give him glory. [Revelation 16:8-9]

The great variety of terms used to translate *blasphemia* and *blasphemeo* can add depth to our understanding of the gospel accounts that report charges of blasphemy leveled at Jesus:

> Jesus was silent. Then the high priest said to him, "I put you under oath before the living God, tell us if you are the Messiah, the Son of God." Jesus said to him, "You have said so. But I tell you, from now on you will see the Son of Man seated at the right hand of Power and coming on the clouds of heaven." Then the high priest tore his clothes and said, "He has **blasphemed**! Why do we still need witnesses? You have now heard his **blasphemy**. What is your verdict?" They answered, "He deserves death." [Matthew 26:63-66]

> Now some of the scribes were sitting there, questioning in their hearts, "Why does this fellow speak in this way? It is **blasphemy**! Who can forgive sins but God alone?" [Mark 2:6-7]

> Jesus replied, "I have shown you many good works from the Father. For which of these are you going to stone me?" The Jews answered, "It is not for a good work that we are going to stone you, but for **blasphemy**, because you, though only a human being, are making yourself God." [John 10:32-33]

According to the gospels, some who opposed Jesus thought that by his words and actions he was slandering, deriding, insulting, reviling, denouncing, abusing, discrediting, maligning, or cursing God. These connotations of *blasphemia* and *blasphemeo* can help explain the strength of the resistance that the gospel writers saw in some of the people Jesus encountered.

blessed, *adjective*; **bless**, *verb*; **blessing**, *noun* Of all the biblical metaphors, the ones that lie behind the English forms of bless may be the most difficult to grasp. The idea in Hebrew and Greek as well as English can be attached to people, things, or God. The original Hebrew metaphor, *barak,* developed from a verb that meant to bend—in this case, to bend the knee, which suggests an attitude of humility or subjection. One of the Greek words of this sort can appear in different forms, all based on the verb *eulogeo—eu,* good + *logeo,* speak.

The other Greek word, with somewhat different connotations, is *makarios,* which appears only as an adjective and which meant happy, fortunate, or lucky. The English word bless apparently has its roots in blood, the blood of sacrifice, but early on it got mixed up in peoples' minds with bliss, meaning blitheness, joy, or happiness.

The knee-bending metaphor when applied to people suggests that this was an ancient ceremonial form in which slaves acknowledged the power of their masters, or warriors admitted defeat in the presence of the victors. In each case, the ones with bended knees hoped for leniency, a little kindness, and perhaps ultimately their freedom. Apparently, the people of ancient Israel adopted a similar attitude of submissiveness toward God.* When their lives were going well, they seem to have thought that God was being kind, or forgiving, or delivering them from their enemies, or perhaps all three. Many such experiences of *barak* appear in the Hebrew Scriptures.

> God **blessed** Noah and his sons, and said to them, "Be fruitful and multiply, and fill the earth." [Genesis 9:1]

> When the LORD your God has **blessed** you, as he promised you, you will lend to many nations, but you will not borrow; you will rule over many nations, but they will not rule over you. [Deuteronomy 15:6]

> The LORD **blessed** the latter days of Job more than his beginning; and he had fourteen thousand sheep, six thousand camels, a thousand yoke of oxen, and a thousand donkeys. [Job 42:12]

The same attitude of submissiveness apparently lies behind the use of the knee-bending metaphor when people are talking to or about God. That is, the people—not God—do the knee bending. In this context, *barak* takes on connotations of thanks and praise.

> The servant of Abraham bowed his head and worshiped the LORD and said, "**Blessed** be the LORD, the God of my master Abraham, who has not forsaken his steadfast love and his faithfulness toward my master. As for me, the LORD has led me on the way to the house of my master's kin." [Genesis 24:26-27]

---

*Marks a word in the text that has its own entry

> Then the women said to Naomi, "**Blessed** be the LORD, who has not left you this day without next-of-kin; and may his name be renowned in Israel! He shall be to you a restorer of life and a nourisher of your old age; for your daughter-in-law who loves you, who is more to you than seven sons, has borne him." [Ruth 4:14-15]

> **Blessed** be God, because he has not rejected my prayer or removed his steadfast love from me. [Psalm 66:20]

Barak also identifies ritual acts setting apart animals or other forms of food to be used in worship.* Presumably, the metaphor says more about the worshipers than about the things they were about to eat. The worshipers metaphorically bend the knee in thanks for what they are about to offer.

> As soon as you enter the town, you will find the seer, before he goes up to the shrine to eat. For the people will not eat until he comes, since he must **bless** the sacrifice; afterward those eat who are invited. [I Samuel 9:13]

In the Hebrew Scriptures, people pronounce blessings on other people, but the characters in the stories assume that the blessings conferred are of divine origin. The words spoken have such power of their own that, once uttered, cannot be recalled—even when the blessing was a mistake.

> When Esau heard his father's words, he cried out with an exceedingly great and bitter cry, and said to his father, "**Bless** me, me also, father!" But he said, "Your brother came deceitfully, and he has taken away your **blessing**." [Genesis 27:34-35]

Although the Greek metaphors have nothing to do with bending the knee, the followers of Jesus used them in ways that are quite similar to the ways that the Hebrew writers used *barak*. When Christians used *makarios*, they apparently had in mind good fortune or happiness, in the original meaning of that English word. Happiness has the same root as *hap*pen and per*haps*, indicating that the emphasis at one time was on chance or good luck. In more recent times, the word happy more often refers to the feelings aroused when circumstances are favorable. The popular meaning of happy confused some people when they found the New English Bible using happy in place of the expected blessed in the section of Matthew's gospel, which is often called the Beatitudes.

> "**Blessed** are the poor in spirit, for theirs is the kingdom of heaven.
> "**Blessed** are those who mourn, for they will be comforted.
> "**Blessed** are the meek, for they will inherit the earth.
> "**Blessed** are those who hunger and thirst for righteousness, for they will be filled.
> "**Blessed** are the merciful, for they will receive mercy.
> "**Blessed** are the pure in heart, for they will see God.
> "**Blessed** are the peacemakers, for they will be called children of God.
> "**Blessed** are those who are persecuted for righteousness' sake, for theirs is the kingdom of heaven.
> "**Blessed** are you when people revile you and persecute you and utter all kinds of evil against you falsely on my account." [Matthew 5:3-11]

These sayings attributed to Jesus are in the form of aphorisms, insights expressed in short, pithy sentences. As Clifton Fadiman wrote in an introduction to a collection of aphorisms by a Polish writer: "An aphorism contains only as much wisdom as an overstatement will permit."[8] When understood as aphorisms, these blessings make people stop and think. How can the poor, the mourners, and the meek be counted among the lucky ones? How can the hungry and thirsty, the merciful, and the peacemakers ever be happy? How can the persecuted and the reviled possibly be thought of as fortunate? Those questions can lead people into a deeper realization of who among us are the truly well off. The questions also challenge today's materialistic standards of judgment.

While *makarios* most often refers to people, the other word translated blessed—*eulogetos*—is occasionally applied to people.

> Then the king will say to those at his right hand, "Come, you that are **blessed** by my Father, inherit the kingdom prepared for you." [Matthew 25:34]

> When God raised up his servant, he sent him first to you, to **bless** you by turning each of you from your wicked ways. [Acts 3:26]

Some form of *eulogeo*, like its Hebrew equivalent, more often appears as praise or thanks to God.

> **Blessed** be the Lord God of Israel, for he has looked favorably on his people and redeemed them. [Luke 1:68]

> **Blessed** be the God and Father of our Lord Jesus Christ, the Father of mercies and the God of all consolation, who consoles us in all our affliction, so that we may be able to console those who are in any affliction with the consolation with which we ourselves are consoled by God. [II Corinthians 1:3-4]

> **Blessed** be the God and Father of our Lord Jesus Christ! By his great mercy he has given us a new birth into a living hope through the resurrection of Jesus Christ from the dead. [I Peter 1:3]

Eulogeo again follows the lead of *barak* in setting aside food to be used in a ritual act. It may be interesting to notice that the only things blessed in the Bible have to do with meals. Although the practice is common among Christians, in the Bible we find no blessing of hounds, ships, medals, or religious paraphernalia.

> Then he ordered the crowds to sit down on the grass. Taking the five loaves and the two fish, he looked up to heaven, and **blessed** and broke the loaves, and gave them to the disciples, and the disciples gave them to the crowds. [Matthew 14:19]

> While they were eating, Jesus took a loaf of bread, and after **blessing** it he broke it, gave it to the disciples, and said, "Take, eat; this is my body." [Matthew 26:26]

> The cup of **blessing** that we **bless**, is it not a sharing in the blood of Christ? The bread that we break, is it not a sharing in the body of Christ? [I Corinthians 10:16]

Blessings bestowed by people on other people also appear in the Christian writings. In these person-to-person exchanges, however, it is not always clear if the author intends *eulogeo* to mean that the one pronouncing the blessing is speaking kindly or invoking divine protection. When either Jesus or Paul is reported to have urged others to offer blessings, again it is not always clear if the recommended behavior has to do with gentle speech or with an invocation of God's favor.

> Then Simeon **blessed** them and said to his mother Mary, "This child is destined for the falling and the rising of many in Israel, and to be a sign that will be opposed so that the inner thoughts of many will be revealed—and a sword will pierce your own soul too." [Luke 2:34-35]

> Jesus said to them, "Let the little children come to me; do not stop them; for it is to such as these that the kingdom of God belongs. Truly I tell you, whoever does not receive the kingdom of

blessed FROM LITERAL TO LITERARY

God as a little child will never enter it." And he took them up in his arms, laid his hands on them, and **blessed** them. [Mark 10:14-16]

I say to you that listen, Love your enemies, do good to those who hate you, **bless** those who curse you, pray for those who abuse you. [Luke 6:27-28]

Bless those who persecute you; **bless** and do not curse them. [Romans 12:14]

In the present time, the original biblical blessing metaphors offer valuable guidance, even for people who do not think that God intervenes in human affairs. The Hebrew image of bending the knee and the Greek concept of good luck in combination can produce a healthy attitude and constructive behavior. When successful people admit how much luck was involved in their good fortune, and when that realization produces a healthy portion of humility, they are more likely to treat the less fortunate with compassion and respect. When people are less successful, they can console themselves with the observation that they may be simply unlucky and that they might be arrogant in assuming that they alone are responsible for their misfortune.

blood—see **sacrifice**

body, *noun*   The Greek word *soma* appears most often in early Christian writings with the same meaning that body has in English. For Paul, and for those who followed in his footsteps, *soma* became an important metaphor describing the nature of the church.

For as in one **body** we have many members, and not all the members have the same function, so we, who are many, are one **body** in Christ, and individually we are members one of another. [Romans 12:4-5]

For just as the **body** is one and has many members, and all the members of the body, though many, are one **body**, so it is with Christ. For in the one Spirit we were all baptized into one **body**—Jews or Greeks, slaves or free—and we were all made to drink of one Spirit. Indeed, the **body** does not consist of one member but of many. [I Corinthians 12:12-14]

The other metaphorical use of *soma* was in discussions of the ritual meal that was later called the Eucharist.*

The cup of blessing that we bless, is it not a sharing in the blood of Christ? The bread that we break, is it not a sharing in the **body** of Christ? Because there is one bread, we who are many are one **body**, for we all partake of the one bread. [I Corinthians 10:16-17]

For I received from the Lord what I also handed on to you, that the Lord Jesus on the night when he was betrayed took a loaf of bread, and when he had given thanks, he broke it and said, "This is my **body** that is for you. Do this in remembrance of me." [I Corinthians 11:23-24]

Paul used *soma* in yet another figurative sense in his writing about what he thinks may follow death.* He contrasts the physical body, the body animated by the *psyche* or soul,* with a body that is spirit.* It is not altogether clear exactly what he had in mind, but when he writes about a spiritual body, he is obviously not using *soma* in its usual sense of flesh* and blood.

Marks a word in the text that has its own entry

> So it is with the resurrection of the dead. What is sown is perishable, what is raised is imperishable. It is sown in dishonor, it is raised in glory. It is sown in weakness, it is raised in power. It is sown a physical **body**, it is raised a spiritual **body**. If there is a physical **body**, there is also a spiritual **body**. [I Corinthians 15:42-44]

These three figurative uses of *soma* may have played an important role in the development of the resurrection* idea. If the followers of Jesus have become the spiritual body of Christ, then indeed Christ has been raised from the dead with a new body. If the bread that the followers of Jesus share represents the body of Christ, then Christ continues to live in and through them. When the followers of Jesus became accustomed to this kind of figurative speech, they may have begun telling imaginative stories about the tomb of Jesus being found empty—stories that Paul apparently had never heard.

born again, *verb*; **new birth**, *noun*   The story about Nicodemus in the third chapter of the Gospel according to John centers on a phrase with a double meaning—*gennethe anothen. Gennethe* always means be born, but *anothen* can have connotations on the one hand suggesting above, top, or first and on the other hand implying again or anew. The author uses this double meaning in a play on words not readily apparent in the English translations.

> Jesus answered him, "Very truly, I tell you, no one can see the kingdom of God without being **born from above.**" Nicodemus said to him, "How can anyone be born after having grown old? Can one enter a second time into the mother's womb and be born?" [John 3:3-4]

In this account, the author attributes to Jesus the metaphorical use of *gennethe anothen,* suggesting birth in a new dimension while Nicodemus hears Jesus using the phrase to mean a repetition of birth, being born again. Greek-speaking people in the early centuries of the church's life might have been amused by Nicodemus's misunderstanding. They would have been accustomed to hearing *anothen* being used in a variety of ways, as can be seen from the many appearances of the word in the gospels and epistles.

> And the curtain of the temple was torn in two, from **top** to bottom. [Mark 15:38]

> I too decided, after investigating everything carefully from the very **first,** to write an orderly account for you, most excellent Theophilus. [Luke 1:3]

> Every generous act of giving, with every perfect gift, is from **above,** coming down from the Father of lights, with whom there is no variation or shadow due to change. [James 1:17]

> Now, however, that you have come to know God, or rather to be known by God, how can you turn back again to the weak and beggarly elemental spirits? How can you want to be enslaved to them **again**? [Galatians 4:9]

The King James Version of the Bible nearly always translates *anothen* as "again" when it appears in conjunction with "born." This pattern continues when it comes to the translation of the word *anagennao,* which can mean either give new birth or cause to be born again.

New Revised Standard Version	King James Version
Blessed be the God and Father of our Lord Jesus Christ! By his great mercy he has given us a **new birth** into a living hope through the resurrection of Jesus Christ from the dead, . . . [I Peter 1:3]	Blessed be the God and Father of our Lord Jesus Christ, which according to his abundant mercy hath **begotten** us **again** unto a lively hope by the resurrection of Jesus Christ from the dead, . . .
You have been **born anew**, not of perishable but of imperishable seed, through the living and enduring word of God. [I Peter 1:23]	Being **born again**, not of corruptible seed, but of incorruptible, by the word of God, which liveth and abideth for ever.

The birth metaphor standing alone without a direction or repetition indicator also appears in the early Christian writings known as the Johannine literature. Each of these citations helps to explicate the metaphor:

But to all who received him, who believed in his name, he gave power to become children of God, who were **born**, not of blood or of the will of the flesh or of the will of man, but of God. [John 1:12-13]

If you know that he is righteous, you may be sure that everyone who does right has been **born** of him. See what love the Father has given us, that we should be called children of God; and that is what we are. [I John 2:29-3:1]

Beloved, let us love one another, because love is from God; everyone who loves is **born** of God and knows God. [I John 4:7]

Because three of the gospels and Paul do not use the birth metaphor, we might fairly conclude that it emerged relatively late in the formative period of Christian thinking. It may represent an evolution of two other metaphors used quite commonly in the earliest writings that refer to the followers of Jesus as family* and as sisters* and brothers. This could have been a logical development. If the followers of Jesus were metaphorically speaking brothers and sisters, then they must have been born to the same mother* or father.*

In modern times, some Christians have used "born again" as the primary demarcation of those who are acceptable to God. Those who have not been born again are doomed. Another way to employ the metaphor is to follow the example of the first letter attributed to John. We could say that everyone who does what is right and who is capable of love has been born of God, that is, such a person has an added dimension to life not experienced by those who care nothing for acts of justice or loving behavior.

The baptism ritual has long been associated with the birth metaphor. When the church baptizes either infants or adults, it is with the hope that they will discover the dimension of love and of justice in their lives. With the guidance of their new sisters and brothers, they may come to understand that all people are children of God deserving their respect and concern.

*Marks a word in the text that has its own entry

DID YOU KNOW ...

... that *gennethe* is pronounced *gehn-nay-thay*
For more help with pronunciation, see "Pronouncing
Transliterated Hebrew and Greek Words" on page 15.

---

bread, *noun*   The Hebrew language had two words for bread. *Lechem* was bread made with yeast, and *matzah* was unleavened or flat bread. Both were featured in temple rituals. Although both kinds of bread could be offered along with the sacrifices,* most of the rituals called for *matzah*, presumably because of negative attitudes toward yeast.* When *lechem* was offered, the priests were expected to eat it.

> This is the law for the nazirites when the time of their consecration has been completed: they shall be brought to the entrance of the tent of meeting, and they shall offer their gift to the LORD, one male lamb a year old without blemish as a burnt offering, one ewe lamb a year old without blemish as a sin offering, one ram without blemish as an offering of well-being, and a basket of **unleavened bread**, cakes of choice flour mixed with oil and unleavened wafers spread with oil, with their grain offering and their drink offerings. [Numbers 6:13-15]

> With your thanksgiving sacrifice of well-being you shall bring your offering with cakes of **leavened bread**. From this you shall offer one cake from each offering, as a gift to the LORD; it shall belong to the priest who dashes the blood of the offering of well-being. [Leviticus 7:13-14]

Although not part of the sacrifices, *lechem panim*—translated as bread of the presence or showbread—was included in the regulations concerning temple rites. The earliest mention may be the story in I Samuel of David appropriating this holy bread to feed his hungry troops. The regulations concerning the *lechem panim* appear in other books.

> The priest answered David, "I have no ordinary bread at hand, only holy bread—provided that the young men have kept themselves from women." David answered the priest, "Indeed women have been kept from us as always when I go on an expedition; the vessels of the young men are holy even when it is a common journey; how much more today will their vessels be holy?" So the priest gave him the holy bread; for there was no bread there except the **bread of the Presence**, which is removed from before the LORD, to be replaced by hot bread on the day it is taken away. [I Samuel 21:4-6]

> Over the table of the **bread of the Presence** they shall spread a blue cloth, and put on it the plates, the dishes for incense, the bowls, and the flagons for the drink offering; the regular bread also shall be on it; then they shall spread over them a crimson cloth, and cover it with a covering of fine leather, and shall put its poles in place. [Numbers 4:7-8]

In the stories about manna, the miraculous food that God provided the people of Israel on their trek though the desert from Egypt to the promised land, the manna is also called *lechem*.

> Then the LORD said to Moses, "I am going to rain **bread** from heaven for you, and each day the people shall go out and gather enough for that day. In that way I will test them, whether they will follow my instruction or not." [Exodus 16:4]

---

*Marks a word in the text that has its own entry

> For their hunger you gave them **bread** from heaven, and for their thirst you brought water for them out of the rock, and you told them to go in to possess the land that you swore to give them. [Nehemiah 9:15]

With all its associations with ritual and with legend, the use of *lechem* as a metaphor should come as no surprise. The word could stand for any kind of food, for nourishment in general, or for all the necessities of life.

> Then Jacob made a vow, saying, "If God will be with me, and will keep me in this way that I go, and will give me **bread** to eat and clothing to wear, so that I come again to my father's house in peace, then the LORD shall be my God." [Genesis 28:20-21]

> So Potiphar left all that he had in Joseph's charge; and, with him there, he had no concern for anything but the **food** that he ate. [Genesis 39:6]

> Then Naomi started to return with her daughters-in-law from the country of Moab, for she had heard in the country of Moab that the LORD had considered his people and given them **food**. [Ruth 1:6]

Similarly, *lechem* could be used as a metaphor indicating the struggle for survival, the toil and pain sometimes required to produce the bare essentials needed to stay alive.

> To the man God said, "Because you have listened to the voice of your wife, and have eaten of the tree about which I commanded you, 'You shall not eat of it,' cursed is the ground because of you; in toil you shall eat of it all the days of your life; thorns and thistles it shall bring forth for you; and you shall eat the plants of the field. By the sweat of your face you shall eat **bread** until you return to the ground, for out of it you were taken; you are dust, and to dust you shall return." [Genesis 3:17-19]

> Though the Lord may give you the **bread** of adversity and the water of affliction, yet your Teacher will not hide himself any more, but your eyes shall see your Teacher. [Isaiah 30:20]

> O LORD God of hosts, how long will you be angry with your people's prayers? You have fed them with the **bread** of tears, and given them tears to drink in full measure. [Psalm 80:4-5]

> It is in vain that you rise up early and go late to rest, eating the **bread** of anxious toil; for he gives sleep to his beloved. [Psalm 127:2]

The Greek language had the equivalents of the Hebrew words, *artos* for *lechem* and *azumos* for *matzah*. Except when St. Paul uses the yeast* metaphor to make a point about responsible behavior, *azumos* appears in the Bible only in reference to the Festival of Unleavened Bread.

> Clean out the old yeast so that you may be a new batch, as you really are **unleavened**. For our paschal lamb, Christ, has been sacrificed. Therefore, let us celebrate the festival, not with the old yeast, the yeast of malice and evil, but with the **unleavened bread** of sincerity and truth. [I Corinthians 5:7-8]

> On the first day of **Unleavened Bread**, when the Passover lamb is sacrificed, his disciples said to him, "Where do you want us to go and make the preparations for you to eat the Passover?" [Mark 14:12]

The use of the Hebrew *lechem* in ritual, legend, and metaphor apparently had a profound influence on the Christian understanding of *artos*, which also could mean food, nourishment, or the necessities of life.

> Give us this day our daily **bread**. [Matthew 6:11]

> Jesus answered, "It is not fair to take the children's **food** and throw it to the dogs." [Matthew 15:26]

> Jesus ordered them to take nothing for their journey except a staff; no **bread**, no bag, no money in their belts; but to wear sandals and not to put on two tunics. [Mark 6:8-9]

> On one occasion when Jesus was going to the house of a leader of the Pharisees to eat a **meal** on the sabbath, they were watching him closely. [Luke 14:1]

> Now such persons we command and exhort in the Lord Jesus Christ to do their work quietly and to earn their own **living**. [II Thessalonians 3:12]

The story about David and his men eating the bread of the Presence became an important part of Christian lore. The story appears in each of the first three gospels, and a reference to the ritual appears in the letter to the Hebrews.

> Jesus said to them, "Have you never read what David did when he and his companions were hungry and in need of food? He entered the house of God, when Abiathar was high priest, and ate the **bread** of the Presence, which it is not lawful for any but the priests to eat, and he gave some to his companions." [Mark 2:25-26; see also Matthew 12:3-4 and Luke 6:3-4]

> Now even the first covenant had regulations for worship and an earthly sanctuary. For a tent was constructed, the first one, in which were the lampstand, the table, and the **bread** of the Presence; this is called the Holy Place. [Hebrews 9:1-2]

The Gospel according to John uses *artos* to make a connection between the manna stories and Jesus.

> Your ancestors ate the manna in the wilderness, and they died. This is the **bread** that comes down from heaven, so that one may eat of it and not die. I am the living **bread** that came down from heaven. Whoever eats of this **bread** will live forever; and the **bread** that I will give for the life of the world is my flesh. [John 6:49-51]

Although only John dwells on this identification of Jesus with *artos*, many of the early Christian writers focus on bread as a primary Christian symbol. The stories and teachings related to bread probably evolved from the ritual meal that came to be known as the Eucharist.* For the followers of Jesus, the sharing of *artos* became the equivalent of the offering and eating of bread in the temple rituals. The earliest mentions of this practice appear in St. Paul's first letter to the community in Corinth. The ritual was clearly standard practice by the time that the Acts of the Apostles was written.

> The **bread** that we break, is it not a sharing in the body of Christ? Because there is one **bread**, we who are many are one body, for we all partake of the one **bread**. [I Corinthians 10:16-17]

> I received from the Lord what I also handed on to you, that the Lord Jesus on the night when he was betrayed took a loaf of **bread**, and when he had given thanks, he broke it and said, "This is my body that is for you. Do this in remembrance of me." [I Corinthians 11:23-24]

Marks a word in the text that has its own entry

> Those who welcomed Peter's message were baptized, and that day about three thousand persons were added. They devoted themselves to the apostles' teaching and fellowship, to the breaking of **bread** and the prayers. [Acts 2:41-42]

> On the first day of the week, when we met to break **bread**, Paul was holding a discussion. [Acts 20:7]

Many scholars doubt that Jesus said the words about bread being his body that Paul attributes to him. As he indicates, the ritual had been well established by the time Paul came on the scene. The early identification of both the bread and the community with the body* of Jesus could easily have evolved into the story that tells of Jesus himself instituting the ritual. From there it was a only a short step to John's use of bread as one of his many metaphors for Jesus. The ritual may also have laid the groundwork for the stories told of Jesus providing *artos* for a large number of people. The most primitive of such stories may be the first of two in Mark's gospel.

> As Jesus went ashore, he saw a great crowd; and he had compassion for them, because they were like sheep without a shepherd; and he began to teach them many things. When it grew late, his disciples came to him and said, "This is a deserted place, and the hour is now very late; send them away so that they may go into the surrounding country and villages and buy **something** for themselves to eat." But he answered them, "You give them something to eat." They said to him, "Are we to go and buy two hundred denarii worth of **bread**, and give it to them to eat?" And he said to them, "How many **loaves** have you? Go and see." When they had found out, they said, "Five, and two fish." Then he ordered them to get all the people to sit down in groups on the green grass. So they sat down in groups of hundreds and of fifties. Taking the five **loaves** and the two fish, he looked up to heaven, and blessed and broke the **loaves**, and gave them to his disciples to set before the people; and he divided the two fish among them all. And all ate and were filled. [Mark 6:34-42]

Note that in all these biblical references to bread in Christian stories and rituals, the word is *artos*, ordinary bread made with yeast. The use of *azumos* or *matzah* in the ritual breaking of the bread must have been a later development. The practice of using small wafers of unleavened bread has obscured the once-powerful symbolism of a congregation attesting to their unity by sharing one loaf of bread. The practice has also separated the ritual meal from familiar forms of bread. The wafer is a symbol of a symbol and cannot evoke what the early followers of Jesus experienced in the look, texture, smell, and taste of the loaf they broke and shared in Jesus's name.

As a metaphor, bread continues to represent all the necessities of life. People say they work to put bread on the table. Bread has often been a metaphor for money. The metaphor has also worked for many people as they try to explain how their experience of Jesus has been lifegiving. Contact with the Jesus tradition can sometimes allow a person to imagine being a companion of Jesus, being taught, and being fed. Jesus, like bread, can be a primary source of nourishment.

brothers—see **sisters and brothers**

C

call—see **church**

chaos—see **create**

---

                                                 *Marks a word in the text that has its own entry

charisma, *noun*   The Greek word *charisma* has as its root *charis*, meaning favor or grace.* *Charisma* has survived in English virtually unchanged in sound from the Greek but with slightly different connotations. In English versions of the Bible, *charisma* is nearly always translated gift, while in English usage the meaning of charisma is usually restricted to the gift of leadership or authority,* that is, the capacity to inspire loyalty or enthusiasm.

Although the word does not appear in the gospels or in the Acts of the Apostles, St. Paul makes extensive use of the term *charisma*, usually in reference to God* or to the Spirit.*

> For the wages of sin is death, but the free **gift** of God is eternal life in Christ Jesus our Lord. [Romans 6:23]

> We have **gifts** that differ according to the grace given to us: prophecy, in proportion to faith; ministry, in ministering; the teacher, in teaching; the exhorter, in exhortation; the giver, in generosity; the leader, in diligence; the compassionate, in cheerfulness. [Romans 12:6-8]

> Now there are varieties of **gifts**, but the same Spirit; and there are varieties of services, but the same Lord; and there are varieties of activities, but it is the same God who activates all of them in everyone. To each is given the manifestation of the Spirit for the common good. To one is given through the Spirit the utterance of wisdom, and to another the utterance of knowledge according to the same Spirit, to another faith by the same Spirit, to another **gifts** of healing by the one Spirit, to another the working of miracles, to another prophecy, to another the discernment of spirits, to another various kinds of tongues, to another the interpretation of tongues. [I Corinthians 12:4-10]

> God has appointed in the church first apostles, second prophets, third teachers; then deeds of power, then **gifts** of healing, forms of assistance, forms of leadership, various kinds of tongues. Are all apostles? Are all prophets? Are all teachers? Do all work miracles? Do all possess **gifts** of healing? Do all speak in tongues? Do all interpret? But strive for the greater **gifts**. And I will show you a still more excellent way. [I Corinthians 12:28-31]

Some Christians focus particularly on the gift of tongues, which they associate with Pentecost.* This focus in some North American churches has led to the custom of calling such congregations and their worshipers charismatic. For St. Paul, this would be a misleading use of the term. Although he did not deny the validity of the gift of tongues, he insisted that it was just one among many.

In using the gift metaphor to write about various abilities and skills, St. Paul seems to have had two goals in mind. First, he wanted the followers of Jesus to adopt a genuinely humble stance in relationship to each other. Second, he wanted them to appreciate their differences. These two qualities were essential for the healthy functioning of each Christian community.* Most Jesus followers would agree that those qualities are as valuable in the twenty-first century as they were in the first.

Christ   Christ came into English almost unchanged from the Greek *christos*, which was a literal translation of the Hebrew *mashiach*, or messiah. Both words are rooted in verbs meaning to anoint with oil. Anointing with oil was the ritual frequently employed in appointing or commissioning a person for high office.

> You shall **anoint** Aaron and his sons, and consecrate them, in order that they may serve me as priests. [Exodus 30:30]

Marks a word in the text that has its own entry

> Samuel said to Saul, "The LORD sent me to **anoint** you king over his people Israel."
> [I Samuel 15:1]

Anyone who had been appointed with this ritual was thereafter known as *mashiach*, the anointed.

> David said to Saul, "Why do you listen to the words of those who say, 'David seeks to do you harm'? This very day your eyes have seen how the LORD gave you into my hand in the cave; and some urged me to kill you, but I spared you. I said, 'I will not raise my hand against my lord; for he is the Lord's **anointed.**'" [I Samuel 24:9-10]

> Now these are the last words of David: The oracle of David, son of Jesse, the oracle of the man whom God exalted, the **anointed** of the God of Jacob, the favorite of the Strong One of Israel.
> [II Samuel 23:1]

The Anointed One was also used in a purely metaphorical sense to identify someone perceived to be doing the LORD's work, even a foreign conqueror.

> Thus says the LORD to his **anointed,** to Cyrus (king of the Persians), whose right hand I have grasped to subdue nations before him and strip kings of their robes, to open doors before him—and the gates shall not be closed. [Isaiah 45:1]

Curiously enough, the New Revised Standard Version of the Bible never translates *mashiach* as messiah, and the King James Version does so only twice.

> From the going forth of the commandment to restore and to build Jerusalem unto the **Messiah** the Prince shall be seven weeks . . . And after threescore and two weeks shall **Messiah** be cut off. [Daniel 9:25-26, KING JAMES VERSION]

The meaning of the metaphor is further confused by the different translations of *christos* in the Greek portion of the scriptures. The King James Version uses Christ while the New Revised Standard Version generally uses the Hebrew messiah, unless *christos* immediately precedes or follows *iesous*.

New Revised Standard Version	King James Version
When John heard in prison what the **Messiah** was doing, he sent word by his disciples. [Matthew 11:2]	Now when John had heard in the prison the works of **Christ,** he sent two of his disciples.
He said to them, "But who do you say that I am?" Peter answered, "The **Messiah** of God." [Luke 9:20]	He said unto them, But whom say ye that I am? Peter answering said, The **Christ** of God.

At some point, either before or after the death of Jesus, his disciples began to use the anointed metaphor to indicate something about their relationship to him. Some scholars argue that many Judeans were looking for God to commission a new leader, someone like Saul or David, who could lead them to freedom from the oppression of the Roman empire. Others think that those who looked for a new messiah represented only the lunatic fringe of first-century Judean society.

Neither analysis of the evidence, however, explains how the disciples came to regard Jesus as the one appointed by God for their benefit. He made no pretension of functioning as a priest like Aaron. He made no bid for political power like Saul or David. He did not present himself as a conqueror like Cyrus. If the disciples thought of Jesus as a *mashiach* or *christos*, they must have experienced in him a freedom different from the kind promised by priests and kings.

A study of the gospel stories describing encounters with Jesus suggests that Jesus represented a response to a three-fold longing present in most human hearts, which is a deep desire for self-confidence, self-understanding, and a meaningful direction for life. In the presence of Jesus people felt free to face what they had not been able to face, to be honest about their weaknesses and strengths, and to find a new way and a new life. This pattern appears in many stories, but perhaps none more clearly than this highly imaginative reflection on the connection between human longing and the anointed metaphor being applied to Jesus.

> Jesus came to a Samaritan city called Sychar, near the plot of ground that Jacob had given to his son Joseph. Jacob's well was there, and Jesus, tired out by his journey, was sitting by the well. It was about noon.
>
> A Samaritan woman came to draw water, and Jesus said to her, "Give me a drink." (His disciples had gone to the city to buy food.) The Samaritan woman said to him, "How is it that you, a Jew, ask a drink of me, a woman of Samaria?" (Jews do not share things in common with Samaritans.) Jesus answered her, "If you knew the gift of God, and who it is that is saying to you, 'Give me a drink,' you would have asked him, and he would have given you living water."
>
> (1)
>
> The woman said to him, "Sir, you have no bucket, and the well is deep. Where do you get that living water? Are you greater than our ancestor Jacob, who gave us the well, and with his sons and his flocks drank from it?" Jesus said to her, "Everyone who drinks of this water will be thirsty again, but those who drink of the water that I will give them will never be thirsty. The water that I will give will become in them a spring of water gushing up to eternal life." The woman said to him, "Sir, give me this water, so that I may never be thirsty or have to keep coming here to draw water."
>
> (2)
>
> Jesus said to her, "Go, call your husband, and come back." The woman answered him, "I have no husband." Jesus said to her, "You are right in saying, 'I have no husband'; for you have had five husbands, and the one you have now is not your husband. What you have said is true!" The woman said to him, "Sir, I see that you are a prophet. Our ancestors worshiped on this mountain, but you say that the place where people must worship is in Jerusalem." Jesus said to her, "Woman, believe me, the hour is coming when you will worship the Father neither on this mountain nor in Jerusalem. You worship what you do not know; we worship what we know, for salvation is from the Jews. But the hour is coming, and is now here, when the true worshipers will worship the Father in spirit and truth, for the Father seeks such as these to worship him. God is spirit, and those who worship him must worship in spirit and truth." The woman said to him, "I know that **Messiah** is coming" (who is called **Christ**). "When he comes, he will proclaim all things to us." Jesus said to her, "I am he, the one who is speaking to you." Just then his disciples came. They were astonished that he was speaking with a woman, but no one said, "What do you want?" or, "Why are you speaking with her?"
>
> (3)
>
> Then the woman left her water jar and went back to the city. She said to the people, "Come and see a man who told me everything I have ever done! He cannot be the **Messiah**, can he?"
> [John 4:4-29]

People attracted to the life and teachings of Jesus, but who are put off by the Christ and Messiah language, might find the original anointed metaphor useful if they think about Jesus as one commissioned on their behalf. It is as if God appointed Jesus to the role of setting them free from whatever stands in the way of their finding confidence, insight, and direction for their lives.

church, *noun*   The Greek word for church was *ekklesia*, which in secular terminology meant a town meeting. In using that term, the followers of Jesus may have been influenced by the Hebrew word with a similar sound, *qahal*, which was the assembly of God's people. *Qahal* was as sacred a concept to the people of Israel as *ekklesia* was a secular idea to the Greeks.

> No one whose testicles are crushed or whose penis is cut off shall be admitted to the **assembly** of the LORD. Those born of an illicit union shall not be admitted to the **assembly** of the LORD. Even to the tenth generation, none of their descendants shall be admitted to the **assembly** of the LORD. [Deuteronomy 23:1-2]

> I will tell of your name to my brothers and sisters; in the midst of the **congregation** I will praise you. [Psalm 22:22]

> After thinking it over, I brought charges against the nobles and the officials; I said to them, "You are all taking interest from your own people." And I called a great **assembly** to deal with them. [Nehemiah 5:7]

Like the word translated advocate,* *ekklesia* is based on *kaleo*, the verb meaning to call. In this case, the prefix is *ek*, out or from. For the early followers of Jesus, church was neither a place nor a people. *Ekklesia* was a symbolic form through which they came to understand an experience of being called out from their ordinary lives. The experience was something like that of the men of ancient Israel when the people were facing war. At such times, the men were called out (Hebrew *tsa'aq*) of their villages and towns to form an army. They were called out for a special kind of service for their people.

> The men of Israel were **called out** from Naphtali and from Asher and from all Manasseh, and they pursued after the Midianites. [Judges 7:23]

> When all Israel heard that Saul had defeated the garrison of the Philistines, and also that Israel had become odious to the Philistines, the people were **called out** to join Saul at Gilgal. [I Samuel 13:4]

People can be called out or assembled for a variety of reasons. The nature of the assembly mostly depends on the one who does the calling. As the story goes, Jesus called the original disciples to join him.

> Jesus saw two other brothers, James son of Zebedee and his brother John, in the boat with their father Zebedee, mending their nets, and he **called** them. [Matthew 4:21]

> Jesus went up the mountain and **called** to him those whom he wanted, and they came to him. And he appointed twelve, whom he also named apostles, to be with him, and to be sent out to proclaim the message. [Mark 3:13]

Those who followed Jesus in subsequent generations claimed to have had a similar experience of Jesus calling them, the most notable early example being Paul, who used such an expression to describe his own experience. He used the same language to describe what he believed to be the experience of the Jesus followers in Rome to whom he addressed a letter.

> Paul, a servant of Jesus Christ, **called** to be an apostle, set apart for the gospel of God. [Romans 1:1]

> To all God's beloved in Rome, who are **called** to be saints: Grace to you and peace from God our Father and the Lord Jesus Christ. [Romans 1:7]

In time, apparently the Jesus followers came to describe themselves as the called out ones, that is the *ekklesia*, the church.

> And I tell you, you are Peter, and on this rock I will build my **church,** and the gates of Hades will not prevail against it. [Matthew 16:18]

> Then the apostles and the elders, with the consent of the whole **church,** decided to choose men from among their members and to send them to Antioch with Paul and Barnabas. They sent Judas called Barsabbas, and Silas, leaders among the brothers. [Acts 15:22]

> Let anyone who has an ear listen to what the Spirit is saying to the **churches.** [Revelation 2:7]

In describing themselves as the called out ones, the Jesus followers were making a statement. They did not just get together. That is what happens in a club. They felt that they had been assembled for a purpose—to follow a new way and a new life, to continue the work begun by Jesus.

circumcise and **uncircumcised** *verbs;* **circumcision**, *noun*   The surgical removal of the foreskin from a boy's penis is a ritual that probably existed long before its adoption by the people of ancient Israel. Following the admonitions in the story of God's covenant* with Abraham, both Jews and many Moslems circumcise male infants.

> This is my covenant, which you shall keep, between me and you and your offspring after you: Every male among you shall be **circumcised.** You shall **circumcise** the flesh of your foreskins, and it shall be a sign of the covenant between me and you. Throughout your generations every male among you shall be **circumcised** when he is eight days old, including the slave born in your house and the one bought with your money from any foreigner who is not of your offspring. Both the slave born in your house and the one bought with your money must be **circumcised.** So shall my covenant be in your flesh an everlasting covenant. [Genesis 17:10-13]

The custom of circumcising baby boys has continued among some Gentiles (see **heathen**), especially in North America, but as a medical procedure rather than as a religious ritual. The rationale given is no longer the commandment in the Hebrew Scriptures but rather hygiene. Some argue that removing the foreskin reduces the chance of infection and the transmission of pathogens.

Except for Jews and some Moslems, ritual as opposed to medical circumcision exists primarily as a puberty rite. The ritual circumcision of ten- to twelve-year-old boys is practiced by aboriginal tribes in Australia, by native South Sea Islanders, by various ethnic groups in Africa, and by some Moslems, notably the Bedouins. Circumcision in these cultures is an initiation into manhood. The pain of the operation creates the emotional climate for learning the rules and sexual taboos of the particular tribe. The willingness of the young men to endure the procedure, according to Bruno Bettelheim,[9] may be their envy of the genital bleeding experienced by girls of their own age. Of the pain, however, there can be little doubt. One of the earliest descriptions of the agony produced by circumcision is recorded in a story about the sons of Jacob seeking revenge for the rape of their sister Dinah by Shechem son of Hamor the Hivite. When Shechem decided he wanted to marry Dinah, her brothers said that would not be possible unless he and his father and all their men were circumcised—

> And all who went out of the city gate heeded Hamor and his son Shechem; and every male was **circumcised**, all who went out of the gate of his city. On the third day, when they were still in pain, two of the sons of Jacob, Simeon and Levi, Dinah's brothers, took their swords and came against the city unawares, and killed all the males. They killed Hamor and his son Shechem with the sword, and took Dinah out of Shechem's house, and went away. [Genesis 34:24-26]

Although many Gentiles were attracted to the high moral standards and the monotheistic faith of Judaism, the prospect of painful genital surgery was enough to keep them from converting. One part of St. Paul's brilliant missionary strategy was to welcome into the Christian community these Gentile men without requiring them to be circumcised. This move did not meet with universal approval from the first of Jesus's followers, but Paul persisted.

> Then certain individuals came down from Judea and were teaching the brothers, "Unless you are **circumcised** according to the custom of Moses, you cannot be saved." And after Paul and Barnabas had no small dissension and debate with them, Paul and Barnabas and some of the others were appointed to go up to Jerusalem to discuss this question with the apostles and the elders. [Acts 15:1-2]

It seems likely that this painful rite of initiation into the adult community at some point in Israel's history became associated with birth rather than the onset of puberty. A boy baby is initiated into the tribe eight days after he is born. The ceremony today is called *bris,* derived from the Hebrew *berith,* covenant. In the Hebrew Scriptures the name for the procedure is *mul,* which means to cut short. In Greek it is *peritemno,* to cut around. Both terms were used as metaphors indicating those who considered themselves to be God's people. The negative terms in both languages, the words for uncircumcised, became metaphors for other people—strangers, aliens, and enemies. The Hebrew for uncircumcised is *orla* or *arel* and the Greek is *akrobustia,* words that literally meant foreskin. In Greek it also could be *aperitmetos,* the negative particle with a form of *peritemno.*

> Jonathan said to the young man who carried his armor, "Come, let us go over to the garrison of these **uncircumcised**; it may be that the LORD will act for us; for nothing can hinder the LORD from saving by many or by few." [I Samuel 14:6]

> Awake, awake, put on your strength, O Zion! Put on your beautiful garments, O Jerusalem, the holy city; for the **uncircumcised** and the unclean shall enter you no more. [Isaiah 52:1]

> Since God is one; and he will justify the **circumcised** on the ground of faith and the **uncircumcised** through that same faith. [Romans 3:30]

That circumcision was intended to be an outward sign of an attitude leading to appropriate behavior can be seen in the metaphorical uses of circumcision and uncircumcised in relation to the heart or mind.*

> If then their **uncircumcised** heart is humbled and they make amends for their iniquity, then will I remember my covenant with Jacob; I will remember also my covenant with Isaac and also my covenant with Abraham, and I will remember the land. [Leviticus 26:41-42]

> The days are surely coming, says the LORD, when I will attend to all those who are **circumcised** only in the foreskin: Egypt, Judah, Edom, the Ammonites, Moab, and all those with shaven temples who live in the desert. For all these nations are **uncircumcised**, and all the house of Israel is **uncircumcised** in heart. [Jeremiah 9:25-26]

> You stiff-necked people, **uncircumcised** in heart and ears, you are forever opposing the Holy Spirit, just as your ancestors used to do. [Acts 7:51]

> For a person is not a Jew who is one outwardly, nor is true **circumcision** something external and physical. Rather, a person is a Jew who is one inwardly, and real **circumcision** is a matter of the heart—it is spiritual and not literal. Such a person receives praise not from others but from God. [Romans 2:28-29]

Although the words associated with circumcision today are seldom used in a metaphorical sense, their ancient connection to matters of the heart stands as a reminder that ritual forms are of little value if they do not represent attitudes that are manifest in moral behavior.

clean—see purity

comforter—see advocate

community, *noun*   When the word community appears in an English translation of the Hebrew Scriptures, the word in the original is almost always the plural of *ach*, meaning brothers or relatives. Community avoids the masculine bias found in earlier translations that used brethren. The same logic apparently lies behind the two times where a similar word in Greek, the plural of *adelphos*—meaning both sisters* and brothers—has been translated as community.

> If there is among you anyone in need, a member of your **community** in any of your towns within the land that the LORD your God is giving you, do not be hard-hearted or tight-fisted toward your needy neighbor.—*ach* [Deuteronomy 15:7]

> So the rumor spread in the **community** that this disciple would not die. Yet Jesus did not say to him that he would not die, but, "If it is my will that he remain until I come, what is that to you?"—*adelphos* [John 21:23]

> Peace be to the whole **community,** and love with faith, from God the Father and the Lord Jesus Christ.—*adelphos* [Ephesians 6:23]

The other Greek word translated as community is *plethos*, meaning a large number.

> The twelve called together the whole **community** of the disciples and said, "It is not right that we should neglect the word of God in order to wait on tables." [Acts 6:2]

> Festus said, "King Agrippa and all here present with us, you see this man about whom the whole Jewish **community** petitioned me, both in Jerusalem and here, shouting that he ought not to live any longer." [Acts 25:24]

---

*Marks a word in the text that has its own entry

The followers of Jesus for whom the metaphor community has become an important way for understanding the nature of the church may be disappointed to find so little support in English translations of the Bible. If that is the case, their best option is to supply their own translation of *koinonia*, which usually appears in English as sharing or fellowship.*

confess, *verb*; **confession**, *noun*   As is the case with the English words confess and confession, the Hebrew *yadah* can convey an acknowledgment of sin* or be a declaration of faith.* The root of *yadah* meant hand,* and the word itself suggests throwing out the hands in an act of reverence or worship. The original meaning of the word can be seen in these passages:

> Those who were my enemies without cause have hunted me like a bird; they flung me alive into a pit and **hurled** stones on me. [Lamentations 3:52-53]

> These are the horns that scattered Judah, so that no head could be raised; but these have come to terrify them, to **strike down** the horns of the nations that lifted up their horns against the land of Judah to scatter its people. [Zechariah 1:21]

More often the word is used in acknowledging fault:

> When you realize your guilt in any of these, you shall **confess** the sin that you have committed. [Leviticus 5:5]

> Then I acknowledged my sin to you, and I did not hide my iniquity; I said, "I will **confess** my transgressions to the LORD," and you forgave the guilt of my sin. [Psalm 32:5]

> No one who conceals transgressions will prosper, but one who **confesses** and forsakes them will obtain mercy. [Proverbs 28:13]

As a declaration of faith, *yadah* has been translated in a variety of ways:

> Leah conceived again and bore a son, and said, "This time I will **praise** the LORD"; therefore she named him Judah; then she ceased bearing. [Genesis 29:35]

> For this I will **extol** you, O LORD, among the nations, and sing praises to your name. [II Samuel 22:50]

> When your people Israel, having sinned against you, are defeated before an enemy but turn again to you, **confess** your name, pray and plead with you in this house, then hear in heaven, forgive the sin of your people Israel, and bring them again to the land that you gave to their ancestors. [I Kings 8:33-34]

> I will also **acknowledge** to you that your own right hand can give you victory. [Job 40:14]

> I will **give thanks** to the LORD with my whole heart; I will tell of all your wonderful deeds. [Psalm 9:1]

In the Greek texts, words with imagery quite different from the Hebrew convey similar meanings. The basic form is *homologeo—homo*, the same + *logeo*, from *logos*, word or reasoning. One sense of *homolegeo* can be an admission as to the true state of a person's situation.

> This is the testimony given by John when the Jews sent priests and Levites from Jerusalem to ask him, "Who are you?" He **confessed** and did not deny it, but **confessed**, "I am not the Messiah." [John 1:19-20]

This I **admit** to you, that according to the Way, which they call a sect, I worship the God of our ancestors, believing everything laid down according to the law or written in the prophets. [Acts 24:14]

If we **confess** our sins, he who is faithful and just will forgive us our sins and cleanse us from all unrighteousness. [I John 1:9]

Much more often *homologeo* carries the sense of affirmation, usually but not always, with a faith connotation.

Everyone therefore who **acknowledges** me before others, I also will **acknowledge** before my Father in heaven; but whoever denies me before others, I also will deny before my Father in heaven. [Matthew 10:32-33]

When Herod's birthday came, the daughter of Herodias danced before the company, and she pleased Herod so much that he **promised** on oath to grant her whatever she might ask. [Matthew 14:6-7]

For one believes with the heart and so is justified, and one **confesses** with the mouth and so is saved. [Romans 10:10]

To the pure all things are pure, but to the corrupt and unbelieving nothing is pure. Their very minds and consciences are corrupted. They **profess** to know God, but they deny him by their actions. They are detestable, disobedient, unfit for any good work. [Titus 1:15-16]

Let us hold fast to the **confession** of our hope without wavering, for he who has promised is faithful. [Hebrews 10:23]

A variation of the word *homologeo* is *exomologeo*, the *ex* meaning out of. It appears to have been used in much the same way as the simpler word but may have indicated a more personal or intense act.

Then the people of Jerusalem and all Judea were going out to him, and all the region along the Jordan, and they were baptized by him in the river Jordan, **confessing** their sins. [Matthew 3:5-6]

At that time Jesus said, "I **thank** you, Father, Lord of heaven and earth, because you have hidden these things from the wise and the intelligent and have revealed them to infants; yes, Father, for such was your gracious will." [Matthew 11:25-26]

Judas went away and conferred with the chief priests and officers of the temple police about how he might betray him to them. They were greatly pleased and agreed to give him money. So he **consented** and began to look for an opportunity to betray him to them when no crowd was present. [Luke 22:4-6]

It is written, "As I live, says the Lord, every knee shall bow to me, and every tongue shall give **praise** to God." [Romans 14:11]

Therefore God also highly exalted him and gave him the name that is above every name, so that at the name of Jesus every knee should bend, in heaven and on earth and under the earth, and every tongue should **confess** that Jesus Christ is Lord, to the glory of God the Father. [Philippians 2:9-11]

Of all the words, ancient and current, used to convey the sense of confession, the one with the most vivid image is the Hebrew *yadah*. The throwing out of one's hands is a strong and purposeful act and brings to mind both reaching out for help and signaling enthusiastic loyalty. The image is not of a person standing quietly with upraised arms, but a desperate person on the roof of a burning building, reaching out eagerly for the rope ladder being dropped from a helicopter, or a person in a political demonstration whose waving arms accentuate the shouting of the crowd. The *yadah* metaphor is a good reminder that confession, in the biblical sense, cannot be a passive gesture. Confession is an act that requires courage and energy.

covenant, *noun*   The Hebrew word *berith,* usually translated covenant, is of uncertain etymology, but the meaning seems clear. A *berith* was an agreement, contract, or deal. When the Hebrew Bible was translated into Greek, *berith* became *diatheke,* from *dia,* by means of + *tithemi,* to put or place. Besides the sense of agreement, *diatheke* could also mean a will, how a person wants property distributed after death. The first Latin translations of the Bible used *testamentum* in most instances for both *berith* and *diatheke,* which is why some English translations occasionally use testament instead of covenant. The meaning of testament, however, except in references to the Bible, is generally restricted to wills.

The Hebrew Scriptures contain many uses of *berith* as an agreement between individuals.

> When Abraham complained to Abimelech about a well of water that Abimelech's servants had seized, Abimelech said, "I do not know who has done this; you did not tell me, and I have not heard of it until today." So Abraham took sheep and oxen and gave them to Abimelech, and the two men made a **covenant**. Abraham set apart seven ewe lambs of the flock. And Abimelech said to Abraham, "What is the meaning of these seven ewe lambs that you have set apart?" He said, "These seven ewe lambs you shall accept from my hand, in order that you may be a witness for me that I dug this well." [Genesis 21:25-30]

> Then Laban answered and said to Jacob, "The daughters are my daughters, the children are my children, the flocks are my flocks, and all that you see is mine. But what can I do today about these daughters of mine, or about their children whom they have borne? Come now, let us make a **covenant,** you and I; and let it be a witness between you and me." So Jacob took a stone, and set it up as a pillar. [Genesis 31:43-45]

> When David had finished speaking to Saul, the soul of Jonathan was bound to the soul of David, and Jonathan loved him as his own soul. Saul took him that day and would not let him return to his father's house. Then Jonathan made a **covenant** with David, because he loved him as his own soul. Jonathan stripped himself of the robe that he was wearing, and gave it to David, and his armor, and even his sword and his bow and his belt. [I Samuel 18:1-4]

Although a *berith* between individuals was not necessarily a deal struck by equals, when human beings use the term in reference to their understandings of God,* they nearly always picture God as dictating the terms. The humans do not see themselves in a position to negotiate. They can only say yes or no to what God offers.

> "I establish my **covenant** with you, that never again shall all flesh be cut off by the waters of a flood, and never again shall there be a flood to destroy the earth." God said, "This is the sign of the **covenant** that I make between me and you and every living creature that is with you, for all future generations: I have set my bow in the clouds, and it shall be a sign of the **covenant** between me and the earth." [Genesis 9:11-13]

God said to Abraham, "As for you, you shall keep my **covenant**, you and your offspring after you throughout their generations. This is my **covenant**, which you shall keep, between me and you and your offspring after you: Every male among you shall be circumcised. You shall circumcise the flesh of your foreskins, and it shall be a sign of the **covenant** between me and you." [Genesis 17:9-11]

Moses wrote down all the words of the LORD. He rose early in the morning, and built an altar at the foot of the mountain, and set up twelve pillars, corresponding to the twelve tribes of Israel. He sent young men of the people of Israel, who offered burnt offerings and sacrificed oxen as offerings of well-being to the LORD. Moses took half of the blood and put it in basins, and half of the blood he dashed against the altar. Then he took the book of the **covenant**, and read it in the hearing of the people; and they said, "All that the LORD has spoken we will do, and we will be obedient." Moses took the blood and dashed it on the people, and said, "See the blood of the **covenant** that the LORD has made with you in accordance with all these words." [Exodus 24:4-8]

The early followers of Jesus picked up on the covenant metaphor, *diatheke*, in expressing their own understanding of relationship with God.

Such is the confidence that we have through Christ toward God. Not that we are competent of ourselves to claim anything as coming from us; our competence is from God, who has made us competent to be ministers of a new **covenant**, not of letter but of spirit; for the letter kills, but the Spirit gives life. [II Corinthians 3:4-6]

Jesus has now obtained a more excellent ministry, and to that degree he is the mediator of a better **covenant**, which has been enacted through better promises. [Hebrews 8:6]

The Holy Spirit also testifies to us, for after saying, "This is the **covenant** that I will make with them after those days, says the Lord: I will put my laws in their hearts, and I will write them on their minds," he also adds, "I will remember their sins and their lawless deeds no more." [Hebrews 10:15-17]

In the Hebrew Scriptures, a *berith* between individuals required a sign of good faith. As a lawyer will point out today, a contract is not a signed piece of paper; the signed paper is merely evidence that the parties reached an agreement. Before written contracts came into fashion, the evidence of an agreement could be a gift or a pillar of stone, as in the examples above. A *berith* with God was also accompanied by a sign: a rainbow, a circumcision, or the blood of sacrifice.* Following the Hebrew tradition, Christians also wrote of their covenant being accompanied by a sign, sometimes attributing the words to Jesus himself. Although many scholars today doubt that Jesus spoke about his blood being a sign of the new covenant, few could doubt that the metaphor appeared very early in the life of the church.

In the same way Jesus took the cup also, after supper, saying, "This cup is the new **covenant** in my blood. Do this, as often as you drink it, in remembrance of me." [I Corinthians 11:25]

Then Jesus took a cup, and after giving thanks he gave it to them, and all of them drank from it. He said to them, "This is my blood of the **covenant**, which is poured out for many. Truly I tell you, I will never again drink of the fruit of the vine until that day when I drink it new in the kingdom of God." [Mark 14:23-25]

You have come to Mount Zion and to the city of the living God, the heavenly Jerusalem, and to innumerable angels in festal gathering, and to the assembly of the firstborn who are enrolled in

---

heaven, and to God the judge of all, and to the spirits of the righteous made perfect, and to Jesus, the mediator of a new **covenant**, and to the sprinkled blood that speaks a better word than the blood of Abel. [Hebrews 12:22-24]

Much can be said in favor of the continued use of the covenant metaphor by followers of Jesus. People calling their relationship with God a covenant are making at least three assertions. First, they are declaring that they experience God as dependable, always with them. Second, they are saying that to accept God's presence in their lives, they must acknowledge their own individual and collective responsibility to live up to what they believe God expects of them. Third, they are acknowledging the importance of renewing the covenant through a ritual that points to the sign, in this case a communal meal often called Eucharist.*

Another use of the covenant metaphor can be seen in the way some Christians talk about the Bible.* Taking their lead from St. Paul and the letter to the Hebrews, they talk as if their new covenant has superceded the old covenant made with the Israelites. This way of using the metaphor has been a point of friction between Christians and Jews.

create, *verb*; **creator** and **creation**, *nouns*; see also **creature**. The Greek root behind the creation words is *ktizo*, which means to fabricate or manufacture. The Hebrew root, *bara*, is rich with other connotations, some of which seem the opposite of create. For example, *bara* is sometimes translated as to cut trees, clear the ground, or cut down people.

> Joshua said to them, "If you are a numerous people, go up to the forest, and **clear ground** there for yourselves in the land of the Perizzites and the Rephaim, since the hill country of Ephraim is too narrow for you." . . . Then Joshua said to the house of Joseph, to Ephraim and Manasseh, "You are indeed a numerous people, and have great power; you shall not have one lot only, but the hill country shall be yours, for though it is a forest, you shall **clear** it and possess it to its farthest borders." [Joshua 17:15, 17-18]

> The assembly shall stone them and with their swords they shall **cut them down**; they shall kill their sons and their daughters, and burn up their houses. [Ezekiel 23:47]

The first use of the word *bara* as a creation metaphor appears at the beginning of the Hebrew Bible. The poem in the first chapter of Genesis reflects the human experience of feeling sustained in the midst of turmoil, as if the chaos of existence has been made suitable for human habitation. This theme is picked up later by Isaiah.

> In the beginning when God **created** the heavens and the earth, the earth was a formless void and darkness covered the face of the deep, while a wind from God swept over the face of the waters. Then God said, "Let there be light"; and there was light. [Genesis 1:1-3]

> For thus says the LORD, who **created** the heavens (he is God!), who formed the earth and made it (he established it; he did not create it a chaos, he formed it to be inhabited!): I am the LORD, and there is no other. [Isaiah 45:18]

The creation metaphor also reflects the experience of awe and wonder that arises in the contemplation of the intricacy and magnitude of nature. Although Albert Einstein did not profess religious beliefs, in reflecting on his work in astrophysics, he sometimes referred to "the old one." In much the same fashion, people over the ages have found it helpful to personify nature.

> Praise the LORD from the heavens; praise him in the heights! Praise him, all his angels; praise him, all his host! Praise him, sun and moon; praise him, all you shining stars! Praise him, you highest heavens, and you waters above the heavens! Let them praise the name of the LORD, for he commanded and they were **created**. He established them forever and ever; he fixed their bounds, which cannot be passed. [Psalm 148:4-6]

> Lift up your eyes on high and see: Who **created** these? He who brings out their host and numbers them, calling them all by name; because he is great in strength, mighty in power, not one is missing. [Isaiah 40:26]

Another use of the creation metaphor reflects the experience of new possibilities, fresh beginnings.

> I am about to **create** new heavens and a new earth; the former things shall not be remembered or come to mind. But be glad and rejoice forever in what I am **creating**; for I am about to create Jerusalem as a joy, and its people as a delight. [Isaiah 65:17-18]

> So if anyone is in Christ, there is a new **creation**: everything old has passed away; see, everything has become new! [II Corinthians 5:17]

Taking the creation metaphor literally, that is, as a scientific description of reality, has brought the church into disrepute in many quarters of the industrialized world. In writing to a friend, Charles Darwin stated the problem of accepting literally the claim that a divine creator designed the universe and all that is in it.

> "I own I cannot see, as plainly as others do, & as I shd. wish to, evidence of design & beneficence on all sides of us. There seems too much misery in the world. I cannot persuade myself that a beneficent & omnipotent God would have designedly created the Ichneumonidae with the express intention of their feeding within the living bodies of caterpillars, or that a cat should play with mice."[10]

Anyone willing to put aside the notion that the creation terms have something to do with natural history can find meaning in their use as religious or spiritual metaphors—on at least three levels: what it means to find stability in the midst of chaos, as an expression of awe and wonder in the experience of the natural world, and the willingness to look for new possibilities.

When using the creation metaphor, however, a person might keep in mind one meaning of *bara*, to cut down—a reminder that in any manufacturing or fabrication process, the original form of something must be destroyed. Creation always has a dark side.

creature, *noun*   The biblical words translated creature are not formed from the same root as create,* creator, or creation.

> God said, "This is the sign of the covenant that I make between me and you and every living **creature** that is with you, for all future generations."—*nephesh*, from a root meaning to breathe [Genesis 9:12]

> When any one of you touches any unclean thing—human uncleanness or an unclean animal or any unclean **creature**—and then eats flesh from the Lord's sacrifice of well-being, you shall be cut off from your kin.—*behemah*, probably from a root meaning mute, i.e., a dumb beast [Leviticus 7:21]

> Make a distinction between the unclean and the clean, and between the living **creature** that may be eaten and the living **creature** that may not be eaten.—*chay*, from a root meaning to be alive
> [Leviticus 11:47]

> You may eat any clean winged **creature**.—*oph*, from a root suggesting feathers
> [Deuteronomy 14:20]

> Wild animals will lie down there, and its houses will be full of howling **creatures**; there ostriches will live, and there goat-demons will dance.—*oach*, from a root that expresses grief or surprise
> [Isaiah 13:21]

The metaphors used to indicate animals do not necessarily imply a creator. They are formed on roots that have nothing to do with intelligent design or manufacture or fabrication. Using the creature metaphor may be a mistake for people who take a Darwinian view of species differentiation. When they use the word creature, instead of bird or beast, they may unwittingly reinforce the creationist point of view.

creed—see **faith**

cross, *noun;* **crucify**, *verb*   The noun translated as cross in Greek is *stauros,* an upright post or a stake. The verb translated as crucify is formed from the noun. *Stauros* had a more general meaning than the English word cross, which indicates a post or stake with a horizontal piece attached near the top. When the Romans executed prisoners, they often fastened them to a *stauros* that had such a bar across the very top, forming a T, or had one a little below the top. The fastening was done either with nails or cords. The prisoner was then left in place until nature took its course and the condemned man died. Although the Romans did not invent this form of execution, they made extensive use of it to keep conquered people in line. The obvious advantage was that the government officials were not only ridding themselves of a troublesome criminal or rebel, they also were putting on display a warning to the entire populace that they had better abide by Roman law or suffer Roman punishment.

Although the people of ancient Israel used a post of some sort to display the bodies of those they executed, stoning was their means of killing the prisoner. The Hebrew word usually translated as tree in the following passage is *ets,* which could meaning a living tree or a walking stick or a gallows.

> If someone has a stubborn and rebellious son who will not obey his father and mother, who does not heed them when they discipline him, then his father and his mother shall take hold of him and bring him out to the elders of his town at the gate of that place. They shall say to the elders of his town, "This son of ours is stubborn and rebellious. He will not obey us. He is a glutton and a drunkard." Then all the men of the town shall stone him to death. So you shall purge the evil from your midst; and all Israel will hear, and be afraid. When someone is convicted of a crime punishable by death and is executed, and you hang him on a **tree**, his corpse must not remain all night upon the tree; you shall bury him that same day, for anyone hung on a **tree** is under God's curse. You must not defile the land that the LORD your God is giving you for possession. [Deuteronomy 21:18-23]

Both systems of displaying the corpse intentionally degraded the memory of the prisoner who was executed. Having one's body hanging on a post instead of being properly buried was particularly shameful. The shame of crucifixion in Roman times was so great that it was reserved for punishing conquered people. No citizen of Rome could be disposed of in this fashion no matter what the crime. In ancient Israel, the sense of the curse* that went with the displaying of the body was so profound that one day of display had to be enough. When the first followers of Jesus tried to make sense of his death on the Romans' cross, they dwelt heavily on the shame* involved and turned it to their advantage. For tree they used *xylon*, the Greek root of such English words as xylographer (a wood engraver) and xylophone (a musical instrument consisting of wooden bars). *Xylon* was equivalent of the Hebrew *ets*.

> The God of our ancestors raised up Jesus, whom you had killed by hanging him on a **tree**.
> [Acts 5:30]

> Christ redeemed us from the curse of the law by becoming a curse for us—for it is written, "Cursed is everyone who hangs on a **tree**"—in order that in Christ Jesus the blessing of Abraham might come to the Gentiles, so that we might receive the promise of the Spirit through faith. [Galatians 3:13-14]

> Christ was **crucified** in weakness, but lives by the power of God. For we are weak in him, but in dealing with you we will live with him by the power of God. [II Corinthians 13:4]

> Therefore, since we are surrounded by so great a cloud of witnesses, let us also lay aside every weight and the sin that clings so closely, and let us run with perseverance the race that is set before us, looking to Jesus the pioneer and perfecter of our faith, who for the sake of the joy that was set before him endured the **cross**, disregarding its shame, and has taken his seat at the right hand of the throne of God. [Hebrews 12:1-2]

Even before Jesus was executed Roman style, the cross may have been a metaphor generally employed to express shame. Many people, even those who did not attend the public spectacle of a crucifixion, could have seen a condemned person being forced to carry his cross or the horizontal piece that would be attached to the stake at the place of execution. The metaphorical use of *stauros* attributed to Jesus may reflect the impact his death had on the use of the term by his followers, but he could have made such a statement without knowing what was in store for him.

> Jesus called the crowd with his disciples, and said to them, "If any want to become my followers, let them deny themselves and take up their **cross** and follow me. For those who want to save their life will lose it, and those who lose their life for my sake, and for the sake of the gospel, will save it. For what will it profit them to gain the whole world and forfeit their life? Indeed, what can they give in return for their life?" [Mark 8:34-36]

> Those who belong to Christ Jesus have **crucified** the flesh with its passions and desires. If we live by the Spirit, let us also be guided by the Spirit. [Galatians 5:24-25]

> May I never boast of anything except the cross of our Lord Jesus Christ, by which the world has been **crucified** to me, and I to the world. [Galatians 6:14]

As the above passages suggest, the figurative use of *stauros* has led in different directions. Taking up one's cross may be facing whatever happens to befall without falling victim to shame,* for example facing disease, disfigurement, or unemployment. The metaphor can also be a reminder that a kind of death* is involved in any major change in the direction of one's life, especially curbing certain self-destructive appetites that St. Paul identified with flesh.* Finally, the cross metaphor can lead to an awareness of one's ultimate unity with the world, in Greek the *kosmos*.

Marks a word in the text that has its own entry

crucifixion—see **cross**

cup—see **wine**

curse, *noun* and *verb*   In ancient times, the mirror image of bless* was curse. Both were understood to have power. A blessing could bring prosperity, health, and long life, while a curse could call down disease, destruction, and death. The basic word for curse in Hebrew was *arar*.

A list in Deuteronomy gives a sense of who the ancients thought deserved *arar*.

> **Cursed** be anyone who makes an idol or casts an image, anything abhorrent to the LORD, the work of an artisan, and sets it up in secret.
> **Cursed** be anyone who dishonors father or mother.
> **Cursed** be anyone who moves a neighbor's boundary marker.
> **Cursed** be anyone who misleads a blind person on the road.
> **Cursed** be anyone who deprives the alien, the orphan, and the widow of justice.
> **Cursed** be anyone who lies with his father's wife, because he has violated his father's rights.
> **Cursed** be anyone who lies with any animal.
> **Cursed** be anyone who lies with his sister, whether the daughter of his father or the daughter of his mother.
> **Cursed** be anyone who lies with his mother-in-law.
> **Cursed** be anyone who strikes down a neighbor in secret.
> **Cursed** be anyone who takes a bribe to shed innocent blood.
> **Cursed** be anyone who does not uphold the words of this law by observing them.
> [Deuteronomy 27:15-26]

In case individuals thought that God was not paying sufficient attention to those deserving *arar*, they could pronounce the curse in the Lord's name.

> When Noah awoke from his wine and knew what his youngest son had done to him, he said, **"Cursed** be Canaan; lowest of slaves shall he be to his brothers." [Genesis 9:24-25]

> Joshua then pronounced this oath, saying, **"Cursed** before the LORD be anyone who tries to build this city—this Jericho! At the cost of his firstborn he shall lay its foundation, and at the cost of his youngest he shall set up its gates!" [Joshua 6:26]

> Thus says the LORD: **Cursed** are those who trust in mere mortals and make mere flesh their strength, whose hearts turn away from the LORD. They shall be like a shrub in the desert, and shall not see when relief comes. They shall live in the parched places of the wilderness, in an uninhabited salt land. [Jeremiah 17:5-6]

Other words in the Hebrew Scripture are translated as curse, notably *qalal* and its variation *qelalah*, to make light or trivial, and *naqab*, to puncture or pierce.

> The Philistine said to David, "Am I a dog, that you come to me with sticks?" And the Philistine **cursed** David by his gods.—*qalal* [I Samuel 17:43]

> I will make them a horror, an evil thing, to all the kingdoms of the earth—a disgrace, a byword, a taunt, and a **curse** in all the places where I shall drive them.—*qelalah* [Jeremiah 24:9]

> The people **curse** those who hold back grain, but a blessing is on the head of those who sell it.—*naqab* [Proverbs 11:26]

Marks a word in the text that has its own entry

> Whoever says to the wicked, "You are innocent," will be **cursed** by peoples, abhorred by nations; but those who rebuke the wicked will have delight, and a good blessing will come upon them.—*naqab* [Proverbs 24:24-25]

Because of the power attributed to cursing, one of the primary offenses was cursing God. When this violation of the sacred comes up, the word may be *qalal*, meaning to treat lightly.

> Speak to the people of Israel, saying: Anyone who **curses** God shall bear the sin. One who blasphemes (*naqab*) the name of the LORD shall be put to death; the whole congregation shall stone the blasphemer. Aliens as well as citizens, when they blaspheme (*naqab*) the Name, shall be put to death. [Leviticus 24:15-16]

More often when on the subject of cursing God, the writers avoid using a dreadful word and substitute the opposite, *barak*, the word for bless. This is similar to the English colloquial use of bless, meaning curse, as in the expression "blessed him out."

> Jezebel wrote in the letters, "Proclaim a fast, and seat Naboth at the head of the assembly; seat two scoundrels opposite him, and have them bring a charge against him, saying, 'You have **cursed** God and the king.' Then take him out, and stone him to death." [I Kings 21:9-10]

> Job took a potsherd with which to scrape himself, and sat among the ashes. Then his wife said to him, "Do you still persist in your integrity? **Curse** God, and die." [Job 2:8-9]

In the specifically Christian portions of the Bible, several Greek words appear in English as curse. *Katara* and *kataraomai* are formed from *kata*, against + *airo*, raise, suggesting the raising of a voice. *Epikataratos* adds the prefix *epi*, which means over. *Anathematizo*—the verb form of *anathema*, from *ana*, upon + *tithemi*, to put or place—meant to bind with an oath, especially a vow invoking a curse as a penalty for failure. *Katanathematizo*, by adding the prefix meaning against, is a more intensive form of *anathematizo*. *Ouai*, usually translated as woe,* could also mean curse. The concept of cursing among the followers of Jesus seems to have closely followed the Hebrew tradition.

> All who rely on the works of the law are under a **curse** (*katara*); for it is written, "**Cursed** (*epikataratos*) is everyone who does not observe and obey all the things written in the book of the law." [Galatians 3:10]

> I say to you that listen, Love your enemies, do good to those who hate you, bless those who **curse** (*kataraomai*) you, pray for those who abuse you. [Luke 6:27-28]

> Therefore I want you to understand that no one speaking by the Spirit of God ever says "Let Jesus be **cursed** (*anathema*)!" and no one can say "Jesus is Lord" except by the Holy Spirit. [I Corinthians 12:3]

> After a little while the bystanders again said to Peter, "Certainly you are one of them; for you are a Galilean." But he began to **curse** (*anathematizo*), and he swore an oath, "I do not know this man you are talking about." [Mark 14:70-71]

> Then Peter began to **curse** (*katanathematizo*), and he swore an oath, "I do not know the man!" At that moment the cock crowed. [Matthew 26:74]

The ancients appear to have taken cursing quite seriously. With them casual cussing would have been out of the question. They had a sense of what was right and proper, and wanted God to bring

---

misery upon anyone who stood against them. Although the early followers of Jesus thought that he had taught them to forgo cursing, they freely cursed those who remained loyal to the traditions of Judaism. As time went on, when Christians disagreed with one another, they were quick to pronounce anathema on their opponents. From the perspective of the twenty-first century, we might understand the feelings of those ancient Israelites and early Christians who cursed their enemies, but we might also conclude that the followers of Jesus should have paid more attention to the teaching about blessing and cursing attributed to him.

Perhaps the Hebrew metaphors used in places to convey the sense of curse offer the best ways of understanding the destructive power of cursing. To make light of another person or to trivialize that person's point of view, as suggested by *qalal*, can certainly carry a destructive intent. The intent is to belittle the other person so that the speaker can feel bigger or more important by comparison. The intent of many excoriations, especially those uttered in great distress or anger, may also be *naqab*, that is, to puncture another person's defenses in order to inflict pain. These two images of cursing may help to identify which expressions are really curses and which are merely evidence of strong feelings.

D

darkness—see **light**

deacon, *noun*   The English title for a recognized secondary role in the functioning of a Christian community is often deacon, a word derived from the Greek *diakonos*. The root of *diakonos* was probably *diako*, which meant to run errands. At the time of Jesus, a *diakonos* could have been something other than an errand boy. As the various translations of the word suggest, a *diakonos* could be a person providing almost any kind of service.

> Jesus called them to him and said, "You know that the rulers of the Gentiles lord it over them, and their great ones are tyrants over them. It will not be so among you; but whoever wishes to be great among you must be your **servant,** and whoever wishes to be first among you must be your slave; just as the Son of Man came not to be served but to serve, and to give his life a ransom for many." [Matthew 20:25-28]

> For rulers are not a terror to good conduct, but to bad. Do you wish to have no fear of the authority? Then do what is good, and you will receive its approval; for it is God's **servant** for your good. But if you do what is wrong, you should be afraid, for the authority does not bear the sword in vain! It is the servant of God to execute wrath on the wrongdoer. [Romans 13:3-4]

> Then the king said to the **attendants,** "Bind him hand and foot, and throw him into the outer darkness, where there will be weeping and gnashing of teeth." [Matthew 22:13]

> Not that we are competent of ourselves to claim anything as coming from us; our competence is from God, who has made us competent to be **ministers** of a new covenant, not of letter but of spirit; for the letter kills, but the Spirit gives life. [II Corinthians 3:5-6]

> We sent Timothy, our brother and **co-worker** for God in proclaiming the gospel of Christ, to strengthen and encourage you for the sake of your faith. [I Thessalonians 3:2]

Late in the first century, *diakonos* apparently took on more the sense of a job title in the church, a job open to both men and women.

> I commend to you our sister Phoebe, a **deacon** of the church at Cenchreae, so that you may welcome her in the Lord as is fitting for the saints, and help her in whatever she may require from you, for she has been a benefactor of many and of myself as well. [Romans 16:1-2]

> **Deacons** likewise must be serious, not double-tongued, not indulging in much wine, not greedy for money; they must hold fast to the mystery of the faith with a clear conscience. [I Timothy 3:8-9]

The word in a slightly different form—*diakonia*—referred to the service performed by a *diakonos*. This term *diakonia* appears frequently in the Acts of the Apostles and has had a profound impact on the way Christians understand the nature of ministry.

> Now during those days, when the disciples were increasing in number, the Hellenists complained against the Hebrews because their widows were being neglected in the daily **distribution** of food. And the twelve called together the whole community of the disciples and said, "It is not right that we should neglect the word of God in order to wait on tables. Therefore, friends, select from among yourselves seven men of good standing, full of the Spirit and of wisdom, whom we may appoint to this task, while we, for our part, will devote ourselves to prayer and to **serving** the word." What they said pleased the whole community, and they chose Stephen, a man full of faith and the Holy Spirit, together with Philip, Prochorus, Nicanor, Timon, Parmenas, and Nicolaus, a proselyte of Antioch. [Acts 6:1-5]

Anyone who reads on in the narrative will discover that these seven deacons did much more than wait on tables. Stephen, at least, was said to have done great wonders and signs and to have preached and proselytized in public. According to the story, he was so effective that he got himself martyred, the first follower of Jesus said to have died for his faith. Elsewhere in Acts, *diakonia* does not seem to be equated with waiting on tables, as is reflected in the English words chosen for the translation.

> The disciples determined that according to their ability, each would send **relief** to the believers living in Judea; this they did, sending it to the elders by Barnabas and Saul. [Acts 11:29-30]

> Then after completing their **mission** Barnabas and Saul returned to Jerusalem and brought with them John, whose other name was Mark. [Acts 12:25]

> I do not count my life of any value to myself, if only I may finish my course and the **ministry** that I received from the Lord Jesus, to testify to the good news of God's grace. [Acts 20:24]

In a way, when *diakonos* became a title, the church lost the use of a metaphor indicating what it means to be a follower of Jesus: willing to run errands, or to wait on tables, or to take care of those in need of assistance.

death, *noun*; **die**, *verb*; **dead**, *adjective*   The Hebrew word *mawet* and the Greek *thanatos* refer most obviously to the state of a human being when the undertaker comes for the body. A Latin phrase from the Office of the Dead speaks to the heart of the subject. *Timor mortis conturbat me.* "The fear of death troubles me." Reflecting on the phrase, Michael Dirda wrote:

> "We have all experienced such intimations of mortality, usually after awaking from uneasy dreams, when we are jabbed into sudden consciousness by the irrefutable, ice-

cold realization that someday we too must die. Lying there in the tremulous darkness, our minds find the prospect inconceivable, terrifying, and for a shuddering moment close at hand. But the spiritual vertigo eventually passes, and we return to our sleepy lives, once more temporarily forgetful of death's bright dart."[11]

Perhaps, just as poignantly, the book Ecclesiastes draws attention to the finality of death.

> For the fate of humans and the fate of animals is the same; as one **dies**, so **dies** the other. They all have the same breath, and humans have no advantage over the animals; for all is vanity. All go to one place; all are from the dust, and all turn to dust again. [Ecclesiastes 3:19-20]

In the ancient world, religions prospered by offering deliverance from death. Witness St. Paul and the anonymous Letter to the Hebrews:

> Listen, I will tell you a mystery! We will not all **die**, but we will all be changed, in a moment, in the twinkling of an eye, at the last trumpet. For the trumpet will sound, and the **dead** will be raised imperishable, and we will be changed. [I Corinthians 15:51-52]

> Since, therefore, the children share flesh and blood, Jesus himself likewise shared the same things, so that through **death** he might destroy the one who has the power of **death**, that is, the devil. [Hebrews 2:14]

Curiously enough, although Christians held out the promise of deliverance from the fate of all living things, they had difficulty talking about the subject directly. In many instances, they avoided using direct language and substituted a euphemism, *koimao*, which meant to sleep.

> The tombs also were opened, and many bodies of the saints who had **fallen asleep** were raised. [Matthew 27:52]

> After that, he was seen of above five hundred brethren at once; of whom the greater part remain unto this present, but some are **fallen asleep**. [I Corinthians 15:6, KING JAMES VERSION]

In avoiding the direct mention of death, Christians were following an ancient Jewish tradition. The editors of the books we call Kings and Chronicles used the same euphemism for death, in Hebrew *shakab*.

> Then David **slept** with his ancestors, and was buried in the city of David. [I Kings 2:10]

> Solomon **slept** with his ancestors and was buried in the city of his father David; and his son Rehoboam succeeded him. [I Kings 11:43]

When the earliest Christian writers employed the words death and dead, often they were using them as metaphors. The death imagery suggested that human beings, while they went on breathing, could lose the substance and meaning of their lives. The avoidance of reality and responsibility, which is what the Bible means by sin,* produces a condition that is something like being dead. Life becomes empty and insubstantial.

> I see in my members another law at war with the law of my mind, making me captive to the law of sin that dwells in my members. Wretched man that I am! Who will rescue me from this body of **death**? [Romans 7:23-24]

> You were **dead** through the trespasses and sins in which you once lived, following the course of this world. [Ephesians 2:1-2]

Marks a word in the text that has its own entry

> And to the angel of the church in Sardis write: These are the words of him who has the seven spirits of God and the seven stars: "I know your works; you have a name of being alive, but you are **dead**." [Revelation 3:1]

To make sense out of the Bible, it is important to recognize when the death words are being used to indicate what happens when the last breath is drawn and when the words are metaphors for some existential condition. When death is a metaphor, resurrection* becomes a genuine possibility rather than a way of coping with mortality.

demon, *noun*   The Hebrew word translated demon, *shed*, seems to have been a derogatory term for the gods of other tribes. The root of the term had to do with swelling up, which then as now is a picture of insolence. The foreign gods who thought that they were as good as the God* of Israel were obviously being insolent, as were any Israelites who chose to honor them.

> They sacrificed to **demons**, not God, to deities they had never known, to new ones recently arrived, whom your ancestors had not feared. [Deuteronomy 32:17]

> They sacrificed their sons and their daughters to the **demons**; they poured out innocent blood, the blood of their sons and daughters, whom they sacrificed to the idols of Canaan; and the land was polluted with blood. [Psalm 106:37-38]

The Greek *daimon*, the origin of the English term, in classical times meant simply a divinity. In the rare appearances *daimon* makes in the Bible, however, it is always about evil spirits.

> The **demons** begged Jesus, "If you cast us out, send us into the herd of swine." [Matthew 8:31]

> After this I saw another angel coming down from heaven, having great authority; and the earth was made bright with his splendor. He called out with a mighty voice, "Fallen, fallen is Babylon the great! It has become a dwelling place of **demons**, a haunt of every foul spirit, a haunt of every foul bird, a haunt of every foul and hateful beast." [Revelation 18:1-2]

The more common Greek word in the Bible translated as demon is *daimonion*, which at one time was also a neutral expression. It appears in at least two places in the Bible to be the generic term for gods.

> Also some Epicurean and Stoic philosophers debated with Paul. Some said, "What does this babbler want to say?" Others said, "He seems to be a proclaimer of foreign **divinities**." [Acts 17:18]

> I imply that what pagans sacrifice, they sacrifice to **demons** and not to God. I do not want you to be partners with **demons**. You cannot drink the cup of the Lord and the cup of demons. You cannot partake of the table of the Lord and the table of **demons**. [I Corinthians 10:20-21]

Another term related to *daimon* is *daimonizomai,* a verb meaning to be possessed or tormented by a demon. When the verb form refers to a person who is demon possessed, the phrase is often translated as demoniac. For the early Christian writers, *daimonion* usually and *daimonizomai* always refer to evil spirits that are the causes of disease. In Matthew's gospel, where the symptoms of demon possession are sometimes described, the diseases seem to be neurological disorders affecting sight or speech or mental health.

> After they had gone away, a **demoniac** who was mute was brought to Jesus. And when the **demon** had been cast out, the one who had been mute spoke; and the crowds were amazed and said, "Never has anything like this been seen in Israel." [Matthew 9:32-33]

> Then they brought to Jesus a **demoniac** who was blind and mute; and he cured him, so that the one who had been mute could speak and see. [Matthew 12:22]

> When they came to the crowd, a man came to Jesus, knelt before him, and said, "Lord, have mercy on my son, for he is an epileptic and he suffers terribly; he often falls into the fire and often into the water. And I brought him to your disciples, but they could not cure him." Jesus answered, "You faithless and perverse generation, how much longer must I be with you? How much longer must I put up with you? Bring him here to me." And Jesus rebuked the **demon**, and it came out of him, and the boy was cured instantly. [Matthew 17:14-18]

In the last example, the father's diagnosis of his son's illness as epilepsy is the translators' interpretation. The Greek word attributed to the father is *seleniazomai*, literally moon-struck, the equivalent of the English lunatic, derived from the Latin word for moon. The association of demons with mental illness is further confirmed by the description of a cured demoniac as being in his right mind and by Jesus's opponents accusing him of being paranoid.

> They came to Jesus and saw the **demoniac** sitting there, clothed and in his right mind, the very man who had had the legion; and they were afraid. [Mark 5:15]

> Jesus said, "Did not Moses give you the law? Yet none of you keeps the law. Why are you looking for an opportunity to kill me?" The crowd answered, "You have a **demon**! Who is trying to kill you?" [John 7:19-20]

Two other characteristics of demons as understood by the gospel writers and editors are scattered throughout the narratives. Demons can operate singly or in groups, and demons are the minions of Satan.*

> Soon afterwards he went on through cities and villages, proclaiming and bringing the good news of the kingdom of God. The twelve were with him, as well as some women who had been cured of evil spirits and infirmities: Mary, called Magdalene, from whom seven **demons** had gone out, and Joanna, the wife of Herod's steward Chuza, and Susanna, and many others, who provided for them out of their resources. [Luke 8:1-3]

> Jesus then asked him, "What is your name?" He said, "Legion"; for many **demons** had entered him. [Luke 8:30]

> Some of them said, "He casts out **demons** by Beelzebul, the ruler of the **demons**." [Luke 11:15]

> The Pharisees said, "By the ruler of the **demons** he casts out the **demons**." [Matthew 9:34]

Besides being an adversary for Jesus, demons play an important role in developing the plot in both Mark and Luke. At the beginning of their narratives, the writers of these two gospels artfully use the demons to remind their readers that Jesus of Nazareth is something more than an ordinary person.

> Jesus cured many who were sick with various diseases, and cast out many demons; and he would not permit the **demons** to speak, because they knew him. [Mark 1:34]

> In the synagogue there was a man who had the spirit of an unclean **demon,** and he cried out with a loud voice, "Let us alone! What have you to do with us, Jesus of Nazareth? Have you come to destroy us? I know who you are, the Holy One of God." [Luke 4:33-34]

Assuming that to the first-century Christian writers demons were something more than a literary device, the twenty-first century follower of Jesus has to decide how to interpret the demon stories. Of course, for those who believe that the Bible is accurate, both historically and scientifically, demons are not a problem. They are the cause of neurological and mental illness, the cure for which is exorcism—not modern medicine or psychotherapy. For those who cannot accept demons as actual beings, however, their presence in the gospels may be a cause for concern.

One way to deal with the demons is to accept the fact that the understanding of disease in the first century was radically different from what it is today. To be an honest follower of Jesus, a person has to separate out the portions of the gospel that are bound up in the mindset of a prescientific culture, and then discard those portions entirely or make use of them metaphorically.

Demons as metaphor can be useful. When people are sick, when they are not themselves, they may indeed feel like they are in the grip of an external force. They also may appear that way to friends and relatives. The demon metaphor can help prevent underestimating the seriousness of an illness. The metaphor can prompt caregivers to listen to what mentally disturbed people are saying. Sometimes, as in the demon stories of the gospels, truths emerge that the mentally balanced people have been unable or unwilling to address. Also, the demon metaphor can remind Christians who have chosen to think of God as the source of life and health that they have a responsibility to carry on the work of Jesus, opposing the forces that spread disease and death.

despair, *noun* and *verb*; **desperate**, *adjective*   The words for being without hope* came into the English language from the French and are reasonable equivalents of the Hebrew word *ya'ash* and the Greek *exaporeomai*. The Greek word literally means to have no way out.

> I turned and gave my heart up to **despair** concerning all the toil of my labors under the sun, because sometimes one who has toiled with wisdom and knowledge and skill must leave all to be enjoyed by another who did not toil for it. [Ecclesiastes 2:20-21]

> How forceful are honest words! But your reproof, what does it reprove? Do you think that you can reprove words, as if the speech of the **desperate** were wind? [Job 6:25-26]

> We do not want you to be unaware, brothers and sisters, of the affliction we experienced in Asia; for we were so utterly, unbearably crushed that we **despaired** of life itself. [II Corinthians 1:8]

Despair has many recognizable forms of expression that do not use the word itself: I've had it. I'm at the end of my rope. That's the last straw. I give up. All these statements indicate an experience of extreme conditions, the sort of experience the Bible people sometimes were talking about when they used the phrase "the end," in Hebrew *qatseh* or *acharit* and in Greek *telos*.

> Hear my cry, O God; listen to my prayer. From **the end** of the earth I call to you, when my heart is faint. [Psalm 61:1-2]

> What your eyes have seen do not hastily bring into court; for what will you do in **the end**, when your neighbor puts you to shame? [Proverbs 25:8-9]

> **The end** of all things is near; therefore be serious and discipline yourselves for the sake of your prayers. [I Peter 4:7]

Out of such an experience, St. Paul was driven to ask:

> Wretched man that I am! Who will rescue me from this body of death? [Romans 7:24]

When people are in extremity, they have at least four possible responses—

1. **Shrug it off.** Say it doesn't matter. That is, they can refuse to be aware of their condition, but if that is their response, they may be lost. If they refuse to be aware, they have placed themselves beyond any kind of help. Just how lost early Christians thought such people might be shows up in observations about the Holy Spirit* attributed to Jesus. Frequently, when the Holy Spirit is mentioned in the gospels, people are becoming aware, learning to see and to hear the truth. So, using the Holy Spirit metaphor, if people refuse to pay attention to what is going on in their lives, they lose their connection with everyone and everything that matters. Or, as Jesus is supposed to have put it:

> "Whoever blasphemes against the Holy Spirit can never have forgiveness, but is guilty of an eternal sin." [Mark 3:29]

2. **Face their despair for a moment and then rush off into an illusion.** They tell themselves things like, "Everything always works out for the best" or "Something is bound to turn up." As long as they base their lives on an illusion, they are not likely to take any positive action that will allow them to move beyond their despair.

3. **Face their despair for a moment and then fall into despondency.** Their only desire is to numb their senses so that they will not feel the pain. They may escape into sleep or television or a chemically induced haze where all reality is blurred beyond recognition.

4. **Affirm both their despair and the freedom from fear that is born when hope disappears.** Hopelessness can free them from fear, can allow them to find the courage necessary to take whatever action may be necessary, and find meaning in their action without regard to how things turn out. The discovery of the possibility that in extremity they can affirm both despair and freedom from fear* may have led the followers of Jesus to make exuberant, symbolic claims:

> The time is fulfilled, and the kingdom of God has come near. [Mark 1:15]

> This is indeed the will of my Father, that all who see the Son and believe in him may have eternal life; and I will raise them up on the last day. [John 6:40]

The above quote from the Gospel according to John provides an excellent example of how the early followers of Jesus may have coped with despair. The word translated "last" is from the Greek *eschatos,* which can mean any extreme situation—the farthest, the poorest, the lowest, or the least. The day of extremity is a metaphor much like death or the end. Only in extreme circumstances does the possibility of a resurrection* experience arise. When people realize that they are utterly empty, unable by their own will to make their lives work, they find themselves raised up to do whatever needs to be done.

Many people confuse the first three responses with faith.* Some have made a virtue out of being imperturbable. For others, faith is the illusion that God always will intervene to make things work out right. Some equate misery and suffering with faith because they assume that the worse they feel the more they deserve God's love, or they adopt the poetic idealization of despondency and revel in their misery.

Devil—see Satan

disciple, *noun*   The word for disciple, *limmud*, occurs only once in the Hebrew Scriptures, but the practice of teachers being surrounded by pupils was widespread by the time of Jesus. *Limmud*, like its Greek equivalent, *mathetes*, meant one who learns. In its sole occurrence, *limmud* illustrates the importance of wisdom being passed down from one generation to another, especially before the advent of the printing press.

> Bind up the testimony, seal the teaching among my **disciples**. I will wait for the LORD, who is hiding his face from the house of Jacob, and I will hope in him. See, I and the children whom the LORD has given me are signs and portents in Israel from the LORD of hosts, who dwells on Mount Zion. [Isaiah 8:16-18]

The gospels and the Acts of the Apostles frequently use *mathetes* to identify followers of Jesus, but St. Paul and the other Christian authors included in the Bible never do. This difference raises the question about when *mathetes* entered the Christian vocabulary.

Another question has to do with exactly what the writers who did use the term meant by it. Matthew and Mark usually seem to mean a small group that was especially close to Jesus and who traveled about with him. The group was distinct from the larger crowd of followers. It was small enough to fit into a house* or a boat.

> Jesus said, "Go into the city to a certain man, and say to him, 'The Teacher says, My time is near; I will keep the Passover at your house with my **disciples**.'" [Matthew 26:18]

> Then Jesus called the crowd again and said to them, "Listen to me, all of you, and understand: there is nothing outside a person that by going in can defile, but the things that come out are what defile." When he had left the crowd and entered the house, his **disciples** asked him about the parable. [Mark 7:14-17]

> Immediately Jesus made the **disciples** get into the boat and go on ahead to the other side, while he dismissed the crowds. [Matthew 14:22]

> Now the **disciples** had forgotten to bring any bread; and they had only one loaf with them in the boat. [Mark 8:14]

Luke seems to have a different understanding of *mathetes*. Luke pictures a large crowd of disciples from whom Jesus picked twelve to be his inner circle. According to Luke, the small group of disciples were called apostles.*

> Now during those days Jesus went out to the mountain to pray; and he spent the night in prayer to God. And when day came, he called his **disciples** and chose twelve of them, whom he also named apostles. [Luke 6:12-13]

> He came down with them and stood on a level place, with a great crowd of his **disciples** and a great multitude of people from all Judea, Jerusalem, and the coast of Tyre and Sidon. [Luke 6:17]

The Gospel according to John uses *mathetes* both ways: to identify a crowd of followers and to indicate the intimate group especially close to Jesus.

> Jesus said, "For this reason I have told you that no one can come to me unless it is granted by the Father." Because of this many of his **disciples** turned back and no longer went about with him. So Jesus asked the twelve, "Do you also wish to go away?" [John 6:65-67]

> Jesus, knowing that the Father had given all things into his hands, and that he had come from God and was going to God, got up from the table, took off his outer robe, and tied a towel around himself. Then he poured water into a basin and began to wash the **disciples'** feet and to wipe them with the towel that was tied around him. [John 13:3-5]

One curious thing about John's use of the term is his designation of one person as the disciple whom Jesus loved. What the author meant by disciple and by love* in this context has been the subject of debate over the centuries.

> Jesus was troubled in spirit, and declared, "Very truly, I tell you, one of you will betray me." The **disciples** looked at one another, uncertain of whom he was speaking. One of his **disciples**—the one whom Jesus loved—was reclining next to him; Simon Peter therefore motioned to him to ask Jesus of whom he was speaking. [John 13:21-24]

Another oddity is his category of the secret disciple.

> Joseph of Arimathea, who was a **disciple** of Jesus, though a secret one because of his fear of the Jews, asked Pilate to let him take away the body of Jesus. Pilate gave him permission; so he came and removed his body. [John 19:38]

The Acts of the Apostles, probably written by the same person who wrote the Gospel according to Luke, follows the custom established in that gospel of using *mathetes* in reference to any follower of Jesus.

> Now during those days, when the **disciples** were increasing in number, the Hellenists complained against the Hebrews because their widows were being neglected in the daily distribution of food. And the twelve called together the whole community of the **disciples** and said, "It is not right that we should neglect the word of God in order to wait on tables." [Acts 6:1-2]

> Then Barnabas went to Tarsus to look for Saul, and when he had found him, he brought him to Antioch. So it was that for an entire year they met with the church and taught a great many people, and it was in Antioch that the **disciples** were first called "Christians." [Acts 11:25-26]

The metaphor based on learning to identify followers of Jesus has much to recommend it, even if St. Paul never picked up the term. To be a follower of Jesus is to be a perpetual student, studying in the company of others who are so inclined. Using this metaphor, a follower of Jesus is defined not by a willingness to believe doctrines about Jesus but by a commitment to learn from Jesus.

discipline, *noun* and *verb*   Both the Greek noun and verb translated discipline have the same root as the word for child. The noun is *paideia* and the verb is *paideuo*. The meaning of these two words can be illuminated by a closely related word, *paidagogos*, which has found its way into English as pedagogue. Contrary to English usage, however, the *paidagogos* was not a teacher but a trusted slave who escorted a child to school, making sure that the child arrived safely and did not get his toga dirty. The *paidagogos* enforced the boundaries established by the parents and applied the pressure necessary to make the child behave. Consequently, in the Bible *paidagogos* is not translated as pedagogue but as guardian or disciplinarian.

> I am not writing this to make you ashamed, but to admonish you as my beloved children. For though you might have ten thousand **guardians** in Christ, you do not have many fathers. Indeed, in Christ Jesus I became your father through the gospel. [I Corinthians 4:14-15]

> Therefore the law was our **disciplinarian** until Christ came, so that we might be justified by faith. But now that faith has come, we are no longer subject to a **disciplinarian**, for in Christ Jesus you are all children of God through faith. [Galatians 3:24-26]

With the role of the pedagogue in mind, a student of the Bible can understand why the verb *paideuo* has been translated in so many ways. What the translations have in common is that each of the words chosen indicates a way of putting on pressure.

> Pilate then called together the chief priests, the leaders, and the people, and said to them, "You brought me this man as one who was perverting the people; and here I have examined him in your presence and have not found this man guilty of any of your charges against him. Neither has Herod, for he sent him back to us. Indeed, he has done nothing to deserve death. I will therefore have him **flogged** and release him." [Luke 23:13-16]

> So Moses was **instructed** in all the wisdom of the Egyptians and was powerful in his words and deeds. [Acts 7:22]

> I am a Jew, born in Tarsus in Cilicia, but brought up in this city at the feet of Gamaliel, **educated** strictly according to our ancestral law, being zealous for God, just as all of you are today. [Acts 22:3]

> When we are judged by the Lord, we are **disciplined** so that we may not be condemned along with the world. [I Corinthians 11:32]

> We are putting no obstacle in anyone's way, so that no fault may be found with our ministry, but as servants of God we have commended ourselves in every way . . . as unknown, and yet are well known; as dying, and see—we are alive; as **punished**, and yet not killed. [II Corinthians 6:3-4, 9]

> By rejecting conscience, certain persons have suffered shipwreck in the faith; among them are Hymenaeus and Alexander, whom I have turned over to Satan, so that they may **learn** not to blaspheme. [I Timothy 1:19-20]

> The Lord's servant must not be quarrelsome but kindly to everyone, an apt teacher, patient, **correcting** opponents with gentleness. [II Timothy 2:24-25]

The noun form, *paideia*, nearly always appears as discipline in the New Revised Standard Version.

> Fathers, do not provoke your children to anger, but bring them up in the **discipline** and instruction of the Lord. [Ephesians 6:4]

> And you have forgotten the exhortation that addresses you as children—"My child, do not regard lightly the **discipline** of the Lord, or lose heart when you are punished by him; for the Lord disciplines those whom he loves, and chastises every child whom he accepts." Endure trials for the sake of **discipline**. God is treating you as children; for what child is there whom a parent does not discipline? [Hebrews 12:5-7]

These last two passages raise the question as to how the authors envisioned the discipline of the Lord. What kind of pressure does the Lord apply? What kind of pressure do parents apply when exercising the Lord's discipline? Perhaps the writers interpreted every difficult or painful experi-

---

Marks a word in the text that has its own entry

ence as the Lord putting on pressure for the purpose of shaping their lives in conformity with God's will. If so, then it was the responsibility of parents to provide difficult and painful experiences for their children to achieve the same purpose. That point of view may comfort some people who wonder why bad things happen, but it leaves them with a picture of God who is not only a stern but a mean, even cruel, Father.*

For the followers of Jesus who reject the idea of a cruel God arbitrarily inflicting misery, another possibility exists for using the *paideia* metaphor. *Paideia* may be the right word for the built-in pressures of daily existence. Difficult or painful experiences do not have to be accepted as God's punishment, but such occasions may provide an opportunity for learning. Certain kinds of behavior invite misery, but misery also happens randomly. Faithful people in the aftermath of tragedy do their best to figure out how they might have brought trouble on themselves and how they might avoid similar consequences in the future. If the trouble seems to be mostly the random sort of tragedy that has befallen, they look to God for the strength to cope with their suffering.

Parents who love their children do not try to shield them from all the consequences of their behavior and from all the random pain that life inflicts. Rather, good parents try to help their children live responsibly within the boundaries imposed by human existence. That is one way to think about what it means to bring up children in the *paideia* of the Lord.

doctrine, *noun*   Both the English word doctrine and the Greek word it translates once meant simply that which is taught. The Greek word is *didaskalia* from the verb *didasko*, which also is the root of *didache*, one of the biblical words translated as instruction.* In recent times, doctrine has taken on the same connotations as dogma.* To many minds, doctrine is that which must be believed in order to be in good standing with the church. Perhaps because of this shift, the New Revised Standard Version less often than the King James Version translates *didaskalia* as doctrine.

> You hypocrites! Isaiah prophesied rightly about you when he said: "This people honors me with their lips, but their hearts are far from me; in vain do they worship me, teaching human precepts as **doctrines.**" [Matthew 15:7-9]

> Whatever was written in former days was written for our **instruction,** so that by steadfastness and by the encouragement of the scriptures we might have hope. [Romans 15:4]

> We must no longer be children, tossed to and fro and blown about by every wind of **doctrine,** by people's trickery, by their craftiness in deceitful scheming. [Ephesians 4:14]

> All these regulations refer to things that perish with use; they are simply human commands and **teachings.** [Colossians 2:22]

> Now the Spirit expressly says that in later times some will renounce the faith by paying attention to deceitful spirits and **teachings** of demons, through the hypocrisy of liars whose consciences are seared with a hot iron. [I Timothy 4:1-2]

A word translated as sound appears several times in the late epistles as a qualification for doctrine.

> Hold to the standard of **sound teaching** that you have heard from me, in the faith and love that are in Christ Jesus. [II Timothy 1:13]

> As for you, teach what is consistent with **sound doctrine.** [Titus 2:1]

Marks a word in the text that has its own entry

The Greek word for sound is *hygiaino*, which originally meant to be in good physical health. It has the same root as such English words as hygiene and hygienist.

> Jesus answered, "Those who **are well** have no need of a physician, but those who are sick; I have come to call not the righteous but sinners to repentance." [Luke 5:31-32]

> When those who had been sent returned to the house, they found the slave **in good health.** [Luke 7:10]

For the followers of Jesus, teaching has always been at the center of their common life. Good health—mental, physical, and social—has from the earliest days been the standard by which to evaluate any teaching.

dogma, *noun*   Reading the Bible in English, a person would never know that the word *dogma* occurs in several places in the original Greek text. The reason dogma does not appear in English is because, like doctrine,* it has taken on the connotation of that which must be believed in order to have good standing in the church. The various translations of *dogma* convey what the word once meant.

> In those days a **decree** went out from Emperor Augustus that all the world should be registered. [Luke 2:1]

> As Paul and Timothy went from town to town, they delivered to them for observance the **decisions** that had been reached by the apostles and elders who were in Jerusalem. [Acts 16:4]

> He has abolished the law with its commandments and **ordinances**, that he might create in himself one new humanity in place of the two, thus making peace. [Ephesians 2:15]

> When you were dead in trespasses and the uncircumcision of your flesh, God made you alive together with him, when he forgave us all our trespasses, erasing the record that stood against us with its **legal demands.** [Colossians 2:13-14]

From these examples, it is clear that dogma had nothing to do with beliefs and that the early Christians generally had a negative view of dogma. Dogma had to do with arbitrary imperial decrees and oppressive legal systems.

doubt, *noun* and *verb*   Doubt appears in the Bible as a characteristic evident only in the followers of Jesus. The concept of doubt does not appear in the Hebrew Scriptures. According to the gospels, Jesus's disciples had four kinds of doubt.

> When the disciples saw it, they were amazed, saying, "How did the fig tree wither at once?" Jesus answered them, "Truly I tell you, if you have faith and do not **doubt**, not only will you do what has been done to the fig tree, but even if you say to this mountain, 'Be lifted up and thrown into the sea,' it will be done."—*diakrino*, separate thoroughly, discriminate, judge*
> [Matthew 21:20-21]

> Now the eleven disciples went to Galilee, to the mountain to which Jesus had directed them. When they saw him, they worshiped him; but some **doubted.**—*distazo*, wavered, hesitated
> [Matthew 28:16-17]

---

*Marks a word in the text that has its own entry

> While they were talking about this, Jesus himself stood among them and said to them, "Peace be with you." They were startled and terrified, and thought that they were seeing a ghost. He said to them, "Why are you frightened, and why do **doubts** arise in your hearts?"—*dialogismos*, discussions, debates, thoughts [Luke 24:36-38]

> A week later his disciples were again in the house, and Thomas was with them. Although the doors were shut, Jesus came and stood among them and said, "Peace be with you." Then he said to Thomas, "Put your finger here and see my hands. Reach out your hand and put it in my side. Do not **doubt** but believe."—*apistos*, be without confidence or trust [John 20:26-27]

Each of these kinds of doubt provides some insight into what seems to have been characteristic of Jesus's early followers. The people who wrote or edited the stories that appear in the gospels presumably saw themselves in the attitude and behavior attributed to the first disciples. In the case of *diakrino*, they saw themselves as people capable of making fine distinctions. They were thoughtful and at times cautious. As *distazo* indicates, this caution caused them to waver or hesitate before committing themselves to a particular enterprise. In the face of perplexing circumstances, they would carry on an internal dialogue, *dialogismos*, before coming to a conclusion. They probably were never as confident or trusting as they wanted to be. That is, they were *apistos*, the Greek word for faith preceded by the negative particle *a*.

The Jesus story continues after his death through the lives of the doubting disciples. People of great faith* appear in the gospel accounts, but they drop out of the story.

> Just then a Canaanite woman from that region came out and started shouting, "Have mercy on me, Lord, Son of David; my daughter is tormented by a demon." But he did not answer her at all. And his disciples came and urged him, saying, "Send her away, for she keeps shouting after us." He answered, "I was sent only to the lost sheep of the house of Israel." But she came and knelt before him, saying, "Lord, help me." He answered, "It is not fair to take the children's food and throw it to the dogs." She said, "Yes, Lord, yet even the dogs eat the crumbs that fall from their masters' table." Then Jesus answered her, "Woman, great is your faith! Let it be done for you as you wish." [Matthew 15:22-28]

> When he entered Capernaum, a centurion came to him, appealing to him and saying, "Lord, my servant is lying at home paralyzed, in terrible distress." And he said to him, "I will come and cure him." The centurion answered, "Lord, I am not worthy to have you come under my roof; but only speak the word, and my servant will be healed. For I also am a man under authority, with soldiers under me; and I say to one, 'Go,' and he goes, and to another, 'Come,' and he comes, and to my slave, 'Do this,' and the slave does it." When Jesus heard him, he was amazed and said to those who followed him, "Truly I tell you, in no one in Israel have I found such faith." [Matthew 8:5-10]

Although Jesus never seems to affirm the importance of doubting, according to the stories told about him, he preferred the company of doubters to that of believers. Understanding that Jesus recruited people capable of doubt and let the people of faith go on about their business can be very reassuring to people who are attracted to Jesus but who cannot believe much of what they have heard about him. If they can picture themselves to be the sort of people Jesus liked to have around, they may be able to hear what the early followers thought Jesus had to teach.

E

Easter, *noun*   The word Easter does not appear in the Greek texts of the Bible, but the King James Version in one place uses it for *pascha*, which is normally translated Passover. (For more on *pascha*, see **bread** and **passion**.)

> Now about that time Herod the king stretched forth his hands to vex certain of the church. And he killed James the brother of John with the sword. And because he saw it pleased the Jews, he proceeded further to take Peter also. (Then were the days of unleavened bread.) And when he had apprehended him, he put him in prison, and delivered him to four quaternions of soldiers to keep him; intending after **Easter** to bring him forth to the people. [Acts 12:1-4, KING JAMES VERSION]

In this one instance, the seventeenth-century English translators followed the German custom of using Easter instead of Passover when *pascha* appears in the text. The reasoning of both the English and German translators may have been that the people in their regions had for centuries, long before the Christians came, called the spring festival by its old Teutonic name, Easter. Easter was the goddess of the dawn who arose in the East. She was also the goddess of fertility whose blessing was especially invoked at the spring equinox, when the planting was getting underway. She was so important that the Christians in Germany and England kept her name for the celebration of the resurrection,* which took place soon after the Jewish observance of Passover. At the festival, they continued to employ her symbols: the signs of fertility, such as flowers and bunnies.

In English- and German-speaking countries, the resurrection of Jesus is often referred to as the first Easter. As some say, the first Easter marked the point at which the Jesus of history became the Christ of faith. Christianity began to separate itself from Judaism at the first Easter, but the use of the term is a reminder that the Christian faith is a combination of both Jewish and pagan* traditions.

elder—see **priest**

Emmanuel, *noun*   One of the titles acquired by Jesus, probably long after his death, was a Hebrew word that Matthew's gospel transliterated into Greek, *emmanouel*, and then provided a translation.

> "Look, the virgin shall conceive and bear a son, and they shall name him Emmanuel," which means, "God is with us." [Matthew 1:23]

Matthew picked up the title *immanuel* from a prophesy of Isaiah that he was using to support his view that the birth of Jesus must have been exceptional, that is a virgin* birth. His translation of the Hebrew is accurate, *immanu*, with us + *el*, god.

> Therefore the Lord himself will give you a sign. Look, the young woman is with child and shall bear a son, and shall name him **Immanuel**. [Isaiah 7:14]

Emmanuel has been a favorite metaphor in Christian circles for good reason. Many followers of Jesus have had experiences when they felt that God was with them. Then they read the stories about Jesus's disciples and realize that when the disciples looked back on their times with Jesus, they felt that God had been with them. Calling Jesus Emmanuel is one way Christians today can form a connection between their experiences and the experiences of the first people who followed Jesus.

Marks a word in the text that has its own entry

epiphany, *noun* In contemporary American English, an epiphany is a sudden insight into the essential meaning of an ordinary event or situation. That meaning is very close to the Greek word *epiphaneia*, derived from the verb *epiphaino*—*epi*, on or over + *phaino*, to shine, give light. Both the noun and the verb occur in the Christian portions of the Bible, but they are disguised in translation.

> By the tender mercy of our God, the dawn from on high will break upon us, to **give light** to those who sit in darkness and in the shadow of death, to guide our feet into the way of peace. [Luke 1:78-79]

> When neither sun nor stars **appeared** for many days, and no small tempest raged, all hope of our being saved was at last abandoned. [Acts 27:20]

> In the presence of God, who gives life to all things, and of Christ Jesus, who in his testimony before Pontius Pilate made the good confession, I charge you to keep the commandment without spot or blame until the **manifestation** of our Lord Jesus Christ. [I Timothy 6:13-14]

> This grace was given to us in Christ Jesus before the ages began, but it has now been revealed through the **appearing** of our Savior Christ Jesus, who abolished death and brought life and immortality to light through the gospel. [II Timothy 1:9-10]

> For the grace of God has **appeared**, bringing salvation to all, training us to renounce impiety and worldly passions, and in the present age to live lives that are self-controlled, upright, and godly, while we wait for the blessed hope and the **manifestation** of the glory of our great God and Savior, Jesus Christ. [Titus 2:11-13]

In the third century, Epiphany took on a technical meaning in the eastern regions of the church, being the name of a festival held on January 6 in commemoration of Jesus's baptism.* In the fourth century, the feast of the Epiphany found its way into western Europe, but it lost its association with baptism and became a celebration of Christ's manifestation to the Gentiles.* The gospel passage always read on Epiphany is the story of the Magi and the star* they followed.

Although the followers of Jesus have no special claim on the epiphany metaphor when talking about sudden insights, the word has special meaning to those who know its history in the life of the church.

eternal, *adjective* To many ears, eternal sounds as if it should always precede life, but in the Bible the Hebrew equivalent always modifies other nouns. While the Greek for eternal often appears as a modifier for the word life, it also often appears with other nouns. The Hebrew word is *olam*, which suggests persisting to the vanishing point in either time or space.

> The blessings of your father are stronger than the blessings of the eternal mountains, the bounties of the **everlasting** hills; may they be on the head of Joseph, on the brow of him who was set apart from his brothers. [Genesis 49:26]

> Remember your creator in the days of your youth, before the days of trouble come, and the years draw near when you will say, "I have no pleasure in them"; . . . when one is afraid of heights, and terrors are in the road; the almond tree blossoms, the grasshopper drags itself along and desire fails; because all must go to their **eternal** home, and the mourners will go about the streets. [Ecclesiastes 12:1, 5]

> The LORD is with me like a dread warrior; therefore my persecutors will stumble, and they will not prevail. They will be greatly shamed, for they will not succeed. Their **eternal** dishonor will never be forgotten. [Jeremiah 20:11]

The Greek word translated eternal is usually *aionios*, from *aion*, or age. Nearly two-thirds of the occurrences of *aionios* are linked with *zoe*, or life, but the other third help to illuminate the possible meaning of eternal life.

> If your hand or your foot causes you to stumble, cut it off and throw it away; it is better for you to enter life maimed or lame than to have two hands or two feet and to be thrown into the **eternal fire**. [Matthew 18:8] See also **hell**.

> Ever since the creation of the world his **eternal power** and divine nature, invisible though they are, have been understood and seen through the things he has made. [Romans 1:20] See also **power**.

> For this slight momentary affliction is preparing us for an **eternal weight of glory** beyond all measure, because we look not at what can be seen but at what cannot be seen; for what can be seen is temporary, but what cannot be seen is eternal. [II Corinthians 4:17-18]

> Now may our Lord Jesus Christ himself and God our Father, who loved us and through grace gave us **eternal comfort** and good hope, comfort your hearts and strengthen them in every good work and word. [II Thessalonians 2:16-17] See also **advocate**.

> Although he was a Son, he learned obedience through what he suffered; and having been made perfect, he became the source of **eternal salvation** for all who obey him. [Hebrews 5:8-9] See also **save**.

> Therefore let us go on toward perfection, leaving behind the basic teaching about Christ, and not laying again the foundation: repentance from dead works and faith toward God, instruction about baptisms, laying on of hands, resurrection of the dead, and **eternal judgment**. [Hebrews 6:1-2] See also **judge**.

> Christ entered once for all into the Holy Place, not with the blood of goats and calves, but with his own blood, thus obtaining **eternal redemption**. [Hebrews 9:12] See also **redeem**.

> Now may the God of peace, who brought back from the dead our Lord Jesus, the great shepherd of the sheep, by the blood of the **eternal covenant**, make you complete in everything good so that you may do his will, working among us that which is pleasing in his sight, through Jesus Christ, to whom be the glory forever and ever. [Hebrews 13:20-21] See also **covenant**.

> Then I saw another angel flying in midheaven, with an **eternal gospel** to proclaim to those who live on the earth—to every nation and tribe and language and people. [Revelation 14:6] See also **gospel**.

From these examples, it appears that eternal has to do with looking back into the past as well as looking forward into the future. Eternal life is like an everflowing stream in which a person might at any time take a dip. Life began farther back in the past than we can see with clarity and will probably continue into the future longer than we can imagine. From the teaching attributed to Jesus, we can gather that he showed the way to an aware participation in the eternal phenomenon of life.

Marks a word in the text that has its own entry

FROM LITERAL TO LITERARY

> Everyone who has left houses or brothers or sisters or father or mother or children or fields, for my name's sake, will receive a hundredfold, and will inherit **eternal life**. [Matthew 19:29] See also **soul**.

> Just then a lawyer stood up to test Jesus. "Teacher," he said, "what must I do to inherit **eternal life**?" He said to him, "What is written in the law? What do you read there?" He answered, "You shall love the Lord your God with all your heart, and with all your soul, and with all your strength, and with all your mind; and your neighbor as yourself." And he said to him, "You have given the right answer; do this, and you will live." [Luke 10:25-28]

> For God so loved the world that he gave his only Son, so that everyone who believes in him may not perish but may have **eternal life**. [John 3:16]

> Very truly, I tell you, anyone who hears my word and believes him who sent me has **eternal life**, and does not come under judgment, but has passed from death to life. [John 5:24]

Some Christians see in these passages a promise of life after physical death,* but others understand eternal life as a powerful metaphor pointing to a quality of existence to be experienced here and now. Or, as John's gospel put it, anyone who has confidence in God already has eternal life. The first followers of Jesus may have heard in the promise of eternal life a guarantee that they would survive the grave, but the focus of the gospels seems to be much more on the present.

Eucharist, *noun*   The followers of Jesus have had many names for the commemoration of the last meal he shared with his inner circle of disciples*—Lord's Supper, Holy Communion, Mass, the Liturgy*—but the one that may come the closest to a biblical understanding of the event is Eucharist, in Greek *eucharistia*. The word is formed from *eu*, good + *charizomai*, to offer thanks. The root of *charizomai* is *charis*, meaning gift or grace.*

Although the Christian writers whose works are included in the Bible do not use *eucharistia* as the name of the celebration, they frequently use the term and the verb from the stem root, *eucharisteo*.

> Jesus took the seven loaves and the fish; and after **giving thanks** he broke them and gave them to the disciples, and the disciples gave them to the crowds. [Matthew 15:36]

> Then one of the lepers, when he saw that he was healed, turned back, praising God with a loud voice. He prostrated himself at Jesus' feet and **thanked** him. And he was a Samaritan. [Luke 17:15-16]

> When Paul had been summoned, Tertullus began to accuse him, saying: "Your Excellency, because of you we have long enjoyed peace, and reforms have been made for this people because of your foresight. We welcome this in every way and everywhere with utmost **gratitude**." [Acts 24:2-3]

> Yes, everything is for your sake, so that grace, as it extends to more and more people, may increase **thanksgiving**, to the glory of God. [II Corinthians 4:15]

> Do not worry about anything, but in everything by prayer and supplication with **thanksgiving** let your requests be made known to God. [Philippians 4:6]

The verb *eucharisteo* is included in three biblical accounts of the last supper and probably provided the basis for the later practice of calling the celebration a eucharist.

Marks a word in the text that has its own entry

> Then Jesus took a cup, and after **giving thanks** he gave it to them, saying, "Drink from it, all of you; for this is my blood of the covenant, which is poured out for many for the forgiveness of sins." [Matthew 26:27-28]

> Jesus took a cup, and after **giving thanks** he said, "Take this and divide it among yourselves; for I tell you that from now on I will not drink of the fruit of the vine until the kingdom of God comes." Then he took a loaf of bread, and when he had given thanks, he broke it and gave it to them, saying, "This is my body, which is given for you. Do this in remembrance of me." [Luke 22:17-19]

> For I received from the Lord what I also handed on to you, that the Lord Jesus on the night when he was betrayed took a loaf of bread, and when he **had given thanks,** he broke it and said, "This is my body that is for you. Do this in remembrance of me." [I Corinthians 11:23-24]

Some scholars have cast doubt on the assumption that Jesus actually said the words attributed to him in these accounts. They believe that the words represent a ritual form that developed after the death of Jesus and after his followers had identified themselves as the risen body* of Christ. No one doubts, however, that Jesus frequently ate with his inner circle of followers or that as the teacher he would have followed the custom of his people and given thanks for the food at each meal. After Jesus's death, his close friends might have met from time to time for a meal and for talk about what their time with Jesus had meant to them. At such a meal, perhaps someone had the realization that the work Jesus had begun could continue through them. In a way, Jesus was alive again. They were to be his new body.* Such an epiphany* may have been the source of a story in Luke's gospel about the two disciples who encountered a mysterious stranger on their way from Jerusalem to their home in Emmaus. After an intensive conversation on the road, they invited the stranger to have supper with them.

> When he was at the table with them, he took bread, blessed and broke it, and gave it to them. Then their eyes were opened, and they recognized him; and he vanished from their sight. They said to each other, "Were not our hearts burning within us while he was talking to us on the road, while he was opening the scriptures to us?" That same hour they got up and returned to Jerusalem; and they found the eleven and their companions gathered together . . . Then they told what had happened on the road, and how he had been made known to them in the breaking of the bread. [Luke 24:30-33, 35]

By the time St. Paul was writing about it in his letter to the community in Corinth, the meal had taken on a ritual form that included giving thanks, *eucharisteo*. In time, the ritual meal became known as the *eucharistia*, but the metaphor had implications far beyond the meal itself. Giving thanks had become central to the lives of the Jesus followers. They had discovered that pausing now and then to be grateful had a way of enhancing their lives. Offering thanks for all the blessings* of life, both large and small, helps to keep life in perspective and to keep hope alive in the midst of trouble.

evangelism—see gospel

Eve, *noun*   In the stories found in the second and third chapters of Genesis, *adam*—the sexually undifferentiated human being—becomes divided into male and female parts. The female part in the story at first has no name. She is simply *ishah,* woman.

> Now the serpent was more crafty than any other wild animal that the LORD God had made. He said to the **woman,** "Did God say, 'You shall not eat from any tree in the garden'?" The **woman** said to the serpent, "We may eat of the fruit of the trees in the garden; but God said, 'You shall not eat of the fruit of the tree that is in the middle of the garden, nor shall you touch it, or you shall die.'" But the serpent said to the **woman,** "You will not die; for God knows that when you eat of it your eyes will be opened, and you will be like God, knowing good and evil." So when the **woman** saw that the tree was good for food, and that it was a delight to the eyes, and that the tree was to be desired to make one wise, she took of its fruit and ate; and she also gave some to her husband, who was with her, and he ate. Then the eyes of both were opened, and they knew that they were naked; and they sewed fig leaves together and made loincloths for themselves. [Genesis 3:1-7]

Later in the story the woman receives a name.

> The man named his wife **Eve,** because she was the mother of all living. [Genesis 3:20]

The Hebrew for the woman's name is *Chavah*. The word appears to be related to *chay*, here translated as living. Some scholars think that *Chavah* is also related to a word for snake, associating her name with an earlier myth that all life originated in a primeval serpent. *Chavah* could also mean a settlement or village.

> So Moses gave Gilead to Machir son of Manasseh, and he settled there. Jair son of Manasseh went and captured their **villages,** and renamed them Havvoth-jair. [Numbers 32:40-41]

Eve appears twice in the early Christian writings, once in a letter by Paul and once in a later letter by a person calling himself Paul. Both use *Eua*, a transliteration of the Hebrew.

> I am afraid that as the serpent deceived **Eve** by its cunning, your thoughts will be led astray from a sincere and pure devotion to Christ. [II Corinthians 11:3]

> For Adam was formed first, then **Eve**; and Adam was not deceived, but the woman was deceived and became a transgressor. [I Timothy 2:13-14]

Both of these citations represent the transition of Eve from the name of a mythological character to Eve as a metaphor, indicating a curious person who is easily duped. Although the word Eveish has not been used much in recent years, there was a time when it was standard English for curious.

evil, *adjective* and *noun*   All the words in the Bible that are translated evil were originally descriptive of bad conditions but came to be used metaphorically to identify what is morally offensive. The Hebrew word most often translated evil is *ra*, and the Greek words are *poneros, phaulos,* and *kakos.*

To differentiate among the three Greek words, we might note that the first evolved from a verb meaning to work and apparently acquired the implication of working so hard that a person was worn out, used up, no longer able to function. When applied to inanimate objects, *poneros* could mean that something was no longer usable for what was intended. The point is that these words could be used descriptively as well as morally, whereas evil has only moral connotations. For that reason, the translators of the New Revised Standard Version decided not to follow earlier English translations that spoke of evil fruit but used the all-purpose word bad to stand for *poneros* in this passage. They also used bad to translate *sapros*, which means decayed, spoiled, or rotten.

> Beware of false prophets, who come to you in sheep's clothing but inwardly are ravenous wolves. You will know them by their fruits. Are grapes gathered from thorns, or figs from thistles? In the same way, every good tree bears good fruit, but the bad (*sapros*) tree bears bad fruit. A good tree cannot bear **bad** fruit, nor can a bad (*sapros*) tree bear good fruit. Every tree that does not bear good fruit is cut down and thrown into the fire. Thus you will know them by their fruits. [Matthew 7:15-20]

For the same reason, the new version does not speak of an eye being evil but in this context assumes that *poneros* means diseased:

> The eye is the lamp of the body. So, if your eye is healthy, your whole body will be full of light; but if your eye is **unhealthy,** your whole body will be full of darkness. [Matthew 6:22-23]

When the Greek words are used as metaphors, the New Revised Standard Version continues to translate them evil.

> Blessed are you when people revile you and persecute you and utter all kinds of **evil** against you falsely on my account.— *poneros* [Matthew 5:11]

> For all who do **evil** hate the light and do not come to the light, so that their deeds may not be exposed.—*phaulos* [John 3:20]

> And Paul said, "I did not realize, brothers, that he was high priest; for it is written, 'You shall not speak **evil** of a leader of your people.'"—*kakos* [Acts 23:5]

In the Hebrew Scriptures, the translators sometimes use evil for *ra* even when the context suggests the use is descriptive rather than moral. For example, this passage probably does not imply an ability to make moral distinctions but rather practical ones, differentiating between what is useful and what might be harmful:

> Out of the ground the LORD God made to grow every tree that is pleasant to the sight and good for food, the tree of life also in the midst of the garden, and the tree of the knowledge of good and **evil**. [Genesis 2:9]

In the same way, when the writers say that God sends *ra*, they do not mean that God is wicked but that they attribute harmful experiences to God. Recent translations of the Hebrew Scriptures sometimes avoid the possible misunderstanding by using another word for *ra*.

> The next day an **evil** spirit from God rushed upon Saul, and he raved within his house, while David was playing the lyre, as he did day by day. [I Samuel 18:10]

> I form light and create darkness, I make weal and create **woe**; I the LORD do all these things. [Isaiah 45:7]

> Then his wife said to him, "Do you still persist in your integrity? Curse God, and die." But he said to her, "You speak as any foolish woman would speak. Shall we receive the good at the hand of God, and not receive the **bad**?" [Job 2:9-10]

Although evil is not personified in the Hebrew Scriptures, the later writings in Greek appear to use *poneros* as another way of identifying Satan.*

> Let your word be "Yes, Yes" or "No, No"; anything more than this comes from the **evil one**. [Matthew 5:37]

*Marks a word in the text that has its own entry

With all of these, take the shield of faith, with which you will be able to quench all the flaming arrows of the **evil one**. [Ephesians 6:16]

Because today evil always means morally depraved, wicked, and vicious, the word should probably be used with caution. Talk of evil empires or an axis of evil can dehumanize whole nations in the minds of those who use such terms. We might be better off if we returned to the original biblical metaphors when attempting to make moral judgments. Saying that people are not living up to their potential or that their behavior is unhealthy or harmful might get the point across without creating additional barriers to reconciliation.*

example, *noun*   The Greek word often translated as example is *typos*. The word originally meant a blow, as from a hammer, and later the mark left by the blow or the shape left from repeated blows. *Typos* is the root of our English word type.

I do not want you to be unaware, brothers and sisters, that our ancestors were all under the cloud, and all passed through the sea, and all were baptized into Moses in the cloud and in the sea, and all ate the same spiritual food, and all drank the same spiritual drink. For they drank from the spiritual rock that followed them, and the rock was Christ. Nevertheless, God was not pleased with most of them, and they were struck down in the wilderness. Now these things occurred as **examples** for us, so that we might not desire evil as they did. Do not become idolaters as some of them did; as it is written, "The people sat down to eat and drink, and they rose up to play." We must not indulge in sexual immorality as some of them did, and twenty-three thousand fell in a single day. We must not put Christ to the test, as some of them did, and were destroyed by serpents. And do not complain as some of them did, and were destroyed by the destroyer. These things happened to them to serve as an **example**, and they were written down to instruct us, on whom the ends of the ages have come. [I Corinthians 10:1-11]

Brothers and sisters, join in imitating me, and observe those who live according to the **example** you have in us. [Philippians 3:17]

You became imitators of us and of the Lord, for in spite of persecution you received the word with joy inspired by the Holy Spirit, so that you became an **example** to all the believers in Macedonia and in Achaia. [I Thessalonians 1:6-7]

The richness of the *typos* metaphor becomes clear with the variety of English words that stand for it in translation:

So the other disciples told Thomas, "We have seen the Lord." But he said to them, "Unless I see the **mark** of the nails in his hands, and put my finger in the mark of the nails and my hand in his side, I will not believe." [John 20:25]

Yet death exercised dominion from Adam to Moses, even over those whose sins were not like the transgression of Adam, who is a **type** of the one who was to come. [Romans 5:14]

Thanks be to God that you, having once been slaves of sin, have become obedient from the heart to the **form** of teaching to which you were entrusted. [Romans 6:17]

Show yourself in all respects a **model** of good works, and in your teaching show integrity, gravity, and sound speech that cannot be censured; then any opponent will be put to shame, having nothing evil to say of us. [Titus 2:7-8]

> They offer worship in a sanctuary that is a sketch and shadow of the heavenly one; for Moses, when he was about to erect the tent, was warned, "See that you make everything according to the **pattern** that was shown you on the mountain." [Hebrews 8:5]

> Therefore I intend to keep on **reminding** you of these things, though you know them already and are established in the truth that has come to you. [II Peter 1:12]

Example can have negative connotations in English. An older brother or sister told to be a good example for the younger children resents the burden. If the younger ones are told to follow the good example of the older one, they are not likely to increase their affection for the one to whom they are supposed to compare themselves. *Typos*, however, can bring to mind the mark of an ax left on an occasional tree to mark a trail. In this image, no one is compared to anyone else. The older are the trailblazers, and they can keep those who follow from getting totally lost.

In much the same way, the *typos* metaphor provides a perspective on scripture. The ancient writings do not tell the modern reader what to do or how to behave, but they provide marks along the way to help modern readers stay on the path to a fulfilling life.

F

faith, *noun;* **believe**, *verb*   Some people like to make a distinction between having faith and believing, but the Bible does not offer that possibility. In the Hebrew Scriptures, the words translated faith and believe are formed from the same root, *aman*. Both the noun and the verb also have the same root in the Greek Scriptures. The noun translated faith is *pistis* and the verb usually rendered believe is *pisteuo*.

The core of the Hebrew concept appears to have been firmness, steadiness, reliability. To believe what another person has said is to grant a strong affirmation of the statement. To believe in another person or in God is to affirm the relationship. To live by faith is to affirm what is.

> They rose early in the morning and went out into the wilderness of Tekoa; and as they went out, Jehoshaphat stood and said, "Listen to me, O Judah and inhabitants of Jerusalem! **Believe** in the LORD your God and you will be established; **believe** his prophets." [II Chronicles 20:20]

> Look at the proud! Their spirit is not right in them, but the righteous live by their **faith**. [Habakkuk 2:4]

That sense of strong affirmation implied by the Hebrew concept of faith or believing carries over into the Greek portion of the Bible. Although most of the words attributed to Jesus were preserved only in Greek, one word he is said to have used frequently was kept in the Hebrew form. The word is *amen*, virtually the same word as the Hebrew verb *aman*. In the King James Version of the Bible, *amen* is translated verily. Every child in Sunday school two generations ago could hear "Verily, I say unto you," and know that these were the words of Jesus. The children did not know, however, that in the language Jesus used, verily and faith had the same root meaning, nor did they guess that the Amen at the end of their prayers was the same word that Jesus probably used to introduce many of his observations about the human situation.

When readers of more recent translations come across "Truly, I tell you" or "I swear to you," they are no more likely to make the connection with faith or believing. The connection between a strong affirmation and faith, however, can help doubters reclaim the metaphor. They can quite justifiably think of faith as noticing, accepting, and acknowledging what is true in their experience. Faith may be an attitude toward life based on a willingness to say yes to what is. In this sense, the opposite of faith is not doubt* but sin,* that is, a refusal to face the facts.

The Greek words of the Bible translated as faith and believe have connotations of their own. *Pistis* can mean trust or confidence. See what a different ring the following statements have when *pistis* becomes confidence instead of faith. Note also that in these examples *pistis* is not followed by in or that.

> Then some people came, bringing to him a paralyzed man, carried by four of them. And when they could not bring him to Jesus because of the crowd, they removed the roof above him; and after having dug through it, they let down the mat on which the paralytic lay. When Jesus saw their **confidence,** he said to the paralytic, "Son, your sins are forgiven." [Mark 2:3-5]

> When Jesus heard the centurion, he was amazed and said to those who followed him, "Truly I tell you, in no one in Israel have I found such **confidence.**" [Matthew 8:10]

> Then he said to the Samaritan, "Get up and go on your way; your **confidence** has made you well."[Luke 17:19]

> For I am not ashamed of the gospel; it is the power of God for salvation to everyone who has **confidence,** to the Jew first and also to the Greek. [Romans 1:16]

If doubters cannot relate to the idea of faith even when understood as affirmation or confidence, they need not give up on Christianity. With the exception of the Gospel according to John and some of the later epistles, faith and believing to do not seem to have been very important to the early followers of Jesus. According to one tradition, Jesus's pet name for his disciples was *oligopistoi*—*oligo,* a few, or little + *pistis* = the little faith ones. Then Luke tells his readers that when Jesus's followers asked for more faith, he kidded them by suggesting that they already had more faith than they knew what to do with. If they had more faith (or confidence) they would probably do something silly, like trying to get mulberry trees to uproot themselves and fly out to sea.

> He said, "Come." So Peter got out of the boat, started walking on the water, and came toward Jesus. But when he noticed the strong wind, he became frightened, and beginning to sink, he cried out, "Lord, save me!" Jesus immediately reached out his hand and caught him, saying to him, "You of **little faith,** why did you doubt?" [Matthew 14:29-31]

> A windstorm arose on the sea, so great that the boat was being swamped by the waves; but he was asleep. And they went and woke him up, saying, "Lord, save us! We are perishing!" And he said to them, "Why are you afraid, you of **little faith**?" Then he got up and rebuked the winds and the sea; and there was a dead calm. [Matthew 8:24-26]

> The apostles said to the Lord, "Increase our **faith!**" The Lord replied, "If you had **faith** the size of a mustard seed, you could say to this mulberry tree, 'Be uprooted and planted in the sea,' and it would obey you." [Luke 17:5-6]

It is interesting to note that the people congratulated for their faith—the Samaritan, the centurion, and the four friends of the paralytic—drop out of the story. It was the little faith people who carried on the tradition initiated by Jesus.

Marks a word in the text that has its own entry

St. Paul did not seem to think that faith was a requirement for being a follower of Jesus. When he listed gifts of the Spirit,* faith was just one of the possibilities. According to St. Paul, faith is not a gift that everybody gets.

> To one is given through the Spirit the utterance of wisdom, and to another the utterance of knowledge according to the same Spirit, to another **faith** by the same Spirit, to another gifts of healing by the one Spirit, . . . [I Corinthians 12:8-9]

Another contribution St. Paul made to an understanding of the faith/believe metaphor was his identification of *pisteuo* with the heart, in Greek *kardia*. In his time, the *kardia* had a variety of meanings. Paul could have been using the term to refer to the seat of either mental or emotional functions. The heart was thought to be the center of grief and longing, but it never seems to have been the place assigned for logical processing or analysis. Apparently for Paul, believing was a recognition of a desire for God rather than an intellectual assent to opinions about God that cannot be supported by empirical evidence.

> If you confess with your lips that Jesus is Lord and **believe** in your heart that God raised him from the dead, you will be saved. [Romans 10:9]

When Latin-speaking Christians attempted to articulate what they had discovered in Jesus, they made regular use of the heart imagery. Their word *credo*—which the English in the seventh century translated "I believe in"—is the verb formed from *cordis*, the genitive of *cor*, their word for "heart." In other words, for Christians to believe is to set the heart rather than the mind.

Some skeptical readers cannot make sense of the business of faith and believing even when informed about other possible connotations. To them, the use of other language for these concepts amounts to little more than linguistic gymnastics employed by those who are trying to make religion more respectable. If such skeptics feel superior to those whom they think are spiritually gullible, they may recognize a soul mate in the person who preserved this proverb, which is enshrined in holy scripture.

> The simple **believe** everything, but the clever consider their steps. [Proverbs 14:15]

Others may find new avenues of exploration in pursuing an understanding of what it means to face the facts, to live with confidence, and to set the heart.

family, *noun*   The Greek word usually translated family is *patria*, a feminine form derived from *pater*, the word for father.* It could also mean a clan or a nation.

> Joseph also went from the town of Nazareth in Galilee to Judea, to the city of David called Bethlehem, because he was descended from the house and **family** of David. [Luke 2:4]

> You are the descendants of the prophets and of the covenant that God gave to your ancestors, saying to Abraham, "And in your descendants all the **families** of the earth shall be blessed." [Acts 3:25]

The author of the letter to the Ephesians used *patria* as a metaphor to identify all the people of God.

> For this reason I bow my knees before the Father, from whom every **family** in heaven and on earth takes its name. [Ephesians 3:14-15]

The other Greek passages referring to family use other words, but they are all metaphors for the group of Jesus followers.

> Paul an apostle . . . and all the members of God's **family** who are with me, To the churches of Galatia: Grace to you and peace from God our Father and the Lord Jesus Christ. [Galatians 1:1-3]

> So then, whenever we have an opportunity, let us work for the good of all, and especially for those of the **family** of faith. [Galatians 6:10]

> Honor everyone. Love the **family** of believers. Fear God. Honor the emperor. [I Peter 2:17]

The first and third of these quotes from the New Revised Standard Version of the Bible have used family instead of sisters and brothers* to translate *adelphoi*. The translators added believers in the verse from I Peter so the readers would know what family the author had in mind. In the second passage, family appears instead of household, the usual translation for *oikeios*.

This consistent use of the word family as a metaphor, meaning the followers of Jesus, offers a clue as to what Jesus probably taught about family life. If he ever had a positive thing to say about life in the families he observed, nobody bothered to preserve his remarks. On the contrary, he is reported to have broken away from his family of origin in favor of creating a new set of communal relationships with people whom he called his new sisters and brothers. According to Matthew and Luke, he urged his followers to do the same.

> I have come to set a man against his father, and a daughter against her mother, and a daughter-in-law against her mother-in-law; and one's foes will be members of one's own household. Whoever loves father or mother more than me is not worthy of me; and whoever loves son or daughter more than me is not worthy of me. [Matthew 10:35-37]

> Whoever comes to me and does not hate father and mother, wife and children, brothers and sisters, yes, and even life itself, cannot be my disciple. [Luke 14:26]

These strong words ascribed to Jesus may have an explanation in an account Matthew and Luke have provided concerning a brief exchange between Jesus and a person who seemed to have a good excuse for not dropping everything to follow him.

> Another of his disciples said to him, "Lord, first let me go and bury my father." But Jesus said to him, "Follow me, and let the dead bury their own dead."
> [Matthew 8:21-22; see also Luke 9:59-60]

Anyone not acquainted with the customs of the region in which Jesus lived and taught might think that Jesus was being unduly harsh. To western ears, it sounds as if someone who wanted to follow Jesus had left the corpse of his father laid out in the front room and was asking for just enough time to take care of the interment, certainly a reasonable request. In all probability, however, Luke and Matthew intended the story to convey the strong sense of family loyalty that kept children bound to their parents until their parents died. The disciple in the story was asking permission to delay a break with the family until the father's death and the burial that would end the filial obligation.

As Matthew and Luke understood Jesus's teaching, those who stay bound to their parents until their parents die are themselves dead.* They have no life of their own. Their sense of identity, meaning, and purpose are derived from their place in the family. The family is their religion. Jesus had apparently observed that family loyalty, which appeared to be a virtue, was in reality an obstacle to developing confidence in God. The family metaphor works quite well in getting across the message the authors intended.

It was this new understanding of family that scandalized the neighbors of the early Christians. According to long-established custom throughout Roman society, a woman could not function apart from a man, her father, or her husband. Having claimed the family metaphor in identifying their community, the women as well as the men who followed Jesus had the confidence to live independently, separated from their families of origin.

In a strange twist of tradition, some Christians now say that God ordained the family and gave it his blessing. They believe that the family is the focus of Christian faith and work.

father, *noun*   According to the gospels, Father was the metaphor Jesus most often employed in praying to God* and in talking about God. If Jesus spoke Aramaic, the word he used would have been *Abba,** but if he taught in Greek, he would have said *Pater*. The Hebrew word for father, *ab*, appears frequently in the scriptures and conveys the same characteristics that we find associated with God the father in the exclusively Christian parts of the Bible.

The vision of God as a gentle, protective father inspired the ancient Hebrew poets and prophets as well as Jesus.

> **Father** of orphans and protector of widows is God in his holy habitation. [Psalm 68:5]

> You are my **Father**, my God, and the Rock of my salvation! [Psalm 89:26]

> With weeping they shall come, and with consolations I will lead them back, I will let them walk by brooks of water, in a straight path in which they shall not stumble; for I have become a **father** to Israel, and Ephraim is my firstborn. [Jeremiah 31:9]

> Look at the birds of the air; they neither sow nor reap nor gather into barns, and yet your heavenly **Father** feeds them. Are you not of more value than they? [Matthew 6:26]

> As the **Father** has loved me, so I have loved you; abide in my love. [John 15:9]

The ancients also saw the father as the one who established the rules governing the relationships in the family. These rules are part of the covenant* between the father and his children. Some of Jesus's early followers thought that the covenant had been amended by a new rule that required acceptance of Jesus.

> Have we not all one **father**? Has not one God created us? Why then are we faithless to one another, profaning the covenant of our ancestors? [Malachi 2:10]

> This is indeed the will of my **Father**, that all who see the Son and believe in him may have eternal life; and I will raise them up on the last day. [John 6:40]

> Everyone who does not abide in the teaching of Christ, but goes beyond it, does not have God; whoever abides in the teaching has both the **Father** and the Son. [II John 1:9]

For the relationship between the father and the children to hold, the rules must be obeyed. The children honor their father by obeying his rules. The children must fear the consequences of disobedience.

> As a **father** has compassion for his children, so the LORD has compassion for those who fear him. [Psalm 103:13]

Marks a word in the text that has its own entry

> A son honors his father, and servants their master. If then I am a **father**, where is the honor due me? And if I am a master, where is the respect due me? says the LORD of hosts. [Malachi 1:6]

> Not everyone who says to me, "Lord, Lord," will enter the kingdom of heaven, but only the one who does the will of my **Father** in heaven. [Matthew 7:21]

> I declare what I have seen in the **Father's** presence; as for you, you should do what you have heard from the Father. [John 8:38]

> If you invoke as **Father** the one who judges all people impartially according to their deeds, live in reverent fear during the time of your exile. [I Peter 1:17]

Those who disobey the Father will surely be punished.

> Yet, O LORD, you are our **Father**; we are the clay, and you are our potter; we are all the work of your hand. Do not be exceedingly angry, O LORD, and do not remember iniquity forever. Now consider, we are all your people. Your holy cities have become a wilderness, Zion has become a wilderness, Jerusalem a desolation. Our holy and beautiful house, where our ancestors praised you, has been burned by fire, and all our pleasant places have become ruins. After all this, will you restrain yourself, O LORD? Will you keep silent, and punish us so severely? [Isaiah 64:8-12]

> And in anger his lord handed him over to be tortured until he would pay his entire debt. So my heavenly **Father** will also do to every one of you, if you do not forgive your brother or sister from your heart. [Matthew 18:34-35]

Two pictures of the father appear in the Bible. In one picture, the father sets down the rules for his household. He demands obedience. He instills fear in the hearts of his children, rewarding compliance and punishing disobedience. In the other picture, the father provides protection, nurturance, compassion, and love. He is infinitely forgiving, always willing to welcome back those who have strayed. In thinking and speaking about God, people today tend to stress one aspect of the metaphor at the expense of the other. For some, God is a stern father, so they conclude that any misery experienced is deserved, a punishment for some infraction of the rules. For others, God is a loving father to whom they look for continuing encouragement and for comfort in times of trouble.

fear, *noun* and *verb*; **afraid**, *adjective*   Over one hundred times in the Bible, people are told not to fear or be afraid. From the frequency of such admonitions in both the Greek and Hebrew portions of the Bible, the obvious conclusion is that fear was a major issue for the people of the ancient world. Both the Hebrew *yare* and the Greek *phobos* (the verb is *phobeo*) were the basic words for fear. A sampling of passages on the subject of fear indicates that mostly people were receiving divine reassurance in the face of military and political enemies.

> Then they turned and went up the road to Bashan; and King Og of Bashan came out against them, he and all his people, to battle at Edrei. But the LORD said to Moses, "Do not be **afraid** of him; for I have given him into your hand, with all his people, and all his land. You shall do to him as you did to King Sihon of the Amorites, who ruled in Heshbon." [Numbers 21:33-34]

> And the Gibeonites sent to Joshua at the camp in Gilgal, saying, "Do not abandon your servants; come up to us quickly, and save us, and help us; for all the kings of the Amorites who live in the hill country are gathered against us." So Joshua went up from Gilgal, he and all the fighting force with him, all the mighty warriors. The LORD said to Joshua, "Do not **fear** them, for I have handed them over to you; not one of them shall stand before you." [Joshua 10:6-8]

Do not be **afraid** when some become rich, when the wealth of their houses increases. For when they die they will carry nothing away; their wealth will not go down after them. [Psalm 49:16-17]

Do not be **afraid** of the king of Babylon, as you have been; do not be **afraid** of him, says the LORD, for I am with you, to save you and to rescue you from his hand. [Jeremiah 42:11]

Do not **fear** those who kill the body but cannot kill the soul; rather **fear** him who can destroy both soul and body in hell. [Matthew 10:28]

Do not **fear** what you are about to suffer. Beware, the devil is about to throw some of you into prison so that you may be tested, and for ten days you will have affliction. Be faithful until death, and I will give you the crown of life. [Revelation 2:10]

Such passages suggest that, for the faithful, fear is an inappropriate emotion. One of the letters attributed to someone named John goes even further. The author claims that a person experiences fear because of a deficiency in love.*

There is no **fear** in love, but perfect love casts out **fear**; for **fear** has to do with punishment, and whoever **fears** has not reached perfection in love. [I John 4:18]

While such sentiments have a lofty sound, on a practical level they make no sense. Fear evolved as a warning device to protect living beings from danger and death. Perhaps the ancients were as well acquainted with the life-saving necessity of fear as people are today. Perhaps the problem is in translation. Their words make sense if they were talking about excessive fear, controlling fear, fear that overrides rational evaluation of circumstances. If indeed irrational fear is the problem, then faith* and love are the ways to put fear in perspective.

A close look at some of the other do-not-fear passages reveals that often the fear people were told to put aside was a fear produced by some manifestation of the divine.

After these things the word of the LORD came to Abram in a vision, "Do not be **afraid**, Abram, I am your shield; your reward shall be very great." [Genesis 15:1]

Then Gideon perceived that it was the angel of the LORD; and Gideon said, "Help me, Lord GOD! For I have seen the angel of the LORD face to face." But the LORD said to him, "Peace be to you; do not **fear**, you shall not die." [Judges 6:22-23]

I called on your name, O LORD, from the depths of the pit; you heard my plea, "Do not close your ear to my cry for help, but give me relief!" You came near when I called on you; you said, "Do not **fear**!" [Lamentations 3:55-57]

Suddenly Jesus met his disciples and said, "Greetings!" And they came to him, took hold of his feet, and worshiped him. Then Jesus said to them, "Do not be **afraid**; go and tell my brothers to go to Galilee; there they will see me." [Matthew 28:9-10]

Then there appeared to him an angel of the Lord, standing at the right side of the altar of incense. When Zechariah saw him, he was terrified; and fear overwhelmed him. But the angel said to him, "Do not be **afraid**, Zechariah, for your prayer has been heard. Your wife Elizabeth will bear you a son, and you will name him John." [Luke 1:11-13]

Last night there stood by me an angel of the God to whom I belong and whom I worship, and he said, "Do not be **afraid**, Paul; you must stand before the emperor; and indeed, God has granted safety to all those who are sailing with you." [Acts 27:23-24]

Any students of the Bible who take such injunctions seriously will find themselves caught in a contradiction. They will come across many passages that give the opposite instructions. They are supposed to fear God.

> The **fear** of the Lord is the beginning of wisdom, and the knowledge of the Holy One is insight. [Proverbs 9:10]

> Though sinners do evil a hundred times and prolong their lives, yet I know that it will be well with those who **fear** God, because they stand in **fear** before him. [Ecclesiastes 8:12]

> Honor everyone. Love the family of believers. **Fear** God. Honor the emperor. [I Peter 2:17]

> **Fear** God and give him glory, for the hour of his judgment has come; and worship him who made heaven and earth, the sea and the springs of water. [Revelation 14:7]

Some scholars say that fear in these last passages actually means to have respect or to hold in awe. If that is the case, the authors of such passages may have been reminding their readers that a relationship with God includes accountability for their behavior. If they respect God, they will have a healthy fear of the possible negative consequences of their actions.

DID YOU KNOW . . .

. . . that *yare* is pronounced *yah-ray*?
For more help with pronunciation, see "Pronouncing
Transliterated Hebrew and Greek Words" on page 15.

---

feet, *plural noun*   The Hebrew and Greek metaphorical uses of feet are similar in many ways, but the Hebrew Scriptures have three that do not appear in the Greek portions of the Bible. Covering of the feet, in Hebrew *regel* (singular), was a euphemism for defecation. Since the nineteenth century, some scholars have argued that *regel* and its cognate *margelah* were also metaphors for the external genitals. Most of the examples could be read either way, literally feet or metaphorically genitals. Unless the Israelites were like J. R. R. Tolkien's hairy-footed Hobbits, however, it seems unlikely that the Lord was going to shave their feet. The third Hebrew figurative use of feet that does not appear in the later, Greek parts of the Bible concerns metaphors of trouble or distress.

covering the feet

New Revised Standard Version	King James Version
After Eglon had gone, the servants came. When they saw that the doors of the roof chamber were locked, they thought, "He must be **relieving** himself in the cool chamber." [Judges 3:24]	When he was gone out, his servants came; and when they saw that, behold, the doors of the parlour were locked, they said, Surely he covereth his **feet** in his summer chamber.
He came to the sheepfolds beside the road, where there was a cave; and Saul went in to **relieve** himself. Now David and his men were sitting in the innermost parts of the cave. [I Samuel 24:3]	He came to the sheepcotes by the way, where was a cave; and Saul went in to cover his **feet**: and David and his men remained in the sides of the cave.

feet meaning genitals

Zipporah took a flint and cut off her son's foreskin, and touched Moses' **feet** with it, and said, "Truly you are a bridegroom of blood to me!" [Exodus 4:25]

"When he lies down, observe the place where he lies; then, go and uncover his **feet** and lie down; and he will tell you what to do." Ruth said to Naomi, "All that you tell me I will do." So she went down to the threshing floor and did just as her mother-in-law had instructed her. When Boaz had eaten and drunk, and he was in a contented mood, he went to lie down at the end of the heap of grain. Then she came stealthily and uncovered his feet, and lay down.—*margelah* [Ruth 3:4-7]

In the year that King Uzziah died, I saw the Lord sitting on a throne, high and lofty; and the hem of his robe filled the temple. Seraphs were in attendance above him; each had six wings: with two they covered their faces, and with two they covered their **feet**, and with two they flew. [Isaiah 6:1-2]

On that day the Lord will shave with a razor hired beyond the River—with the king of Assyria—the head and the hair of the **feet**, and it will take off the beard as well. [Isaiah 7:20]

Thou hast built thy high place at every head of the way, and hast made thy beauty to be abhorred, and hast opened thy **feet** to every one that passed by, and multiplied thy whoredoms. [Ezekiel 16:25, KING JAMES VERSION]

In both the primary biblical languages, feet appear in a metaphor indicating conquest of subjugation. Both use the image of the defeated being under the feet of the victor. The metaphor may have evolved from a ritual of surrender in which the conqueror put his feet on the necks of the vanquished as in the Joshua passage below. Or it may have been the other way around: the metaphor may have preceded the use of the surrender ritual. In the Greek version of the metaphor, the word for feet is *podes,* from which we get our English words podiatry and pedal.

feet in metaphors of domination

When they brought the kings out to Joshua, Joshua summoned all the Israelites, and said to the chiefs of the warriors who had gone with him, "Come near, put your **feet** on the necks of these kings." Then they came near and put their **feet** on their necks. [Joshua 10:24]

You know that my father David could not build a house for the name of the LORD his God because of the warfare with which his enemies surrounded him, until the LORD put them under the soles of his **feet**. [I Kings 5:3]

For the LORD, the Most High, is awesome, a great king over all the earth. He subdued peoples under us, and nations under our **feet**. [Psalm 47:2-3]

You shall tread down the wicked, for they will be ashes under the soles of your **feet**, on the day when I act, says the LORD of hosts. [Malachi 4:3]

The Lord said to my Lord, "Sit at my right hand, until I put your enemies under your **feet**." [Matthew 22:44]

The God of peace will shortly crush Satan under your **feet**. The grace of our Lord Jesus Christ be with you. [Romans 16:20]

FROM LITERAL TO LITERARY

> Someone has testified somewhere, "What are human beings that you are mindful of them, or mortals, that you care for them? You have made them for a little while lower than the angels; you have crowned them with glory and honor, subjecting all things under their **feet**." [Hebrews 2:6-8, from Psalm 8:4-6]

Similarly, in the Hebrew Scriptures, the word for feet was also used in figures of speech for trouble or distress.

feet in metaphors of distress

> For the lips of a loose woman drip honey, and her speech is smoother than oil; but in the end she is bitter as wormwood, sharp as a two-edged sword. Her **feet** go down to death; her steps follow the path to Sheol. [Proverbs 5:3-5]

> Give glory to the LORD your God before he brings darkness, and before your **feet** stumble on the mountains at twilight; while you look for light, he turns it into gloom and makes it deep darkness. [Jeremiah 13:16]

> May a cry be heard from their houses, when you bring the marauder suddenly upon them! For they have dug a pit to catch me, and laid snares for my **feet**. [Jeremiah 18:22]

> Your trusted friends have seduced you and have overcome you; Now that your **feet** are stuck in the mud, they desert you. [Jeremiah 38:22]

Feet in both Hebrew and Greek could be used in metaphors with connotations that are the opposite of domination and trouble. These figures of speech may suggest divine support: guidance, steadiness, or even salvation.* Or they may suggest a way of life that opens a person to such support.

feet in metaphors of support

> You have made me stride freely, and my **feet** do not slip. [II Samuel 22:37]

> You have delivered my soul from death, and my **feet** from falling, so that I may walk before God in the light of life. [Psalm 56:13]

> Your word is a lamp to my **feet** and a light to my path. [Psalm 119:105]

> Keep straight the path of your **feet**, and all your ways will be sure. [Proverbs 4:26]

> By the tender mercy of our God, the dawn from on high will break upon us, to give light to those who sit in darkness and in the shadow of death, to guide our **feet** into the way of peace. [Luke 1:78-79]

> Then he poured water into a basin and began to wash the disciples' **feet** and to wipe them with the towel that was tied around him. He came to Simon Peter, who said to him, "Lord, are you going to wash my **feet**?" Jesus answered, "You do not know now what I am doing, but later you will understand." Peter said to him, "You will never wash my **feet**." Jesus answered, "Unless I wash you, you have no share with me." Simon Peter said to him, "Lord, not my **feet** only but also my hands and my head!" Jesus said to him, "One who has bathed does not need to wash, except for the **feet**, but is entirely clean. And you are clean, though not all of you." [John 13:5-10]

> Therefore lift your drooping hands and strengthen your weak knees, and make straight paths for your **feet**, so that what is lame may not be put out of joint, but rather be healed. [Hebrews 12:12-13]

In the specifically Christian portions of the Bible, feet appear in two contexts that have no antecedents in the Hebrew Scriptures: sitting at the feet of someone and shaking the dust off one's feet. At one time these phrases may have described physical gestures. A person of inferior status, such as a student, may well have sat on the floor while the teacher sat in a chair (see **throne**). Disgusted or disappointed people may have actually made a ceremonial gesture showing that they did not want to take with them even a particle of dust from the place that had refused them hospitality. In time, however, these two expressions became primarily metaphors that brought to mind the original, literal meaning.

Feet in metaphors of status

Then people came out to see what had happened, and when they came to Jesus, they found the man from whom the demons had gone sitting at the **feet** of Jesus, clothed and in his right mind. [Luke 8:35]

I am a Jew, born in Tarsus in Cilicia, but brought up in this city at the **feet** of Gamaliel, educated strictly according to our ancestral law, being zealous for God, just as all of you are today. [Acts 22:3]

For if a person with gold rings and in fine clothes comes into your assembly, and if a poor person in dirty clothes also comes in, and if you take notice of the one wearing the fine clothes and say, "Have a seat here, please," while to the one who is poor you say, "Stand there," or, "Sit at my **feet**," have you not made distinctions among yourselves, and become judges with evil thoughts? [James 2:2-4]

dust of the feet

If anyone will not welcome you or listen to your words, shake off the dust from your **feet** as you leave that house or town. [Matthew 10:14]

If any place will not welcome you and they refuse to hear you, as you leave, shake off the dust that is on your **feet** as a testimony against them. [Mark 6:11]

Whenever you enter a town and they do not welcome you, go out into its streets and say, "Even the dust of your town that clings to our **feet**, we wipe off in protest against you. Yet know this: the kingdom of God has come near." [Luke 10:11]

The Jews incited the devout women of high standing and the leading men of the city, and stirred up persecution against Paul and Barnabas, and drove them out of their region. So they shook the dust off their **feet** in protest against them, and went to Iconium. [Acts 13:50-51]

Of all the body parts, feet appear to have been the most versatile in the making of biblical metaphors. From the low comedy of King Eglon's death to the lofty expressions of faith in the Psalms, the figures of speech involving feet helped the authors of scripture say what they wanted to convey.

fellowship, *noun*   The Greek word usually translated fellowship has become popular among Christians as a name for their camps and communities*: *koinonia*. The word is based on the verb *koinoneo*, which meant to share, in the sense of dividing up or distributing.

The original meaning of share stands in stark contrast to one of the modern meanings, to talk about a personal experience or to reveal private thoughts. Share came from the same root as shear and meant to cut into pieces. What one person has cannot be possessed by another; each has only a

---

part of the whole. In the 1930s, a movement called Moral Rearmament introduced into the language the use of share, meaning to talk about intimate concerns. This usage has become popular with therapy and encounter groups as well as with church people. The shift in meaning has had a way of debasing *koinoneo* and the two nouns derived from it. One is *koinonia*. The other is *koinonos*, one who shares—a participant, associate, or partner. When people today hear about sharing, they do not pick up the sense of pain or loss that may accompany cutting things into pieces.

The verb *koinoneo* appears at several points in the Greek texts of the Bible.

> **Contribute** to the needs of the saints; extend hospitality to strangers. [Romans 12:13]

> At present, however, I am going to Jerusalem in a ministry to the saints; for Macedonia and Achaia have been pleased to **share** their resources with the poor among the saints at Jerusalem. [Romans 15:25-26]

> Those who are taught the word must **share** in all good things with their teacher. [Galatians 6:6]

Even more frequent is the use of *koinonia*, such as:

> So those who welcomed his message were baptized, and that day about three thousand persons were added. They devoted themselves to the apostles' teaching and **fellowship**, to the breaking of bread and the prayers. [Acts 2:41-42]

> God is faithful; by him you were called into the **fellowship** of his Son, Jesus Christ our Lord. [I Corinthians 1:9]

> The cup of blessing that we bless, is it not a **sharing** in the blood of Christ? The bread that we break, is it not a **sharing** in the body of Christ? [I Corinthians 10:16]

> When James and Cephas and John, who were acknowledged pillars, recognized the grace that had been given to me, they gave to Barnabas and me the right hand of **fellowship**, agreeing that we should go to the Gentiles and they to the circumcised. [Galatians 2:9]

> I thank my God every time I remember you, constantly praying with joy in every one of my prayers for all of you, because of your **sharing** in the gospel from the first day until now. [Philippians 1:3-5]

Those who share, *koinonoi* in the plural, is less common, but the use of the word can help to illuminate the concept of sharing.

> Simon Peter and all who were with him were amazed at the catch of fish that they had taken; and so also were James and John, sons of Zebedee, who were **partners** with Simon. Then Jesus said to Simon, "Do not be afraid; from now on you will be catching people." [Luke 5:9-10]

> Our hope for you is unshaken; for we know that as you **share** in our sufferings, so also you share in our consolation. [II Corinthians 1:7]

> Recall those earlier days when, after you had been enlightened, you endured a hard struggle with sufferings, sometimes being publicly exposed to abuse and persecution, and sometimes being **partners** with those so treated. [Hebrews 10:32-33]

Even with the problems that have arisen because of the shift in meaning associated with share, many Christians continue to find that fellowship works as a useful metaphor pointing to the essential nature of community. Other Jesus followers have as much trouble with fellowship as they do with share. Because of these problems with share and fellowship, for some church people the Greek word *koinonia* has become the preferred metaphor in discussions about their gatherings.

fire, *noun*   Fire is one of the most frequently employed metaphors in both the Hebrew and the Greek portions of the Bible, twenty-five times in the book of Revelation alone. The fascination of early people with fire is not hard to understand. Before Joseph Priestly in England and Antoine Lavoisier in France isolated oxygen in the late eighteenth century, fire was a mystery. As a natural disaster and as a means of waging war, fire could be terrifying. As the only source of light and heat, other than the sun, fire was also a necessity for survival.

In ancient times, fire was a part of religious ritual in the burning of incense, grain, and portions of animal carcasses. The burning of ritual offerings, *thuo* in Greek, provided the basis for the metaphors translated into English as patience* and lust.*

Even in the modern world, fire holds a certain fascination. Brush fires, forest fires, and chemical fires can be terrifying, especially as they threaten to destroy people's homes and businesses. Fire continues to be one of the horrors of war. At the same time, many people find comfort in a campfire or a fire in a fireplace. The flames of candles give a meal more of a sense of romance or gentility than artificial light can provide.

The English word fire may be etymologically related to the Greek word *pyr*. Most of our fire-related words—such as pyre, pyrotechnic, and pyromaniac—use the Greek root. *Pyr* is the equivalent of the Hebrew *esh*. The two biblical words for fire have the same connotations and appear in the same kind of metaphorical expressions.

FIRE USED LITERALLY

They shall eat the lamb that same night; they shall eat it roasted over the **fire** with unleavened bread and bitter herbs. [Exodus 12:8]

The sons of the priest Aaron shall put **fire** on the altar and arrange wood on the fire. Aaron's sons the priests shall arrange the parts, with the head and the suet, on the wood that is on the **fire** on the altar. [Leviticus 1:7-8]

Aaron shall take a censer full of coals of **fire** from the altar before the LORD, and two handfuls of crushed sweet incense, and he shall bring it inside the curtain and put the incense on the **fire** before the LORD. [Leviticus 16:12-13]

Hazael asked, "Why does my lord weep?" Elisha answered, "Because I know the evil that you will do to the people of Israel; you will set their fortresses on **fire**, you will kill their young men with the sword, dash in pieces their little ones, and rip up their pregnant women." [II Kings 8:12]

A man said, "Lord, have mercy on my son, for he is an epileptic and he suffers terribly; he often falls into the **fire** and often into the water." [Matthew 17:15]

When they had kindled a **fire** in the middle of the courtyard and sat down together, Peter sat among them. [Luke 22:55]

FIRE USED METAPHORICALLY

Fire identified with God

For the LORD your God is a devouring **fire**, a jealous God. [Deuteronomy 4:24]

Indeed our God is a consuming **fire**. [Hebrews 12:29]

Fire as an indication of God's presence

There the angel of the Lord appeared to him in a flame of **fire** out of a bush; he looked, and the bush was blazing, yet it was not consumed. [Exodus 3:2]

The Lord went in front of them in a pillar of cloud by day, to lead them along the way, and in a pillar of **fire** by night, to give them light, so that they might travel by day and by night. [Exodus 13:21]

Now Mount Sinai was wrapped in smoke, because the Lord had descended upon it in **fire**; the smoke went up like the smoke of a kiln, while the whole mountain shook violently. [Exodus 19:18]

Then the angel of the Lord reached out the tip of the staff that was in his hand, and touched the meat and the unleavened cakes; and **fire** sprang up from the rock and consumed the meat and the unleavened cakes; and the angel of the Lord vanished from his sight. [Judges 6:21]

As they continued walking and talking, a chariot of **fire** and horses of **fire** separated the two of them, and Elijah ascended in a whirlwind into heaven. [II Kings 2:11]

Divided tongues, as of **fire**, appeared among them, and a tongue rested on each of them. [Acts 2:3]

God declares that I will show portents in the heaven above and signs on the earth below, blood, and **fire**, and smoky mist. [Acts 2:19]

For it is indeed just of God to repay with affliction those who afflict you, and to give relief to the afflicted as well as to us, when the Lord Jesus is revealed from heaven with his mighty angels in flaming **fire**. [II Thessalonians 1:6-8]

Fire as an indication of God's displeasure

Then the Lord rained on Sodom and Gomorrah sulfur and **fire** from the Lord out of heaven. [Genesis 19:24]

Thus says the Lord: For three transgressions of Damascus, and for four, I will not revoke the punishment; because they have threshed Gilead with threshing sledges of iron. So I will send a **fire** on the house of Hazael, and it shall devour the strongholds of Ben-hadad. [Amos 1:3-4]

Just as the weeds are collected and burned up with **fire**, so will it be at the end of the age. The Son of Man will send his angels, and they will collect out of his kingdom all causes of sin and all evildoers, and they will throw them into the furnace of **fire**, where there will be weeping and gnashing of teeth. [Matthew 13:40-42]

If your hand causes you to stumble, cut it off; it is better for you to enter life maimed than to have two hands and to go to hell, to the unquenchable **fire**. [Mark 9:43]

If we willfully persist in sin after having received the knowledge of the truth, there no longer remains a sacrifice for sins, but a fearful prospect of judgment, and a fury of **fire** that will consume the adversaries. [Hebrews 10:26-27]

And the devil who had deceived them was thrown into the lake of **fire** and sulfur, where the beast and the false prophet were, and they will be tormented day and night forever and ever. [Revelation 20:10]

Fire related to human attributes assigned to God

Wait for me, says the LORD, for the day when I arise as a witness. For my decision is to gather nations, to assemble kingdoms, to pour out upon them my indignation, all the heat of my anger; for in the **fire** of my passion all the earth shall be consumed. [Zephaniah 3:8]

In my distress I called upon the LORD; to my God I cried for help. . . . Smoke went up from his nostrils, and devouring **fire** from his mouth; glowing coals flamed forth from him. [Psalm 18:6, 8]

His eyes are like a flame of **fire**, and on his head are many diadems; and he has a name inscribed that no one knows but himself. [Revelation 19:12]

Fire as purification or testing

In the whole land, says the LORD, two-thirds shall be cut off and perish, and one-third shall be left alive. And I will put this third into the **fire**, refine them as one refines silver, and test them as gold is tested. They will call on my name, and I will answer them. I will say, "They are my people"; and they will say, "The LORD is our God." [Zechariah 13:8-9]

Who can endure the day of his coming, and who can stand when he appears? For he is like a refiner's **fire** and like fullers' soap; he will sit as a refiner and purifier of silver, and he will purify the descendants of Levi and refine them like gold and silver, until they present offerings to the LORD in righteousness. [Malachi 3:2-3]

John answered all of them by saying, "I baptize you with water; but one who is more powerful than I is coming; I am not worthy to untie the thong of his sandals. He will baptize you with the Holy Spirit and **fire**. His winnowing fork is in his hand, to clear his threshing floor and to gather the wheat into his granary; but the chaff he will burn with unquenchable fire." [Luke 3:16-17]

The work of each builder will become visible, for the Day will disclose it, because it will be revealed with **fire**, and the **fire** will test what sort of work each has done. [I Corinthians 3:13]

In this you rejoice, even if now for a little while you have had to suffer various trials, so that the genuineness of your faith being more precious than gold that, though perishable, is tested by **fire**—may be found to result in praise and glory and honor when Jesus Christ is revealed. [I Peter 1:6-7]

Fire as human emotion

I was silent and still; I held my peace to no avail; my distress grew worse, my heart became hot within me. While I mused, the **fire** burned; then I spoke with my tongue. [Psalm 39:2-3]

They are kindled like an oven, their heart burns within them; all night their anger smolders; in the morning it blazes like a flaming **fire**. [Hosea 7:6]

Set me as a seal upon your heart, as a seal upon your arm; for love is strong as death, passion fierce as the grave. Its flashes are flashes of **fire**, a raging flame. [Song of Solomon 8:6]

Fire associated with offensive people

They surrounded me like bees; they blazed like a **fire** of thorns; in the name of the LORD I cut them off! [Psalm 118:12]

Scoundrels concoct evil, and their speech is like a scorching **fire**. [Proverbs 16:27]

As charcoal is to hot embers and wood to **fire**, so is a quarrelsome person for kindling strife. [Proverbs 26:21]

If your enemies are hungry, feed them; if they are thirsty, give them something to drink; for by doing this you will heap **burning** coals on their heads. [Romans 12:20]

So also the tongue is a small member, yet it boasts of great exploits. How great a forest is set ablaze by a small **fire**! And the tongue is a **fire**. [James 3:5-6]

Even a quick look at the fire metaphors in each of the above sections will suggest that the followers of Jesus drew on Hebrew imagery in telling the story about the impact of Jesus on their lives. They presented Jesus as a second Moses by saying that tongues of fire had affirmed the authenticity of Jesus just as fire had revealed the divine presence in the life of Moses. The Jesus followers also drew on the Hebrew Scripture for the fire metaphors indicating the nature of God's displeasure and the ideas of purification and testing. The continued use of the fire metaphor was one way Christians laid claim to being a legitimate expression of the Hebrew tradition.

Although Christians have always understood how fire works as a figure of speech, they have had a tendency to take literally references to fire in connection with stories they take to be historical. Many also have had a literal understanding of fire identified with hell* and Satan.* For the past two hundred years, however, a critical approach to the Bible has suggested that these passages may have more power when fire is recognized as a metaphor for an experience of the divine presence or for the present-life result of destructive behavior than when they are taken literally. Fire as a description of torment in an existence after death may have had a positive effect on some people's conduct, but over the centuries all too few Christians have been frightened sufficiently by the prospect of eternal fire to mold their lives according to the teachings of Jesus.

fish, *noun* and *verb*; **fisherman**, *noun*   Most present-day followers of Jesus are aware of the fish as a central metaphor and symbol in their tradition. Long before the cross became the primary sign of a Christian presence, a simple outline of a fish identified a person or a group with Jesus.

One reason for the popularity of the fish was that anyone could draw it with one stroke of a pen on paper or one swift motion of a toe in the sand. Another was that, in Greek, fish was the acronym for Jesus Christ God's Son Savior.

Iesous	Jesus	If you understand that English-speaking people use the letter H
Christos	Christ*	to express the aspirated U in the Greek for Son, you can see that
Theou	God's	the initials of these words spell *ichthus*, the Greek word for fish.
hUios	Son*	
Soter	Savior*	

Perhaps the most important reason for the popularity of the fish symbol was the frequent use of the fish and fisherman metaphors in the life and teaching of Jesus as represented in the gospels. Each of these figures of speech has its origin in the Hebrew Scriptures. In Greek, the word for fisherman appears to be unrelated to *ichthus*. It is *halieus*, which comes from *hals*, or salt, and originally meant anyone who worked at sea, a sailor. In Hebrew fish is *dag* and a fisherman is *davvag*.

In the metaphors of both languages, the people are the fish and God's agents are the fishermen. These figures of speech can represent either rescue or punishment.

I will bring them back to their own land that I gave to their ancestors. I am now sending for many **fishermen**, says the LORD, and they shall catch them. [Jeremiah 16:15-16]

The Lord GOD has sworn by his holiness: The time is surely coming upon you, when they shall take you away with hooks, even the last of you with **fishhooks**. [Amos 4:2]

You have made people like the **fish** of the sea, like crawling things that have no ruler. The enemy brings all of them up with a hook; he drags them out with his net, he gathers them in his seine; so he rejoices and exults. [Habakkuk 1:14-15]

As Jesus passed along the Sea of Galilee, he saw Simon and his brother Andrew casting a net into the sea—for they were **fishermen**. And Jesus said to them, "Follow me and I will make you **fish** for people." [Mark 1:16-17]

Again, the kingdom of heaven is like a net that was thrown into the sea and caught **fish** of every kind; when it was full, they drew it ashore, sat down, and put the good into baskets but threw out the bad. [Matthew 13:47-48]

In several Bible stories, plentiful fish seem to indicate the abundance of God's grace.* Jesus feeding fish to great crowds of people reflects this tradition. The feeding of the crowds with fish was so significant that the story is told six times in the gospels, twice each in Mark and in Matthew and once in Luke and once in John. The feeding of the disciples at the end of John's gospel features the same food that appeared in the feeding of the crowds, bread* and fish.

Wherever the river goes, every living creature that swarms will live, and there will be very many **fish**, once these waters reach there. It will become fresh; and everything will live where the river goes. People will stand **fishing** beside the sea from En-gedi to En-eglaim; it will be a place for the spreading of nets; its **fish** will be of a great many kinds, like the **fish** of the Great Sea. [Ezekiel 47:9-10]

When he had finished speaking, Jesus said to Simon, "Put out into the deep water and let down your nets for a catch." Simon answered, "Master, we have worked all night long but have caught nothing. Yet if you say so, I will let down the nets." When they had done this, they caught so many **fish** that their nets were beginning to break. [Luke 5:4-6]

Jesus said to them, "Children, you have no **fish**, have you?" They answered him, "No." He said to them, "Cast the net to the right side of the boat, and you will find some." So they cast it, and now they were not able to haul it in because there were so many **fish**. [John 21:5-6]

Taking the five loaves and the two **fish**, he looked up to heaven, and blessed and broke the loaves, and gave them to his disciples to set before the people; and he divided the two **fish** among them all. And all ate and were filled; and they took up twelve baskets full of broken pieces and of the **fish**. [Mark 6:41-43]

Jesus said to them, "Come and have breakfast." Now none of the disciples dared to ask him, "Who are you?" because they knew it was the Lord. Jesus came and took the bread and gave it to them, and did the same with the **fish**. [John 21:12-13]

The stories of spectacular individual fish also seem to be expressions of the power and presence of God as do the stories about the availability of a single fish for food at a critical moment.

The LORD provided a large **fish** to swallow up Jonah; and Jonah was in the belly of the **fish** three days and three nights. [Jonah 1:17]

When they reached Capernaum, the collectors of the temple tax came to Peter and said, "Does your teacher not pay the temple tax?" He said, "Yes, he does." And when he came home, Jesus spoke of it first, asking, "What do you think, Simon? From whom do kings of the earth take toll or tribute? From their children or from others?" When Peter said, "From others," Jesus said to him, "Then the children are free. However, so that we do not give offense to them, go to the sea and cast a hook; take the first **fish** that comes up; and when you open its mouth, you will find a coin; take that and give it to them for you and me." [Matthew 17:24-27]

Is there anyone among you who, if your child asks for a **fish**, will give a snake instead of a fish? Or if the child asks for an egg, will give a scorpion? If you then, who are evil, know how to give good gifts to your children, how much more will the heavenly Father give the Holy Spirit to those who ask him!" [Luke 11:11-13]

While in their joy they were disbelieving and still wondering, Jesus said to them, "Have you anything here to eat?" They gave him a piece of broiled **fish**, and he took it and ate in their presence. [Luke 24:41-43]

For some Christians, these stories about fish tell of miracles* that are historical events. When coming across one of these accounts, however, readers can decide for themselves whether to take the story as a description of an event or an extended metaphor that evolved from figurative language used by both Jesus and the people of ancient Israel.

firstborn—see sacrifice

flesh, *noun*   The Hebrew *basar* and the Greek *sarx*, both traditionally translated as flesh, have approximately the same variety of meanings. Modern translations vary in an attempt to get the correct connotation. Here are some of the possible meanings of *basar* and *sarx*, in each pair of examples the Hebrew being first, followed by the Greek.

The soft parts of an animal or human body

You shall take the ram of ordination, and boil its **flesh** in a holy place; and Aaron and his sons shall eat the **flesh** of the ram and the bread that is in the basket, at the entrance of the tent of meeting. [Exodus 29:31-32]

So then, remember that at one time you Gentiles by birth, called "the uncircumcision" by those who are called "the circumcision"—a physical circumcision made in the **flesh** by human hands. [Ephesians 2:11]

The body* itself

You shall say to the Israelites, "This shall be my holy anointing oil throughout your generations. It shall not be used in any ordinary anointing of the **body**, and you shall make no other like it in composition; it is holy, and it shall be holy to you." [Exodus 30:31-32]

Since therefore Christ suffered in the **flesh**, arm yourselves also with the same intention (for whoever has suffered in the **flesh** has finished with sin). [I Peter 4:1]

Human beings

Then the glory of the LORD shall be revealed, and all **people** shall see it together, for the mouth of the LORD has spoken. [Isaiah 40:5]

After Jesus had spoken these words, he looked up to heaven and said, "Father, the hour has come; glorify your Son so that the Son may glorify you, since you have given him authority over all **people**, to give eternal life to all whom you have given him." [John 17:1-2]

Kinship

Then Judah said to his brothers, "What profit is it if we kill our brother and conceal his blood? Come, let us sell him to the Ishmaelites, and not lay our hands on him, for he is our brother, our own **flesh**." And his brothers agreed. [Genesis 37:26-27]

Now I am speaking to you Gentiles. Inasmuch then as I am an apostle to the Gentiles, I glorify my ministry in order to make my own **people** jealous, and thus save some of them. [Romans 11:13-14]

Existence

Then the LORD said, "My spirit shall not abide in mortals forever, for they are **flesh**; their days shall be one hundred twenty years." [Genesis 6:3]

If you marry, you do not sin, and if a virgin marries, she does not sin. Yet those who marry will experience distress in this **life**, and I would spare you that. [I Corinthians 7:28]

Human nature

Thus says the LORD: Cursed are those who trust in mere mortals and make mere **flesh** their strength, whose hearts turn away from the LORD. [Jeremiah 17:5]

They are Israelites, and to them belong the adoption, the glory, the covenants, the giving of the law, the worship, and the promises; to them belong the patriarchs, and from them, according to the **flesh**, comes the Messiah, who is over all, God blessed forever. Amen. [Romans 9:4-5]

Sexual union

Therefore a man leaves his father and his mother and clings to his wife, and they become one **flesh**. [Genesis 2:24]

Do you not know that whoever is united to a prostitute becomes one body with her? For it is said, "The two shall be one **flesh**." [I Corinthians 6:16]

The realm of emotions and desires

When I think of it I am dismayed, and shuddering seizes my **flesh**. [Job 21:6]

All of us once lived among them in the passions of our **flesh**, following the desires of flesh and senses, and we were by nature children of wrath, like everyone else. [Ephesians 2:3]

The sphere of sin*

The earth was corrupt in God's sight, and the earth was filled with violence. And God saw that the earth was corrupt; for all **flesh** had corrupted its ways upon the earth. [Genesis 6:11-12]

Live by the Spirit, I say, and do not gratify the desires of the **flesh**. For what the **flesh** desires is opposed to the Spirit, and what the Spirit desires is opposed to the **flesh**; for these are opposed to each other, to prevent you from doing what you want. [Galatians 5:16-17]

If the original meaning of *basar* and *sarx* was the soft parts of an animal or human body, then the other uses of the terms came into being as metaphors. In the twenty-first century, some may question the usefulness of the flesh metaphor in understanding the nature of the body, kinship, existence, human nature, sex, emotions and desires, and sin. One difficulty lies in what appears to be a false separation of flesh and spirit.* If the spirit does not dwell in the physical body, where is spirit to be found? If the spirit acts primarily in mental processes, that means that the spirit resides in the brain, one of the soft parts of the body.

Adding to the difficulty of using the flesh metaphor has been the tendency of some Christians to disparage the physical aspects of human existence, especially the desire for sexual intimacy. This tendency has worked against women ever achieving equal status with men in the church. Because women evoke sexual desires in men, the argument goes, women are the cause of sin and must be kept under tight control. As long as men in authority* equate sinful flesh with the feelings stirred up by women, the male leadership will continue, using all their power to subjugate women.

The one area in which the flesh metaphor might be useful for Jesus followers is kinship. Now that the science of genetics is better understood, people can appreciate how much of their inheritance is in their flesh, in the DNA (deoxyribonucleic acid), which resides in every cell of their bodies. This realization has begun to put into perspective the influences of environment and training on human development. To a real extent, every person has some particular limitations and unique potential because of the genes inherited from ancestors. Figuratively speaking, the boundaries and the potential of a human being are located in the flesh.

follow—see progress

fool, *noun*; **foolish**, *adjective*   The Hebrew Scriptures have several words that mean foolish or silly, but they are not as vivid as the Greek metaphor dealing with the same concept. One Hebrew word, *nabal*, comes from a root meaning to wilt or to faint. Another, *kesil*, originally meant fat. The origins of the other Hebrew words are not clear, but the Greek word *aphron* presents the reader with a vivid image. The root of the word is *phren*, indicating the part of the body usually known as the midriff. The Greeks located thought and understanding in this part of the body so their term for sensible or prudent was *phronimos*. With the negative particle *a* preceding *phron*, the picture is of person with a fluttering midriff, one unable to hold a firm opinion, a fool.

In whichever language they wrote, the biblical authors held fools in great contempt.

Fools say in their hearts, "There is no God." They are corrupt, they do abominable deeds; there is no one who does good.—*nabal* [Psalm 14:1]

Marks a word in the text that has its own entry

> The wise of heart will heed commandments, but a babbling **fool** will come to ruin.—*evil* (not to be confused with the English word spelled the same way) [Proverbs 10:8]

> The clever do all things intelligently, but the **fool** displays folly. —*kesil* [Proverbs 13:16]

> Do not be too wicked, and do not be a **fool**; why should you die before your time?—*sakal*, same root as *kesil* [Ecclesiastes 7:17]

Aphron appears frequently in the early Christian writings. The following are fairly typical:

> You **fools**! Did not the one who made the outside make the inside also? So give for alms those things that are within; and see, everything will be clean for you. [Luke 11:40-41]

> I have been a **fool**! You forced me to it. Indeed you should have been the ones commending me, for I am not at all inferior to these super-apostles, even though I am nothing.
> [II Corinthians 12:11]

> Be careful then how you live, not as unwise people but as wise, making the most of the time, because the days are evil. So do not be **foolish**, but understand what the will of the Lord is.
> [Ephesians 5:15-17]

> For it is God's will that by doing right you should silence the ignorance of the **foolish**.
> [I Peter 2:15]

The fluttering midriff metaphor may be more useful for people in assessing their own condition than in forming opinions about others. Sometimes when people are unable to make an obvious decision, they get a physical sensation in the region below the heart. Avoidance of clear thinking that might lead to responsible behavior can create a fluttering in the midriff. Even without the physical symptoms, foolishness is often the refusal to develop understanding and to form opinions rather that simply being silly or stupid.

forgive, *verb*; **forgiveness**, *noun*   Three Hebrew words and three Greek words are translated forgive. The original image behind one Hebrew word, *nasa,* was the lifting of a burden. Another Hebrew word, *salach*, meant to spare, as in to spare the life of a prisoner. The third word, *kaphar,* is often translated atone* and perhaps once meant to cover.

> Relieve the troubles of my heart, and bring me out of my distress. Consider my affliction and my trouble, and **forgive** all my sins.—*nasa* [Psalm 25:17-18]

> Hear the plea of your servant and of your people Israel when they pray toward this place; O hear in heaven your dwelling place; heed and **forgive**.—*salach* [I Kings 8:30]

> Yet you, O LORD, know all their plotting to kill me. Do not **forgive** their iniquity, do not blot out their sin from your sight. Let them be tripped up before you; deal with them while you are angry.— *kaphar* [Jeremiah 18:23]

The three Greek words employ slightly different imagery. Two of them, *aphiemi* and *apoluo*, in their simplest forms meant to let go or to send away. The third, *charizomai,* has the same root as the English words charisma and charity; it seems to suggest a graceful sort of interaction, freeing two people for a renewed relationship.

---

*Marks a word in the text that has its own entry

> Then Peter came and said to him, "Lord, if another member of the church sins against me, how often should I **forgive**? As many as seven times?" Jesus said to him, "Not seven times, but, I tell you, seventy-seven times."—*aphiemi* [Matthew 18:21-22]

> "Do not judge, and you will not be judged; do not condemn, and you will not be condemned. **Forgive**, and you will be **forgiven**; give, and it will be given to you. A good measure, pressed down, shaken together, running over, will be put into your lap; for the measure you give will be the measure you get back."— *apoluo* [Luke 6:37-38]

> Anyone whom you **forgive**, I also **forgive**. What I have **forgiven**, if I have forgiven anything, has been for your sake in the presence of Christ.—*charizomai* [II Corinthians 2:10]

Some people today assume that forgiveness is what you ask for from a person who is upset with you, but nothing in the Bible would support that assumption. None of the gospels suggests that Jesus ever urged people to ask those whom they offended to forgive them. In all the advice that St. Paul so readily offered in his letters that have survived, not once did he urge his readers to ask other people for forgiveness.

In the Hebrew Scriptures, only twice do we find people asking other people to forgive them. In one instance, the request was not genuine. When Abigail learned that David was going to destroy everything she held dear because her husband Nabal had insulted some of David's men, she tried to put the blame on herself and asked David to forgive her.

> Please **forgive** the trespass of your servant; for the Lord will certainly make my lord a sure house, because my lord is fighting the battles of the Lord; and evil shall not be found in you so long as you live.— *nasa* [I Samuel 25:28]

The only other plea for a human being to forgive an offense resulted in an absolute, but well reasoned, refusal. After the death of the patriarch Jacob—or Israel, as he came to be called—his older sons were afraid that their brother Joseph would decide to take his revenge upon them for selling him into slavery when he was a young man.

> Realizing that their father was dead, Joseph's brothers said, "What if Joseph still bears a grudge against us and pays us back in full for all the wrong that we did to him?" So they approached Joseph, saying, "Your father gave this instruction before he died, 'Say to Joseph: I beg you, **forgive** the crime of your brothers and the wrong they did in harming you.' Now therefore please **forgive** the crime of the servants of the God of your father." Joseph wept when they spoke to him. Then his brothers also wept, fell down before him, and said, "We are here as your slaves." But Joseph said to them, "Do not be afraid! Am I in the place of God?"—*nasa* [Genesis 50:15-19]

Only God* can forgive. By asking Joseph to forgive them, his brothers were putting Joseph in the place of God. The followers of Jesus were aware of this conviction that only God can forgive sins when they told stories about Jesus announcing that a person's sins were forgiven. The point of the stories seems to be that Jesus stood in a special relationship to God. If Jesus did indeed make such pronouncements, all but his followers would have been scandalized. For those who put their trust in Jesus, he was the exception to the rule that only God can forgive sins.

> When Jesus saw their faith, he said, "Friend, your sins are **forgiven** you." Then the scribes and the Pharisees began to question, "Who is this who is speaking blasphemies? Who can **forgive** sins but God alone?" [Luke 5:20-21]

                                                                              Marks a word in the text that has its own entry

Both believers and agnostics can see the danger in asking another person to forgive an offense. To ask another for release from the burden of shame* or guilt* would be to put the other person in control of their souls' health, in charge of their spiritual well-being. Even people who have no confidence in a forgiving God can see that they will make their ruptured relationships worse if they make gods out of those whom they have hurt. Rather than turning over to human beings the authority that the Bible assigns to God, they can act as if they were confident that only God can forgive them. Seeking God's forgiveness requires repentance.*

Although granting another person the authority to release you from the misery created by offenses or lapses may be inappropriate, you can seek forgiveness by offering an apology or saying that you are sorry. If you can do so within the original meaning of those terms, you will not be asking another person to make you feel better. An apology, or *apologia*, was originally a strong defense of a position taken and did not carry an admission of fault. Sometimes it helps to explain what you did and why you did it, and to let the other person decide if your explanation has cleared up the trouble between you. You also can say you are sorry, if indeed looking back at your behavior makes you sad or sore at heart. If your sorrow was produced by the other person's upset over what you did or did not do, rather than by a reflection on your actions, then saying you are sorry probably will not help, nor will saying that you are sorry do much good if you do not feel at all sad about your conduct.

Another popular misconception entails a willingness to forgive yourself. If you are looking for wisdom in the Bible to guide your actions, you will look in vain for any suggestion that forgiving yourself is an appropriate way to get out from under the burdens of guilt and shame. The Bible does not mention the subject directly, but it is safe to say that any author or editor who contributed to either the Hebrew or Christian scriptures would consider self-forgiveness to be a form of blasphemy,* putting oneself in the place of God. Besides, as many people have discovered, they cannot by an act of will gain their release from the spiritual prison that has been the result of their misbehavior. If people could forgive themselves, they would never have developed religious rituals that would help them experience a lifting of the burdens they imposed on themselves by their destructive behavior.

As people learn to accept forgiveness, they often find the freedom to forgive other people. Granting forgiveness is not necessarily playing God. It should not be an attempt to restore the soul's health of an offending party but rather a willingness to restore the relationship. When people are obsessed by their shame and guilt, they are often afraid to forgive the people who have offended them. Having a low opinion of themselves, they attempt to bolster their self-esteem by savoring every hurt they have suffered. To forgive would be to give up their only way of claiming moral superiority and to be left with nothing but their own sense of unworthiness

In the paradoxical fashion that is typical of them, the gospels never quote Jesus as saying anything at all about asking other people to forgive you, but they all say Jesus taught that you should forgive other people. Both Matthew and Luke make absolute the command to forgive other members of the community.

With our contemporary concepts of human relations, we might wonder how all this forgiving can go on if no one is asking anyone else for forgiveness. Apparently, the offended person has the responsibility to forgive if the offending party expresses sorrow or makes an apology. The offended person may even initiate the forgiving process. This responsibility makes sense in terms of the biblical metaphors.

Nasa—If one person feels hurt by another, the relationship suffers under a burden that only the injured party can lift.

Salach—If the relationship matters more than getting even, the injured person can spare the offender the hurt that would have been inflicted by retaliation.

Kaphar—To cover the offense would mean that the person who felt wronged would put the incident out of sight, smell, and hearing so that it cannot continue to poison the relationship.

Aphiemi and *apoluo*—Offended people have a peculiar kind of power over those who love them and have hurt them; to restore the broken relationship, they have to let it go.

Charizomai—Although the person who has been hurt has the primary responsibility for restoring the relationship, this metaphor suggesting mutual interaction can remind both parties to a dispute that neither one of them alone can bring things back to equilibrium.

The richness of the metaphors can open up fresh ways of thinking and behaving when people have hurt each other and do not know how to repair the cherished connections that once had bound them together.

free—see **redeem, slave**

G

gate, *noun* Although the Hebrew Scriptures sometimes employ the word *sha'ar* as a metaphor, it appears most frequently in its primary sense as a gate placed in the wall of a town or city. *Sha'ar* could refer to the panels that swing open or closed, or to the opening itself, but most significantly it identified the space in and near the gate. Archeologists have found that the earliest towns built in the Bible lands had only one gate in the wall to make them easier to defend. The streets within the walls were narrow and twisted, leaving the area near the gate the only space large enough for public gatherings. This was the place where the community handled legal proceedings. For example, the law* made provision for parents who had incorrigible sons.

> If someone has a stubborn and rebellious son who will not obey his father and mother, who does not heed them when they discipline him, then his father and his mother shall take hold of him and bring him out to the elders of his town at the **gate** of that place. [Deuteronomy 21:18-19]

The events that took place at the gate may well have influenced the metaphorical use of *sha'ar*. At the gate, people sought justice or safety and experienced shame* or approval.

> Then all the people who were at the **gate**, along with the elders, said, "We are witnesses. May the LORD make the woman who is coming into your house like Rachel and Leah, who together built up the house of Israel. May you produce children in Ephrathah and bestow a name in Bethlehem." [Ruth 4:11]

> Say to the Israelites, "Appoint the cities of refuge, of which I spoke to you through Moses, so that anyone who kills a person without intent or by mistake may flee there; they shall be for you a refuge from the avenger of blood. The slayer shall flee to one of these cities and shall stand at the entrance of the **gate** of the city, and explain the case to the elders of that city; then the fugitive shall be taken into the city, and given a place, and shall remain with them." [Joshua 20:2-4]

> I am the subject of gossip for those who sit in the **gate**, and the drunkards make songs about me. [Psalm 69:12]

Marks a word in the text that has its own entry

> A capable wife who can find? She is far more precious than jewels . . . Her husband is known in the city **gates**, taking his seat among the elders of the land. [Proverbs 31:10, 23]

When *sha'ar* appears as a metaphor pointing to an experience of God, it suggests far more than simply the door to the kingdom* or realm of God. The gate is a figurative place into which a person can project a longing for justice and safety, a fear of shame, and a hunger for approval.

> Open to me the **gates of** righteousness, that I may enter through them and give thanks to the LORD. This is the **gate** of the LORD; the righteous shall enter through it. [Psalm 118:19-20]

> Then Jacob woke from his sleep and said, "Surely the LORD is in this place—and I did not know it!" And he was afraid, and said, "How awesome is this place! This is none other than the house of God, and this is the **gate** of heaven." [Genesis 28:16-17]

The gospels and other early Christian writings assume an understanding of the gate imagery found in the Hebrew Scriptures. One of the Greek words for gate—*pyle,* the root of the English word pylon—appears in both its primary and metaphorical sense.

> Soon afterwards Jesus went to a town called Nain, and his disciples and a large crowd went with him. As he approached the **gate** of the town, a man who had died was being carried out. He was his mother's only son, and she was a widow; and with her was a large crowd from the town. [Luke 7:11-12]

> Enter through the narrow **gate**; for the **gate** is wide and the road is easy that leads to destruction, and there are many who take it. For the **gate** is narrow and the road is hard that leads to life, and there are few who find it. [Matthew 7:13-14]

The gate imagery is somewhat obscured, however, for people reading English translations. Another of the Greek words for gate is *thura.* It often is translated door, and means just that, but when used as a metaphor, *thura* sometimes appears in English as door and sometimes as gate.

> I will stay in Ephesus until Pentecost, for a wide **door** for effective work has opened to me, and there are many adversaries. [I Corinthians 16:8-9]

> After this I looked, and there in heaven a **door** stood open! And the first voice, which I had heard speaking to me like a trumpet, said, "Come up here, and I will show you what must take place after this." [Revelation 4:1]

> So again Jesus said to them, "Very truly, I tell you, I am the **gate** for the sheep. All who came before me are thieves and bandits; but the sheep did not listen to them. I am the **gate**. Whoever enters by me will be saved, and will come in and go out and find pasture." [John 10:7-9]

In each of the three examples of *thura*, the emphasis is not on the hinged panels but on the portal opened wide to new possibilities. The line from I Corinthians suggests the feasibility of new work. The verse from Revelation points to greater clarity of insight. The passage from John adds another layer of imagery to the gate metaphor. Here the gate is to the sheep pen, but it functions for the sheep as the city gate does for people. The gate is both the way in to safety and the way out to the wider world.

In each case, there is coming and going. By going through the gate into the pen, the sheep are saved from bandits and wolves; by going out to pasture, they are saved from starvation. From what will the followers of Jesus be saved*? The come-and-go language suggests that they will be saved

---

Marks a word in the text that has its own entry

from being trapped on the inside of the gate in their quest for ultimate safety and approval, and saved from being stuck outside with the constant stress and anxiety of proving their worth to the world. For people who picture Jesus as the gate to the realm of God, participation in that realm cannot be a static achievement but must be a dynamic realization.

DID YOU KNOW . . .

. . . that *pyle* is pronounced *puh-lay*?
For more help with pronunciation, see "Pronouncing
Transliterated Hebrew and Greek Words" on page 15.

---

gift—see **charisma**

Gentile—see **heathen**

God In English Bibles, the word God stands for three Hebrew expressions—*el, elohim*, and *YHWH*—as well as for *theos* in the Greek Scriptures.

In the Hebrew Scriptures *el,* or more commonly the plural *elohim,* denotes divine powers of various kinds. When Arabic-speaking Christians and Muslims pray, they address their prayers to Allah, a word from the same root. *El* and *elohim* could also be used in reference to the other deities worshiped by the tribes in the neighborhood of the ancient Israelites.

> And King Melchizedek of Salem brought out bread and wine; he was priest of **God** Most High.— *el* [Genesis 14:18]

> When all the lords of the Tower of Shechem heard of it, they entered the stronghold of the temple of **El**-berith. [Judges 9:46]

> Then Solomon built a high place for Chemosh the abomination of Moab, and for Molech the abomination of the Ammonites, on the mountain east of Jerusalem. He did the same for all his foreign wives, who offered incense and sacrificed to their **gods**.—*elohim* [I Kings 11:7-8]

Thunder is the roaring of *elohim* and paralyzing fear is the terror of *elohim*.

> Then Pharaoh summoned Moses and Aaron, and said to them, "This time I have sinned; the LORD is in the right, and I and my people are in the wrong. Pray to the LORD! Enough of **God's** thunder and hail! I will let you go; you need stay no longer." [Exodus 9:27-28]

> They gave to Jacob all the foreign **gods** that they had, and the rings that were in their ears; and Jacob hid them under the oak that was near Shechem. As they journeyed, a terror from **God** fell upon the cities all around them, so that no one pursued them. [Genesis 35:4-5]

The ancestral God of Israel, *YHWH* usually translated LORD,* is also identified as one of the *elohim*. Like the other *elohim*, *YHWH* could intervene in nature and in history, could create and destroy, usually keeping in mind the best interests of the people who worshiped *YHWH*. When surrounding tribes threatened Israel, they appealed to *YHWH tsebaot*, that is, the LORD of hosts, or more literally, the commander of the army. Some translators express this divine title in English as Yahweh Sabaoth.

Marks a word in the text that has its own entry

> Then the LORD God formed man from the dust of the ground, and breathed into his nostrils the breath of life; and the man became a living being. And the LORD God planted a garden in Eden, in the east; and there he put the man whom he had formed.– *YHWH elohim* [Genesis 2:7-8]

> Moses prayed to the LORD and said, "Lord GOD, do not destroy the people who are your very own possession, whom you redeemed in your greatness, whom you brought out of Egypt with a mighty hand."—*adonai YHWH* [Deuteronomy 9:26]

> Therefore thus says the Lord GOD: My anger and my wrath shall be poured out on this place, on human beings and animals, on the trees of the field and the fruit of the ground; it will burn and not be quenched.—*adonai YHWH* [Jeremiah 7:20]

> Thus says the LORD of hosts, "I will punish the Amalekites for what they did in opposing the Israelites when they came up out of Egypt."—*YHWH tsebaot* [I Samuel 15:2]

> In the year that King Uzziah died, I saw the Lord sitting on a throne, high and lofty; and the hem of his robe filled the temple. Seraphs were in attendance above him; each had six wings: with two they covered their faces, and with two they covered their feet, and with two they flew. And one called to another and said: "Holy, holy, holy is the LORD of hosts; the whole earth is full of his glory."—*YHWH tsebaot* [Isaiah 6:1-3]

Apparently at one time *YHWH elohim* had to compete with other *elohim* for the loyalty and affection of the Israelites. The people of Israel may well have been attracted to *elohim* of neighboring tribes because they were more clearly connected with the fertility of the soil and of the flocks. In addition, their rituals may have had the appeal of offering intercourse with cult prostitutes, wrongly identified by the King James Version of the Bible as sodomites.*

> The Israelites again did what was evil in the sight of the LORD, worshiping the Baals and the Astartes, the **gods** of Aram, the **gods** of Sidon, the gods of Moab, the **gods** of the Ammonites, and the **gods** of the Philistines. Thus they abandoned the LORD, and did not worship him. [Judges 10:6]

As in the above passage from Judges, the foreign *elohim* are often identified as Baals (two syllables "bah-als"), in Hebrew *ba'alim*. Perhaps because the translators wanted to make a case for monotheism, they obscured the fact that *YHWH* in many passages is also referred to as a *ba'al*. When *YHWH* is identified as *ba'al*, they translate the word as master, lord, or even husband.

> Return, O faithless children, says the LORD, for I am your **master**; I will take you, one from a city and two from a family, and I will bring you to Zion. [Jeremiah 3:14]

> O LORD our God, other **lords** besides you have ruled over us, but we acknowledge your name alone. [Isaiah 26:13]

> For your Maker is your **husband**, the LORD of hosts is his name; the Holy One of Israel is your Redeemer, the God of the whole earth he is called. [Isaiah 54:5]

Although present-day Jews and Christians usually claim to be monotheistic, their sacred literature suggests that many deities are at work in the universe. Over time, apparently they exalted *YHWH* to a position above the other tribal *ba'alim* or *elohim*, relegating them to the status of elemental spirits or demons.* Even to the early Christians, these other deities were still around and could be called in Greek *theos*, but they were subject to the authority of the one God, who was identified with the *YHWH* of Hebrew Scripture.

> Indeed, even though there may be so-called **gods** in heaven or on earth—as in fact there are many **gods** and many lords—yet for us there is one **God**, the Father, from whom are all things and for whom we exist, and one Lord, Jesus Christ, through whom are all things and through whom we exist. [I Corinthians 8:5-6]

> Formerly, when you did not know **God**, you were enslaved to beings that by nature are not **gods**. Now, however, that you have come to know God, or rather to be known by God, how can you turn back again to the weak and beggarly elemental spirits? [Galatians 4:8-9]

Making reasonable use of the god metaphors today presents most doubters and skeptics with a challenge. People today have no way of being sure what the spiritual ancestors of Jews and Christians had in mind when they used any of the terms that in English are lumped together under the heading of God or gods. For the people who first used these expressions, presumably the words pointed to what they imagined was a reality of some sort.

For some Jesus followers, the intense experience of feeling responsibly connected with other people cannot be expressed using ordinary language in ordinary ways. In such instances, talking about the presence of God seems to make sense. They are emboldened to make this use of the metaphor by a theme that runs through scripture: where love* and justice* are present, there is God.

> Joseph's master took him and put him into the prison, the place where the king's prisoners were confined; he remained there in prison. But the Lord was with Joseph and showed him **steadfast love**; he gave him favor in the sight of the chief jailer. [Genesis 39:20-21]

> The alien who resides with you shall be to you as the citizen among you; you shall **love** the alien as yourself, for you were aliens in the land of Egypt: I am the Lord your God. [Leviticus 19:34]

> As for you, return to your God, hold fast to **love** and **justice**, and wait continually for your God. [Hosea 12:6]

> Jesus said to him, "'You shall **love** the Lord your God with all your heart, and with all your soul, and with all your mind.' This is the greatest and first commandment. And a second is like it: 'You shall **love** your neighbor as yourself.'" [Matthew 22:37-39]

> Be imitators of God, as beloved children, and live in **love**, as Christ loved us. [Ephesians 5:1-2]

> So we have known and believe the love that God has for us. God is **love**, and those who abide in love abide in God, and God abides in them. [I John 4:16]

Jesus followers often have experiences of being similarly connected with nature—such as observing a particularly brilliant sunrise or sitting quietly near the top of a mountain with the valley spread out below—experiences that sometimes can best be expressed in the creation* poetry of scripture. In talking about experiences of God in nature, some call it panentheism.*

Of all the English words that are used to stand for biblical metaphors, God may be the least helpful for post-modern skeptics. For those of a more religious inclination, those three letters—g, o, and d—represent the very foundation of their world. These people seem to forget, or perhaps they never knew, that this is a Germanic word, which in origin probably meant simply what is invoked or what is worshiped. The word stood for a great variety of supernatural beings invented long before the coming of the Christians, including those for whom the days of the week are named, such as Wednesday for Woden and Thursday for Thor. Using this all-purpose little word to translate biblical imagery has created serious problems for many people who might like to take religion seriously.

Today the word god is most often used as an expression of exasperation or annoyance. Not only sailors and construction laborers, but also businessmen and women, find the word a convenient way of letting off steam. The only other people who use the word with much frequency are preachers and politicians who are attempting to give their rhetoric the ring of authority without the necessity of being precise. In short, the word as used in formal speeches or in expostulations stands for no reality beyond itself. It is a ritual noise like hello, which long ago lost its purpose of blessing, of wishing for the good health of people being greeted. The impact of the word on many people comes through clearly in a caption Robert Mankoff added to one of his cartoons: "Good sermon, Reverend, but all that God stuff was pretty far-fetched."

As inadequate and confused as the god metaphor may be in the Christian tradition, no other word has yet appeared to replace it.

For other biblical metaphors associated with God, see **Abba**, **father**, **fire**, **king**, **lion**, **mother**, **rock**, **savior**, and **shepherd**.

good, *adjective*   Two Greek words appear in English versions of the Bible as good. One of them, *kalos*, originally meant beautiful, free from defects, but it appears in its primary sense only once.

> When some were speaking about the temple, how it was adorned with **beautiful** stones and gifts dedicated to God, he said, "As for these things that you see, the days will come when not one stone will be left upon another; all will be thrown down." [Luke 21:5-6]

In all of the other occurrences, *kalos* appears as a metaphor indicating what is useful or praiseworthy or morally sound. In its metaphorical use, *kalos* becomes almost indistinguishable from the second word for good, *agathos*, which, in its most primitive sense, meant useful, fit, or capable. In the plural, it meant goods or possessions. As a metaphor, *agathos* was also used to suggest moral goodness or virtue. When either word appears as an adverb, the translation is well; when a comparison is called for, the word better is used. The scholars who translated the Hebrew Bible into Greek used both *kalos* and *agathos* for the Hebrew word *tob,* which was an all-purpose word like good.

Some passages take on new richness when the original metaphors appear instead of the commonplace good. Here are a few examples of *kalos* returned to its most basic meaning.

> Let your light shine before others, so that they may see your **beautiful** works and give glory to your Father in heaven. [Matthew 5:16]

> Jesus said, "Let her alone; why do you trouble her? She has performed a **beautiful** service for me." [Mark 14:6]

> Just as they were leaving him, Peter said to Jesus, "Master, it is **beautiful** for us to be here; let us make three dwellings, one for you, one for Moses, and one for Elijah"—not knowing what he said. [Luke 9:33]

> I do not understand my own actions. For I do not do what I want, but I do the very thing I hate. Now if I do what I do not want, I agree that the law is **beautiful**. [Romans 7:15-16]

The same exercise is possible substituting useful for *kalos*, but since useful is the primary meaning of *agathos*, the following examples are from this second word for good.

> Then someone came to him and said, "Teacher, what **useful** deed must I do to have eternal life?" [Matthew 19:16]
>
> He said to him, "Well done, **useful** slave! Because you have been trustworthy in a very small thing, take charge of ten cities." [Luke 19:17]
>
> Nathanael said to him, "Can anything **useful** come out of Nazareth?" Philip said to him, "Come and see." [John 1:46]
>
> Now in Joppa there was a disciple whose name was Tabitha, which in Greek is Dorcas. She was devoted to **useful** works and acts of charity. [Acts 9:36]
>
> So the law is holy, and the commandment is holy and just and **useful**. [Romans 7:12]

The problem with translating either of these two words with good is that in today's English, good often means the opposite of practical and sensible, while in the Bible the opposite of useful is evil.* No one calls a person a do-gooder when intending a compliment. The same goes for Goody Two Shoes, taken from the title of an eighteenth-century, highly moralistic tale for children. Both phrases now refer to a self-righteous, smugly virtuous person.

When running across good—or well or better—in an English version of the Bible, the serious reader can always try the useful metaphor to see if that would make better sense of the text.

gospel, *noun;* **evangelize**, *verb*   Although the connection is not so obvious in modern English, gospel is a perfect translation of the Greek *euangelion*, which was formed from *eu*, good + *angelia*, message. In much the same way, the English word originally was formed from good + spell, discourse or story. Early on, when people heard the preacher say good spell, many thought he was saying God's spell, so by the Middle Ages the word entered the language as *godspell*, which evolved into gospel.

The verb form in English, evangelize, more closely resembles the Greek, *euangelizo*. The verbs mean to bring or to announce good news.

Although in English the gospel and all the words related to it—evangelize, evangelism, evangelist, evangelical—have a specifically Christian connotation, that was not so in the ancient world. For example, proclamations of the emperor were frequently issued as good news. Birth announcements were good news. In the Bible, *euangelizo* is sometimes used in this generic sense. The same is true of *basar*, the Hebrew equivalent of *euangelizo*. When *basar* is used as a noun, it is usually translated as flesh.* The connection between good news and flesh may have been the color rose. Meat is rose colored, and a rosy or ruddy complexion is associated with good health. This is the same sort of logic that lies behind the English word sanguine, or bloody, meaning optimistic, but the connection between flesh and good news in Hebrew may have been that they happened to use the same letters.

> David answered Rechab and his brother Baanah, the sons of Rimmon the Beerothite, "As the LORD lives, who has redeemed my life out of every adversity, when the one who told me, 'See, Saul is dead,' thought he **was bringing good news,** I seized him and killed him at Ziklag—this was the reward I gave him for his news." [II Samuel 4:9-10]
>
> While Joab was still speaking, Jonathan son of the priest Abiathar arrived. Adonijah said, "Come in, for you are a worthy man and surely you **bring good news.**" [I Kings 1:42]

Marks a word in the text that has its own entry

> Zechariah said to the angel, "How will I know that this is so? For I am an old man, and my wife is getting on in years." The angel replied, "I am Gabriel. I stand in the presence of God, and I have been sent to speak to you and to **bring you this good news.**" [Luke 1:18-19]

> Timothy has just now come to us from you, and **has brought us the good news** of your faith and love. He has told us also that you always remember us kindly and long to see us—just as we long to see you. [I Thessalonians 3:6]

More frequently in the specifically Christian portions of the Bible, *euangelizo* refers to an announcement of divine concern for the welfare of the world.

> Jesus answered them, "Go and tell John what you hear and see: the blind receive their sight, the lame walk, the lepers are cleansed, the deaf hear, the dead are raised, and the poor **have good news brought** to them." [Matthew 11:4-5]

> Jesus said to them, "I must **proclaim the good news** of the kingdom of God to the other cities also; for I was sent for this purpose." [Luke 4:43]

> Thus I make it my ambition to **proclaim the good news,** not where Christ has already been named, so that I do not build on someone else's foundation. [Romans 15:20]

> Now I would remind you, brothers and sisters, of the **good news that I proclaimed** to you, which you in turn received, in which also you stand, through which also you are being saved, if you hold firmly to the **message that I proclaimed** to you—unless you have come to believe in vain. [I Corinthians 15:1-2]

Basar in the Hebrew Scriptures also can convey this sense of making a proclamation in the name of God.

> The spirit of the Lord God is upon me, because the Lord has anointed me; he has sent me **to bring good news** to the oppressed, to bind up the brokenhearted, to proclaim liberty to the captives, and release to the prisoners; to proclaim the year of the Lord's favor, and the day of vengeance of our God; to comfort all who mourn; to provide for those who mourn in Zion—to give them a garland instead of ashes, the oil of gladness instead of mourning, the mantle of praise instead of a faint spirit. They will be called oaks of righteousness, the planting of the Lord, to display his glory. [Isaiah 61:1-3]

> Look! On the mountains the feet of one who **brings good tidings,** who proclaims peace! Celebrate your festivals, O Judah, fulfill your vows, for never again shall the wicked invade you; they are utterly cut off. [Nahum 1:15]

The early Christian writers frequently used the noun *euangelion* in reference to their message about Jesus. In some places, they add specific content using other popular metaphors—such as kingdom,* grace,* salvation,* peace,* hope,* glory, and life.

> Jesus went throughout Galilee, teaching in their synagogues and proclaiming the **good news** of the kingdom and curing every disease and every sickness among the people. [Matthew 4:23]

> I do not count my life of any value to myself, if only I may finish my course and the ministry that I received from the Lord Jesus, to testify to the **good news** of God's grace. [Acts 20:24]

> For I am not ashamed of the **gospel;** it is the power of God for salvation to everyone who has faith, to the Jew first and also to the Greek. [Romans 1:16]

As shoes for your feet put on whatever will make you ready to proclaim the **gospel** of peace. [Ephesians 6:15]

We have heard of your faith in Christ Jesus and of the love that you have for all the saints, because of the hope laid up for you in heaven. You have heard of this hope before in the word of the truth, the **gospel** that has come to you. [Colossians 1:4-6]

For this purpose he called you through our proclamation of the **good news,** so that you may obtain the glory of our Lord Jesus Christ. [II Thessalonians 2:14]

This grace was given to us in Christ Jesus before the ages began, but it has now been revealed through the appearing of our Savior Christ Jesus, who abolished death and brought life and immortality to light through the **gospel**. [II Timothy 1:9-10]

Perhaps starting with Mark, *euangelion* became the designation for any composition about the life and teachings of Jesus. Mark opened his narrative this way:

The beginning of the **good news** of Jesus Christ, the Son of God. [Mark 1:1]

Mark and the authors of the other gospels and of the Acts of the Apostles employed one of the most popular literary forms of their era, a form that today would be called a novella, that is, a fictional piece that is longer and more complicated than a short story but not as long as a typical novel. Each gospel attempts to engage the interest of a particular segment of the literate population by using language and images that would have been familiar. For example, Matthew seems to assume that his readers were familiar with the Hebrew Scriptures, while Luke makes his appeal to a well-informed Greek audience. In either case, the form is a reminder that the authors may not have been intending to write from an historical or a scientific perspective, but attempting to convey the life and teachings of Jesus in a compelling manner.

The good news metaphor to identify the Jesus story challenges all teachers and preachers to examine their messages and to ask themselves if the news they bring will be good in the minds of their listeners.

grace, *noun*   Both grace and the biblical words it translates suggest a quality of an attractive gift or of a favorable impression. The Hebrew word is *chen*, often translated as favor. In British English, grace and favor are sometimes linked, as in the expression grace and favor housing, residences supplied rent free to civil servants or military personnel. The Greek word is *charis*, the root of charisma* and Eucharist.*

Chen appears frequently in the Hebrew Scriptures, both in human interactions and in experiences attributed to the presence of God.* A few examples of *chen* in human interactions . . .

Esau said, "What do you mean by all this company that I met?" Jacob answered, "To find **favor** with my lord." [Genesis 33:8]

Then Ruth fell prostrate, with her face to the ground, and said to Boaz, "Why have I found **favor** in your sight, that you should take notice of me, when I am a foreigner?" [Ruth 2:10]

As soon as the king saw Queen Esther standing in the court, she won his **favor** and he held out to her the golden scepter that was in his hand. Then Esther approached and touched the top of the scepter. [Esther 5:2]

. . . and in relationship to God.

Moses said to the LORD, "Why have you treated your servant so badly? Why have I not found **favor** in your sight, that you lay the burden of all this people on me?" [Numbers 11:11]

You are the most handsome of men; **grace** is poured upon your lips; therefore God has blessed you forever. [Psalm 45:2]

Thus says the LORD: The people who survived the sword found **grace** in the wilderness; when Israel sought for rest, the LORD appeared to him from far away. I have loved you with an everlasting love; therefore I have continued my faithfulness to you. [Jeremiah 31:2-3]

Charis also can appear in human relationships . . .

After two years had passed, Felix was succeeded by Porcius Festus; and since he wanted to grant the Jews a **favor**, Felix left Paul in prison. [Acts 24:27]

I wanted to come to you first, so that you might have a double **favor**; I wanted to visit you on my way to Macedonia, and to come back to you from Macedonia and have you send me on to Judea. [II Corinthians 1:15-16]

. . . or in human appreciation of God.

The angel said to her, "Do not be afraid, Mary, for you have found **favor** with God." [Luke 1:30]

With great power the apostles gave their testimony to the resurrection of the Lord Jesus, and great **grace** was upon them all. [Acts 4:33]

When James and Cephas and John, who were acknowledged pillars, recognized the **grace** that had been given to me, they gave to Barnabas and me the right hand of fellowship, agreeing that we should go to the Gentiles and they to the circumcised. [Galatians 2:9]

Charis also became part of a fixed formula used by Christians in opening and closing their letters. Whether they gave more thought in following the practice than today's correspondents do in writing Dear or Sincerely is hard to say, but here are a few examples.

To all God's beloved in Rome, who are called to be saints: **Grace** to you and peace from God our Father and the Lord Jesus Christ . . . The **grace** of our Lord Jesus Christ be with you. [Romans 1:7 and 16:20]

Grace to you and peace from God our Father and the Lord Jesus Christ . . . May the **grace** of our Lord Jesus Christ be with your spirit, brothers and sisters. [Galatians 1:3 and 6:18]

May **grace** and peace be yours in abundance in the knowledge of God and of Jesus our Lord . . . Grow in the **grace** and knowledge of our Lord and Savior Jesus Christ. To him be the glory both now and to the day of eternity. [II Peter 1:2 and 3:18]

To see what the biblical writers had in mind when they used *chen* and *charis* as metaphors to illuminate their understanding of God, it is first necessary to recognize how the words were used in everyday human interactions. Usually the person extending grace or favor was of a higher station—because of wealth, prestige, or political power—than the recipient. The expected response of the recipient was gratitude. Gratitude became so inseparable from *charis* that *charis* could also mean thanks.

Do you **thank** the slave for doing what was commanded? [Luke 17:9]

> Therefore, since we are receiving a kingdom that cannot be shaken, let us give **thanks,** by which we offer to God an acceptable worship with reverence and awe. [Hebrews 12:28]

> **Thanks** be to God for his indescribable gift! [II Corinthians 9:15]

> Let the word of Christ dwell in you richly; teach and admonish one another in all wisdom; and with **gratitude** in your hearts sing psalms, hymns, and spiritual songs to God. [Colossians 3:16]

The advantage of using the grace/favor metaphor in discussing God is that it centers a person's understanding of life on gratitude. Gratitude has way of helping a person keep things in perspective. As St. Paul put it:

> For by the **grace** given to me I say to everyone among you not to think of yourself more highly than you ought to think, but to think with sober judgment, each according to the measure of faith that God has assigned. [Romans 12:3]

In Paul's way of thinking, faith* comes to a person through grace or favor. Everybody gets enough so that no one has reason to feel superior or inferior to others. Whatever measure of faith a person has received, the appropriate response is gratitude.

guilt, *noun;* **guilty**, *adjective*   No Hebrew or Greek words carry quite the same connotations as guilt in modern English. Today, guilt is both the existential condition of being in the wrong and the bad feelings that arise from having done something wrong or having failed to do what is right. While several of the biblical words have to do with the existential condition of being in the wrong, none has anything to do with bad feelings.

Of the several Hebrew words translated guilt, the most common is *asham*, which is the word used to identify a person who was responsible for an offense and subject to punishment.

> So Abimelech called for Isaac, and said, "So she is your wife! Why then did you say, 'She is my sister'?" Isaac said to him, "Because I thought I might die because of her." Abimelech said, "What is this you have done to us? One of the people might easily have lain with your wife, and you would have brought **guilt** upon us." [Genesis 26:9-10]

> When a ruler sins, doing unintentionally any one of all the things that by commandments of the LORD his God ought not to be done and incurs **guilt,** once the sin that he has committed is made known to him, he shall bring as his offering a male goat without blemish. [Leviticus 4:22-23]

Two of the Hebrew words have been translated both as guilt and as punishment. One is *avon*, from a root that meant to make crooked; the other is *chet*, which means crime or fault.

> Judah said, "What can we say to my lord? What can we speak? How can we clear ourselves? God has found out the **guilt** of your servants; here we are then, my lord's slaves, both we and also the one in whose possession the cup has been found."—*avon* [Genesis 44:16]

> Be careful that you do not entertain a mean thought, thinking, "The seventh year, the year of remission, is near," and therefore view your needy neighbor with hostility and give nothing; your neighbor might cry to the LORD against you, and you would incur **guilt.**—*chet* [Deuteronomy 15:9]

> Cain said to the LORD, "My **punishment** is greater than I can bear!"—*avon* [Genesis 4:13]

> Why should any who draw breath complain about the **punishment** of their sins?—*chet* [Lamentations 3:39]

Two other Hebrew words are frequently translated as guilt or guilty: *rasha*, which meant to have caused wrong, and *ashmah*, derived from *asham*.

> Are your days like the days of mortals, or your years like human years, that you seek out my iniquity and search for my sin, although you know that I am not **guilty,** and there is no one to deliver out of your hand?—*rasha* [Job 10:5-7]

> He did not humble himself before the LORD, as his father Manasseh had humbled himself, but this Amon incurred more and more **guilt.**—*ashmah* [II Chronicles 33:23]

The word guilt does not occur in English translations of the Greek texts. Guilty occurs only four times, but in three of these, guilty does not translate a Greek word at all but has been inserted as an interpretation of the text.

> Whoever blasphemes against the Holy Spirit can never have forgiveness, but is **guilty** of an eternal sin.—literally, in danger of eternal judgment. [Mark 3:29]

> Jesus answered Pilate, "You would have no power over me unless it had been given you from above; therefore the one who handed me over to you is **guilty** of a greater sin."—literally, has a greater sin. [John 19:11]

> Everyone who commits sin is **guilty** of lawlessness; sin is lawlessness.—literally, does lawlessness. [I John 3:4]

In the one place where guilty actually translates a Greek word in the text, the word is *aition*, which meant the cause of or the responsibility for.

> Pilate then called together the chief priests, the leaders, and the people, and said to them, "You brought me this man as one who was perverting the people; and here I have examined him in your presence and have not found this man **guilty** of any of your charges against him." [Luke 23:13-14]

The earliest Christian writers had little to say about guilt, but the Hebrew metaphors can help people today avoid mixing existential guilt with psychological guilt or shame.* Following the Hebrew metaphors, guilt is the condition of having let down people who had a reasonable expectation of being upheld. To discourage such behavior, a community may inflict punishment on a person who is the cause of a problem, which practice adds another dimension to guilt—deserving punishment. To determine guilt in the Hebrew sense requires a careful assessment of the evidence and a concerted effort to separate feelings from behavior. If the behavior in question falls under the heading of sin,* then a discussion of repentance* may be in order.

H

hand, *noun*   In both Hebrew and Greek, metaphors incorporating the word hand tend to be identifications of power,* most often expressing an author's sense of God's might. These figures of speech based on hand, *yad* in Hebrew and *cheir* in Greek, can suggest awe in the presence of divine power experienced in three distinct ways. The first has to do with feelings of wonder inspired by encounters with the natural world (see **create**). The second type of hand metaphor reflects an experience of survival from a catastrophe or the anticipated capacity to survive an ordeal. The third type

---

arose from an experience in seeing justice* done or a confidence that vindication was possible. In many cases, justice for the writers and editors of the Bible meant seeing their enemies punished.

God's hand in nature metaphors

The heavens are telling the glory of God; and the firmament proclaims his **handiwork**. [Psalm 19:1]

Ask the animals, and they will teach you; the birds of the air, and they will tell you; ask the plants of the earth, and they will teach you; and the fish of the sea will declare to you. Who among all these does not know that the **hand** of the Lord has done this? [Job 12:7-9]

I will put in the wilderness the cedar, the acacia, the myrtle, and the olive; I will set in the desert the cypress, the plane and the pine together, so that all may see and know, all may consider and understand, that the **hand** of the Lord has done this, the Holy One of Israel has created it. [Isaiah 41:19-20]

God's hand in metaphors of survival

The Lord your God dried up the waters of the Jordan for you until you crossed over, as the Lord your God did to the Red Sea, which he dried up for us until we crossed over, so that all the peoples of the earth may know that the **hand** of the Lord is mighty, and so that you may fear the Lord your God forever. [Joshua 4:23-24]

There is nothing better for mortals than to eat and drink, and find enjoyment in their toil. This also, I saw, is from the **hand** of God. [Ecclesiastes 2:24]

The **hand** of the Lord was with them, and a great number became believers and turned to the Lord. [Acts 11:21]

Humble yourselves therefore under the mighty **hand** of God, so that he may exalt you in due time. Cast all your anxiety on him, because he cares for you. [I Peter 5:6-7]

God's hand in metaphors of justice

The Lord said to Moses, "Go to Pharaoh, and say to him, 'Thus says the Lord, the God of the Hebrews: Let my people go, so that they may worship me. For if you refuse to let them go and still hold them, the **hand** of the Lord will strike with a deadly pestilence your livestock in the field: the horses, the donkeys, the camels, the herds, and the flocks.'" [Exodus 9:1-3]

The people of Ekron sent therefore and gathered together all the lords of the Philistines, and said, "Send away the ark of the God of Israel, and let it return to its own place, that it may not kill us and our people." For there was a deathly panic throughout the whole city. The **hand** of God was very heavy there. [I Samuel 5:11]

It will be said on that day, Lo, this is our God; we have waited for him, so that he might save us. This is the Lord for whom we have waited; let us be glad and rejoice in his salvation. For the **hand** of the Lord will rest on this mountain. The Moabites shall be trodden down in their place as straw is trodden down in a dung-pit. [Isaiah 25:9-10]

"Now listen—the **hand** of the Lord is against you, and you will be blind for a while, unable to see the sun." Immediately mist and darkness came over him, and he went about groping for someone to lead him by the hand. [Acts 13:11]

Hand also appears in biblical metaphors identifying human power over others, either hostile powers or the power of the people for whom the author speaks. Perhaps because of the associations with power, *yad* was also used as a metaphor for the penis, the organ representing male sexual dominance.

hand in metaphors of hostile human power

The enemy said, "I will pursue, I will overtake, I will divide the spoil, my desire shall have its fill of them. I will draw my sword, my **hand** shall destroy them." [Exodus 15:9]

He saved them from the **hand** of the foe, and delivered them from the **hand** of the enemy. [Psalm 106:10]

In this place I will make void the plans of Judah and Jerusalem, and will make them fall by the sword before their enemies, and by the **hand** of those who seek their life. [Jeremiah 19:7]

Jesus was teaching his disciples, saying to them, "The Son of Man is to be betrayed into human **hands**, and they will kill him." [Mark 9:31]

He has raised up a mighty savior for us in the house of his servant David, as he spoke through the mouth of his holy prophets from of old, that we would be saved from our enemies and from the **hand** of all who hate us. [Luke 1:69-71]

They tried to arrest Jesus again, but he escaped from their **hands**. [John 10:39]

hand in metaphors of human power over others

King Melchizedek blessed him and said, "Blessed be Abram by God Most High, maker of heaven and earth; and blessed be God Most High, who has delivered your enemies into your **hand**!" [Genesis 14:19-20]

When the Canaanite, the king of Arad, who lived in the Negeb, heard that Israel was coming by the way of Atharim, he fought against Israel and took some of them captive. Then Israel made a vow to the LORD and said, "If you will indeed give this people into our **hands**, then we will utterly destroy their towns." [Numbers 21:1-2]

Joshua said, "Roll large stones against the mouth of the cave, and set men by it to guard them; but do not stay there yourselves; pursue your enemies, and attack them from the rear. Do not let them enter their towns, for the LORD your God has given them into your **hand**." [Joshua 10:18-19]

Ehud said to them, "Follow after me; for the LORD has given your enemies the Moabites into your **hand**." [Judges 3:28]

hand as a sexual metaphor

Behind the door and the doorpost you have set up your symbol; for, in deserting me, you have uncovered your bed, you have gone up to it, you have made it wide; and you have made a bargain for yourself with them, you have loved their bed, you have gazed on their **nakedness**.—*yad* [Isaiah 57:8]

In English versions of the Bible, the term right hand often appears when the words for hand, *yad* and *cheir*, are not in the original text. In these passages, the adjective for right stands as a noun. In Hebrew the word for right is *yamin* and in Greek *dexios*, from which we get our English word dexterity, meaning skill or cleverness. Since ancient times, the right hand has been a metaphor indicating who or what is favored. The reason may be that the majority of human beings are right handed. Added to the fact that most people are more skillful with their right hands is the custom in some cultures for the left hand to be used exclusively in cleaning the parts of the body soiled by emptying the bowels. For whatever reason, the right hand indicated favor or blessing, usually that bestowed by God. To be seated at God's right hand was the favorite metaphor employed by the early followers of Jesus in expressing their feelings about Jesus in relation to the God of Abraham, Isaac, and Jacob.

right hand in human relations

So Bathsheba went to King Solomon, to speak to him on behalf of Adonijah. The king rose to meet her, and bowed down to her; then he sat on his throne, and had a throne brought for the king's mother, and she sat on his **right**. [I Kings 2:19]

When James and Cephas and John, who were acknowledged pillars, recognized the grace that had been given to me, they gave to Barnabas and me the right hand of fellowship, agreeing that we should go to the Gentiles and they to the circumcised. [Galatians 2:9]

God's right hand

Look on all who are proud, and bring them low; tread down the wicked where they stand. Hide them all in the dust together; bind their faces in the world below. Then I will also acknowledge to you that your own **right hand** can give you victory. [Job 40:12-14]

You show me the path of life. In your presence there is fullness of joy; in your **right hand** are pleasures forevermore. [Psalm 16:11]

Wondrously show your steadfast love, O savior of those who seek refuge from their adversaries at your **right hand**. [Psalm 17:7]

The LORD has sworn by his **right hand** and by his mighty arm: I will not again give your grain to be food for your enemies, and foreigners shall not drink the wine for which you have labored. [Isaiah 62:8]

Jesus said to him, "You have said so. But I tell you, From now on you will see the Son of Man seated at the **right hand** of Power and coming on the clouds of heaven." [Matthew 26:64]

So then the Lord Jesus, after he had spoken to them, was taken up into heaven and sat down at the **right hand** of God. [Mark 16:19]

The God of our ancestors raised up Jesus, whom you had killed by hanging him on a tree. God exalted him at his **right hand** as Leader and Savior that he might give repentance to Israel and forgiveness of sins. [Acts 5:30-31]

Who is to condemn? It is Christ Jesus, who died, yes, who was raised, who is at the **right hand** of God, who indeed intercedes for us. [Romans 8:34]

The right hand indicating favor also shows up in the psalms that employ metaphors indicating the desired relationship of a person with God.

God at my right hand

I keep the L ORD always before me; because he is at my **right hand,** I shall not be moved. [Psalm 16:8]

I was stupid and ignorant; I was like a brute beast toward you. Nevertheless I am continually with you; you hold my **right hand.**—*yamin + yad* [Psalm 73:22-23]

Look on my **right hand** and see—there is no one who takes notice of me; no refuge remains to me; no one cares for me. I cry to you, O L ORD; I say, "You are my refuge, my portion in the land of the living." [Psalm 142:4-5]

Metaphors that incorporate the word hand can be expressive of profound human experiences and can offer comfort in times of trouble. Because of their focus on power, however, the hand metaphors can produce undesirable side effects. The conviction that God is on my side can lead to political and personal attitudes that justify suppression of other people's aspirations. Such attitudes foster cruelty, violence, war, and torture. Those followers of Jesus who reject a theology of domination use the hand metaphors with great caution.

hear—see **obey**

heart—see **faith, mind**

heathen, *noun* and *adjective*   Since the fourth century, many translations of the Bible have used heathen for the Hebrew *goy* and for the Greek *ethnos* and *ethnikos.* As has been the case with pagan,* many people have thought that heathen was derived from heath and was the name for rustics or villagers as opposed to city dwellers. As Christianity spread through the cities of Europe, the country people often kept to the older religions, so, according to this theory, non-Christians were known as the heathen. The theory cannot explain, however, why Ulphilas—the apostle to the Goths (311-383)—used heathen to translate both *goy* and the Greek equivalents into Gothic. The likely explanation is that heathen reflects the influence of the Armenian *hetanos,* which in turn evolved from the Greek *ethnikos.* Following the example of Ulphilas, until quite recently all editions of the Bible in Germanic languages, including English, usually translated *goy, ethnos,* and *ethnikos* as heathen.

The two original Bible words translated as heathen had approximately the same meaning: nation, clan, or tribe. In many places in the text, however, *goy* and *ethnikos* refer to the nations, clans, and tribes that were not part of the ancient kingdoms of Israel and Judah. They were what people using modern English would call those who are not Jews: Gentiles. The word Gentile comes from the Latin *gentilis,* which had nearly the same meaning as *goy* and *ethnikos* and which stood for them in the earliest Latin translations.

As Gentile has changed its meaning to become the name for non-Jews, so has heathen taken on specific connotations in modern usage. Heathen has come to mean specifically any person or group that is not Christian, Muslim, or Jewish. Moreover, heathen nearly always carries a negative judgment: anyone who does not worship the God of the Jews, Muslims, and Christians is by definition unenlightened and inferior. These changes in the use of words are apparent in the differences between the seventeenth-century King James Version and the late twentieth-century New Revised Standard Version.

Marks a word in the text that has its own entry   **135**

New Revised Standard Version	King James Version

goy

Why do the **nations** conspire, and the peoples plot in vain? [Psalm 2:1]	Why do the **heathen** rage, and the people imagine a vain thing?
Then you shall know that I am the LORD, whose statutes you have not followed, and whose ordinances you have not kept, but you have acted according to the ordinances of the **nations** that are around you. [Ezekiel 11:12]	And ye shall know that I am the LORD: for ye have not walked in my statutes, neither executed my judgments, but have done after the manners of the **heathen** that are round about you.
And I am extremely angry with the **nations** that are at ease; for while I was only a little angry, they made the disaster worse. [Zechariah 1:15]	I am very sore displeased with the **heathen** that are at ease: for I was but a little displeased, and they helped forward the affliction.

ethnikos

When you are praying, do not heap up empty phrases as the **Gentiles** do; for they think that they will be heard because of their many words. [Matthew 6:7]	When ye pray, use not vain repetitions, as the **heathen** do: for they think that they shall be heard for their much speaking.
If the member refuses to listen to them, tell it to the church; and if the offender refuses to listen even to the church, let such a one be to you as a **Gentile** and a tax collector. [Matthew 18:17]	And if he shall neglect to hear them, tell it unto the church: but if he neglect to hear the church, let him be unto thee as a **heathen** man and a publican.

ethnos

On frequent journeys, in danger from rivers, danger from bandits, danger from my own people, danger from **Gentiles**, danger in the city, danger in the wilderness, danger at sea, danger from false brothers and sisters. [II Corinthians 11:26]	In journeyings often, in perils of waters, in perils of robbers, in perils by mine own countrymen, in perils by the **heathen**, in perils in the city, in perils in the wilderness, in perils in the sea, in perils among false brethren.
When God, who had set me apart before I was born and called me through his grace, was pleased to reveal his Son to me, so that I might proclaim him among the **Gentiles**, I did not confer with any human being. [Galatians 1:15-16]	When it pleased God, who separated me from my mother's womb, and called me by his grace, To reveal his Son in me, that I might preach him among the **heathen**; immediately I conferred not with flesh and blood.

In an effort to respect differences in culture and religion, many Christians have discarded the term heathen as being unnecessarily derisive.

Marks a word in the text that has its own entry

heaven, *noun*   In the Hebrew version of the Bible, the word heaven always appears in the plural, *shamayim*. It is usually, but not always, translated as the heavens. The reader can usually tell from the context if the word refers to the apparent arch above the earth where the clouds float or to the starry skies above.

> In the beginning when God created the **heavens** and the earth . . . [Genesis 1:1]

> The windows of the **heavens** were opened. The rain fell on the earth forty days and forty nights. [Genesis 7:11-12]

In early Hebrew writing, we find mention of the skies above being the dwelling place of their God and the angels.* Although the people of Israel once may have taken these images of God above the stars or riding on the clouds as accurate descriptions, they work best as metaphors, indicating a presence accessible throughout the universe.

> So acknowledge today and take to heart that the LORD is God in **heaven** above and on the earth beneath; there is no other. [Deuteronomy 4:39]

> Sing to God, sing praises to his name; lift up a song to him who rides upon the clouds—his name is the LORD—be exultant before him. [Psalm 68:4]

> The angel of the LORD called to him from **heaven**, and said, "Abraham, Abraham!" And he said, "Here I am." [Genesis 22:11]

In the Greek, heaven was used in much the same way as in the Hebrew. The word, *ouranos*, could mean the sky above and is sometimes translated that way.

> From one person, and this one as good as dead, descendants were born, "as many as the stars of **heaven** and as the innumerable grains of sand by the seashore." [Hebrews 11:12]

> The Pharisees and Sadducees came, and to test Jesus they asked him to show them a sign from **heaven**. He answered them, "When it is evening, you say, 'It will be fair weather, for the **sky** is red.' And in the morning, 'It will be stormy today, for the sky is red and threatening.' You know how to interpret the appearance of the **sky**, but you cannot interpret the signs of the times." [Matthew 16:1-3]

Notice that, in the second citation, the translators decided that Matthew intended for the Pharisees and the Sadducees to be understood as using *ouranos* in a religious or metaphorical sense, but Matthew wanted Jesus to respond using the same word in its everyday sense of sky.

The early Christians used the sky imagery of Hebrew Scriptures in telling their story. They wrote as if heaven were the dwelling place of God and the angels, whom Jesus joined after his death. Although they generally refrained from making the suggestion that heaven is where Jesus's followers would go after they die, they sometimes indicate that heaven is the place where records of individual behavior are kept.

> When the angels had left them and gone into **heaven**, the shepherds said to one another, "Let us go now to Bethlehem and see this thing that has taken place, which the Lord has made known to us." [Luke 2:15]

---

*Marks a word in the text that has its own entry

> For Christ did not enter a sanctuary made by human hands, a mere copy of the true one, but he entered into **heaven** itself, now to appear in the presence of God on our behalf. [Hebrews 9:24]

> Jesus, looking at him, loved him and said, "You lack one thing; go, sell what you own, and give the money to the poor, and you will have treasure in **heaven**; then come, follow me." [Mark 10:21]

> Do not rejoice at this, that the spirits submit to you, but rejoice that your names are written in **heaven**. [Luke 10:20]

In the teaching attributed to Jesus, the word heaven is frequently used in connection with Father.* In this case, the word in Matthew's gospel is most often in the plural.

> Pray then in this way: Our Father in **heaven**, hallowed be your name. [Matthew 6:9]

> Again, truly I tell you, if two of you agree on earth about anything you ask, it will be done for you by my Father in **heaven**. [Matthew 18:19]

A present-day reader will have to wonder what Matthew thought Jesus was teaching. Was he saying that God lived in the skies, out in space? Possibly Matthew pictured the Father much as his ancestors had—a god who could ride the clouds or move among the stars—but neither he nor any of the other gospel writers came right out and said, "Your Father is in heaven."

The structure of the sentences suggests that Matthew wanted to make clear what father Jesus was talking about. In these instances, Jesus was not talking about biological fathers or heroes of the past, such as Father Abraham. According to Matthew, Jesus was talking about a father whom we experience in a dimension of reality other than the human levels of history or science. The authors of the Bible may have used the heaven metaphor as way of pointing to the most profound human experiences in this life: being connected with all other human beings and all other creatures, who have the same father in heaven.

In association with the word kingdom,* the importance of the sky metaphor to the early Jesus followers may become even more clear. Human beings may have a shaping power in their lives other than the genes they inherit and the traditions they learn. Most people have a sense that there may be more to life than what they can see, hear, touch, or smell. Ordinary language used in ordinary ways will always fail to convey this sense of what Matthew described as another realm, that is, a kingdom that can be experienced within present time and space.

> From that time Jesus began to proclaim, "Repent, for the kingdom of **heaven** has come near." [Matthew 4:17]

> As you go, proclaim the good news, "The kingdom of **heaven** has come near." [Matthew 10:7]

When heaven appears in this context, the metaphor clearly points to a place of life, not death. This perspective can be helpful in dealing with the metaphor in other contexts where the reader might think that heaven is about dying rather than living more intensely. When people sitting in church hear the word heaven, many of them think of it as a place out there where God is supposed to live and where they are supposed to go when life on earth is over. That understanding of heaven as a place of the dead may not have been in every case what the biblical authors had in mind.

hell, *noun*   Three words in the Bible—one Hebrew and two Greek—have appeared in English versions as hell.

The Hebrew term, *sheol,* in modern versions is often simply transliterated. Although attitudes toward *sheol* changed over time, all the usages point to the idea of a place under the ground where the shades of the dead reside. The idea probably arose from the practice of burying the bodies of the dead in the ground. The ancient Israelites had no concept of life after death or resurrection* from the dead until quite late in their history. The dead had no life, but something of their former selves had a shadowy existence under the earth.

> **Sheol** beneath is stirred up to meet you when you come; it rouses the shades to greet you, all who were leaders of the earth; it raises from their thrones all who were kings of the nations. All of them will speak and say to you: "You too have become as weak as we! You have become like us!" Your pomp is brought down to **Sheol**, and the sound of your harps; maggots are the bed beneath you, and worms are your covering. [Isaiah 14:9-11]

Sheol also appears in the Hebrew Scriptures as a metaphor for suffering or despair.*

> The snares of death encompassed me; the pangs of **Sheol** laid hold on me; I suffered distress and anguish. [Psalm 116:3]

> You have said, "We have made a covenant with death, and with **Sheol** we have an agreement; when the overwhelming scourge passes through it will not come to us; for we have made lies our refuge, and in falsehood we have taken shelter." [Isaiah 28:15]

> Then Jonah prayed to the LORD his God from the belly of the fish, saying, "I called to the LORD out of my distress, and he answered me; out of the belly of **Sheol** I cried, and you heard my voice." [Jonah 2:1-2]

By the time of Jesus, popular notions about the fate of the dead had evolved under the influence of Greek mythology and the dualistic religions indigenous to the east of Palestine. Greek mythology included *hades,* the place of all who have died. Dualism—imagining good and evil realms in a state of constant warfare—pictured a separation of the dead, the shades of the wicked sent beneath the earth and those of the good lifted to heaven.* This merger of traditions lies behind the use of *hades* in the early Christian writings.

> And you, Capernaum, will you be exalted to heaven? No, you will be brought down to **Hades**. For if the deeds of power done in you had been done in Sodom, it would have remained until this day. [Matthew 11:23]

> The poor man died and was carried away by the angels to be with Abraham. The rich man also died and was buried. In **Hades**, where he was being tormented, he looked up and saw Abraham far away with Lazarus by his side. [Luke 16:22-23]

> For David says concerning him, "I saw the Lord always before me, for he is at my right hand so that I will not be shaken; therefore my heart was glad, and my tongue rejoiced; moreover my flesh will live in hope. For you will not abandon my soul to **Hades**, or let your Holy One experience corruption." [Acts 2:25-27]

Although some English versions of the Bible translate both *sheol* and *hades* as hell, the only biblical word consistently rendered as hell is the Greek *gehenna.* At the time of Jesus, Gehenna—literally the Valley of the Hinnon—was the Jerusalem city dump. In earlier times, this had been a place of human sacrifice to the Canaanite god Moloch.

> You shall not give any of your offspring to sacrifice them to Molech, and so profane the name of your God: I am the LORD. [Leviticus 18:21]

By making the cult site a dumping ground for rubbish, the Judeans had thoroughly desecrated what had once been sacred space, but Gehenna lived on in their writings as a place of torment for great sinners and others who had betrayed their God. In the gospel, several teachings attributed to Jesus mention Gehenna.

> I say to you that if you are angry with a brother or sister, you will be liable to judgment; and if you insult a brother or sister, you will be liable to the council; and if you say, "You fool," you will be liable to the **hell** of fire. [Matthew 5:22]

> If your hand causes you to stumble, cut it off; it is better for you to enter life maimed than to have two hands and to go to **hell,** to the unquenchable fire. And if your foot causes you to stumble, cut it off; it is better for you to enter life lame than to have two feet and to be thrown into **hell.** And if your eye causes you to stumble, tear it out; it is better for you to enter the kingdom of God with one eye than to have two eyes and to be thrown into **hell,** where their worm never dies, and the fire is never quenched. [Mark 9:43-48]

From this distance, no one can say for certain what Jesus had in mind when he spoke of Gehenna. He could have been speaking about a place of future punishment, but his teachings make good sense if he was using Gehenna as a metaphor. His hearers would have been familiar with the characteristics of a garbage dump, the perpetually smoldering fires* and the little organisms that slowly consume the rubbish. People who violate basic principles of responsible behavior can find themselves alienated from society, on the trash heap of life.

Today's followers of Jesus have to decide what to make of the three hell words. They can take all three biblical references to mean the place of the dead, especially the wicked, or they can see them as powerful metaphors. They can take Sheol and Hades as expressions of despair and Gehenna as a vivid image of life gone astray.

heresy, *noun*   Although the English word heresy comes from the Greek *hairesis*, which appears several times in the Bible, the English has lost most of the original meaning of the term. In English, heresy means holding an opinion contrary to the established or orthodox doctrine of the Christian church. *Hairesis* originally meant a choice and evolved to mean that which was chosen, such as a religious party, sect, school, opinion, or faction. In the Acts of the Apostles, *hairesis* is the term used for the Sadducees, the Pharisees, and the Way of Jesus.

> Then the high priest took action; he and all who were with him (that is, the **sect** of the Sadducees), being filled with jealousy, arrested the apostles and put them in the public prison. [Acts 5:17-18]

> They have known for a long time, if they are willing to testify, that I have belonged to the strictest **sect** of our religion and lived as a Pharisee. [Acts 26:5]

> But this I admit to you, that according to the Way, which they call a **sect,** I worship the God of our ancestors, believing everything laid down according to the law or written in the prophets. [Acts 24:14]

In his letters, Paul uses *hairesis* in another way, one with a negative connotation.

> Indeed, there have to be **factions** among you, for only so will it become clear who among you are genuine. [I Corinthians 11:19]

> Now the works of the flesh are obvious: fornication, impurity, licentiousness, idolatry, sorcery, enmities, strife, jealousy, anger, quarrels, dissensions, **factions**, envy, drunkenness, carousing, and things like these. I am warning you, as I warned you before: those who do such things will not inherit the kingdom of God. [Galatians 5:19-21]

In the second letter attributed to Peter, commonly thought to be one of the latest bits to make it into the Christian Bible,* *hairesis* continues to carry a negative connotation.

> But false prophets also arose among the people, just as there will be false teachers among you, who will secretly bring in destructive **opinions**. They will even deny the Master who bought them—bringing swift destruction on themselves. [II Peter 2:1]

Although *hairesis* implied a negative judgment early in the life of the church, it did not imply utter condemnation until the fourth century, when Constantine made Christianity the official religion of the empire. The emperor was not pleased with the great variety of opinions present in the religion he wanted to use as the glue for holding his empire together. When he decided to back the majority present at the Council of Nicea in 315, the views of the party that could not muster enough votes to prevail were labeled heresy.

In 380, Emperor Theodosius I announced that all who were not in agreement with the majority vote were "foolish madmen . . . branded with the ignominious name of heretics." He went on to say, "They will suffer in the first place the chastisement of the divine condemnation, and in the second the punishment which our authority, in accordance with the will of Heaven, shall decide to inflict." In 385, the authorities for the first time executed a Christian, Bishop Abila of Spain, for heresy. From then until the seventeenth century, death was the usual punishment for heresy.

The authorities in various branches of the Christian church, even in the twenty-first century, continue to deal with contrary opinions by labeling them heresies and forcing their proponents out of the church. The church might be a stronger and more trustworthy institution if it could recover the original meaning of the heresy metaphor: that all opinions are to be respected and understood as a matter of choice.

holy, *adjective*; **saints**, *noun* The Hebrew Scriptures contain many stories about people encountering the holy, which in that language is *qadosh*.

> When the LORD saw that he had turned aside to see, God called to him out of the bush, "Moses, Moses!" And he said, "Here I am." Then he said, "Come no closer! Remove the sandals from your feet, for the place on which you are standing is **holy** ground." [Exodus 3:4-5]

> In the year that King Uzziah died, I saw the Lord sitting on a throne, high and lofty; and the hem of his robe filled the temple. Seraphs were in attendance above him; each had six wings: with two they covered their faces, and with two they covered their feet, and with two they flew. And one called to another and said: "**Holy, holy, holy** is the LORD of hosts; the whole earth is full of his glory." [Isaiah 6:1-3]

> Once when Joshua was by Jericho, he looked up and saw a man standing before him with a drawn sword in his hand. Joshua went to him and said to him, "Are you one of us, or one of our adversaries?" He replied, "Neither; but as commander of the army of the LORD I have now come."

> And Joshua fell on his face to the earth and worshiped, and he said to him, "What do you command your servant, my lord?" The commander of the army of the LORD said to Joshua, "Remove the sandals from your feet, for the place where you stand is **holy**." And Joshua did so. [Joshua 5:13-15]

Often for people in these early times, religion* was literally a falling down in fear before what they believed to be the divine presence. As places came to be set aside for worship, they partook of the holy quality. As the leaders of worship came to set aside instruments and other things to be used in the cult rituals, these also were thought to be holy. Finally, the people who had entered into the awesome yet beckoning experience of the terrible mystery were themselves called holy. (For another understanding of holy people, see also **sodomite**.)

> The LORD is in his **holy** temple; let all the earth keep silence before him! [Habakkuk 2:20]

> You shall say to the Israelites, "This shall be my **holy** anointing oil throughout your generations. It shall not be used in any ordinary anointing of the body, and you shall make no other like it in composition; it is holy, and it shall be **holy** to you." [Exodus 30:31-32]

> Thus shall Aaron come into the **holy** place: with a young bull for a sin offering and a ram for a burnt offering. He shall put on the holy linen tunic, and shall have the linen undergarments next to his body, fasten the linen sash, and wear the linen turban; these are the **holy** vestments. [Leviticus 16:3-4]

> The LORD will establish you as his **holy** people, as he has sworn to you, if you keep the commandments of the LORD your God and walk in his ways. [Deuteronomy 28:9]

In the Greek Scriptures, *hagios* is used in much the same way as *qadosh* in the examples above, but the word most often appears in conjunction with words such as spirit,* angels,* or prophets.

> If you then, who are evil, know how to give good gifts to your children, how much more will the heavenly Father give the **Holy** Spirit to those who ask him! [Luke 11:13]

> Those who are ashamed of me and of my words in this adulterous and sinful generation, of them the Son of Man will also be ashamed when he comes in the glory of his Father with the **holy** angels. [Mark 8:38]

> This is now, beloved, the second letter I am writing to you; in them I am trying to arouse your sincere intention by reminding you that you should remember the words spoken in the past by the **holy** prophets, and the commandment of the Lord and Savior spoken through your apostles. [II Peter 3:1-2]

What is not so obvious, however, is the frequency with which *hagios* refers to people. In most of these instances, the plural form is translated saints.

> Ananias answered, "Lord, I have heard from many about this man, how much evil he has done to your **saints** in Jerusalem; and here he has authority from the chief priests to bind all who invoke your name." [Acts 9:13-14]

> To all God's beloved in Rome, who are called to be **saints**: Grace to you and peace from God our Father and the Lord Jesus Christ. [Romans 1:7]

To use saints, from the Latin *sanctus*, instead of holy ones obscures the connection between the various usages of the holy metaphor. The metaphor has the most power when the users understand that the saints, the holy ones, are those people who are willing to affirm both their fascination and their terror in the face of the terrible mystery of life and death.

Switching to a Latin-based word also obscures all the connections with other Anglo-Saxon words that come from the same root as holy: whole, hale, health, and, of course, ale. A holy one is an individual who is not only open to the mystery, but one who is also on the way to fulfillment as a whole person. In Celtic and Anglo-Saxons lands, those Christians known to subsequent generations as saints were not necessarily sweet or gentle but were remembered for their wisdom and the guidance they had offered ordinary people who were coping with the issues of everyday life.

The concept of holiness has its roots in the fear of the unknown. Rudolph Otto,[12] one of the most influential thinkers about religion in the first half of the twentieth century, identified an experience of the holy with what he called an encounter with *mysterium tremendum*. The encounter provokes terror because *mysterium tremendum* presents itself as overwhelming power as well as what is merciful and gracious. As nearly as anyone can tell, the first human beings stood in awe of the terrible mystery of life and death* and of the powers of nature. At the same time, they were fascinated by what struck such terrible fear* in their hearts. This double-sided experience, being in terror and being beckoned, is the nature of an encounter with the holy.

Holy Spirit, *noun*   Since ancient times, spirit* had been understood as one of the manifestations of God.* Equally established in tradition was the association of holy* with the divine presence. Since people perceived all kinds of spirits around them, it is not surprising that, in time, someone identified the spirit of God as the holy spirit. The term appears three times in the Hebrew Scriptures.

> Do not cast me away from your presence, and do not take your **holy spirit** from me. [Psalm 51:11]

> They rebelled and grieved his **holy spirit**; therefore he became their enemy; he himself fought against them. Then they remembered the days of old, of Moses his servant. Where is the one who brought them up out of the sea with the shepherds of his flock? Where is the one who put within them his **holy spirit**. [Isaiah 63:10-11]

By the time that the followers of Jesus began putting their thoughts into written form, Holy Spirit had evolved to be the name for God's primary agent in the world. The Gospel according to John uses the term three times, Mark four, and Matthew five. Luke outdoes the others by using the term thirteen times in his gospel* and forty-one times in the Acts of the Apostles. The term also crops up in many of the epistles. None of the writers, however, equates Holy Spirit with God. That was a post-biblical development. A few examples illustrate how the followers of Jesus used the Holy Spirit metaphor in making sense out of their experience.

> Now the birth of Jesus the Messiah took place in this way. When his mother Mary had been engaged to Joseph, but before they lived together, she was found to be with child from the **Holy Spirit**. [Matthew 1:18]

> When they bring you to trial and hand you over, do not worry beforehand about what you are to say; but say whatever is given you at that time, for it is not you who speak, but the **Holy Spirit**. [Mark 13:11]

> Now when all the people were baptized, and when Jesus also had been baptized and was praying, the heaven was opened, and the **Holy Spirit** descended upon him in bodily form like a dove.

Marks a word in the text that has its own entry

> And a voice came from heaven, "You are my Son, the Beloved; with you I am well pleased." [Luke 3:21-22]

> I have said these things to you while I am still with you. But the Advocate, the **Holy Spirit**, whom the Father will send in my name, will teach you everything, and remind you of all that I have said to you. [John 14:25-26]

> When they had prayed, the place in which they were gathered together was shaken; and they were all filled with the **Holy Spirit** and spoke the word of God with boldness. [Acts 4:31]

> May the God of hope fill you with all joy and peace in believing, so that you may abound in hope by the power of the **Holy Spirit**. [Romans 15:13]

Holy Spirit was such a popular metaphor among Jesus followers that, by the fourth century, many were using the term to refer not simply to an agent of God but to the Lord God of Israel, the God and Father of Jesus Christ. This evolution of the holy spirit metaphor coincided with the gradual development of the son* of God metaphor to the point at which some Christians thought of Jesus as God. Slowly, the three most common metaphors for God had so merged in the minds of some Christians that they wanted to make logical, literal sense of the terms. The result of this process was the formulation of the idea of Trinity, which was more literal than logical. God was supposed to be three—Father, Son, and Holy Spirit—yet still one God. The Council of Nicaea in 325 codified this formula, but the appearance of worshiping three Gods alienated many of the faithful and made Christianity vulnerable to the advances of Islam with its doctrine of radical monotheism.

Holy Spirit as a metaphor conveys valuable insights about the way human beings experience God—as an unseen, empowering presence.

homosexual   The words homosexual and homosexuality do not appear in most English translations of the Bible. The Bible has nothing to say about homosexual orientation or about committed homosexual relationships. If Jesus had anything to say on the subject of people being attracted to those of the same sex, nobody bothered to record his words. Through a misunderstanding of the story about the unsavory behavior of the men of Sodom found in Genesis 19:4-5 and the mistranslation of a Hebrew word that the King James Version renders Sodomite,* some Christians have come to the conclusion that the Bible was more concerned about same-sex relationships than it actually is. Having set aside these questionable references to homosexuality, the student of the Bible is left with only five passages that mention homosexual behavior.

The only two verses in the Hebrew Scripture that refer to homosexual acts appear in the Holiness Code.

> You shall not lie with a male as with a woman; it is an abomination. [Leviticus 18:22]

> If a man lies with a male as with a woman, both of them have committed an abomination; they shall be put to death; their blood is upon them. [Leviticus 20:13]

The Holiness Code, found in Leviticus 17-26, outlines the behavior expected of the people of Israel to keep themselves separate from the Canaanites and Egyptians. The code covers such areas as diet, proper rituals for sacrifice, religious duties, the obligations of the priests, and the celebration of festivals. The code strictly forbids the participation of the people of Israel in the worship of the local fertility gods. Their sense of identity depended on their differentiating themselves from their neighbors whose religious practices included participation in fertility cults where worship may have included sexual intercourse with the same as well as the opposite sex. The Holiness Code taught that to the God of Israel such conduct was an abomination.* The language of the two verses and their position in the Holiness Code indicate that certain homosexual acts, along with certain heterosexual acts, were proscribed because of ritual as well as moral concerns.

The remaining three passages appear in letters to early Christian communities. The most lengthy passage occurs at the beginning of Paul's letter to the Romans. The context makes clear that his concern was similar to that of the priests who wrote the ancient Holiness Code. He did not want the followers of Jesus participating in the fertility cults that were everywhere abundant and enticing, so he tries to point out the self-destructive tendencies of people who worship in the temples of the cults where the idols could be in the form of humans, birds, animals, or reptiles.

> Claiming to be wise, they became fools; and they exchanged the glory of the immortal God for images resembling a mortal human being or birds or four-footed animals or reptiles. Therefore God gave them up in the lusts of their hearts to impurity, to the degrading of their bodies among themselves, because they exchanged the truth about God for a lie and worshiped and served the creature rather than the Creator, who is blessed forever! Amen. For this reason God gave them up to degrading passions. Their women exchanged natural intercourse for unnatural, and in the same way also the men, giving up natural intercourse with women, were consumed with passion for one another. Men committed shameless acts with men and received in their own persons the due penalty for their error. And since they did not see fit to acknowledge God, God gave them up to a debased mind and to things that should not be done. [Romans 1:22-28]

Then as now, the primary substitute for the worship of God was the pursuit of sexual satisfaction. Both promise deliverance from isolation and emptiness, but the satisfaction that comes from casual sexual encounters tends to be of short duration. As Paul wrote, those who pursue sex as a form of religion can easily find themselves debased and miserable, but that reality has nothing to do with homosexual orientation or stable homosexual relationships. Paul's observations are as true for heterosexual people as for gays and lesbians, as can be seen from the second passage—a list of people who have put themselves outside of God's realm.

> Do you not know that wrongdoers will not inherit the kingdom of God? Do not be deceived! Fornicators, idolaters, adulterers, **male prostitutes, sodomites**, thieves, the greedy, drunkards, revilers, robbers—none of these will inherit the kingdom of God. [I Corinthians 6:9-10]

In this list, two of the ten categories refer to homosexual practice. The first, *malakoi* in Greek and here translated male prostitutes, refers to passive homosexuality. As an adjective, it originally meant soft and then, by derivation, effeminate. In the literature of the time, it was used especially for catamites, men and boys who allowed themselves to be used by men for sex, most often for money. The second, inappropriately translated sodomite, in Paul's Greek was *arsenokoitai*. This word generally refers to men who used, and frequently abused, the *malakoi*. This pair of words, indicating those whose behavior Paul condemns, clearly says nothing about relationships between equals of the same sex any more than the mention of fornicators and adulterers suggests that he condemned stable relationships between those of opposite sexes.

The final passage, from a letter attributed to Paul, but probably not by him, is also a list of people whose behavior is unacceptable. Once again, in a long list, sodomite appears as the translation for *arsenokoitai.*

Marks a word in the text that has its own entry

> This means understanding that the law is laid down not for the innocent but for the lawless and disobedient, for the godless and sinful, for the unholy and profane, for those who kill their father or mother, for murderers, fornicators, **sodomites**, slave traders, liars, perjurers, and whatever else is contrary to the sound teaching. [I Timothy 1:9-10]

In summary, it is safe to say that while the people who wrote and edited the Bible probably were opposed to homosexual practices, most of them had no interest in the subject. In the five passages where homosexuality is mentioned, the primary concern seems to be for sex used as a substitute for God. Perhaps the five passages are useful in that they provide a worthwhile warning for today's sex-obsessed culture. Whether these five verses, however, provide an adequate basis for condemning all homosexual relationships has been the subject of heated debate in recent times.

honor, *verb* and *noun*   In Hebrew, the words most often translated as honor are *kabad* and *kabod*, both of which evolved from *kabed*, the liver. Anyone involved in slaughtering animals could see that the liver was the most dense, the weightiest of the entrails. To honor, then, meant to treat as a weighty matter a relationship to one's parents, to other people, or to God.

> **Honor** your father and your mother, so that your days may be long in the land that the LORD your God is giving you. [Exodus 20:12]

> Like snow in summer or rain in harvest, so **honor** is not fitting for a fool. [Proverbs 26:1]

> Therefore the LORD the God of Israel declares: "I promised that your family and the family of your ancestor should go in and out before me forever"; but now the LORD declares: "Far be it from me; for those who **honor** me I will **honor**, and those who despise me shall be treated with contempt." [I Samuel 2:30]

Another Hebrew word sometimes translated as honor, *yeqar*, also originally meant heavy but became a metaphor indicating value or wealth.

> So Haman said to the king, "For the man whom the king wishes to **honor**, let royal robes be brought, which the king has worn, and a horse that the king has ridden, with a royal crown on its head." [Esther 6:7-8]

The Greek verb meaning to honor, *timao*, appears frequently in ancient documents related to jewelry transactions. Similar in use to the Hebrew *yaqar*, it meant to place a high value on something. As a metaphor, it could mean to place a high value on one's parents, other people, or God.

> "**Honor** your father and mother"—this is the first commandment with a promise: "so that it may be well with you and you may live long on the earth." [Ephesians 6:2-3]

> **Honor** widows who are really widows. [I Timothy 5:3]

> The Father judges no one but has given all judgment to the Son, so that all may **honor** the Son just as they **honor** the Father. Anyone who does not **honor** the Son does not **honor** the Father who sent him. [John 5:22-23]

The original metaphors of weight and value do not carry several of the connotations related to the English word honor, such as an allegiance to what is morally right or virtuous, a reputation for chastity and purity, or a form of address indicating title or rank. To understand the biblical concepts, a present-day reader must put aside the accumulated associations with honor and get back to the liver and to jewelry transactions.

For example, the commandment to honor one's parents in ancient Israel may have been a break with custom among nomadic tribes, leaving the old people alongside the trail to die when they could no longer keep up with the others. It was not to be so among the Israelites. Their responsibility for their parents was to be a weighty matter. The author of the letter to the Ephesians understood the implications. Jesus's followers were to treat their parents as being people of great value, no matter what their age or abilities. In much the same way, the ancient honor metaphors can illuminate the nature of relationships among people and with God.

hope, *verb* and *noun*   At least seven Hebrew words have been translated as hope. Two are based on the root word *qavah*, which originally meant to bind together. *Qavah* became a metaphor used when the meaning was to expect, to look for, to wait for, or to hope. The two words that evolved from this root are *tiqvah* and *miqveh*. Two other words, *yachal* and *tocheleth*, stressed the idea of waiting, while *seber* emerged from the idea of watchful waiting. *Bittachon* emphasized trust. All seven words could be used to indicate either a desire for a stated objective or a feeling of trust, confidence. The same possibilities were present in the Greek verb *elpizo* and the noun *elpis*, both based on the root *elpo*, which meant to anticipate with pleasure.

First, a few examples when these words are translated as hope and used in the sense of a desire for a particular result.

> Turn back, my daughters, go your way, for I am too old to have a husband. Even if I thought there was **hope** for me, even if I should have a husband tonight and bear sons, would you then wait until they were grown?—*tiqvah* [Ruth 1:12-13]

> Lay hands on Leviathon; think of the battle; you will not do it again! Any **hope** of capturing it will be disappointed; were not even the gods overwhelmed at the sight of it?—*tocheleth* [Job 41:8-9]

> I do not want to see you now just in passing, for I **hope** to spend some time with you, if the Lord permits.—*elpizo* [I Corinthians 16:7]

> When her owners saw that their **hope** of making money was gone, they seized Paul and Silas and dragged them into the marketplace before the authorities.—*elpis* [Acts 16:19]

When such words are used without a stated objective, they often are an expression of trust or confidence in God's good will.

> Can any idols of the nations bring rain? Or can the heavens give showers? Is it not you, O LORD our God? We set our **hope** on you, for it is you who do all this.—*qavah* [Jeremiah 14:22]

> So the poor have **hope**, and injustice shuts its mouth.—*tiqvah* [Job 5:16]

> Let your steadfast love, O LORD, be upon us, even as we **hope** in you.—*yachal* [Psalm 33:22]

> Happy are those whose help is the God of Jacob, whose **hope** is in the LORD their God, who made heaven and earth, the sea, and all that is in them; who keeps faith forever.—*seber* [Psalm 146:5-6]

> The **hope** of the righteous ends in gladness, but the expectation of the wicked comes to nothing.—*tocheleth* [Proverbs 10:28]

Whoever is joined with all the living has **hope**, for a living dog is better than a dead lion.—*bittachon* [Ecclesiastes 9:4]

O **hope** of Israel! O LORD! All who forsake you shall be put to shame; those who turn away from you shall be recorded in the underworld, for they have forsaken the fountain of living water, the LORD.—*miqveh* [Jeremiah 17:13]

Here is my servant, whom I have chosen, my beloved, with whom my soul is well pleased. I will put my Spirit upon him, and he will proclaim justice to the Gentiles. He will not wrangle or cry aloud, nor will anyone hear his voice in the streets. He will not break a bruised reed or quench a smoldering wick until he brings justice to victory. And in his name the Gentiles will **hope**.—*elpizo* [Matthew 12:18-21]

Now faith is the assurance of things **hoped** for, the conviction of things not seen.—*elpizo* [Hebrews 11:1]

And not only that, but we also boast in our sufferings, knowing that suffering produces endurance, and endurance produces character, and character produces **hope**, and **hope** does not disappoint us, because God's love has been poured into our hearts through the Holy Spirit that has been given to us.—*elpis* [Romans 5:3-5]

For the hope to be a useful concept, people need to be aware that the two possible meanings are easily confused. The practical, everyday meaning of a desire for a particular outcome can get mixed up with religious meaning of trust or confidence in God. The first can produce disappointment when circumstances fail to satisfy the desire. Hope in the religious sense cannot disappoint because it does not depend on future circumstances. In this second sense, hope is a present experience of waiting with patient expectation.

If hope for particular results becomes part of a person's religion*—be it hope for wealth, health, or approval—the person suffers more than disappointment if the results are not forthcoming. Such a person also loses a sense of God's presence and may no longer look to the future with eager anticipation. The other kind of hope may not come easily, but it can be cultivated. A person can choose to live in hope through all the changes and chances of this life.

house, *noun*   Of all the metaphors in the Bible, house is perhaps the most common and the most versatile. As a result of the various connotations, a passage like this one is subject to interpretation:

In my Father's **house** there are many dwelling places [many mansions, in the KING JAMES VERSION]. If it were not so, would I have told you that I go to prepare a place for you?—*oikia* [John 14:2]

Seeing these words, which the gospel according to John attributes to Jesus, few people would take literally house as meaning a building for human occupation. Many suppose that house as a metaphor indicates a dwelling place for the dead, but the use of the metaphor in the Hebrew Scriptures suggests other possibilities. The words for house in Hebrew, *beth,* and in Greek, *oikia* and *oikos,* have similar uses as figurative language.

(*Note:* In Medieval theater, craft and trade guilds performed liturgical dramas on the steps or the porch of a church. Across the acting area, they placed a number of booths representing specific locations, with Hell's Mouth and Heaven's Gate at opposite ends. These booths were known as mansions. The actors would move from mansion to mansion as the play demanded. The area in front of and between the mansions was neutral and was presumed to be part of whichever mansion

Marks a word in the text that has its own entry

was being featured. The translators of the King James Version would have been familiar with this practice.[13])

More often than not, *beth* is translated as house or home and clearly refers to a building where a person or a family* lives. When *beth* is being used as a metaphor, however, the New Revised Standard Version may use house or another word that clarifies the meaning of the metaphor.

beth as a group of related people

Tell the whole congregation of Israel that on the tenth of this month they are to take a lamb for each **family,** a lamb for each **household.** [Exodus 12:3]

Now Sisera had fled away on foot to the tent of Jael wife of Heber the Kenite; for there was peace between King Jabin of Hazor and the **clan** of Heber the Kenite. [Judges 4:17]

A man from each tribe shall be with you, each man the head of his ancestral **house.**
[Numbers 1:4]

For the cloud of the LORD was on the tabernacle by day, and fire was in the cloud by night, before the eyes of all the **house** of Israel at each stage of their journey. [Exodus 40:38]

And he said, "Hear my words: When there are prophets among you, I the LORD make myself known to them in visions; I speak to them in dreams. Not so with my servant Moses; he is entrusted with all my **house.**" [Numbers 12:6-7]

beth as a space with a specific use

So the Philistines seized Samson and gouged out his eyes. They brought him down to Gaza and bound him with bronze shackles; and he ground at the mill in the **prison.** [Judges 16:21]

At midnight the LORD struck down all the firstborn in the land of Egypt, from the firstborn of Pharaoh who sat on his throne to the firstborn of the prisoner who was in the **dungeon,** and all the firstborn of the livestock. [Exodus 12:29]

Then King Darius made a decree, and they searched the **archives** where the documents were stored in Babylon. [Ezra 6:1]

Let the cost be paid from the royal **treasury.** [Ezra 6:4]

Every day Mordecai would walk around in front of the court of the **harem,** to learn how Esther was and how she fared. [Esther 2:11]

Hezekiah welcomed them; he showed them his treasure **house,** the silver, the gold, the spices, the precious oil, his whole **armory.** [Isaiah 39:2]

beth as a safe place

"Send, therefore, and have your livestock and everything that you have in the open field brought to a **secure place;** every human or animal that is in the open field and is not brought under **shelter** will die when the hail comes down upon them." Those officials of Pharaoh who feared the word of the LORD hurried their slaves and livestock off to a **secure place.** [Exodus 9:19-20]

Incline your ear to me; rescue me speedily. Be a rock of refuge for me, a strong **fortress** to save me. [Psalm 31:2]

---

beth as a holy place

Jacob was afraid, and said, "How awesome is this place! This is none other than the **house** of God, and this is the gate of heaven." [Genesis 28:17]

The choicest of the first fruits of your ground you shall bring into the **house** of the LORD your God. [Exodus 23:19]

These I will bring to my holy mountain, and make them joyful in my **house** of prayer; their burnt offerings and their sacrifices will be accepted on my altar; for my **house** shall be called a **house** of prayer for all peoples. [Isaiah 56:7]

They gave him seventy pieces of silver out of the **temple** of Baal-berith with which Abimelech hired worthless and reckless fellows, who followed him. [Judges 9:4]

The LORD said to me: Mortal, mark well, look closely, and listen attentively to all that I shall tell you concerning all the ordinances of the **temple** of the LORD and all its laws. [Ezekiel 44:5]

This man Micah had a **shrine**, and he made an ephod and teraphim, and installed one of his sons, who became his priest. [Judges 17:5]

beth as bondage

When in the future your child asks you, "What does this mean?" you shall answer, "By strength of hand the LORD brought us out of Egypt, from the **house** of slavery." [Exodus 13:14]

Like *beth* in the Hebrew Scriptures, *oikos* and *oikia* in the Greek portions of the Bible usually are translated as house or home and clearly refer to buildings where a person or a family lives. When appearing as metaphors, they also sometimes are expressed by other words. Originally the two Greek words for house had slightly different meanings. *Oikos* referred to the whole estate while *oikia* meant simply a dwelling place. By the time of Jesus, however, the distinction seems to have been forgotten.

oikos/oikia as a group of related people

In the sixth month the angel Gabriel was sent by God to a town in Galilee called Nazareth, to a virgin engaged to a man whose name was Joseph, of the **house** of David.—*oikos* [Luke 1:26-27]

Therefore let the entire **house** of Israel know with certainty that God has made him both Lord and Messiah, this Jesus whom you crucified.—*oikos* [Acts 2:36]

The father realized that this was the hour when Jesus had said to him, "Your son will live." So he himself believed, along with his whole **household**.—*oikia* [John 4:53]

They must be silenced, since they are upsetting whole **families** by teaching for sordid gain what it is not right to teach.—*oikia* [Titus 1:11]

If I am delayed, you may know how one ought to behave in the **household** of God, which is the church of the living God, the pillar and bulwark of the truth.—*oikos* [I Timothy 3:15]

Now Moses was faithful in all God's **house** as a servant, to testify to the things that would be spoken later.—*oikos* [Hebrews 3:5]

Like living stones, let yourselves be built into a spiritual **house**, to be a holy priesthood, to offer spiritual sacrifices acceptable to God through Jesus Christ.—*oikos* [I Peter 2:5]

oikos/oikia as a holy place

David entered the **house** of God and ate the bread of the Presence, which it was not lawful for him or his companions to eat, but only for the priests.—*oikos* [Matthew 12:4]

This generation may be charged with the blood of all the prophets shed since the foundation of the world, from the blood of Abel to the blood of Zechariah, who perished between the altar and the **sanctuary**.—*oikos* [Luke 11:50-51]

Jesus told those who were selling the doves, "Take these things out of here! Stop making my Father's **house** a marketplace!"—*oikos* [John 2:16]

oikos/oikia as a human body

When the unclean spirit has gone out of a person, it wanders through waterless regions looking for a resting place, but not finding any, it says, "I will return to my **house** from which I came." —*oikos* [Luke 11:24]

For we know that if the earthly **tent** we live in is destroyed, we have a building from God, a **house** not made with hands, eternal in the heavens.—*oikia* [II Corinthians 5:1]

From this review of the house metaphor in the Bible, it should be obvious that when John has Jesus refer to his father's* house with many dwelling places, the house intended might not be a place for the dead. If the father's house is taken to be a physical structure, this saying could be a reference to the temple in Jerusalem, but it seems unlikely that John thought Jesus was preparing the temple as a place where his followers one day would reside. The other possibility is that house is being used as a group of related people, the whole people of God,* as above in Numbers 12:6-7, I Timothy 3:15, Hebrews 3:5, and I Peter 2:5. If John understood Jesus correctly, perhaps Jesus was preparing the way for his followers to find a place to live out their lives among God's people.

If John was using the house metaphor in one of its most common applications, a group of related people, the father's house with many dwelling places may be the most radically inclusive statement in the gospels. Jesus was making room for his followers among all the other people in God's household. For some, that interpretation of the house metaphor contradicts the exclusive sounding pronouncement that follows a few verses later.

Jesus said, "I am the way, and the truth, and the life. No one comes to the Father except through me." [John 14:6]

John may have thought that the only way* to God was through Jesus and that anyone who did not follow Jesus could not be part of the father's household. Or John may have intended his readers to see this statement as a song of praise expressing his faith and the faith of his community. Jesus was the only way for them to find a place among God's people. When they found their place, they would also realize that among God's people were those who had found their places in God's household by following different ways.

husband—see marriage

hypocrite, *noun* Although the English word hypocrite comes directly from the Greek *hypokrites*, scholars disagree about the meaning of the word in the teachings attributed to Jesus. The majority hold to the classical understanding that the word came from *hypokrinomai*, which

---

originally meant to pretend or act. Actors performed under masks to distinguish the characters they portrayed, hence the word *hypo*, under + *krino*, distinguish, separate, or judge. In this understanding, hypocrites are dissemblers, imposters, phonies. Some scholars, however, say that in the time of Jesus the word had a different meaning, not at all connected with classical Greek. *Hypo* could also mean by, indicating a cause or agent. In this understanding, a hypocrite is someone who lives by making judgments about all things large and small, who is guilty of scrupulosity—a petty fogger, hair-splitter or nitpicker. Whichever definition may be correct, if Jesus called his listeners hypocrites, he was not passing out compliments.

> "So whenever you give alms, do not sound a trumpet before you, as the **hypocrites** do in the synagogues and in the streets, so that they may be praised by others. Truly I tell you, they have received their reward . . . And whenever you pray, do not be like the **hypocrites**; for they love to stand and pray in the synagogues and at the street corners, so that they may be seen by others. Truly I tell you, they have received their reward. [Matthew 6:2, 5]

> "Woe to you, scribes and Pharisees, **hypocrites**! For you tithe mint, dill, and cummin, and have neglected the weightier matters of the law: justice and mercy and faith. It is these you ought to have practiced without neglecting the others." [Matthew 23:23]

> So the Pharisees and the scribes asked him, "Why do your disciples not live according to the tradition of the elders, but eat with defiled hands?" He said to them, "Isaiah prophesied rightly about you **hypocrites**, as it is written, 'This people honors me with their lips, but their hearts are far from me; in vain do they worship me, teaching human precepts as doctrines.'" [Mark 7:5-7]

> "How can you say to your neighbor, 'Friend, let me take out the speck in your eye,' when you yourself do not see the log in your own eye? You **hypocrite**, first take the log out of your own eye, and then you will see clearly to take the speck out of your neighbor's eye." [Luke 6:42]

> The leader of the synagogue, indignant because Jesus had cured on the sabbath, kept saying to the crowd, "There are six days on which work ought to be done; come on those days and be cured, and not on the sabbath day." But the Lord answered him and said, "You **hypocrites**! Does not each of you on the sabbath untie his ox or his donkey from the manger, and lead it away to give it water? And ought not this woman, a daughter of Abraham whom Satan bound for eighteen long years, be set free from this bondage on the sabbath day?" [Luke 13:14-16]

The use of *hypokrites* attributed to Jesus might well reflect the attitudes of his followers at a later time when their writings took on a polemical tone in their attempts to discredit the Jews* with whom they were competing for converts among the Gentiles. At any rate, the word used as a metaphor suggesting either hair splitting or play acting can underscore the destructive nature of certain attitudes and actions.

I

idol, idolatry, idolater, *nouns*   The religions* with whom the people of Israel were competing had representations of their gods in shrines and in temples as a focus for worship.* One way the Israelites had of maintaining their identity was to be different. They did not allow the making of an idol, *tselem,* let alone the using of one as an aid to devotion.

> You shall not make for yourself an **idol**, whether in the form of anything that is in heaven above, or that is on the earth beneath, or that is in the water under the earth. [Exodus 20:4]

> You shall make for yourselves no **idols** and erect no carved images or pillars, and you shall not place figured stones in your land, to worship at them; for I am the LORD your God. [Leviticus 26:1]

In order to strengthen the loyalty of the faltering, some of the prophets heaped ridicule on the religious practices of their neighbors.

> What use is an **idol** once its maker has shaped it—a cast image, a teacher of lies? For its maker trusts in what has been made, though the product is only an idol that cannot speak! Alas for you who say to the wood, "Wake up!" to silent stone, "Rouse yourself!" Can it teach? See, it is gold and silver plated, and there is no breath in it at all. [Habakkuk 2:18-19]

Another way they showed their contempt for other religions was to call their images *elil*, good for nothing, which is the word for idol in these passages from Isaiah.

> Their land is filled with **idols**; they bow down to the work of their hands, to what their own fingers have made. [Isaiah 2:8]

> An oracle concerning Egypt. See, the LORD is riding on a swift cloud and comes to Egypt; the **idols** of Egypt will tremble at his presence, and the heart of the Egyptians will melt within them. [Isaiah 19:1]

The book Deuteronomy, which reflects an attempt by the priests in Jerusalem to wrest control of religion away from the cult sites scattered about the countryside, has three other, less-than-complimentary terms for images used in worship. *Pesel* was anything carved in wood or stone. *Gillul* was something round, like a log. *Hebel* meant emptiness or nothingness.

> When you have had children and children's children, and become complacent in the land, if you act corruptly by making an **idol** in the form of anything, thus doing what is evil in the sight of the LORD your God, and provoking him to anger, I call heaven and earth to witness against you today that you will soon utterly perish from the land that you are crossing the Jordan to occupy; you will not live long on it, but will be utterly destroyed.—*pesel* [Deuteronomy 4:25-26]

> You know how we lived in the land of Egypt, and how we came through the midst of the nations through which you passed. You have seen their detestable things, the filthy **idols** of wood and stone, of silver and gold, that were among them.—*gillul* [Deuteronomy 29:16-17]

> They made me jealous with what is no god, provoked me with their **idols**. So I will make them jealous with what is no people, provoke them with a foolish nation.—*hebel* [Deuteronomy 32:21]

The reason for the continuous denunciation of idols over a long period of Israel's history should be obvious. In times of distress, the people wanted a concrete focus for their worship. The Hebrew Scriptures give ample evidence of the continuing fascination of idols for the people of Israel.

> Then the Danites set up the **idol** for themselves. Jonathan son of Gershom, son of Moses, and his sons were priests to the tribe of the Danites until the time the land went into captivity. —*pesel* [Judges 18:30]

> Asa did what was right in the sight of the Lord, as his father David had done. He put away the male temple prostitutes out of the land, and removed all the **idols** that his ancestors had made.—*gillul* [I Kings 15:11-12]

> Israel served **idols,** of which the Lord had said to them, "You shall not do this."—*gillul* [II Kings 17:12]

> As my hand has reached to the kingdoms of the idols whose images were greater than those of Jerusalem and Samaria, shall I not do to Jerusalem and her **idols** what I have done to Samaria and her images?—*elil* [Isaiah 10:10-11]

The followers of Jesus used the same strategy as the people of Israel in their competition with other religions. They called an image used in worship *eidolon,* which often carried the connotation of a phantom or fantasy. They were as adept as the Israelites in heaping contempt on anyone who was an idolater, *eidololatres,* or whose worship involved idolatry, *eidololatria.*

> Hence, as to the eating of food offered to idols, we know that "no **idol** in the world really exists," and that "there is no God but one." [I Corinthians 8:4]

> What agreement has the temple of God with **idols**? For we are the temple of the living God; as God said, "I will live in them and walk among them, and I will be their God, and they shall be my people. Therefore come out from them, and be separate from them, says the Lord, and touch nothing unclean; then I will welcome you, and I will be your father, and you shall be my sons and daughters, says the Lord Almighty." [II Corinthians 6:16-18]

> For the word of the Lord has sounded forth from you not only in Macedonia and Achaia, but in every place your faith in God has become known, so that we have no need to speak about it. For the people of those regions report about us what kind of welcome we had among you, and how you turned to God from **idols,** to serve a living and true God, and to wait for his Son from heaven, whom he raised from the dead—Jesus, who rescues us from the wrath that is coming. [I Thessalonians 1:8-10]

> Now the works of the flesh are obvious: fornication, impurity, licentiousness, **idolatry,** sorcery, enmities, strife, jealousy, anger, quarrels, dissensions, factions, envy, drunkenness, carousing, and things like these. I am warning you, as I warned you before: those who do such things will not inherit the kingdom of God. [Galatians 5:19-21]

> Be sure of this, that no fornicator or impure person, or one who is greedy (that is, an **idolater**), has any inheritance in the kingdom of Christ and of God. [Ephesians 5:5]

Although the Christians adopted the strategy of ancient Israel in dealing with religious rivals, they were more flexible in responding to the desire for a visual focus for worship. In time they approved the use of images, but a Christian image was not called an *eidolon* but an *eikon.* Although paintings or sculptures as aides to Christian devotion are not mentioned in the Bible, the word *eikon* does appear, usually with neutral or positive connotations.

> They came and said to him, "Teacher, we know that you are sincere, and show deference to no one; for you do not regard people with partiality, but teach the way of God in accordance with truth. Is it lawful to pay taxes to the emperor, or not? Should we pay them, or should we not?" But knowing their hypocrisy, he said to them, "Why are you putting me to the test? Bring me a denarius and let me see it." And they brought one. Then he said to them, "Whose **head** is this, and whose title?" They answered, "The emperor's." [Mark 12:14-16]

> The Father has rescued us from the power of darkness and transferred us into the kingdom of his beloved Son, in whom we have redemption, the forgiveness of sins. He is the **image** of the invisible God, the firstborn of all creation. [Colossians 1:13-15]

Muslims, Jews, and Christians have often banded together in dismissing the indigenous religions of Asia, Africa, and the Pacific Rim as idolatrous. At the same time, art dealers in the predominantly monotheistic cultures have traded in stolen religious images, calling them native works of art.

Using the idol metaphor as way of showing contempt for other religious traditions may have been a justifiable strategy in the past, but it may not be appropriate in a pluralistic society. To put aside the metaphor, however, would leave a gap in religious language. Idolatry has been a useful metaphor in identifying unhealthy substitutes for God—such as money, possessions, and social status.

instruct, *verb*; **instruction**, *noun*   Both the Hebrew and the Greek languages provide a rich variety of metaphors that often appear in English Bibles as instruct or instruction. These images suggest a wide range of connotations associated with religious instruction.

Some of the metaphors indicate that instruction is the passing along of important information.

> The sons of Israel did so. Joseph gave them wagons according to the **instruction** of Pharaoh, and he gave them provisions for the journey.—*peh*, mouth [Genesis 45:21]

> So David went up following Gad's **instructions**, which he had spoken in the name of the LORD.—*dabar*, word* [I Chronicles 21:19]

> And those who err in spirit will come to understanding, and those who grumble will accept **instruction**.—*leqach*, take or receive [Isaiah 29:24]

> These twelve Jesus sent out with the following **instructions**: "Go nowhere among the Gentiles, and enter no town of the Samaritans, but go rather to the lost sheep of the house of Israel."—*parangello*, send a message, from *para*, with + *angelos*, messenger or angel* [Matthew 10:5-6]

> I too decided, after investigating everything carefully from the very first, to write an orderly account for you, most excellent Theophilus, so that you may know the truth concerning the things about which you have been **instructed**.—*katecheo*, make a sound down into the ears, from *kata*, down + *echo*, a loud noise; the origin of the word catechism [Luke 1:3-4]

Other metaphors emphasize the development of an appropriate mindset or attitude toward life.

> Carry out exactly the decision that they announce to you from the place that the LORD will choose, diligently observing everything they **instruct** you.—*yarah*, flow as water, throw, or shoot an arrow; a reminder that missing the target is a metaphor for sin* [Deuteronomy 17:10]

When they have a dispute, they come to me and I decide between one person and another, and I make known to them the statutes and **instructions** of God.—*torah*, law,* from *yarah* [Exodus 18:16]

You gave your good spirit to **instruct** them, and did not withhold your manna from their mouths, and gave them water for their thirst.—*sakal*, make circumspect or intelligent [Nehemiah 9:20]

In the first book, Theophilus, I wrote about all that Jesus did and taught from the beginning until the day when he was taken up to heaven, after giving **instructions** through the Holy Spirit to the apostles whom he had chosen.—*entellomai*, enjoin or charge, from *en*, in + *telos*, end point or goal [Acts 1:1-2]

I myself feel confident about you, my brothers and sisters, that you yourselves are full of goodness, filled with all knowledge, and able to **instruct** one another.—*noutheteo*, from *nous*, mind + *tithemi*, put or place [Romans 15:14]

These things happened to them to serve as an example, and they were written down to **instruct** us, on whom the ends of the ages have come.—*nouthesia*, same as *noutheteo* [I Corinthians 10:11]

Some of the instruction metaphors suggest developing clarity of thought, putting ideas in order so that they make better sense.

Uzziah set himself to seek God in the days of Zechariah, who **instructed** him in the fear of God; and as long as he sought the LORD, God made him prosper.—*bin*, separate mentally, distinguish [II Chronicles 26:5]

Now when Jesus had finished **instructing** his twelve disciples, he went on from there to teach and proclaim his message in their cities.—*diatasso*, from *dia*, by or for + *tasso*, arrange [Matthew 11:1]

But as for you, continue in what you have learned and firmly believed, knowing from whom you learned it, and how from childhood you have known the sacred writings that are able to **instruct** you for salvation through faith in Christ Jesus.—*sophizo*, make wise, from *sophia*, wisdom, a word related to *saphes*, clarity [II Timothy 3:14-15]

Educating both children and adults is stressed by some of the Bible words translated as instruct or instruction.

Whenever a case comes to you from your kindred who live in their cities, concerning bloodshed, law or commandment, statutes or ordinances, then you shall **instruct** them, so that they may not incur guilt before the LORD and wrath may not come on you and your kindred.—*zahar*, shine or enlighten [II Chronicles 19:10]

For among them are those who make their way into households and captivate silly women, overwhelmed by their sins and swayed by all kinds of desires, who are always being **instructed** and can never arrive at a knowledge of the truth.—*manthano*, learn [II Timothy 3:6-7]

Therefore let us go on toward perfection, leaving behind the basic teaching about Christ, and not laying again the foundation: repentance from dead works and faith toward God, **instruction** about baptisms, laying on of hands, resurrection of the dead, and eternal judgment.—*didache*, from *didasko*, teach; *Didache* is the name of an early Christian book on morals and church practice. [Hebrews 6:1-2]

Those who are spiritual discern all things, and they are themselves subject to no one else's scrutiny. "For who has known the mind of the Lord so as to **instruct** him?" But we have the mind of Christ.—*symbibazo*, from *sym*, with + *baino*, walk [I Corinthians 2:15-16]

Finally, some of the biblical images suggest that the purpose of instruction is to improve behavior, getting people to act in a more responsible manner by following orders.

Joseph settled his father and his brothers, and granted them a holding in the land of Egypt, in the best part of the land, in the land of Rameses, as Pharaoh had **instructed**.—*tsavah*, appoint or command [Genesis 47:11]

Do not let anyone enter the house of the Lord except the priests and ministering Levites; they may enter, for they are holy, but all the other people shall observe the **instructions** of the Lord.—*mishmereth*, sentry or guard [II Chronicles 23:6]

See, you have **instructed** many; you have strengthened the weak hands.—*yasar*, chastise with blows or words. [Job 4:3]

Poverty and disgrace are for the one who ignores **instruction**, but one who heeds reproof is honored.—*musar*, warning, from *yasar* [Proverbs 13:18]

The king made Joseph lord of his house, and ruler of all his possessions, to **instruct** his officials at his pleasure, and to teach his elders wisdom.—*asar*, yoke or hitch [Psalm 105:21-22]

So Moses was **instructed** in all the wisdom of the Egyptians and was powerful in his words and deeds.—*paideuo*, train a child [Acts 7:22]

When followers of Jesus today want to follow the Bible in offering instruction, they would do well by considering what sort of instructing they intend. They might note a big difference between, on the one hand, getting people to follow orders and, on the other hand, offering them information, an attitude toward life, a way of ordering their thoughts, or an education.

interest (on loans)—see **usury**

J

jealous, *adjective;* **jealousy**, *noun*   In Hebrew, the word *qana* and its derivatives have two related but quite different meanings: jealous and zealous. If the root is the same as that in other Semitic languages, *qana* originally meant to be dyed dark red or black. These are the colors of a person's face showing strong emotions. According to the Hebrew Scriptures, both God and human beings can experience the strong emotions of jealousy and zeal.

Take care not to make a covenant with the inhabitants of the land to which you are going, or it will become a snare among you. You shall tear down their altars, break their pillars, and cut down their sacred poles (for you shall worship no other god, because the Lord, whose name is **Jealous**, is a **jealous** God). [Exodus 34:12-14]

This is the law in cases of **jealousy**, when a wife, while under her husband's authority, goes astray and defiles herself, or when a spirit of jealousy comes on a man and he is **jealous** of his wife; then he shall set the woman before the Lord, and the priest shall apply this entire law to her. [Numbers 5:29-30]

> Elijah answered, "I have been very **zealous** for the LORD, the God of hosts; for the Israelites have forsaken your covenant, thrown down your altars, and killed your prophets with the sword. I alone am left, and they are seeking my life, to take it away." [I Kings 19:10]

> The surviving remnant of the house of Judah shall again take root downward, and bear fruit upward; for from Jerusalem a remnant shall go out, and from Mount Zion a band of survivors. The **zeal** of the LORD of hosts will do this. [II Kings 19:30-31]

The Greek word *zelos* has the same double meaning, both jealousy and zeal. The root of *zelos* was probably the verb *zeo*, which meant to be hot, to boil. Although the adjective form of *zelos* appears infrequently, the noun is fairly common in the Christian part of the Bible.

> Then the high priest took action; he and all who were with him (that is, the sect of the Sadducees), being filled with **jealousy**, arrested the apostles and put them in the public prison. [Acts 5:17-18]

> Brothers and sisters, my heart's desire and prayer to God for them is that they may be saved. I can testify that they have a **zeal** for God, but it is not enlightened. [Romans 10:1-2]

> I feel a divine **jealousy** for you, for I promised you in marriage to one husband, to present you as a chaste virgin to Christ. [II Corinthians 11:2]

Attributing human emotions to God can be troublesome. Jealousy is especially unattractive. To use such a term, people have to keep in mind that the description of God being dark red in the face is a figurative use of language. Jealousy is a metaphor pointing to the conviction that looking for ultimate meaning from that which is not God leads to self-destructive behavior. The metaphor is more about human experience than it is about the nature of God. When enough people substitute wealth, power, and status for God, society has a way of self-destructing. An individual who, consciously or unconsciously, adopts a substitute for God is at the same risk.

Jehovah—see **Lord**

Jerusalem, *noun*　According to tradition, one thousand years before the birth of Jesus, King David unified twelve Hebrew-speaking tribes. For his capital, he ultimately chose an as-yet unconquered Jebusite stronghold called Jerusalem.

> At Hebron he reigned over Judah seven years and six months; and at **Jerusalem** he reigned over all Israel and Judah thirty-three years. The king and his men marched to **Jerusalem** against the Jebusites, the inhabitants of the land, who said to David, "You will not come in here, even the blind and the lame will turn you back"—thinking, "David cannot come in here." Nevertheless David took the stronghold of Zion, which is now the city of David. [II Samuel 5:5-7]

As both the political and religious center of the unified kingdom of Israel, Jerusalem had an almost mystical meaning. That meaning carried over after the collapse of the unified kingdom when Jerusalem was the capital of only the southern region, Judah, as can be seen from this psalm.

> I was glad when they said to me, "Let us go to the house of the LORD!"
> Our feet are standing within your gates, O **Jerusalem**.
> **Jerusalem**—built as a city that is bound firmly together.
> To it the tribes go up, the tribes of the LORD, as was decreed for Israel, to give thanks to the name of the LORD.

> For there the thrones for judgment were set up, the thrones of the house of David.
> Pray for the peace of **Jerusalem**: "May they prosper who love you.
> Peace be within your walls, and security within your towers."
> For the sake of my relatives and friends I will say, "Peace be within you."
> For the sake of the house of the LORD our God, I will seek your good. [Psalm 122]

The interest in Jerusalem expressed by the early followers of Jesus was more metaphorical than actual. For them, the city became a symbol of God's realm, the kingdom of heaven.*

> Now Hagar is Mount Sinai in Arabia and corresponds to the present **Jerusalem**, for she is in slavery with her children. But the other woman corresponds to the **Jerusalem** above; she is free, and she is our mother. [Galatians 4:25-26]

> You have come to Mount Zion and to the city of the living God, the heavenly **Jerusalem**, and to innumerable angels in festal gathering. [Hebrews 12:22]

> If you conquer, I will make you a pillar in the temple of my God; you will never go out of it. I will write on you the name of my God, and the name of the city of my God, the new **Jerusalem** that comes down from my God out of heaven, and my own new name. [Revelation 3:12]

As a metaphor, Jerusalem still has power to evoke the human longing for joy and peace, whether to be fulfilled soon or in the mythical future.

The power of the metaphor for the adherents to three of the world's major religions has brought disaster to the actual city. Jerusalem has been the scene of bloody battles between Christians and Muslims and Muslims and Jews. The bloodshed continues. As a figure of speech, Jerusalem now stands for tragedy and despair as well as for the promise of love and prosperity.

Jesus—see **advocate, blasphemy, bread, Christ, gate, judge, king, lamb, light, lord, name, priest, redeem, rock, sacrifice, savior, shepherd, Son of David, Son of Man, Son of God, teacher, throne, truth, vine, way,** and **word**

Jew, Judean, *nouns*   The English word Jews often appears in the Bible as a translation of the Hebrew *yehudim* and always of the Greek *ioudaioi*. The Hebrew word originally appeared in reference to the tribe descended from the patriarch *yehudah*, or Judah. In the older parts of the Hebrew Scriptures, *yehudim* is translated as Judeans.

> At that time the king of Edom recovered Elath for Edom, and drove the **Judeans** from Elath; and the Edomites came to Elath, where they live to this day. [II Kings 16:6]

> King Zedekiah said to Jeremiah, "I am afraid of the **Judeans** who have deserted to the Chaldeans, for I might be handed over to them and they would abuse me." [Jeremiah 38:19]

The tribe of Judah was briefly united with ten other Hebrew-speaking tribes under David and Solomon. After the death of Solomon in 926 BCE, Judah became a separate kingdom with its political capital and cult center in Jerusalem.* Anyone who lived within the realm was known as a Judean.

The other tribes, to the north of Judah, formed a kingdom that was the first of the two to be conquered by foreign invaders. Judah held out until 587, when Jerusalem was invaded and the temple destroyed. The Judeans rebuilt their temple in 520. At this point in the story, however, the translators of the New Revised Standard Version begin translating *yehudim* as Jews. They also use Jews as the translation in works that appear to have been written after the rebuilding of the temple.

> Now the prophets, Haggai and Zechariah son of Iddo, prophesied to the **Jews** who were in Judah and Jerusalem, in the name of the God of Israel who was over them. [Ezra 5:1]

> Now when Sanballat heard that we were building the wall, he was angry and greatly enraged, and he mocked the **Jews**. He said in the presence of his associates and of the army of Samaria, "What are these feeble **Jews** doing? Will they restore things? Will they sacrifice? Will they finish it in a day? Will they revive the stones out of the heaps of rubbish—and burned ones at that?" [Nehemiah 4:1-2]

> There are certain **Jews** whom you have appointed over the affairs of the province of Babylon: Shadrach, Meshach, and Abednego. These pay no heed to you, O King. They do not serve your gods and they do not worship the golden statue that you have set up. [Daniel 3:12]

Soon after the Maccabean revolt in 165 BCE, the designation *yehudim* or *ioudaioi* acquired an additional meaning that was neither territorial nor tribal. People whose worship life centered in the Jerusalem temple also became known as Judeans, even if their ancestors belonged to one of the other tribes. The Romans destroyed the temple in 70 CE and, by the end of the first century, a religion centered on the synagogues, and the teachings of the rabbis had evolved from the practice of the Pharisees.* Any adherent of this religion was known as a Judean.

Some have suggested that the English word Jew, which lost the "d" during the Middle Ages, is appropriate only for translating the Hebrew *yehudim* or the Greek *ioudaios* when the word is used primarily in a religious sense. Those using this approach always would use Judean when the reference could be tribal or territorial.

At the same time that rabbinic Judaism was taking form, the followers of Jesus under the leadership of Paul began welcoming Gentiles into their communities without insisting that they conform their diet and dress to rabbinic rules. Neither did they require Gentile men to be circumcised.* The leaders of the synagogues, however, were not willing to make such concessions for their Gentile converts.

In order to preserve their spiritual identity, the rabbis came to the conclusion that they could no longer tolerate the confusion caused by the Jesus followers in their midst. Even the Christians who were born Judeans and followed the rules were no longer accepted. Their rejection from the synagogues left many followers of Jesus feeling hurt and angry, but there was another reason for the hostility that developed between the two groups, Jews and Christians, that emerged from the Pharisee tradition. They found themselves in fierce competition for converts among the Gentiles. The depth of the animosity on the Christian side is reflected in a curse Matthew attributes to Jesus. In *The Five Gospels,* the curse reads:

> "You scholars and Pharisees, you imposters! Damn you! You scour land and sea to make one convert, and when you do, you make that person more a child of Hell than you are." [Matthew 23:15]

Another use of the word further complicates an appropriate understanding of Judean. During the first century, people in the southern part of Herod's realm were called Judeans, while people in the north were Samaritans or Galileans. Apparently the division was as important for them as the division between the northern and southern parts of Ireland are today. In *Angela's Ashes*, Frank McCourt says that, living in Limerick, he was always suspect because his father, although a Catholic, was from the north. His own grandmother accused him of having Presbyterian hair.[14] According to John's gospel, the Judeans challenged Jesus with a similar kind of guilt by geographical association.

> The **Jews** answered him, "Are we not right in saying that you are a Samaritan and have a demon?" [John 8:48]

Apparently, the people from Galilee and Samaria spoke with an accent different from that spoken in the south. The servant-girl accused Peter:

> "Certainly you are also one of them, for your accent betrays you." [Matthew 26:73]

According to the gospels, most of Jesus's early followers were Galileans so, to outsiders, Greeks and Romans, the later followers of Jesus—even the Gentiles—were called Galileans to differentiate them from the Jews. When these second- and third-generation Christians wrote their Jesus stories, they naturally identified themselves with the Galileans, in their minds the good people, while they pictured the Judeans as the bad people.

Because of the animosity of the Jesus followers toward rabbinic Judaism and because of their ingrained antagonism toward the people of Judah, the early Christian writings have a polemical tone that continues to feed Christian hostility toward the Jews. Because of the peculiar evolution of our language, English-speaking people have the opportunity of blunting the anti-Semitism of their holy writings by always substituting Judean for Jew. That reform by itself, however, will not be enough to remove all the anti-Semitic influences of the Christian Bible. The modern followers of Jesus need constant reminders to recognize and to reject their Bible's negative comments about Judeans, Pharisees, and Jews.

As a metaphor indicating undesirable human traits, any form of the word Jew should be totally out of bounds for any follower of Jesus. Sad to say, the vulgar and offensive metaphorical uses of Jew and Jewish have continued even after the atrocities of World War II showed what horrors anti-Semitic attitudes could produce. People who take seriously the admonition to love their neighbors will not use such language, nor will they permit the misuse of Jew or Jewish to go unchallenged in their presence.

Judas Iscariot—one of the Twelve identified as Jesus's first disciples.* Judas was a fairly common Hebrew name derived from the name of the tribe Judah. Iscariot probably meant that he was from the region of Kerioth. Although his name has become a metaphor applied to traitors, his betrayal of Jesus in the gospel stories is peculiar since neither a motive nor a precise act of treachery is attributed to him. What finally happened to Judas is a matter of some dispute. Mark and John are silent on the subject, while Matthew has him hanging himself. Only in the Acts of the Apostles do we find a vivid description of his death.

> When **Judas,** his betrayer, saw that Jesus was condemned, he repented and brought back the thirty pieces of silver to the chief priests and the elders. He said, "I have sinned by betraying innocent blood." But they said, "What is that to us? See to it yourself." Throwing down the pieces of silver in the temple, he departed; and he went and hanged himself. [Matthew 27:3-5]

> Now this man acquired a field with the reward of his wickedness; and falling headlong, he burst open in the middle and all his bowels gushed out. This became known to all the residents of Jerusalem, so that the field was called in their language Hakeldama, that is, Field of Blood. [Acts 1:18-19]

Marks a word in the text that has its own entry

As far as St. Paul is concerned, Jesus—at some point after his death—appeared to the Twelve, not to only eleven. Judas has no place in Paul's letters. In the light of this evidence, it seems possible that the treason of Judas followed rather than preceded the arrest and execution of Jesus. Judas may have betrayed the community, which saw itself as the new body* of Christ, rather than Jesus himself.

We can never know precisely what happened to the original group of Jesus's followers, but we can assume that they experienced difficult times soon after his death. Not only were they disappointed in their hope that Jesus would return, but they were also subject to persecution and abuse. In the face of disappointment and persecution, it would not be surprising if some members of the group walked away, but if one of the original Twelve betrayed the movement by leaving, those remaining would have been deeply upset. The shock and horror at the betrayal of Judas easily could have led the little community to project his crime back into the period of Jesus's life.

If the faithful followers of Jesus wrote the betrayal of Judas back into history, they had an obvious precedent in the way the priests of the second temple in Jerusalem dealt with the revolt by the clan of Korah. The revolt is described in the book Numbers as if it had taken place at the time of Moses. The account gives the reasons for the revolt in the answer Moses gives to Korah and his family.

> Moses said to Korah, "Hear now, you Levites! Is it too little for you that the God of Israel has separated you from the congregation of Israel, to allow you to approach him in order to perform the duties of the LORD's tabernacle, and to stand before the congregation and serve them? He has allowed you to approach him, and all your brother Levites with you; yet you seek the priesthood as well! [Numbers 16:8-10]

The swift punishment for their presumptuous claims to the priesthood understandably terrified all the bystanders.

> As soon as he finished speaking all these words, the ground under them was split apart. The earth opened its mouth and swallowed them up, along with their households—everyone who belonged to Korah and all their goods. So they with all that belonged to them went down alive into Sheol; the earth closed over them, and they perished from the midst of the assembly. [Numbers 16:31-33]

So the clan of Korah was totally destroyed before the children of Israel ever reached the promised land. How then to explain the psalms attributed to them and the many references to Korahites in the Chronicles, identifying them as musicians and incense makers and outlining their other duties, such as these:

> Shallum son of Kore, son of Ebiasaph, son of Korah, and his kindred of his ancestral house, the Korahites, were in charge of the work of the service, guardians of the thresholds of the tent, as their ancestors had been in charge of the camp of the LORD, guardians of the entrance. [I Chronicles 9:19]

The only reasonable explanation is that the revolt of Korah's clan took place centuries later than the time of Moses. In all probability, the Korahites were minor temple functionaries who were not forced into exile with the priests when the Babylonians destroyed the temple in 587. They may have carried on rituals at the ruined temple site for nearly fifty years, but when the families of the exiled priests returned and rebuilt the temple, they were forced to give up their priestly status and go back to being minor functionaries. When they complained, they were sent packing. At this time, the priests were promulgating a new edition of the sacred Hebrew texts. In their editing of older material, they included the story that supported their exclusive authority and control of worship and political life.

Projecting a conflict back into history is one way a community has of getting through a difficult experience and preparing itself for the future. This may have been the fate of Judas Iscariot, making his name a metaphor for traitor.

judge, *noun and verb*; **judgment**, *noun*   Hebrew has three words, along with their derivatives, that can be translated as judge or judgment. *Din* and *shaphat* have to do with governance, which can include settling disagreements, and *mishpat* is the rendering of a judicial verdict. Generally speaking, *din* and *shaphat* have to do with the immediate demands for managing the affairs of the people, while *mishpat* can be about the here and now or the mythical future.

The responsibility of human leaders and an understanding of God's presence both can be expressed as *din*.

> And you, Ezra, according to the God-given wisdom you possess, appoint magistrates and **judges** who may **judge** all the people in the province Beyond the River who know the laws of your God; and you shall teach those who do not know them. All who will not obey the law of your God and the law of the king, let **judgment** be strictly executed on them, whether for death or for banishment or for confiscation of their goods or for imprisonment. [Ezra 7:25-26]

> See, he scatters his lightning around him and covers the roots of the sea. For by these he **governs** peoples; he gives food in abundance. [Job 36:30-31]

> Then Rachel said, "God has **judged** me, and has also heard my voice and given me a son"; therefore she named him Dan. [Genesis 30:6]

> The Lord! His adversaries shall be shattered; the Most High will thunder in heaven. The Lord will **judge** the ends of the earth; he will give strength to his king, and exalt the power of his anointed. [I Samuel 2:10]

Mishpat, sometimes translated as justice,* is also used for both human interactions and for a sense of the divine in everyday events.

> At that time Deborah, a prophetess, wife of Lappidoth, was judging (*shaphat*) Israel. She used to sit under the palm of Deborah between Ramah and Bethel in the hill country of Ephraim; and the Israelites came up to her for **judgment**. [Judges 4:4-5]

> Absalom used to rise early and stand beside the road into the gate; and when anyone brought a suit before the king for **judgment**, Absalom would call out and say, "From what city are you?" When the person said, "Your servant is of such and such a tribe in Israel," Absalom would say, "See, your claims are good and right; but there is no one deputed by the king to hear you." [II Samuel 15:2-3]

> You must not be partial in **judging**: hear out the small and the great alike; you shall not be intimidated by anyone, for the **judgment** is God's. Any case that is too hard for you, bring to me, and I will hear it. [Deuteronomy 1:17]

> From the heavens you uttered judgment (*din*); the earth feared and was still when God rose up to establish **judgment**, to save all the oppressed of the earth. [Psalm 76:8-9]

Some of the prophets seemed to think that God's *mishpat* had been postponed but that a day of reckoning would eventually come.

> Therefore the LORD waits to be gracious to you; therefore he will rise up to show mercy to you. For the LORD is a God of **justice**; blessed are all those who wait for him. [Isaiah 30:18]

> Are you not from of old, O LORD my God, my Holy One? You shall not die. O LORD, you have marked them for **judgment**; and you, O Rock, have established them for punishment. [Habakkuk 1:12]

The Greek words corresponding to *mishpat* are based on the verb *krino*, which meant to separate, distinguish, or decide. *Krima* often assumes a negative judgment, that is, a condemnation. *Krisis* can be translated either justice or judgment, depending on the context. *Krites* is the word for the person making the decisions, the judge. In these examples of the separation metaphor in reference to human interactions, note that the authors took a dim view of Jesus's followers making judgments about each other or other people.

> You have heard that it was said to those of ancient times, "You shall not murder"; and "whoever murders shall be liable to **judgment**." But I say to you that if you are angry with a brother or sister, you will be liable to **judgment**; and if you insult a brother or sister, you will be liable to the council; and if you say, "You fool," you will be liable to the hell of fire.—*krisis* [Matthew 5:21-22]

> Come to terms quickly with your accuser while you are on the way to court with him, or your accuser may hand you over to the **judge**, and the **judge** to the guard, and you will be thrown into prison.—*krites* [Matthew 5:25]

> Do not **judge**, so that you may not be **judged**. For with the **judgment** you make you will be **judged,** and the measure you give will be the measure you get. Why do you see the speck in your neighbor's eye, but do not notice the log in your own eye? Or how can you say to your neighbor, "Let me take the speck out of your eye," while the log is in your own eye? You hypocrite, first take the log out of your own eye, and then you will see clearly to take the speck out of your neighbor's eye.—judge, *krino*; judgment, *krima* [Matthew 7:1-5]

> For we know the one who said, "Vengeance is mine, I will repay." And again, "The Lord will **judge** his people."—*krino* [Hebrews 10:30]

When the separation metaphor is used in reference to God, sometimes the sense is of an immediate experience.

> We ourselves boast of you among the churches of God for your steadfastness and faith during all your persecutions and the afflictions that you are enduring. This is evidence of the righteous **judgment** of God, and is intended to make you worthy of the kingdom of God, for which you are also suffering.—*krisis* [II Thessalonians 1:4-5]

> For the time has come for **judgment** to begin with the household of God; if it begins with us, what will be the end for those who do not obey the gospel of God?—*krima* [I Peter 4:17]

More often, however, the followers of Jesus pursued the line taken by the Hebrew prophets and wrote of God's *krisis* being announced in the future.

> If anyone will not welcome you or listen to your words, shake off the dust from your feet as you leave that house or town. Truly I tell you, it will be more tolerable for the land of Sodom and Gomorrah on the day of **judgment** than for that town. [Matthew 10:14-15]

Marks a word in the text that has its own entry

> The queen of the South will rise at the **judgment** with the people of this generation and condemn them, because she came from the ends of the earth to listen to the wisdom of Solomon, and see, something greater than Solomon is here! The people of Nineveh will rise up at the **judgment** with this generation and condemn it, because they repented at the proclamation of Jonah, and see, something greater than Jonah is here! [Luke 11:31-32]

> By the same word the present heavens and earth have been reserved for fire, being kept until the day of **judgment** and destruction of the godless. [II Peter 3:7]

> Love has been perfected among us in this: that we may have boldness on the day of **judgment**, because as he is, so are we in this world. [I John 4:17]

Some of them wrote as if God had delegated the future *krisis* to Jesus for him to handle as he saw fit.

> The Father **judges** no one but has given all **judgment** to the Son, so that all may honor the Son just as they honor the Father. Anyone who does not honor the Son does not honor the Father who sent him.— *krino* and *krisis* [John 5:22-23]

> They show that what the law requires is written on their hearts, to which their own conscience also bears witness; and their conflicting thoughts will accuse or perhaps excuse them on the day when, according to my gospel, God, through Jesus Christ, will **judge** the secret thoughts of all.—*krino* [Romans 2:15-16]

> In the presence of God and of Christ Jesus, who is to **judge** the living and the dead, and in view of his appearing and his kingdom, I solemnly urge you: proclaim the message; be persistent whether the time is favorable or unfavorable; convince, rebuke, and encourage, with the utmost patience in teaching.—*krino* [II Timothy 4:1-2]

Both the people of Israel and the early Christians used metaphors taken from the legal systems of their times to express something about their relationship with God. They may well have assumed that God had intervened in past history and that, in the future, God would set things straight, separating the good* people from those who did not obey* the commandments. Even so, their words may convey wisdom to those for whom the picture of an intervening God makes no sense. The most fulfilling life possible is that lived as if one were accountable to a chosen lord.* Accountability gives life form and direction. Just as a society without mechanisms for judging behavior will produce chaos, so an individual's life without a sense of impending judgment can become unmanageable.

justice, *noun*   In the Bible, the concept of justice is inseparable from the ideas of judgment* and of justification.* The Hebrew word *mishpat* and the Greek word *krisis* are translated as either justice or judgment, depending on the context. Hebrew words based on *tsadaq* and Greek words with the *dike* root appear in English as either justice or justification.

In human affairs, the justice demanded in the Hebrew Scripture seems to have been a balance between the sort that today is called distributive and the other kind known as retributive or vindictive justice. That is, the law* and the prophets were as interested in seeing that the poor and oppressed received fair treatment as they were in getting criminals punished.

> You shall not render an unjust judgment; you shall not be partial to the poor or defer to the great: with **justice** you shall judge your neighbor.—*tsedeq* [Leviticus 19:15]

> If you see in a province the oppression of the poor and the violation of **justice** and right, do not be amazed at the matter; for the high official is watched by a higher, and there are yet higher ones over them.—*tsedeq* [Ecclesiastes 5:8]

> Thus says the LORD: Act with **justice** and righteousness, and deliver from the hand of the oppressor anyone who has been robbed. And do no wrong or violence to the alien, the orphan, and the widow, or shed innocent blood in this place.—*mishpat* [Jeremiah 22:3]

> Hate evil and love good, and establish **justice** in the gate; it may be that the LORD, the God of hosts, will be gracious to the remnant of Joseph.—*mishpat* [Amos 5:15]

The followers of Jesus picked up on the same understanding of justice as found in the Hebrew Scriptures. Presumably, this was the view of justice that Jesus taught.

> Here is my servant, whom I have chosen, my beloved, with whom my soul is well pleased. I will put my Spirit upon him, and he will proclaim **justice** to the Gentiles.—*krisis* [Matthew 12:18]

> But woe to you Pharisees! For you tithe mint and rue and herbs of all kinds, and neglect **justice** and the love of God; it is these you ought to have practiced, without neglecting the others.—*krisis* [Luke 11:42]

> Some days later when Felix came with his wife Drusilla, who was Jewish, he sent for Paul and heard him speak concerning faith in Christ Jesus. And as he discussed **justice**, self-control, and the coming judgment, Felix became frightened and said, "Go away for the present; when I have an opportunity, I will send for you."—*krima* [Acts 24:24-25]

> If our injustice serves to confirm the **justice** of God, what should we say? That God is unjust to inflict wrath on us?—*dikaiosune* [Romans 3:5]

Paul writing to the Romans about the justice of God* demonstrated that he held the same understanding as that found in the Hebrew Scriptures. Justice is an attribute of God, as is made clear by these examples:

> The LORD works vindication and **justice** for all who are oppressed.—*mishpat* [Psalm 103:6]

> The LORD is exalted, he dwells on high; he filled Zion with **justice** and righteousness; he will be the stability of your times, abundance of salvation, wisdom, and knowledge; the fear of the LORD is Zion's treasure.—*mishpat* [Isaiah 33:5-6]

The justice metaphors imply that those who consider themselves to be God's people live under an obligation to see justice done in human affairs. All political and economic decisions are to be based on the standard of what is fair, especially what is fair to the poor and powerless.

justification, *noun*; **just**, *adjective* and *noun*; **justify**, *verb*   Both the Hebrew and Greek expressions that are translated with some form of the word just often appear in English as some form of the word right. In Hebrew, most of the words in this category are related to the verb *tsadaq* and in Greek to *dikaioo*. Although the translators have used a variety of English words, a few examples illustrate the two most common ways of translating the verbs in question.

> If you have anything to say, answer me; speak, for I desire to **justify** you. [Job 33:32]

> How then can a mortal **be righteous** before God? How can one born of woman be pure? [Job 25:4]

> For we hold that a person is **justified** by faith apart from works prescribed by the law. Or is God the God of Jews only? Is he not the God of Gentiles also? Yes, of Gentiles also, since God is one; and he will **justify** the circumcised on the ground of faith and the uncircumcised through that same faith. [Romans 3:28-30]

> Let the evildoer still do evil, and the filthy still be filthy, and the righteous still **do right,** and the holy still be holy. [Revelation 22:11]

What is true of the verb forms also shows up in the adjectives, and in the adjectives used as nouns.

> Therefore walk in the way of the good, and keep to the paths of the **just.** [Proverbs 2:20]

> Give instruction to the wise, and they will become wiser still; teach the **righteous** and they will gain in learning. [Proverbs 9:9]

> Finally, beloved, whatever is true, whatever is honorable, whatever is **just,** whatever is pure, whatever is pleasing, whatever is commendable, if there is any excellence and if there is anything worthy of praise, think about these things. [Philippians 4:8]

> I say to you, Love your enemies and pray for those who persecute you, so that you may be children of your Father in heaven; for he makes his sun rise on the evil and on the good, and sends rain on the **righteous** and on the unrighteous. [Matthew 5:44-45]

Only in the letter of St. Paul to the Christian community in Rome does the word justification appear in English versions. This particular form of the Greek word does not lend itself to a smooth translation based on right, but someone once tried and came up with the awkward term rightwizing.

> Therefore just as one man's trespass led to condemnation for all, so one man's act of righteousness leads to **justification** and life for all. [Romans 5:18]

Although the use of these right and just terms in the Bible appears always to have a moral or religious connotation, they might make more sense to the modern reader who can treat them as metaphors taken from the everyday use of the English words. To justify margins is to make the edges of a document straight up and down. To right a listing ship is to make it float at right angles to the water. To make anything right usually means to make it straight, not bent or crooked. In building, the carpenters frame the walls at right angles with the floor to give them maximum strength and stability.

Using the terms in a metaphorical sense, a community could judge a person to be upright, meaning stable, steady, or firm—a condition to which most people aspire, especially in moments when they feel shaken by unforseen events or difficult decisions.

Human beings have developed several ways of making themselves feel steady or upright within. The name for this activity is self-justification. Take the case of the supervisor whose boss during a slack period tells him to lay off his most unproductive employees. The supervisor knows that one of the most obvious men to go is nearly bankrupt due to the medical expenses of his wife, who is dying of cancer. The supervisor is badly shaken, torn between loyalty to his employer and compassion for the man in trouble.

The supervisor can try to make himself feel steady, that is justify himself, by making absolute the claim of either his employer or of the impoverished worker and discounting the claim of the other. Or he can take another option: firing the man and pretending that, in the end, things will work for the best. Both the method of ignoring one of the conflicting claims and the method of pretending that everything works out for the best are attempts at achieving uprightness by sidestepping responsibility. In other words, this is justification by sin.*

The supervisor, had he known it, had another possibility. He could have seen that no matter what he did, he would be partially wrong and on shaky ground. He could have tried to make the best decision he could on the basis of the facts at hand and allowed himself to be upheld in the manner that people associate with the presence of God.* This last possibility is known as justification by faith.*

DID YOU KNOW . . .

. . . that *dikaioo* is pronounced *deek-ah-yo-oh*?
For more help with pronunciation, see "Pronouncing
Transliterated Hebrew and Greek Words" on page 15.

K

king, *noun*   According to tradition, one of the earliest titles the people of Israel used for their God* was king, in Hebrew *melek*.

> He has not beheld misfortune in Jacob; nor has he seen trouble in Israel. The LORD their God is with them, acclaimed as a **king** among them. [Numbers 23:21]

> Thus says the LORD, the **King** of Israel, and his Redeemer, the LORD of hosts: I am the first and I am the last; besides me there is no god. [Isaiah 44:6]

Some of them took the metaphor so seriously that they objected to the idea of having a human king. The tradition is somewhat suspect, however, because the priestly party in Jerusalem edited the ancient stories to serve their self-interest, which included exalting their own authority at the expense of the monarchy. Still, the story about the controversy over the issue of the king reveals the problem with investing too much power in one human being.

> Samuel reported all the words of the LORD to the people who were asking him for a **king**. He said, "These will be the ways of the **king** who will reign over you: he will take your sons and appoint them to his chariots and to be his horsemen, and to run before his chariots; and he will appoint for himself commanders of thousands and commanders of fifties, and some to plow his ground and to reap his harvest, and to make his implements of war and the equipment of his chariots. He will take your daughters to be perfumers and cooks and bakers. He will take the best of your fields and vineyards and olive orchards and give them to his courtiers. He will take one-tenth of your grain and of your vineyards and give it to his officers and his courtiers. He will take your male and female slaves, and the best of your cattle and donkeys, and put them to his work. He will take one-tenth of your flocks, and you shall be his slaves. And in that day you will cry out because of your **king**, whom you have chosen for yourselves; but the LORD will not answer you in that day." [I Samuel 8:10-18]

Apparently because Jesus frequently mentioned the kingdom* of God in his public statements, he set himself up for the accusation found in all four gospels that he was trying to make himself a king, in Greek *basileus*. Luke tells this story this way:

> Then the assembly rose as a body and brought Jesus before Pilate. They began to accuse him, saying, "We found this man perverting our nation, forbidding us to pay taxes to the emperor, and saying that he himself is the Messiah, a **king**." Then Pilate asked him, "Are you the **king** of the Jews?" He answered, "You say so." [Luke 23:1-3]

According to the Acts of the Apostles, long after Jesus's death, the same accusation was brought up in Thessalonica, where Paul and his companion Silas were preaching. Some ruffians dragged the friends of Paul and Silas before the city authorities, complaining:

> They are all acting contrary to the decrees of the emperor, saying that there is another **king** named Jesus. [Acts 17:7]

Perhaps because calling Jesus a king anywhere in the empire was tantamount to treason, John's gospel includes a brief incident in which Jesus rejects the title.

> When Jesus realized that they were about to come and take him by force to make him **king,** he withdrew again to the mountain by himself. [John 6:15]

By the fourth century, when it was no longer dangerous to call Jesus a king, the metaphor slowly gained popularity. In time, Jesus began to appear in works of art dressed as a monarch, wearing a crown and holding an orb and scepter. In 1925, Pope Pius XI instituted a festival called Christ the King to be celebrated by all Roman Catholics on the last Sunday before the beginning of Advent, the four weeks leading up to Christmas. Some Anglicans also observe the festival.

The king metaphor has much the same appeal and many of the same problems as father.* Whether the king is the God of Israel or is Jesus, the metaphor holds out the promise of peace, stability, and protection. The trouble with the king metaphor, however, was foreshadowed in the words attributed to the prophet Samuel, quoted above. Those who see themselves as servants of the king can believe themselves to be invested with the power to impose their will on the rest of humanity, or for that matter, on the rest of the natural world.

kingdom of God, kingdom of heaven   The teachings about the kingdom of God or the kingdom of heaven attributed to Jesus usually appear in contexts that leave little doubt that the writers were using kingdom—in Greek, *basileia*—in a metaphorical sense. They did not think that Jesus was attempting to compete with either Rome or Jerusalem to establish his rule in a political or geographical sense, but those in authority were not so sure. Any talk about a kingdom not approved by the emperor may have sounded like treason to them.

> Pilate replied, "I am not a Jew, am I? Your own nation and the chief priests have handed you over to me. What have you done?" Jesus answered, "My **kingdom** is not from this world." [John 18:35-36]

> The kingdom of God is not coming with things that can be observed; nor will they say, "Look, here it is!" or "There it is!" For, in fact, the **kingdom of God** is among you. [Luke 17:20-21]

Much of the teaching about God's realm attributed to Jesus has come down to us in the form of parables, but all four gospels also contain many thought-provoking one-liners, associating kingdom with God* or heaven.*

> Truly I tell you, unless you change and become like children, you will never enter the **kingdom of heaven.** [Matthew 18:3]

> Then Jesus looked around and said to his disciples, "How hard it will be for those who have wealth to enter the **kingdom of God**!" [Mark 10:23]

> Then he looked up at his disciples and said: "Blessed are you who are poor, for yours is the **kingdom of God**." [Luke 6:20]

> Jesus answered, "Very truly, I tell you, no one can enter the **kingdom of God** without being born of water and Spirit." [John 3:5]

Each of these statements, and all the other one-line observations about God's realm, challenge conventional ways of understanding status and achievement. If the gospels represent what Jesus taught, his use of the God's realm metaphor was full of disturbing surprises. Financially successful people will have a hard time entering this realm, but poor people and children will find easy access. His one-line statements, sometimes called aphorisms, have a way of standing conventional wisdom on its head. So do his parables.

People living in a modern, democratic society can scarcely imagine the emotional impact that the word kingdom once carried. Long before the time of Jesus, a family attempting to live outside a kingdom was subject to perpetual chaos. Their property was not safe from theft, and they were not safe from intentional or casual extermination by armed men. A kingdom meant established order: protection from enemies, enforcement of contracts, and dependable procedures. A kingdom kept the chaos at bay.

When Jesus used the kingdom metaphor, the Roman authorities may have perceived a threat. The only way they knew of keeping the chaos at bay was through military power. For them, the only way to peace was victory. When Jesus suggested that peace could come through another kind of kingdom—one based on justice—he was asking for trouble. When arrested, Jesus apparently was unsuccessful in convincing his captors that he was using kingdom as a metaphor to teach people about his understanding of God. Getting across the meaning of that metaphor can be difficult even today.

For some, the kingdom even as a metaphor presents a problem common with much biblical imagery. It is not only archaic but sexist. Fortunately, many other translations are possible for the Greek term *basileia*—imperial rule, royal power, sovereignty, dominion, reign, or realm. Any of these terms can be used to indicate the kinds of perceptions and experiences that cannot be described by using the language of logic and analysis. The realm that mattered most to the followers of Jesus is the one that is approached through metaphors,* parables,* myths,* poetry, novels, fantasy, art, drama, music, and dance.

know, lie with, *verbs*   The Hebrew Scriptures have two metaphors for sexual intercourse, *yada* and *shakab*. Both have English equivalents that were common euphemisms when the King James Bible appeared in the seventeenth century: know and lie with, respectively. By the twentieth century, both of these metaphors had fallen into disuse. The only current remnant of earlier usage is the legal term for unwanted sexual intimacy, carnal knowledge. In spite of the shift in language, the translators of the New Revised Standard Version in many instances retained know and lie with.

Examples of passages about sexual intercourse in which New Revised Standard Version translates *yada* as know:

> Now the man **knew** his wife Eve, and she conceived and bore Cain, saying, "I have produced a man with the help of the LORD." [Genesis 4:1]

The girl was very fair to look upon, a virgin, whom no man had **known**. [Genesis 24:16]

They rose early in the morning and worshiped before the LORD; then they went back to their house at Ramah. Elkanah **knew** his wife Hannah, and the LORD remembered her. [I Samuel 1:19]

Occasionally, the New Revised Standard Version uses a more contemporary English expression to translate *yada*.

New Revised Standard Version	King James Version
At the end of two months, she returned to her father, who did with her according to the vow he had made. She had never **slept with** a man. [Judges 11:39]	And it came to pass at the end of two months, that she returned unto her father, who did with her according to his vow which he had vowed: and she **knew** no man.
But the men would not listen to him. So the man seized his concubine, and put her out to them. They wantonly **raped** her, and abused her all through the night until the morning. [Judges 19:25]	But the men would not hearken to him: so the man took his concubine, and brought her forth unto them; and they **knew** her, and abused her all the night until the morning:

More often than not, the translators of the New Revised Standard Version translate *yada* with some form of know, but when they want the word to be taken literally, they sometimes use other English terms with slightly different connotations. All these terms represent aspects of the basic meaning of *yada*, which is to ascertain.

The man gazed at her in silence to **learn** whether or not the LORD had made his journey successful. [Genesis 24:21]

So Pharaoh said to Joseph, "Since God has **shown** you all this, there is no one so discerning and wise as you." [Genesis 41:39]

His sister stood at a distance, to **see** what would happen to him. [Exodus 2:4]

God looked upon the Israelites, and God took **notice** of them. [Exodus 2:25]

Pharaoh's officials said to him, "How long shall this fellow be a snare to us? Let the people go, so that they may worship the LORD their God; do you not yet **understand** that Egypt is ruined?" [Exodus 10:7]

In two critical passages, the context does not make clear whether *yada* is to be taken in the literal sense of ascertain or the metaphorical sense of a sex act. In the first instance, the translators have left the interpretation up to the reader, but because the term know is a matter of law as well as language, people generally assume that the offense of the Sodomites* was homosexual rape. In the second passage, the translators have passed along their interpretation that the demand was indeed that a male guest be produced for the sexual satisfaction of local men. In both cases, the author or editor of the story might have meant by *yada* that the local people wanted to interrogate the guest, perhaps violently.

But before they lay down, the men of the city, the men of Sodom, both young and old, all the people to the last man, surrounded the house; and they called to Lot, "Where are the men who came to you tonight? Bring them out to us, so that we may **know** them." [Genesis 19:4-5]

---

*Marks a word in the text that has its own entry

While they were enjoying themselves, the men of the city, a perverse lot, surrounded the house, and started pounding on the door. They said to the old man, the master of the house, "Bring out the man who came into your house, so that we may have **intercourse** with him." [Judges 19:22]

The early Greek translation of the Hebrew Scriptures, the Septuagint, usually translated *yada* with *ginosko*. In old English the initial consonant k was sounded in know, as was the initial g in the Greek *gno*, one form of *ginosko*. The similarity of the English and Greek verbs suggests the etymological relationship between know and *ginosko*. The metaphorical use of *ginosko* for sexual intercourse appears twice in the gospels.

New Revised Standard Version	King James Version
When Joseph awoke from sleep, he did as the angel of the Lord commanded him; he took her as his wife, but had no **marital relations** with her until she had borne a son; and he named him Jesus. [Matthew 1:24-25]	Then Joseph being raised from sleep did as the angel of the Lord had bidden him, and took unto him his wife: And **knew** her not till she had brought forth her firstborn son: and he called his name JESUS.
Mary said to the angel, "How can this be, since I **am a virgin**?" [Luke 1:34]	Then said Mary unto the angel, How shall this be, seeing I **know** not a man?

As is the case with *yada*, English translations of *ginosko* usually employ a form of know, but sometimes verbs with slightly different connotations show up. Except in the two instances of sexual intimacy, however, *ginosko* never appears to be understood as a metaphor. In every other case, the English words for *ginosko* suggest something to do with ascertaining information. Here are a few examples taken from the four gospels.

When the chief priests and the Pharisees heard his parables, they **realized** that he was speaking about them. [Matthew 21:45]

Jesus said to them, "How many loaves have you? Go and see." When they had **found out**, they said, "Five, and two fish." [Mark 6:38]

If you, even you, had only **recognized** on this day the things that make for peace! But now they are hidden from your eyes. [Luke 19:42]

Jesus used this figure of speech with them, but they did not **understand** what he was saying to them. [John 10:6]

The other Hebrew metaphor used to indicate sexual intercourse is *shakab*, which meant literally to recline in a horizontal position. Besides being a sexual metaphor, *shakab* appears frequently in the Bible as a figure of speech meaning sleep or death.* The association of death and sex is not unknown among English-speaking people. The climax of a sexual act can be described with a phrase imported from the French, *le petit mort*, the little death. Apparently Greek-speaking people made the same association of sex and death. They translated *shakab* with *koimao*, which means literally sleep and metaphorically death or sex. In the Christian writings of the Bible, however, *koimao* never has a sexual connotation. Some examples of *shakab* as a metaphor indicating a sex act:

Now Joseph was handsome and good-looking. And after a time his master's wife cast her eyes on Joseph and said, "**Lie** with me." [Genesis 39:6-7]

*Marks a word in the text that has its own entry

> When a man seduces a virgin who is not engaged to be married, and **lies** with her, he shall give the bride-price for her and make her his wife. [Exodus 22:16]

> If any man's wife goes astray and is unfaithful to him, if a man has had **intercourse** with her but it is hidden from her husband, . . . then the man shall bring his wife to the priest. And he shall bring the offering required for her. [Numbers 5:12-13, 15]

> If there is a young woman, a virgin already engaged to be married, and a man meets her in the town and **lies** with her, you shall bring both of them to the gate of that town and stone them to death, the young woman because she did not cry for help in the town and the man because he violated his neighbor's wife. [Deuteronomy 22:23-24]

> Uriah said to David, "The ark and Israel and Judah remain in booths; and my lord Joab and the servants of my lord are camping in the open field; shall I then go to my house, to eat and to drink, and to **lie** with my wife?" [II Samuel 11:11]

Yada and *shakab* as well as *ginosko* and *koimao* appear to be morally neutral. The other biblical metaphors for sex, however, always convey a connotation of illicit sexual behavior. In Hebrew, the word for adultery, fornication, or prostitution is *zanah,* which can also mean a whore. *Zanah* frequently is the metaphor used to condemn the people of Israel for worshipping foreign gods.

> When the daughter of a priest profanes herself through **prostitution**, she profanes her father; she shall be burned to death. [Leviticus 21:9]

> While Israel was staying at Shittim, the people began to have **sexual relations** with the women of Moab. [Numbers 25:1]

> Then Joshua son of Nun sent two men secretly from Shittim as spies, saying, "Go, view the land, especially Jericho." So they went, and entered the house of a **prostitute** whose name was Rahab, and spent the night there. [Joshua 2:1]

> The LORD said to Moses, "Soon you will lie down with your ancestors. Then this people will begin to **prostitute** themselves to the foreign gods in their midst, the gods of the land into which they are going; they will forsake me, breaking my covenant that I have made with them." [Deuteronomy 31:16]

> If a man divorces his wife and she goes from him and becomes another man's wife, will he return to her? Would not such a land be greatly polluted? You have played the **whore** with many lovers; and would you return to me? says the LORD. [Jeremiah 3:1]

The Greek language could make a distinction between adultery, *moicheia,* and prostitution or fornication, *porneia,* the root of the English word pornography. In the Bible, *moicheia* and *porneia* nearly always appear in their literal sense rather than as religious metaphors. The only exception can be found in the book of Revelation.

> For out of the heart come evil intentions, murder, **adultery, fornication**, theft, false witness, slander. [Matthew 15:19]

> The scribes and the Pharisees brought a woman who had been caught in **adultery**; and making her stand before all of them, they said to him, "Teacher, this woman was caught in the very act of committing **adultery**." [John 8:3-4]

Marks a word in the text that has its own entry

I have reached the decision that we should not trouble those Gentiles who are turning to God, but we should write to them to abstain only from things polluted by idols and from **fornication** and from whatever has been strangled and from blood. [Acts 15:19-20]

Shun **fornication**! Every sin that a person commits is outside the body; but the **fornicator** sins against the body itself. [I Corinthians 6:18]

Then another angel, a second, followed, saying, "Fallen, fallen is Babylon the great! She has made all nations drink of the wine of the wrath of her **fornication**." [Revelation 14:8]

In translating the biblical metaphors for sex, Christians have betrayed a kind of squeamishness that has resulted in the use of archaic expressions. Today, where but in church would you hear such words for sex as know, lie with, or fornication? More contemporary euphemisms would be sleep with for the two neutral terms and recreational sex for the illicit variety.

L

lamb, *noun*   The importance of lambs in the Israelite culture shows up in the Hebrew language, which had at least ten words for identifying young sheep or goats. These words appear in the regulations for offering sacrifice and in stories where animals represent wealth. Several of the words for lamb also appear as metaphors in the Hebrew Scriptures. These examples show the words for lamb first in their original and second in their figurative sense.

seh, from a word that suggests pushed out to graze

Tell the whole congregation of Israel that on the tenth of this month they are to take a **lamb** for each family, a **lamb** for each household. If a household is too small for a whole **lamb**, it shall join its closest neighbor in obtaining one; the **lamb** shall be divided in proportion to the number of people who eat of it. Your **lamb** shall be without blemish, a year-old male; you may take it from the sheep or from the goats. You shall keep it until the fourteenth day of this month; then the whole assembled congregation of Israel shall slaughter it at twilight. [Exodus 12:3-6]

My servant was oppressed, and he was afflicted, yet he did not open his mouth; like a **lamb** that is led to the slaughter, and like a sheep that before its shearers is silent, so he did not open his mouth. [Isaiah 53:7]

kar, suggests plumpness

Saul and the people spared Agag, and the best of the sheep and of the cattle and of the fatlings, and the **lambs**, and all that was valuable, and would not utterly destroy them; all that was despised and worthless they utterly destroyed. [I Samuel 15:9]

I will bring Babylon down like **lambs** to the slaughter, like rams and goats. [Jeremiah 51:40]

kibsah, a female lamb

Abraham set apart seven ewe **lambs** of the flock. And Abimelech said to Abraham, "What is the meaning of these seven ewe **lambs** that you have set apart?" He said, "These seven ewe **lambs** you shall accept from my hand, in order that you may be a witness for me that I dug this well." [Genesis 21:28-30]

Marks a word in the text that has its own entry

The poor man had nothing but one little ewe **lamb,** which he had bought. He brought it up, and it grew up with him and with his children; it used to eat of his meager fare, and drink from his cup, and lie in his bosom, and it was like a daughter to him. [II Samuel 12:3]

kebes, suggests dominance, old enough to butt

Now this is what you shall offer on the altar: two **lambs** a year old regularly each day. One **lamb** you shall offer in the morning, and the other **lamb** you shall offer in the evening. [Exodus 29:38-39]

I was like a gentle **lamb** led to the slaughter. And I did not know it was against me that they devised schemes, saying, "Let us destroy the tree with its fruit, let us cut him off from the land of the living, so that his name will no longer be remembered!" [Jeremiah 11:19]

taleh, perhaps from a word meaning protective covering

Samuel took a sucking **lamb** and offered it as a whole burnt offering to the LORD; Samuel cried out to the LORD for Israel, and the LORD answered him. [I Samuel 7:9]

The wolf and the **lamb** shall feed together, the lion shall eat straw like the ox; but the serpent— its food shall be dust! They shall not hurt or destroy on all my holy mountain, says the LORD. [Isaiah 65:25]

ben tso'n, offspring of sheep

They shall come and sing aloud on the height of Zion, and they shall be radiant over the goodness of the LORD, over the grain, the wine, and the oil, and over the **young of the flock** and the herd; their life shall become like a watered garden, and they shall never languish again. [Jeremiah 31:12]

When Israel went out from Egypt, the house of Jacob from a people of strange language, Judah became God's sanctuary, Israel his dominion. The sea looked and fled; Jordan turned back. The mountains skipped like rams, the hills like **lambs.** [Psalm 114:1-4]

The Hebrew word for a lamb to be sacrificed at passover was *pasach.* Although *pasach* does not appear as a metaphor, its Greek equivalent, *pascha* does.

On the fourteenth day of the first month the returned exiles kept the passover. For both the priests and the Levites had purified themselves; all of them were clean. So they killed the passover **lamb** for all the returned exiles, for their fellow priests, and for themselves. [Ezra 6:19-20]

Clean out the old yeast so that you may be a new batch, as you really are unleavened. For our paschal **lamb,** Christ, has been sacrificed. [I Corinthians 5:7]

The other Greek words for lamb in the early Christian writings are always used as metaphors.

aren

Go on your way. See, I am sending you out like **lambs** into the midst of wolves. [Luke 10:3]

arnion, a diminutive of *aren*

When they had finished breakfast, Jesus said to Simon Peter, "Simon son of John, do you love me more than these?" He said to him, "Yes, Lord; you know that I love you." Jesus said to him, "Feed my **lambs.**" [John 21:15]

Marks a word in the text that has its own entry   **175**

> They will hunger no more, and thirst no more; the sun will not strike them, nor any scorching heat; for the **Lamb** at the center of the throne will be their shepherd, and he will guide them to springs of the water of life, and God will wipe away every tear from their eyes. [Revelation 7:16-17]

amnos

> The next day he saw Jesus coming toward him and declared, "Here is the **Lamb** of God who takes away the sin of the world!" [John 1:29]

> You know that you were ransomed from the futile ways inherited from your ancestors, not with perishable things like silver or gold, but with the precious blood of Christ, like that of a **lamb** without defect or blemish. [I Peter 1:18-19]

In both the Hebrew and Greek languages, the lamb metaphor had two uses. In the first place, lamb could mean an innocent, childlike, or dependent person. In the other usage, lamb meant one whose death was like a sacrifice, that is, one whose life was given for others. In the gospels, both Jesus and his followers are called lambs, the followers in the first sense and Jesus in the second. The author of Revelation was especially fond of the lamb metaphor for Jesus, using it twenty-nine times.

Whether the followers of Jesus are referred to as full-grown sheep or as lambs, the implication is that they must be led by a shepherd* and are unable to take care of themselves. Many people find this image unflattering and unhelpful. When the context makes clear that the metaphor is pointing to childlike playfulness, however, some people might not at all mind seeing themselves as lambs.

The lamb metaphor for Jesus can be helpful in emphasizing that the energy of his life is available to all people, but it has all the disadvantages of the sacrifice* and atonement* metaphors.

law, *noun*   The English word law translates both the Hebrew *torah* and the Greek *nomos*, but they did not have exactly the same meaning.

The root of *torah* is *yarah*, which originally had to do with the flow of water but came to mean to throw something or to shoot an arrow. As a metaphor, *yarah* came to mean to teach or instruct.* *Torah* is the body of teaching or instruction that describes how the Israelites were to live in the community and get along with their foreign neighbors. The same word could also mean the first five books of the Bible,* known as the five books of Moses, or mean the specific commandments that, according to tradition, Moses received on Mt. Sinai.

> If an alien who resides with you wants to celebrate the passover to the LORD, all his males shall be circumcised; then he may draw near to celebrate it; he shall be regarded as a native of the land. But no uncircumcised person shall eat of it; there shall be one **law** for the native and for the alien who resides among you. [Exodus 12:48-49]

> The LORD said to Moses, "Come up to me on the mountain, and wait there; and I will give you the tablets of stone, with the **law** and the commandment, which I have written for their instruction." [Exodus 24:12]

The root of *nomos* is *nemo*, which meant to deal out or distribute. *Nomos* could be a custom, rule, or principle.

> Now if I do what I do not want, it is no longer I that do it, but sin that dwells within me. So I find it to be a **law** that when I want to do what is good, evil lies close at hand. [Romans 7:20-21]

> It is even more obvious when another priest arises, resembling Melchizedek, one who has become a priest, not through a **legal requirement** concerning physical descent, but through the power of an indestructible life. [Hebrews 7:15-16]

Although not the precise equivalent, *nomos* was used for *torah* in the Greek translations of the Hebrew Scriptures, and the early Christians followed the practice. In Matthew, Luke, and Acts, *nomos* generally means *torah*.

> Do not think that I have come to abolish the **law** or the prophets; I have come not to abolish but to fulfill. For truly I tell you, until heaven and earth pass away, not one letter, not one stroke of a letter, will pass from the **law** until all is accomplished. [Matthew 5:17-18]

> When the time came for their purification according to the **law** of Moses, the parents of Jesus brought him up to Jerusalem to present him to the Lord (as it is written in the **law** of the Lord, "Every firstborn male shall be designated as holy to the Lord"), and they offered a sacrifice according to what is stated in the **law** of the Lord, "a pair of turtledoves or two young pigeons." [Luke 2:22-24]

> The next day Paul went with us to visit James; and all the elders were present. After greeting them, he related one by one the things that God had done among the Gentiles through his ministry. When they heard it, they praised God. Then they said to him, "You see, brother, how many thousands of believers there are among the Jews, and they are all zealous for the **law**." [Acts 21:18-20]

St. Paul, however, sometimes uses *nomos* in the narrow sense of the legal system of Israel in order to argue that the Gentile converts to Christianity were not bound by all its precepts. Instead, the followers of Jesus follow a superior law, one that is not codified.

> There is therefore now no condemnation for those who are in Christ Jesus. For the **law** of the Spirit of life in Christ Jesus has set you free from the **law** of sin and of death. For God has done what the **law**, weakened by the flesh, could not do: by sending his own Son in the likeness of sinful flesh, and to deal with sin, he condemned sin in the flesh, so that the just requirement of the **law** might be fulfilled in us, who walk not according to the flesh but according to the Spirit. [Romans 8:1-4]

> Once again I testify to every man who lets himself be circumcised that he is obliged to obey the entire **law**. You who want to be justified by the **law** have cut yourselves off from Christ; you have fallen away from grace. [Galatians 5:3-4]

> Bear one another's burdens, and in this way you will fulfill the **law** of Christ. [Galatians 6:2]

Twenty-first century followers of Jesus may have a difficult time figuring out what to make of the law when they run across the term in the Bible. One way is to focus on the origins of the metaphors. If *torah* was like shooting an arrow, it was about guidance. *Torah* was the collected wisdom of the community passed down from one generation to the next. The people of Israel celebrated *torah* through their stories about Moses. The origin of *nomos* puts the emphasis on distributing the best of what has been learned through experience.

Both the Hebrew and Greek words for law are reminders that law is descriptive before it becomes proscriptive. Law always begins with a description of what works for a particular culture in a particular time and place. Those descriptions may have universal validity, or they may be culture bound. Because of a confusion of language, St. Paul's letters can seem to belittle the Torah, the core of the Jewish faith, but he was doing the work that needed to be done. Like other Jews of his day, he was sorting through the guidance from the past to find what was valuable and necessary for Gentile converts.

Although St. Paul saw no need to codify the new law of Christ, subsequent generations of Christians naturally wrote down the wisdom that they wanted to celebrate and pass along. In time, the new law looked very much like what Paul described as the old law, a set of precepts that must be obeyed.

life—see soul

light, *noun*   In the Bible, light is such a frequently used metaphor that the meaning is not always clear. In general, the Hebrew *or* and the Greek *phos* stand for what is good,* while darkness stands for evil,* but the specific references vary. It is not always possible to tell if the light means the divine presence or some result of the presence, such as knowledge. The following headings, therefore, to some extent represent an interpretation of the passages.

Knowledge

God strips understanding from the leaders of the earth, and makes them wander in a pathless waste. They grope in the dark without **light**; he makes them stagger like a drunkard. [Job 12:24]

O send out your **light** and your truth; let them lead me; let them bring me to your holy hill and to your dwelling. [Psalm 43:3]

It is the God who said, "Let **light** shine out of darkness," who has shone in our hearts to give the **light** of the knowledge of the glory of God in the face of Jesus Christ. [II Corinthians 4:6]

Prosperity

Then Mordecai went out from the presence of the king, wearing royal robes of blue and white, with a great golden crown and a mantle of fine linen and purple, while the city of Susa shouted and rejoiced. For the Jews there was **light** and gladness, joy and honor. [Esther 8:15-16]

Now for a brief moment favor has been shown by the LORD our God, who has left us a remnant, and given us a stake in his holy place, in order that he may **brighten** our eyes and grant us a little sustenance in our slavery. [Ezra 9:8]

Righteousness

He will make your vindication shine like the **light**, and the justice of your cause like the noonday. [Psalm 37:6]

Your eye is the lamp of your body. If your eye is healthy, your whole body is full of **light**; but if it is not healthy, your body is full of darkness. [Luke 11:34]

Do not be mismatched with unbelievers. For what partnership is there between righteousness and lawlessness? Or what fellowship is there between **light** and darkness? [II Corinthians 6:14]

Sphere of the divine

O house of Jacob, come, let us walk in the **light** of the LORD! [Isaiah 2:5]

The name *Uriel*, which appears in the Chronicles, means God (*El*) is my light. Outside of the canonical Hebrew Bible, Uriel became the name of the fourth archangel—along with Gabriel, Michael, and Raphael. See also **angel**.

In the eighteenth year of King Jeroboam, Abijah began to reign over Judah. He reigned for three years in Jerusalem. His mother's name was Micaiah daughter of *Uriel* of Gibeah.
[II Chronicles 13:1-2]

May you be made strong with all the strength that comes from his glorious power, and may you be prepared to endure everything with patience, while joyfully giving thanks to the Father, who has enabled you to share in the inheritance of the saints in the **light**. [Colossians 1:11-12]

He who is the blessed and only Sovereign, the King of kings and Lord of lords: It is he alone who has immortality and dwells in unapproachable **light**, whom no one has ever seen or can see; to him be honor and eternal dominion. [I Timothy 6:15-16]

If we say that we have fellowship with him while we are walking in darkness, we lie and do not do what is true; but if we walk in the **light** as he himself is in the **light**, we have fellowship with one another, and the blood of Jesus his Son cleanses us from all sin. [I John 1:6-7]

Announcement or message

Therefore I have hewn them by the prophets, I have killed them by the words of my mouth, and my judgment goes forth as the **light**. [Hosea 6:5]

While I was on my way and approaching Damascus, about noon a great **light** from heaven suddenly shone about me. [Acts 22:6]

The heavenly Jerusalem*

The city has no need of sun or moon to shine on it, for the glory of God is its light, and its lamp is the Lamb. The nations will walk by its **light**, and the kings of the earth will bring their glory into it. [Revelation 21:23-24]

Public or open

What I say to you in the dark, tell in the **light**; and what you hear whispered, proclaim from the housetops. [Matthew 10:27]

Nothing is covered up that will not be uncovered, and nothing secret that will not become known. Therefore whatever you have said in the dark will be heard in the **light**, and what you have whispered behind closed doors will be proclaimed from the housetops. [Luke 12:2-3]

Take no part in the unfruitful works of darkness, but instead expose them. For it is shameful even to mention what such people do secretly; but everything exposed by the **light** becomes visible, for everything that becomes visible is **light**. [Ephesians 5:11-14]

Torch or lamp

When they had kindled a fire in the middle of the courtyard and sat down together, Peter sat among them. Then a servant-girl, seeing him in the **firelight**, stared at him and said, "This man also was with him." [Luke 22:55-56]

The jailer called for **lights**, and rushing in, he fell down trembling before Paul and Silas.
[Acts 16:29]

Heavenly bodies

O give thanks to the God of gods, for his steadfast love endures forever . . . who made the great **lights,** for his steadfast love endures forever; the sun to rule over the day, for his steadfast love endures forever; the moon and stars to rule over the night, for his steadfast love endures forever. [Psalm 136:2, 7-9]

I looked on the earth, and lo, it was waste and void; and to the heavens, and they had no **light.** [Jeremiah 4:23]

Guide or teacher*

You are the **light** of the world. A city built on a hill cannot be hid. [Matthew 5:14]

If you are sure that you are a guide to the blind, a **light** to those who are in darkness, a corrector of the foolish, a teacher of children, having in the law the embodiment of knowledge and truth, you, then, that teach others, will you not teach yourself? [Romans 2:19-21]

God*

The LORD is my **light** and my salvation; whom shall I fear? The LORD is the stronghold of my life; of whom shall I be afraid? [Psalm 27:1]

The sun shall no longer be your **light** by day, nor for brightness shall the moon give **light** to you by night; but the LORD will be your everlasting **light,** and your God will be your glory. [Isaiah 60:19]

This is the message we have heard from him and proclaim to you, that God is **light** and in him there is no darkness at all. [I John 1:5]

Christ*

In the beginning was the Word, and the Word was with God, and the Word was God. He was in the beginning with God. All things came into being through him, and without him not one thing came into being. What has come into being in him was life, and the life was the **light** of all people. The **light** shines in the darkness, and the darkness did not overcome it. [John 1:1-5]

Again Jesus spoke to them, saying, "I am the **light** of the world. Whoever follows me will never walk in darkness but will have the light of life." [John 8:12]

From this brief sample of the way light was used as a figure of speech in the Bible, the versatility and complexity of the metaphor should be obvious. In each passage, the reader has to sort through the possibilities of interpretation. Was the author making a statement about God or using a common metaphor about some aspect of human experience? Or both?

In an industrialized society, the meaning of light as a metaphor has changed from what it was in Bible times. With the availability of electric lights, people are seldom exposed to genuine darkness. Outdoor lighting is so pervasive that astronomers complain about light pollution obscuring the night sky. In ancient times, the sun was the primary source of light, and darkness severely restricted activity. For thousands of years, humans have worshiped the sun. As Judaism and Christianity developed, they had a tendency to coopt the language of sun worship, to make their God the light and the source of light. Use of the light metaphor can help Jesus followers appreciate their connection with the people, in the past and in the present, for whom the sun has been the focus of their spiritual development.

The light metaphor also has been an issue in discussions of race. Some white people associate light and darkness with skin color. Light is good and dark is bad. Light is intelligent, moral, and favored by God; dark is stupid, depraved, and merely tolerated by God. This use of the metaphor, sometimes intentional and sometimes thoughtless, has encouraged bigotry and racism among those who call themselves Christians.

lion, *noun*   Among biblical authors, a favorite image for invoking fear* was the lion, *ari* in Hebrew and *leon* in Greek. They used it in a positive sense in blessings* and in depictions of God,* and in a negative sense in references to enemies and to the Devil (see **Satan**).

Blessings

Judah is a **lion's** whelp; from the prey, my son, you have gone up. He crouches down, he stretches out like a lion, like a lioness—who dares rouse him up? [Genesis 49:9]

Surely there is no enchantment against Jacob, no divination against Israel; now it shall be said of Jacob and Israel, "See what God has done!" Look a people rising up like a lioness, and rousing itself like a **lion**! It does not lie down until it has eaten the prey and drunk the blood of the slain. [Numbers 23:23-24]

The wicked

Save me from the mouth of the **lion**! From the horns of the wild oxen you have rescued me. [Psalm 22:21]

The Lord stood by me and gave me strength, so that through me the message might be fully proclaimed and all the Gentiles might hear it. So I was rescued from the **lion's** mouth. The Lord will rescue me from every evil attack and save me for his heavenly kingdom. [II Timothy 4:17-18]

Enemies

O LORD my God, in you I take refuge; save me from all my pursuers, and deliver me, or like a **lion** they will tear me apart; they will drag me away, with no one to rescue. [Psalm 7:1-2]

A **lion** has gone up from its thicket, a destroyer of nations has set out; he has gone out from his place to make your land a waste; your cities will be ruins without inhabitant. [Jeremiah 4:7]

God

For thus the LORD said to me, As a **lion** or a young lion growls over its prey, and—when a band of shepherds is called out against it—is not terrified by their shouting or daunted at their noise, so the LORD of hosts will come down to fight upon Mount Zion and upon its hill. [Isaiah 31:4]

I will not execute my fierce anger; I will not again destroy Ephraim; for I am God and no mortal, the Holy One in your midst, and I will not come in wrath. They shall go after the LORD, who roars like a **lion**; when he roars, his children shall come trembling from the west. [Hosea 11:9-10]

The **lion** has roared; who will not fear? The Lord GOD has spoken; who can but prophesy? [Amos 3:8]

The devil

Discipline yourselves, keep alert. Like a roaring **lion** your adversary the devil prowls around, looking for someone to devour. [I Peter 5:8]

Marks a word in the text that has its own entry   **181**

A variation on the lion theme appears in Ezekiel's vision of four-winged creatures, who reappear in the Revelation to John. Christian tradition has assigned each of the figures to one of the gospels, the winged lion being the symbol of St. Mark.

> As for the appearance of their faces: the four had the face of a human being, the face of a **lion** on the right side, the face of an ox on the left side, and the face of an eagle; such were their faces. Their wings were spread out above; each creature had two wings, each of which touched the wing of another, while two covered their bodies. [Ezekiel 1:10-11]

> Around the throne, and on each side of the throne, are four living creatures, full of eyes in front and behind: the first living creature like a **lion**, the second living creature like an ox, the third living creature with a face like a human face, and the fourth living creature like a flying eagle. [Revelation 4:6-7]

The lion has proved to be one of the most versatile images in the Bible. In the early days of Israel, when the only protection from natural dangers was a tent, the people may have lived in constant fear of lions. Or perhaps in the collective unconscious was the memory of an even earlier period when the big cats were the primary threat to the survival of human beings as a species. Even for people who have never had reason to be frightened by a lion, the animal has continued to be an object of fascination. C. S. Lewis used the Christian tradition and the natural interest in lions often displayed by children in his charming book for them, *The Lion, the Witch and the Wardrobe*.[15] The Christ-like figure in the tale is Aslan, a magnificent lion.

liturgy, *noun*   In many Christian traditions, liturgy is another name for a service of worship.* In Orthodox churches, Liturgy is the name for what others call Holy Communion or Eucharist.* The word comes from the Greek *leitourgia*, from *laos*, people + *ergon*, work. *Leitourgia* was originally any form of public service, but it came to be applied to the services of the temple in Jerusalem. The early Christian writers used the term in a variety of ways.

> In the days of King Herod of Judea, there was a priest named Zechariah, who belonged to the priestly order of Abijah . . . Once when he was serving as priest before God and his section was on duty, he was chosen by lot, according to the custom of the priesthood, to enter the sanctuary of the Lord and offer incense . . . When his time of **service** was ended, he went to his home. [Luke 1:5, 8-9, 23]

> You will be enriched in every way for your great generosity, which will produce thanksgiving to God through us; for the rendering of this **ministry** not only supplies the needs of the saints but also overflows with many thanksgivings to God. [II Corinthians 9:11-12]

> Even if I am being poured out as a libation over the sacrifice and the **offering** of your faith, I am glad and rejoice with all of you. [Philippians 2:17]

> Welcome Epaphroditus then in the Lord with all joy, and honor such people, because he came close to death for the work of Christ, risking his life to make up for those **services** that you could not give me. [Philippians 2:29-30]

> Jesus has now obtained a more excellent **ministry,** and to that degree he is the mediator of a better covenant, which has been enacted through better promises. [Hebrews 8:6]

The use of the related word *leitourgos*, a public servant, gives a further indication of how the early Christians thought about *leiturgia*.

Marks a word in the text that has its own entry

FROM LITERAL TO LITERARY

You also pay taxes, for the authorities are God's **servants.** [Romans 13:6]

Nevertheless on some points I have written to you rather boldly by way of reminder, because of the grace given me by God to be a **minister** of Christ Jesus to the Gentiles in the priestly service of the gospel of God, so that the offering of the Gentiles may be acceptable, sanctified by the Holy Spirit. [Romans 15:15-16]

I think it necessary to send to you Epaphroditus—my brother and co-worker and fellow soldier, your messenger and **minister** to my need. [Philippians 2:25]

Of the angels he says, "He makes his angels winds, and his **servants** flames of fire."
[Hebrews 1:7]

At no place in the Bible do the nouns *leitourgia* and *leitourgos* refer to Christian worship. In the context of one passage, however, the verb *leitourgeo* does seem to mean engaging in a service of worship.

Now in the church at Antioch there were prophets and teachers: Barnabas, Simeon who was called Niger, Lucius of Cyrene, Manaen a member of the court of Herod the ruler, and Saul. While they were **worshiping** the Lord and fasting, the Holy Spirit said, "Set apart for me Barnabas and Saul for the work to which I have called them." [Acts 13:1-2]

In the Christian writings of the second century, *leitourgia* refers primarily to acts of charity, such as the collection for the relief of the Jesus followers in Jerusalem referred to in II Corinthians 9:11-12, quoted above. Clement, Bishop of Rome, did use *leitourgia* in writing about the activities of the layman in the church service, a warning not to overstep the fixed boundaries of his ministry.

Possibly because in listening to the Greek translations of the Hebrew Scriptures they heard the temple services referred to as *leitourgia*, the Christians began applying the same metaphor to their own worship. More recently, some church leaders have been using the etymology of the metaphor in an attempt to convince lay people of their responsibility for worship. They tell them that liturgy is the work of the people. That is a fine concept, but it does not fit the facts. In the temple, *leitourgia* was work on behalf of the people, not work done by the people. In the church, the work of the *laos* was not taking responsibility for worship but serving the people in the world around them.

long suffering—see patience

lord, *noun*   The English word lord usually translates two Hebrew words—*adonai* and *adon*—and one Greek word, *kyrios*. The poets who wrote the psalms frequently addressed God* as *adonai*.

O **Lord,** all my longing is known to you; my sighing is not hidden from you. [Psalm 38:9]

Rouse yourself! Why do you sleep, O **Lord**? Awake, do not cast us off forever! [Psalm 44:23]

O **Lord,** open my lips, and my mouth will declare your praise. [Psalm 51:15]

Apparently *adonai*, a form reserved for addressing God, evolved from *adon*, also translated Lord, which indicated a ruler or, in the case of a slave, the master. It was also used simply as a way of showing respect in direct address, much as people trying to be especially polite might today say Sir or Madam.

Hear us, my **lord**; you are a mighty prince among us. [Genesis 23:6]

Marks a word in the text that has its own entry

So the servant put his hand under the thigh of Abraham his **master** and swore to him concerning this matter. [Genesis 24:9]

So Eli said to her, "How long will you make a drunken spectacle of yourself? Put away your wine." But Hannah answered, "No, my **lord,** I am a woman deeply troubled; I have drunk neither wine nor strong drink." [I Samuel 1:14-15]

At some point in their history, the Hebrew-speaking people decided that the ancient name of their tribal God was so sacred that they should refrain from saying it aloud. When the name, indicated by the four letters *YHWH*, appeared in the text, they substituted *adonai*. Originally, written Hebrew had no vowels. In the centuries not long before Jesus, Hebrew scholars added marks to remind them of the vowel sounds required for correct pronunciation. When they came to *YHWH*, they inserted the vowel sounds for *adonai*. Some early Christian translators, not understanding the secret, made up the name Jehovah for God. Later, linguists tried to reconstruct the ancient Hebrew and came up with Yahweh. In recent times, out of respect for the Jewish tradition of never saying aloud the sacred name of God, translators have used LORD, small capital letters, to stand for *YHWH*. This use of LORD appears more than six thousand five hundred times in the Hebrew Scriptures, beginning with the second chapter of Genesis and continuing through the last chapter of Malachi.

These are the generations of the heavens and the earth when they were created. In the day that the LORD God made the earth and the heavens, when no plant of the field was yet in the earth and no herb of the field had yet sprung up—for the LORD God had not caused it to rain upon the earth, and there was no one to till the ground. [Genesis 2:4-5]

Lo, I will send you the prophet Elijah before the great and terrible day of the LORD comes. He will turn the hearts of parents to their children and the hearts of children to their parents, so that I will not come and strike the land with a curse. [Malachi 4:5-6]

The first Christian statement of faith was probably "Jesus is Lord." The context in which St. Paul used the affirmation sounds as if he were quoting something that his readers would immediately recognize.

No one can say "Jesus is **Lord**" except by the Holy Spirit. [I Corinthians 12:3]

When the authors of the Bible or characters in their stories used the term *kyrios iesous,* they were indicating a relationship with Jesus, but the question of what kind of relationship depends upon their understanding of the metaphor. They could have been demonstrating their deep respect for Jesus or they could have been acknowledging Jesus as their master and themselves as servants. They also could have been suggesting that they recognized the presence of God in Jesus. Except for the author of the Gospel according to John, they probably were not implying that Jesus is God, a statement that does not appear in the Bible.

With great power the apostles gave their testimony to the resurrection of the **Lord** Jesus, and great grace was upon them all. [Acts 4:33]

I know and am persuaded in the **Lord** Jesus that nothing is unclean in itself; but it is unclean for anyone who thinks it unclean. [Romans 14:14]

For whoever was called in the **Lord** as a slave is a freed person belonging to the **Lord,** just as whoever was free when called is a slave of Christ. [I Corinthians 7:22]

Marks a word in the text that has its own entry

Therefore God also highly exalted him and gave him the name that is above every name, so that at the name of Jesus every knee should bend, in heaven and on earth and under the earth, and every tongue should confess that Jesus Christ is **Lord**, to the glory of God the Father. [Philippians 2:9-11]

My brothers and sisters, do you with your acts of favoritism really believe in our glorious **Lord** Jesus Christ? [James 2:1]

Jesus said to Thomas, "Put your finger here and see my hands. Reach out your hand and put it in my side. Do not doubt but believe." Thomas answered him, "My **Lord** and my God!" [John 20:27-28]

Originally, Lord was a faithful English translation of the Hebrew *adonai* and the Greek *kyrios*. Until relatively modern times, Lord was in every English-speaking person's common vocabulary. Everyone had a human lord or was a lord. In old English, the word was *hlaford*, a contraction of loaf and warden. A lord was the keeper of the bread.

In the early English social structure, the lord provided protection to the farmers so that they could raise their crops in peace. At the time of the harvest, they brought the grain to the lord's mill for the grinding of the flour that would become their bread. They gave their loyalty to the lord and trusted the lord to protect them and to see that they were fed. Common people owed their lives to their lord. They were fed as long as they did what they were told and could starve if they lost favor. From the perspective of the twenty-first century, social critics might find fault with the social system once established in England, but they should be able to understand why Lord made sense to the English as a way of addressing Jesus and the God to whom Jesus had led them.

love, *noun* and *verb*   Love, one of the most important terms in the Bible, almost defies definition. One word for love in the Hebrew Scriptures, *chesed,* appears in some English versions as steadfast love, an attribute of God.

For the king trusts in the LORD, and through the **steadfast love** of the Most High he shall not be moved. [Psalm 21:7]

For the mountains may depart and the hills be removed, but my **steadfast love** shall not depart from you, and my covenant of peace shall not be removed, says the LORD, who has compassion on you. [Isaiah 54:10]

The Hebrew verb *aheb* and noun *ahabah* are almost always translated love, but they cover a great variety of conditions and relationships. In the two books of Samuel, the words cover impersonal relationships—servants and guests—as well as the affection between two men or an overwhelming sexual desire.

Saul commanded his servants, "Speak to David in private and say, 'See, the king is delighted with you, and all his servants **love** you; now then, become the king's son-in-law.'" [I Samuel 18:22]

Jonathan made David swear again by his **love** for him; for he **loved** him as he **loved** his own life. [I Samuel 20:17]

Jonadab said to him, "O son of the king, why are you so haggard morning after morning? Will you not tell me?" Amnon said to him, "I **love** Tamar, my brother Absalom's sister." [II Samuel 13:4]

With this range of possibilities, what then is the reader supposed to make of commandments to love God and neighbors or a pronouncement that God loves people?

> You shall **love** the LORD your God, therefore, and keep his charge, his decrees, his ordinances, and his commandments always. [Deuteronomy 11:1]

> You shall not take vengeance or bear a grudge against any of your people, but you shall **love** your neighbor as yourself. [Leviticus 19:18]

> Although heaven and the heaven of heavens belong to the LORD your God, the earth with all that is in it, yet the LORD set his heart in **love** on your ancestors alone and chose you, their descendants after them, out of all the peoples, as it is today. [Deuteronomy 10:14-15]

The followers of Jesus inherited the range of possibilities for understanding love. For most of them, the scriptures were the Greek translations of the Hebrew writings (see **Bible**). In almost every case, the scholars who translated the Hebrew into Greek used *agapao* for the verb *aheb* and *agape* for the noun *ahabah*. The origin of these two Greek words remains obscure, but they once may have indicated a concern for another that is not based on the other's worthiness. Something of that connotation may have been present in both the Hebrew and Greek words for love.

The commandment to love God implies a choice, a choice that does not depend on a person's feelings about God, which may vary from day to day or even moment to moment. The commandment to love neighbors implies a similar choice. The context of the verse in Leviticus quoted above—not bearing a grudge or taking vengeance—suggests that choosing love is a possibility even for people who are disgusted or angry with their neighbors.

Being commanded to love or promising to love would make no sense if love were limited to the three kinds of experiences illustrated from the books of Samuel. Nobody can like or admire or fall in love with another because someone in authority issued an order to do so. Love without feeling or passion, however, would be sterile. Look at love from the perspective of the recipient. Who would want to be the object of a logically calculated act of charity? Who would want to be the object of a cold, impersonal sort of love?

The contradictions inherent in using love as the keystone of their overarching symbol system frequently has left the followers of Jesus in a morally precarious position. Because love in the culture is usually of the romantic sort, to identify God with love can be a trivial assertion. In one extreme, the presence of God can be experienced only when a person is having happily excited, or at least warm, fuzzy feelings. In the opposite extreme, God is experienced as a harsh, demanding presence evoking feelings of failure, even of self-loathing. For the love metaphor to work constructively in people's lives, they need to be aware of the danger in the two extremes and to chart a course between them.

The Letter to the Ephesians, attributed to St. Paul but probably written by someone else, has much to say about love. The following examples illustrate the understanding of love as a choice rather than a spontaneous feeling of affection. At the same time, they suggest that love without feeling would be sterile.

> Speaking the truth in **love,** we must grow up in every way into him who is the head, into Christ, from whom the whole body, joined and knit together by every ligament with which it is equipped, as each part is working properly, promotes the body's growth in building itself up in **love.** [Ephesians 4:15-16]

Marks a word in the text that has its own entry

Be imitators of God, as beloved children, and live in **love**, as Christ **loved** us. [Ephesians 5:1-2]

Husbands, **love** your wives, just as Christ **loved** the church and gave himself up for her. [Ephesians 5:25]

Grace be with all who have an undying **love** for our Lord Jesus Christ. [Ephesians 6:24]

The author of this letter addressed to the Christian community in Ephesus has a particular insight into the nature of love that cannot be expressed in English. In the New Revised Standard Version, the line reads:

I therefore, the prisoner in the Lord, beg you to lead a life worthy of the calling to which you have been called, with all humility and gentleness, with patience, bearing with one another in **love**. [Ephesians 4:1-2]

A peculiarity of Greek grammar known as the middle voice allows the author to describe an understanding of love in action. In English, limited by active and passive voice verbs, an author must write about people as subjects or objects. In the active voice, somebody is doing something to someone else. In the passive voice, something is being done to someone by somebody else. The beauty of the middle voice is that it carries the possibility of two subjects engaged in mutual inter-action. The present English translation sounds as if the author's concern was putting up with one another. A more literal although awkward translation would be having one another up in love. In other words, in loving one another, people can be mutually supportive—not taking turns with first the one and then the other having to do the upholding.

Although the Gospel according to John uses *agapao* in contexts that imply a free choice, the author on two occasions uses the word in a way that suggests that Jesus's feelings of affection for some people could be quite spontaneous. Although the Jesus pictured in John's gospel is the most ethereal and supernatural of the four biblical portraits, at moments in John's narrative, Jesus seems completely human in his feelings for special friends.

John uses another verb for spontaneous affection that leads to friendship, *phileo*. Although the word appears in other books of the Greek Scriptures, John makes almost as much use of it as all the others put together. Most of the time, John seems to use *agapao* and *phileo* interchangeably.

Now a certain man was ill, Lazarus of Bethany, the village of Mary and her sister Martha . . . So the sisters sent a message to Jesus, "Lord, he whom you **love** is ill."—*phileo* [John 11:1-3]

Though Jesus **loved** Martha and her sister and Lazarus, after having heard that Lazarus was ill, he stayed two days longer in the place where he was.—*agapao* [John 11:5-6]

One of his disciples—the one whom Jesus **loved**—was reclining next to him;—*agapao* [John 13:23]

Early on the first day of the week, while it was still dark, Mary Magdalene came to the tomb and saw that the stone had been removed from the tomb. So she ran and went to Simon Peter and the other disciple, the one whom Jesus **loved**.—*phileo* [John 20:1-2]

The Father **loves** the Son and shows him all that he himself is doing; and he will show him greater works than these, so that you will be astonished.—*phileo* [John 5:20]

The Father **loves** the Son and has placed all things in his hands.—*agapao* [John 3:35]

Marks a word in the text that has its own entry

> When they had finished breakfast, Jesus said to Simon Peter, "Simon son of John, do you **love** (*agapao*) me more than these?" He said to him, "Yes, Lord; you know that I **love** (*phileo*) you." [John 21:15]

From John's use of the two words, it seems clear that he would have scoffed at the idea that a faithful follower of Jesus could love others without having any friendly feelings toward them. John probably would not have put up with the idea that, for a person's life to be fulfilled, the person could concentrate on loving others without having to worry about liking anyone. The love metaphor is too complex and too rich to be reduced to easy formulas, especially of the sort that allow the followers of Jesus to duck their responsibilities.

Another way to expand an appreciation of the love metaphor is to see how the biblical writers contrasted love with opposing possibilities. As might be expected, the opposite of love is often hate. What is not so well known is that love is also contrasted with lust.* While lust is an overpowering desire to use other people for self-gratification, love is wanting the best for another. Lust obscures the reality of another person, while love is the power to see and meet another person. Lust distorts self-perception, while love is the power to see and meet one's own soul.*

lust, *noun*   In Greek, the word usually translated as lust is *epithumia*. The root of the word is *thuo*, which was fire used for sacrifice. Ritual fire became a metaphor suggesting intense feeling or passion. That root with its prefix *epi* evokes an image of grasping after fire by people who feel that with themselves all is cold and dark The opposite of such grasping is love,* which is open and self-giving.

While extolling the Christian life of love, the author of the Letter to the Ephesians, probably not St. Paul, reminds the followers of Jesus:

> You were taught to put away your former way of life, your old self, corrupt and deluded by its **lusts**. [Ephesians 4:22]

St. Paul himself makes the same contrast between the way of love and the way of lust in his letter to the Romans, but translators have obscured that fact by substituting desires for *epithumia*.

> Owe no one anything, except to love one another; for the one who loves another has fulfilled the law . . . Instead, put on the Lord Jesus Christ, and make no provision for the flesh, to gratify its **desires**. [Romans 13:8, 14]

Writing a generation or two after St. Paul, another writer who used his name marked a similar contrast between two ways of approaching life. In this passage, the plural of *epithumia* becomes passions, but the meaning is clear.

> Shun youthful **passions** and pursue righteousness, faith, love, and peace, along with those who call on the Lord from a pure heart. [II Timothy 2:22]

The ritual fire metaphor takes on further meaning when *epithumia* appears alongside of another word based on the same root, *makrothumia*, which is usually translated long suffering or patience.* Lust is an inner fire burning out of control, while patience is more like a fire in a stove bringing light and warmth.

Marks a word in the text that has its own entry

M

Magdalene, *noun*   A misreading of the gospel stories associated with Mary Magdalene produced a metaphor indicating a reformed and repentant prostitute. The name Magdalene, with or without the final e, has been used to indicate not only women who abandoned their profession as sex workers but also the institutions in which they found refuge and support for changing their lives. In eighteenth and nineteenth century Britain, Magdalen was the shorthand name for a hospital or a hospital ward, a home, a house, an asylum, or a charity devoted to the care of former prostitutes. Magdalen (pronounced Maudlin) College, Oxford, founded in 1448, is the exception to the rule that institutions bearing the name were established for wayward women, but the pronunciation of the college name is a reminder that when the word is spelled as it sometimes sounds, magdalene/maudlin has developed other figurative connotations. To be maudlin is to be weepy and overly sentimental, especially after having had too much alcohol to drink. This development of the metaphor apparently was the result of Mary Magdalene appearing in paintings as a tearful penitent.

Nothing in the gospels, however, links Mary *Magdalene* with prostitution. This Mary, whose last name in English is a transliteration of the Greek, probably came from the village of Magdala near Tiberius on the west side of the Lake of Gennesaret. She appears at the end of all four gospels, but they say very little about her by way of identification. Only Luke introduces her early in his version of the story. Luke, along with Mark and Matthew, identifies Mary Magdalene as one of the women who had "provided for" Jesus. The verb in all three of these gospels is *diakoneo,* from which we get such English words as deacon* and diaconate.

> Soon afterwards he went on through cities and villages, proclaiming and bringing the good news of the kingdom of God. The twelve were with him, as well as some women who had been cured of evil spirits and infirmities: Mary, called **Magdalene,** from whom seven demons had gone out, and Joanna, the wife of Herod's steward Chuza, and Susanna, and many others, who provided for them out of their resources. [Luke 8:1-3]

> Many women were also at Golgotha, looking on from a distance; they had followed Jesus from Galilee and had provided for him. Among them were Mary **Magdalene,** and Mary the mother of James and Joseph, and the mother of the sons of Zebedee. [Matthew 27:55-56]

All four gospels place Mary Magdalene at the crucifixion of Jesus and later at his tomb. Matthew, Luke, and John say that Mary Magdalene was among the women who told the male disciples* that Jesus lived. Only Mark, in what is commonly accepted as the end of his gospel, says that the women refused the assignment of reporting to the other disciples.

> After the sabbath, as the first day of the week was dawning, Mary **Magdalene** and the other Mary went to see the tomb. . . . Suddenly Jesus met them and said, "Greetings!" And they came to him, took hold of his feet, and worshiped him. Then Jesus said to them, "Do not be afraid; go and tell my brothers to go to Galilee; there they will see me." [Matthew 28:1, 9-10]

> Then they remembered Jesus' words, and returning from the tomb, they told all this to the eleven and to all the rest. Now it was Mary **Magdalene,** Joanna, Mary the mother of James, and the other women with them who told this to the apostles. [Luke 24:8-10]

> Mary **Magdalene** went and announced to the disciples, "I have seen the Lord"; and she told them that he had said these things to her. [John 20:18]

> When the sabbath was over, Mary **Magdalene**, and Mary the mother of James, and Salome bought spices, so that they might go and anoint him. . . . As they entered the tomb, they saw a young man, dressed in a white robe, sitting on the right side; and they were alarmed. But he said to them, "Do not be alarmed; you are looking for Jesus of Nazareth, who was crucified. He has been raised; he is not here. Look, there is the place they laid him. But go, tell his disciples and Peter that he is going ahead of you to Galilee; there you will see him, just as he told you." So they went out and fled from the tomb, for terror and amazement had seized them; and they said nothing to anyone, for they were afraid. [Mark 16:1, 5-8]

Apparently the notion that Mary Magdalene was a prostitute was the result of a compound error. John's gospel has a brief account about Mary, the sister of Martha and Lazarus of Bethany, anointing Jesus's feet and wiping them with her hair.

> Mary took a pound of costly perfume made of pure nard, anointed Jesus' feet, and wiped them with her hair. The house was filled with the fragrance of the perfume. [John 12:3]

This account in John is very similar to one in Luke where a nameless woman anointing Jesus's feet is clearly a prostitute. She is described as a sinner, and as in John's account, she carries a tool of her trade, perfumed ointment.

> A woman in the city, who was a sinner, having learned that he was eating in the Pharisee's house, brought an alabaster jar of ointment. She stood behind him at his feet, weeping, and began to bathe his feet with her tears and to dry them with her hair. Then she continued kissing his feet and anointing them with the ointment. [Luke 7:37-38]

The irony of identifying Mary Magdalene with the nameless sex worker of Luke's gospel arises from the possibility that she was particularly close to Jesus, perhaps his wife. Admittedly, the evidence for Jesus being married to anyone is fairly slim, but an intriguing hint appears in John's gospel in the scene where the crucified Jesus appears to her.

> Jesus said to her, "Mary!" She turned and said to him in Hebrew, "Rabbouni!" (which means Teacher). Jesus said to her, "Do not hold on to me, because I have not yet ascended to the Father." [John 20:16-17]

The King James Version at this point is a bit more dramatic. Jesus says, "Touch me not." The Greek verb in question is *hapto,* which can mean take hold of or touch or cling to. *Hapto* could also be used as a euphemism for sexual intercourse as it is in the Greek translation of Genesis and in a letter of St. Paul. (For other sexual metaphors, see **know**.)

> Then God said to Abimelech in the dream, "Yes, I know that you did this in the integrity of your heart; furthermore it was I who kept you from sinning against me. Therefore I did not let you **touch** Abraham's wife." [Genesis 20:6]

> Now concerning the matters about which you wrote: "It is well for a man not to **touch** a woman." But because of cases of sexual immorality, each man should have his own wife and each woman her own husband. [I Corinthians 7:1-2]

In the Hebrew culture of Jesus's time, only two women could claim the right to embrace or even touch a man: his mother and his wife. If Jesus had to admonish Mary Magdalene to refrain from embracing him, the story suggests that both of them recognized her right to do so. Mary Magdalene was not Jesus's mother, so the tradition behind the story indicates that at least some of Jesus's early followers thought she was his wife.

Whether Mary Magdalene was or was not Jesus's wife, the use of her name as a metaphor meaning prostitute seems grossly unfair to her memory. Fortunately, that figurative use of her name has faded. Understanding the origin of the metaphor is now more important for understanding eighteenth and nineteenth century English usage than for understanding the Bible.

man—see **adam**

marriage, *noun*; **marry**, *verb*   The original languages of the Bible have no equivalent for the English word marriage when it means the condition of wedlock or spousehood. They have words that refer to the process or ritual of getting into such a condition—the wedding—but nothing that expresses the state of matrimony. The Hebrew expression for a wedding was literally to give a woman or to take a woman. The Greeks, however, had a word for getting married, *gamos*, which became a metaphor indicating something about the relationship between Christ* and the church.* In the book Revelation, Christ is identified as the Lamb* and the church as the new Jerusalem adorned for marriage.

> Let us rejoice and exult and give him the glory, for the **marriage** of the Lamb has come, and his bride has made herself ready; to her it has been granted to be clothed with fine linen, bright and pure—for the fine linen is the righteous deeds of the saints. [Revelation 19:7-8]

An analogy related to the marriage metaphor appears in the Epistle to the Ephesians, but note that neither Hebrew nor Greek had a special word for husband or wife. In both languages, the ordinary words for woman and man had to do. Woman in Hebrew was *ishah* and in Greek *gyne*, the root of the English word gynecology. Man in Hebrew was *ish* and in Greek *aner*.

> Wives, be subject to your **husbands** as you are to the Lord. For the **husband** is the head of the **wife** just as Christ is the head of the church, the body of which he is the Savior. Just as the church is subject to Christ, so also **wives** ought to be, in everything, to their **husbands. Husbands,** love your **wives,** just as Christ loved the church and gave himself up for her, in order to make her holy by cleansing her with the washing of water by the word, so as to present the church to himself in splendor, without a spot or wrinkle or anything of the kind—yes, so that she may be holy and without blemish. [Ephesians 5:22-27]

The differences between contemporary English and the ancient languages concerning marriage should warn the reader that contemporary concepts of marriage are quite different from the understandings of domestic relationships found in the Bible. An understanding of the marriage metaphor and analogy requires a knowledge of ancient marital practices.

A man could take several wives and keep concubines as well, if he could afford them. Apparently, among the early Christians only bishops were restricted to one woman.

> Now Gideon had seventy sons, his own offspring, for he had many wives (*ishah*). His concubine who was in Shechem also bore him a son, and he named him Abimelech. [Judges 8:30-31]

> In Jerusalem, after he came from Hebron, David took more concubines and wives (*ishah*); and more sons and daughters were born to David. [II Samuel 5:13]

> Now a bishop must be above reproach, married only once.—literally *aner* of one *gyne*
> [I Timothy 3:2]

If a woman could not prove she had been a virgin before her wedding night, not only was her marriage invalid, but also she was subject to the death penalty.

> If, however, this charge is true, that evidence of the young woman's virginity was not found, then they shall bring the young woman out to the entrance of her father's house and the men of her town shall stone her to death, because she committed a disgraceful act in Israel by prostituting herself in her father's house. So you shall purge the evil from your midst. [Deuteronomy 22:20-21]

At times in their history, the people of Israel were not permitted to marry foreigners.

> The land that you are entering to possess is a land unclean with the pollutions of the peoples of the lands, with their abominations. They have filled it from end to end with their uncleanness. Therefore do not give your daughters to their sons, neither take their daughters for your sons. [Ezra 9:11-12]

> We will not give our daughters to the peoples of the land or take their daughters for our sons. [Nehemiah 10:30]

If a married man died without children, his brother was obliged to have sexual intercourse with his sister-in-law. As the quote from Mark's gospel illustrates, this law apparently was still in effect at the time of Jesus.

> Judah took a wife for Er his firstborn; her name was Tamar. But Er, Judah's firstborn, was wicked in the sight of the LORD, and the LORD put him to death. Then Judah said to Onan, "Go in to your brother's wife and perform the duty of a brother-in-law to her; raise up offspring for your brother." [Genesis 38:6-8]

> When brothers reside together, and one of them dies and has no son, the wife of the deceased shall not be married outside the family to a stranger. Her husband's brother shall go in to her, taking her in marriage, and performing the duty of a husband's brother to her, and the firstborn whom she bears shall succeed to the name of the deceased brother, so that his name may not be blotted out of Israel. But if the man has no desire to marry his brother's widow, then his brother's widow shall go up to the elders at the gate and say, "My husband's brother refuses to perpetuate his brother's name in Israel; he will not perform the duty of a husband's brother to me." Then the elders of his town shall summon him and speak to him. If he persists, saying, "I have no desire to marry her," then his brother's wife shall go up to him in the presence of the elders, pull his sandal off his foot, spit in his face, and declare, "This is what is done to the man who does not build up his brother's house." Throughout Israel his family shall be known as "the house of him whose sandal was pulled off." [Deuteronomy 25:5-10]

> Some Sadducees, who say there is no resurrection, came to Jesus and asked him a question, saying, "Teacher, Moses wrote for us that 'if a man's brother dies, leaving a wife but no child, the man shall marry the widow and raise up children for his brother.'" [Mark 12:18-19]

Using the marriage metaphor and analogy can help in understanding the relationship between Christ and the church if people keep in mind that, in ancient times, women were supposed to be subservient and men dominant. At the same time, men were supposed to be caring and protective. The man could take care of any number of women. This image may still make sense in understanding a relationship to the divine. The church is not likely to claim a partnership with Christ based on the equality of the partners.

No matter how well the marriage metaphor and analogy work, however, most Christians would not favor a return to all the marriage laws found in the Bible.

DID YOU KNOW . . .

. . . that *gyne* is pronounced *guh-nay*?
For more help with pronunciation, see "Pronouncing
Transliterated Hebrew and Greek Words" on page 15.

Mary—see **mother**, **virgin birth**

mediator, *noun* Some early followers of Jesus borrowed from Greek legal language to describe their relationship to him. They called Jesus a *mesites*, one who mediates between two parties to resolve a dispute or to achieve a common purpose.

> There is one God; there is also one **mediator** between God and humankind, Christ Jesus, himself human, who gave himself a ransom for all—this was attested at the right time. [I Timothy 2:5-6]

> Jesus has now obtained a more excellent ministry, and to that degree he is the **mediator** of a better covenant, which has been enacted through better promises. [Hebrews 8:6]

Curiously, the only time St. Paul used *mesites* was when he demonstrated the inferiority of Judaism, arguing that the covenant* with Israel required a go-between, which was not necessary for the followers of Jesus.

> Why then the law? It was added because of transgressions, until the offspring would come to whom the promise had been made; and it was ordained through angels by a **mediator**. Now a **mediator** involves more than one party; but God is one. [Galatians 3:19-20]

Apparently, Christians were able to put aside Paul's negative view of *mesites*. The mediator metaphor became one of the popular titles they assigned to Jesus. If God* seemed remote and inaccessible, they could address their prayers to Jesus, whom they could trust to represent their interests before the divine authority.*

mercy, *noun* Three quite different Hebrew words appear in English translation as mercy. *Racham* comes from a verb that meant to caress and indicates tenderness and compassion. *Chesed* could also mean love* or kindness, or both at the same time. *Chanan* evolved from a verb *chanah,* which often meant to pitch a tent, and was used to indicate graciousness. These words referred to aspects of human relationships as well as expressing feelings about God.* Their use in human terms can illuminate the meaning of the words when applied to God.

racham

> The woman whose son was alive said to the king—because **compassion** for her son burned within her—"Please, my lord, give her the living boy; certainly do not kill him!" The other said, "It shall be neither mine nor yours; divide it." [I Kings 3:26]

Marks a word in the text that has its own entry

Look, a people is coming from the north; a mighty nation and many kings are stirring from the farthest parts of the earth. They wield bow and spear, they are cruel and have no **mercy**. [Jeremiah 50:41-42]

To the Lord our God belong **mercy** and forgiveness, for we have rebelled against him. [Daniel 9:9]

chesed

And Lot said to them, "Oh, no, my lords; your servant has found favor with you, and you have shown me great **kindness** in saving my life; but I cannot flee to the hills, for fear the disaster will overtake me and I die." [Genesis 19:18-19]

Ben-Hadad's servants said to him, "Look, we have heard that the kings of the house of Israel are **merciful** kings; let us put sackcloth around our waists and ropes on our heads, and go out to the king of Israel; perhaps he will spare your life." [I Kings 20:31]

Surely goodness and **mercy** shall follow me all the days of my life, and I shall dwell in the house of the LORD my whole life long. [Psalm 23:6]

chanan

A man of God approached and said to the king of Israel, "Thus says the LORD: Because the Arameans have said, 'The LORD is a god of the hills but he is not a god of the valleys,' therefore I will give all this great multitude into your hand, and you shall know that I am the LORD." They **encamped** opposite one another seven days. Then on the seventh day the battle began; the Israelites killed one hundred thousand Aramean foot soldiers in one day.—chanah [I Kings 20:28-29]

The souls of the wicked desire evil; their neighbors find no **mercy** in their eyes. [Proverbs 21:10]

Have **mercy** upon us, O LORD, have **mercy** upon us, for we have had more than enough of contempt. [Psalm 123:3]

The Greek word for mercy was *eleos*. The verb form, to have mercy, was *eleeo*. In the Bible, these words are usually associated with God, but occasionally they are used to suggest that the early Christians expected the same quality to be demonstrated by the followers of Jesus.

Then his lord summoned him and said to him, "You wicked slave! I forgave you all that debt because you pleaded with me. Should you not have had **mercy** on your fellow slave, as I had **mercy** on you?" [Matthew 18:32-33]

For judgment will be without mercy (*anileos*) to anyone who has shown no **mercy**; **mercy** triumphs over judgment. [James 2:13]

Now the time came for Elizabeth to give birth, and she bore a son. Her neighbors and relatives heard that the Lord had shown his great **mercy** to her, and they rejoiced with her. [Luke 1:57-58]

Epaphroditus was indeed so ill that he nearly died. But God had **mercy** on him, and not only on him but on me also, so that I would not have one sorrow after another. [Philippians 2:27]

In several of the gospel stories, petitioners, in asking Jesus for help, used what was a well-known ritual form: *kyrie eleison*, Lord,* have mercy upon us. Not only did worshipers use this phrase in the rituals of their cults, but the populace also shouted the words when they were called out to witness the triumphant procession of a king* or emperor. To use the phrase in addressing Jesus amounted to treason; suggesting that Jesus was heir to the throne* of Israel by adding the title Son of David* was inviting trouble.

> Just then a Canaanite woman from that region came out and started shouting, "Have **mercy** on me, Lord, Son of David; my daughter is tormented by a demon." [Matthew 15:22]

> There were two blind men sitting by the roadside. When they heard that Jesus was passing by, they shouted, "Lord, have **mercy** on us, Son of David!" [Matthew 20:30]

Although this particular language actually may have been avoided in the time of Jesus, from its appearance in the gospels, it is clear that the phrase was in use among Christians soon after his death. By the fourth century, *kyrie eleison* was definitely part of the Christian liturgy* and was also used in private devotions in a repetitive form known as the Jesus Prayer.

In modern English, mercy usually means a person forbearing to inflict punishment on an offender or an enemy. Seldom does mercy bring to mind the qualities suggested by the Hebrew metaphors—tenderness, graciousness, or loving kindness. Today's followers of Jesus might benefit from paying attention to the Hebrew metaphors.

messiah—see **Christ**

metaphor, *noun*   This term is formed from two Greek words, *meta*, over + *pherein*, to carry. A metaphor is a figure of speech in which the characteristics of one thing are carried over to something else; the natural qualities of one thing are transferred to another. Ordinary conversation is filled with metaphors that people seldomly stop to question:

> That idea didn't get to first base.
> The cost of your proposal is in the ball park.
> It rained cats and dogs.
> The candidate waded more deeply into the political debate.
> The old man kicked the bucket.
> He kept his nose to the grindstone.
> The chair called for a vote.

Religious language is by nature metaphorical. In ordinary conversation, people seldomly take metaphors literally, but many have a tendency to do so when the conversation is about religion.

mind, *noun*   No word in biblical Hebrew expresses the concept of mind meaning memory, thought, or mental faculties. When the word mind occurs in English translations, the Hebrew word is most often *lebab* or *leb*, the words for heart. Because the heart was the central organ in the body, the ancients may have seen it as the location of thought processes, or perhaps this was always a convenient figure of speech and they were using heart the way English-speaking people do today when they talk about knowing in their hearts.

> Moses summoned all Israel and said to them: You have seen all that the LORD did before your eyes in the land of Egypt, to Pharaoh and to all his servants and to all his land, the great trials that your eyes saw, the signs, and those great wonders. But to this day the LORD has not given you a **mind** to understand, or eyes to see, or ears to hear. [Deuteronomy 29:2-4]

> Samuel answered Saul, "I am the seer; go up before me to the shrine, for today you shall eat with me, and in the morning I will let you go and will tell you all that is on your **mind**." [I Samuel 9:19]

> O LORD my God, you have made your servant king in place of my father David, although I am only a little child; I do not know how to go out or come in. And your servant is in the midst of the people whom you have chosen, a great people, so numerous they cannot be numbered or counted. Give your servant therefore an understanding **mind** to govern your people, able to discern between good and evil; for who can govern this your great people? [I Kings 3:7-9]

> Mortal, say to the prince of Tyre, Thus says the Lord GOD: Because your **heart** is proud and you have said, "I am a god; I sit in the seat of the gods, in the **heart** of the seas," yet you are but a mortal, and no god, though you compare your **mind** with the **mind** of a god. [Ezekiel 28:2]

In English translations of the Hebrew Scriptures, the word mind also appears in the expressions to change the mind or to repent.* This is a verb form that has nothing to do with the heart but has some connotations that are similar to the Greek word translated with the same phrase.

The early Christians at times used *kardia*, the Greek word for heart, in much the same way that *lebab* and *leb* are used in the Hebrew Scriptures to mean something to do with thinking, reasoning, or believing.

> Jesus, perceiving their thoughts, said, "Why do you think evil in your **hearts**?" [Matthew 9:4]

> Now some of the scribes were sitting there, questioning in their **hearts**. [Mark 2:6]

> The Mighty One has shown strength with his arm; he has scattered the proud in the thoughts of their **hearts**. [Luke 1:51]

> One believes with the **heart** and so is justified, and one confesses with the mouth and so is saved. [Romans 10:10]

They also used a Greek verb *phroneo* to mean using the mind. It is similar to heart in that the verb comes from the noun *phren*, which meant midriff, another location for the center of the body.

> Jesus turned and said to Peter, "Get behind me, Satan! You are a stumbling block to me; for you are setting your **mind** not on divine things but on human things." [Matthew 16:23]

> When I was a child, I spoke like a child, I **thought** like a child, I reasoned like a child; when I became an adult, I put an end to childish ways. [I Corinthians 13:11]

> If then there is any encouragement in Christ, any consolation from love, any sharing in the Spirit, any compassion and sympathy, make my joy complete: be of the same **mind**, having the same love, being in full accord and of one **mind**. [Philippians 2:1-2]

When the early Christians wrote about having a sound mind, they used the verb *sophroneo*, formed from *sozo*, save or keep from harm + *phren*, midriff. A person of sound mind has steady center and is the opposite of a fool,* who has a fluttering *phren*.

> They came to Jesus and saw the demoniac sitting there, clothed and in his **right mind**, the very man who had had the legion; and they were afraid. [Mark 5:15]

> If we are beside ourselves, it is for God; if we are in our **right mind**, it is for you. [II Corinthians 5:13]

For the opposite situation, they had another verb, *mainomai*, from which we have inherited mania and maniac.

> While he was making this defense, Festus exclaimed, "You are **out of your mind**, Paul! Too much learning is driving you insane!" But Paul said, "I am not **out of my mind**, most excellent Festus, but I am speaking the sober truth." [Acts 26:24-25]

> If, therefore, the whole church comes together and all speak in tongues, and outsiders or unbelievers enter, will they not say that you are **out of your mind**? [I Corinthians 14:23]

The Greek words that are most like the English word mind are *nous* and its derivatives *dianoia* and *noema*. *Nous* can also mean understanding or intellect. *Dianoia* can sometimes take on the connotations of intelligence or disposition. Both *dianoia* and *noema* sometimes indicate purpose or plan. First, some examples of the basic word *nous*:

> He said to them, "These are my words that I spoke to you while I was still with you—that everything written about me in the law of Moses, the prophets, and the psalms must be fulfilled." Then he opened their **minds** to understand the scriptures. [Luke 24:44-45]

> I see in my members another law at war with the law of my **mind**, making me captive to the law of sin that dwells in my members. [Romans 7:23]

> Now I appeal to you, brothers and sisters, by the name of our Lord Jesus Christ, that all of you be in agreement and that there be no divisions among you, but that you be united in the same **mind** and the same purpose. [I Corinthians 1:10]

> To the pure all things are pure, but to the corrupt and unbelieving nothing is pure. Their very **minds** and consciences are corrupted. [Titus 1:15]

The words derived from *nous* appear less frequently and are not always translated as mind. From this distance, it is not clear in what ways the writers intended them to be different from *nous*.

> Jesus answered, "The first is, 'Hear, O Israel: the Lord our God, the Lord is one; you shall love the Lord your God with all your heart, and with all your soul, and with all your **mind**, and with all your strength.'"—*dianoia* [Mark 12:29-30]

> You who were once estranged and hostile in **mind**, doing evil deeds, he has now reconciled in his fleshly body through death, so as to present you holy and blameless and irreproachable before him.—*dianoia* [Colossians 1:21-22]

> Even if our gospel is veiled, it is veiled to those who are perishing. In their case the god of this world has blinded the **minds** of the unbelievers, to keep them from seeing the light of the gospel of the glory of Christ, who is the image of God.—*noema* [II Corinthians 4:3-4]

> The peace of God, which surpasses all understanding (*nous*), will guard your hearts and your **minds** in Christ Jesus.—*noema* [Philippians 4:7]

As is apparent from these examples, the early followers of Jesus used both *kardia* and *nous* as the location of thinking, but they could make a distinction between the two. Faith* was a matter of the heart while logic was a matter of the mind, as the word is used in English. For the love* of God to be complete, both the heart and mind are necessary. Both the heart and the mind require God's peace.*

Marks a word in the text that has its own entry

minister—see **bishop**, **deacon**, **liturgy**, **priest**, and **shepherd**

miracle, *noun*   The word miracle does not appear in the New Revised Standard Version of the Bible, but it does in the King James Version. It is the translation once for the Hebrew *mopheth*, which is wonder, and once for the Greek *dynamis*, which is power.* Miracle frequently stands for the Greek *semeion*, which more often is translated as sign. This is the way the New Revised Standard Version handles the miracle passages:

mopheth and *dynamis*

The LORD said to Moses and Aaron, "When Pharaoh says to you, 'Perform a **wonder**,' then you shall say to Aaron, 'Take your staff and throw it down before Pharaoh, and it will become a snake.'"—*mopheth* [Exodus 7:8-9]

John said to him, "Teacher, we saw someone casting out demons in your name, and we tried to stop him, because he was not following us." But Jesus said, "Do not stop him; for no one who does a **deed of power** in my name will be able soon afterward to speak evil of me."—*dynamis* [Mark 9:38-39]

semeion

When Herod saw Jesus, he was very glad, for he had been wanting to see him for a long time, because he had heard about him and was hoping to see him perform some **sign**. [Luke 23:8]

As the official was going down, his slaves met him and told him that his child was alive. So he asked them the hour when he began to recover, and they said to him, "Yesterday at one in the afternoon the fever left him." The father realized that this was the hour when Jesus had said to him, "Your son will live." So he himself believed, along with his whole household. Now this was the second **sign** that Jesus did after coming from Judea to Galilee. [John 4:51-54]

So the crowd that had been with Jesus when he called Lazarus out of the tomb and raised him from the dead continued to testify. It was also because they heard that he had performed this **sign** that the crowd went to meet him. [John 12:17-18]

The man on whom this **sign** of healing had been performed was more than forty years old. [Acts 4:22]

Today's readers are apt to think of miracles as events in which the laws of nature are temporarily suspended, but that could not have been the understanding of the biblical authors. The laws of nature had not yet been discovered. A miracle was a wonder, a surprise, that pointed beyond itself to a particular realization. So a reader might fairly ask if the wonders of the Bible were historical events or literary devices employed to add the elements of surprise and delight to the narratives. Whether reports of historical events or inventions of the authors, the point of including the incidents was the same: to pass on to the reader the author's sense of awe and wonder in considering God's presence in the world.

mother, *noun*   Although, in the Bible, mother is never used as a metaphor indicating God,* three passages compare God to a mother. The first uses the Hebrew word for mother, *em*. The other two compare God not to a human mother but to a mother bird, in Greek *ornis*.

Marks a word in the text that has its own entry

> As a **mother** comforts her child, so I will comfort you; you shall be comforted in Jerusalem. [Isaiah 66:13]

> Jerusalem, Jerusalem, the city that kills the prophets and stones those who are sent to it! How often have I desired to gather your children together as a **hen** gathers her brood under her wings, and you were not willing! [Matthew 23:37; see also Luke 13:34]

Because the Bible reflects a patriarchal view of the world and religion, and because the biblical writers were unanimous in condemning goddess worship, the female aspects of God have been submerged. Perhaps in an unconscious awareness of this deficit, Jesus's followers from an early age began exalting his mother to divine status. The stories about the virgin birth* were just the beginning of the process. By the third century, they were referring to Mary as *theotokos*, the God-bearer. By the fifth century, in the West she was known as *Dei Genitrix*, the Mother of God. In the sixth century, the idea began to circulate that her body had been assumed into heavenly glory. In 1854, Pope Pius XI completed the transformation of Mary by issuing a decree that, from the time she conceived Jesus, she had been kept free from sin. In other words, from the time of her conception, Mary had not been an ordinary mortal.

Although Christians in theory have placed the Trinity at the center of their theology, in practice many of them have worshiped a Quadrinity—Father, Mother, Son, and Holy Spirit.* That tradition still exists among the Orthodox, Roman Catholic, and Anglican faithful. In recent times, other Christians have searched among the goddess traditions for a sense of God as mother. Another place where people have found a mother figure is in the wisdom* tradition, which at times elevated wisdom almost to the state of a goddess.

mystery, *noun*   In the Hebrew Scriptures, the idea of divine mystery occurs only in Daniel, and there in the form of a word borrowed from Chaldean—*raz*.

> Daniel answered the king, "No wise men, enchanters, magicians, or diviners can show to the king the **mystery** that the king is asking, but there is a God in heaven who reveals **mysteries**, and he has disclosed to King Nebuchadnezzar what will happen at the end of days. Your dream and the visions of your head as you lay in bed were these: To you, O king, as you lay in bed, came thoughts of what would be hereafter, and the revealer of **mysteries** disclosed to you what is to be." [Daniel 2:27-29]

The early followers of Jesus, especially St. Paul and his imitators, had a profound sense of what they called *mysterion*, which in their culture often meant the secret rites and secret teachings of other religions. In Christian literature, *mysterion* usually refers to what is normally beyond human comprehension and reason. Through divine dispensation, the faithful on occasion may be privileged to glimpse, although not explain, the *mysterion*.

> Jesus said to them, "To you has been given the **secret** of the kingdom of God, but for those outside, everything comes in parables; in order that 'they may indeed look, but not perceive, and may indeed listen, but not understand; so that they may not turn again and be forgiven.'" [Mark 4:11-12]

> Now to God who is able to strengthen you according to my gospel and the proclamation of Jesus Christ, according to the revelation of the **mystery** that was kept secret for long ages but is now disclosed, and through the prophetic writings is made known to all the Gentiles, according to

> the command of the eternal God, to bring about the obedience of faith—to the only wise God, through Jesus Christ, to whom be the glory forever! Amen. [Romans 16:25-27]

> If I have prophetic powers, and understand all **mysteries** and all knowledge, and if I have all faith, so as to remove mountains, but do not have love, I am nothing. [I Corinthians 13:2]

> Pray also for me, so that when I speak, a message may be given to me to make known with boldness the **mystery** of the gospel, for which I am an ambassador in chains. [Ephesians 6:19-20]

> I want their hearts to be encouraged and united in love, so that they may have all the riches of assured understanding and have the knowledge of God's **mystery**, that is, Christ himself, in whom are hidden all the treasures of wisdom and knowledge. [Colossians 2:2-3]

> Without any doubt, the **mystery** of our religion is great: He was revealed in flesh, vindicated in spirit, seen by angels, proclaimed among Gentiles, believed in throughout the world, taken up in glory. [I Timothy 3:16]

The concept of mystery has been so important for the followers of Jesus that it has become a metaphor not only for the Christian religion but also for the Eucharist*—known in some traditions as the Holy Mysteries. Holy Mystery has also been one of the many names for God.*

myth, *noun*   The Greek word *mythos* meant a tale, story, legend, fable, or myth. The word out of context did not imply a value judgment, but the early Christians used the term only in a negative sense.

> Have nothing to do with profane **myths** and old wives tales. [I Timothy 4:7]

> For the time is coming when people will not put up with sound doctrine, but having itching ears, they will accumulate for themselves teachers to suit their own desires, and will turn away from listening to the truth and wander away to **myths**. [II Timothy 4:3-4]

> There are also many rebellious people, idle talkers and deceivers, especially those of the circumcision; . . . rebuke them sharply, so that they may become sound in the faith, not paying attention to Jewish **myths** or to commandments of those who reject the truth. [Titus 1:10, 13-14]

> We did not follow cleverly devised **myths** when we made known to you the power and coming of our Lord Jesus Christ, but we had been eyewitnesses of his majesty. [II Peter 1:16]

Until recently, myth for Christians usually meant false tales, stories, legends, or fables. The narratives of other religions were myths while those told by Christians were the truth.* Gradually, however, myth has taken on more of the original meaning of *mythos*. Myth is the primary way of talking about the realm of God,* which lies beyond the limits of logical definition or interpretation. Myth is the language of religion.*

N

name, *noun*   One of the most popular metaphors that the Bible applies to God* is name, in Hebrew *shem* and in Greek *onoma*. Name had a significance beyond that of other metaphors in the ancient world. The name participated in the very nature of the personality designated. The name took on the qualities and powers of the human being or god for which it stood. This understanding of name explains the importance of the commandment:

> You shall not make wrongful use of the **name** of the LORD your God, for the LORD will not acquit anyone who misuses his **name**. [Exodus 20:7]

When the name of the Hebrew god became so revered that it was no longer said aloud, using *shem* was as convenient as Lord* in talking about God. The followers of Jesus continued in the tradition of Judaism in referring to God as the name.

> I will give to the LORD the thanks due to his righteousness, and sing praise to the **name** of the LORD, the Most High. [Psalm 7:17]

> I will be glad and exult in you; I will sing praise to your **name**, O Most High . . . And those who know your **name** put their trust in you, for you, O LORD, have not forsaken those who seek you. [Psalm 9:2, 10]

> Pray then in this way: Our Father in heaven, hallowed be your **name**. [Matthew 6:9]

> The sun shall be turned to darkness and the moon to blood, before the coming of the Lord's great and glorious day. Then everyone who calls on the **name** of the Lord shall be saved. [Acts 2:20-21]

> For I tell you that Christ has become a servant of the circumcised on behalf of the truth of God in order that he might confirm the promises given to the patriarchs, and in order that the Gentiles might glorify God for his mercy. As it is written, "Therefore I will confess you among the Gentiles, and sing praises to your **name**." [Romans 15:8-9]

In some places, the name refers to the place where God could be known and worshiped. As in other religions, the place could be marked by a holy* tree, well, or building.

> Abraham planted a tamarisk tree in Beer-sheba, and called there on the **name** of the LORD, the Everlasting God. [Genesis 21:33]

> That very night the LORD appeared to him and said, "I am the God of your father Abraham; do not be afraid, for I am with you and will bless you and make your offspring numerous for my servant Abraham's sake." So he built an altar there, called on the **name** of the LORD, and pitched his tent there. And there Isaac's servants dug a well. [Genesis 26:24-25]

> You shall bring everything that I command you to the place that the LORD your God will choose as a dwelling for his **name**: your burnt offerings and your sacrifices, your tithes and your donations, and all your choice votive gifts that you vow to the LORD. [Deuteronomy 12:11]

The power* of the name was such that it could be conveyed to the people.

> So they shall put my **name** on the Israelites, and I will bless them. [Numbers 6:27]

> Jesus said, "I have made your **name** known to those whom you gave me from the world. They were yours, and you gave them to me, and they have kept your word . . . I made your **name** known to them, and I will make it known, so that the love with which you have loved me may be in them, and I in them." [John 17:6, 26]

Similarly, accepting the name put people under the rule and protection of God. The followers of Jesus had this same understanding of Jesus's name, which they accepted in baptism.*

Marks a word in the text that has its own entry   **201**

> You, O LORD, are our father; our Redeemer from of old is your **name**. [Isaiah 63:16]

> Has Christ been divided? Was Paul crucified for you? Or were you baptized in the **name** of Paul? I thank God that I baptized none of you except Crispus and Gaius, so that no one can say that you were baptized in my **name**. [I Corinthians 1:13-15]

> Therefore God also highly exalted him and gave him the **name** that is above every **name**, so that at the **name** of Jesus every knee should bend, in heaven and on earth and under the earth, and every tongue should confess that Jesus Christ is Lord, to the glory of God the Father. [Philippians 2:9-11]

The ancient understanding of the power in a name shows up in the gospels according to Matthew and Mark in pleas for help, and in John's gospel as the focus for belief.

> Jesus said, "Again, truly I tell you, if two of you agree on earth about anything you ask, it will be done for you by my Father in heaven. For where two or three are gathered in my **name**, I am there among them." [Matthew 18:19-20]

> John said to him, "Teacher, we saw someone casting out demons in your **name**, and we tried to stop him, because he was not following us." [Mark 9:38]

> To all who received him, who believed in his **name**, he gave power to become children of God. [John 1:12]

> When Jesus was in Jerusalem during the Passover festival, many believed in his **name** because they saw the signs that he was doing. [John 2:23]

In some ways, the twenty-first century attitude toward names has little to do with that found in the ancient world, but in other ways the importance of names has remained constant. Politicians accused of malfeasance in office talk about wanting to clear their names. Police officers act in the name of the law. Reporters may write about a successful person who made a name for himself or a social event where all the big names were present. Lawyers can contrast an agent with someone acting in his or her own name. This use of name as a metaphor indicating a person is not dissimilar from the use of name in Christian worship* where a congregation may pray* in the name of Jesus or praise God's holy name.

New Testament—see **Bible**

O

obey, *verb*; **obedient**, *adjective*   Obey is unusual in that it is a literal translation of Hebrew and Greek metaphors found in the Bible. The English word came from the Latin *ob* + *audire* and originally meant to listen intently or to hearken. This is similar to the use of *ob* in observe, which means to watch carefully, or in obnoxious, which means extremely harmful. The Hebrew word *shama* can mean either to do as one is told or to listen carefully. The translators had to make a decision based on the context.

When obey is the preferred translation, *shama* more often has to do with God.

Be careful to **obey** all these words that I command you today, so that it may go well with you and with your children after you forever, because you will be doing what is good and right in the sight of the LORD your God. [Deuteronomy 12:28]

The people said to Joshua, "The LORD our God we will serve, and him we will **obey**." [Joshua 24:24]

Samuel said, "Has the LORD as great delight in burnt offerings and sacrifices, as in **obeying** the voice of the LORD? Surely, to **obey** is better than sacrifice, and to heed than the fat of rams." [I Samuel 15:22]

When *shama* appears in English as hear, the word frequently refers to human communications, but sometimes God is the one to be heard.

Hear, O Israel: The LORD is our God, the LORD alone. You shall love the LORD your God with all your heart, and with all your soul, and with all your might. [Deuteronomy 6:4]

Joshua then said to the Israelites, "Draw near and **hear** the words of the LORD your God." [Joshua 3:9]

Elisha said, "**Hear** the word of the LORD: thus says the LORD, Tomorrow about this time a measure of choice meal shall be sold for a shekel, and two measures of barley for a shekel, at the gate of Samaria." [II Kings 7:1]

The same two sorts of possibilities for translation are present in the Greek word *phylasso*, only in this case the verb can mean obey or can be used in its original sense of observing, keeping watch, or guarding. In two places, *phylasso* clearly seems to be used in the sense of doing what one is told.

"Blessed rather are those who hear the word of God and **obey** it!" [Luke 11:28]

Even the circumcised do not themselves **obey** the law, but they want you to be circumcised so that they may boast about your flesh. [Galatians 6:13]

More frequently, *phylasso* is used in a sense that does not necessarily imply following orders.

In that region there were shepherds living in the fields, **keeping watch** over their flock by night. [Luke 2:8]

While I was with them, I protected them in your name that you have given me. I **guarded** them, and not one of them was lost except the one destined to be lost, so that the scripture might be fulfilled. [John 17:12]

While the blood of your witness Stephen was shed, I myself was standing by, approving and **keeping** the coats of those who killed him. [Acts 22:20]

The other Greek word frequently translated obey has a form quite similar to the English. In this case, the verb *akouo*, which means to hear, has the intensifier *hypo*, giving the language a word that could be used to instruct a servant to listen closely for a knock at the door and to answer it. That is precisely what the translators thought *hypakouo* means in this verse:

When Peter knocked at the outer gate, a maid named Rhoda came **to answer**. [Acts 12:13]

The more usual way of translating *hypakouo* is to use some form of obey. Often, the context clearly indicates that the author had in mind following orders, doing as commanded.

> They were all amazed, and they kept on asking one another, "What is this? A new teaching—with authority! He commands even the unclean spirits, and they **obey** him." [Mark 1:27]

> The word of God continued to spread; the number of the disciples increased greatly in Jerusalem, and a great many of the priests became **obedient** to the faith. [Acts 6:7]

> By faith Abraham **obeyed** when he was called to set out for a place that he was to receive as an inheritance; and he set out, not knowing where he was going. [Hebrews 11:8]

Often, the context is not so clear, raising the possibility that the authors had in mind the literal meaning of *hypakouo*. Some passages have quite a different ring when translated literally.

> Not all have **listened carefully** to the good news; for Isaiah says, "Lord, who has believed our message?" [Romans 10:16]

> Children, **listen carefully** to your parents in the Lord, for this is right. "Honor your father and mother"—this is the first commandment with a promise: "so that it may be well with you and you may live long on the earth." [Ephesians 6:1-3]

> Therefore, my beloved, just as you have **listened attentively** to me, not only in my presence, but much more now in my absence, work out your own salvation with fear and trembling. [Philippians 2:12]

Although obey long ago lost its original meaning of listening attentively, the origins of the word are a reminder that the Greek and Hebrew words translated with some form of obey all originally meant to pay attention. That literal sense of the words can be more useful in attempting a relationship with God than can the derived meaning of do as you are told. In most people's experience, God does not deliver clear, unambiguous orders to those who would be faithful, but listening intently and watching closely to what is going on within and around a person can challenge prejudices and conventional ways of thinking. Paying attention to scripture and tradition can yield more wisdom than using literature from the past as a code of conduct.

Old Testament—see Bible

original sin—see sin

orthodoxy and orthopraxy, *nouns*

Although these two terms do not appear in the Bible, they have had an impact on the way the followers of Jesus understand their religion. They both combine *orthos*, the Greek for straight, with another concept—*doxa*, opinion or *praxis*, action. As orthodontics applies to straightening teeth and orthopedics to straightening the limbs of children, orthodoxy has to do with getting opinions straight and orthopraxy with getting actions straight. Although *doxa*, in the sense of opinion, was in wide use among Greek-speaking people of the first century, the early Christian writers did not use the word that way. They did, however, write about *praxis*.

> Now there was a good and righteous man named Joseph, who, though a member of the council, had not agreed to their plan and **action**. He came from the Jewish town of Arimathea, and he was waiting expectantly for the kingdom of God. [Luke 23:50-51]

> Many of those who became believers confessed and disclosed their **practices**. A number of those who practiced magic collected their books and burned them publicly; when the value of these books was calculated, it was found to come to fifty thousand silver coins. [Acts 19:18-19]

> If you live according to the flesh, you will die; but if by the Spirit you put to death the **deeds** of the body, you will live. [Romans 8:13]

> For as in one body we have many members, and not all the members have the same **function**, so we, who are many, are one body in Christ, and individually we are members one of another. [Romans 12:4-5]

> Do not lie to one another, seeing that you have stripped off the old self with its **practices** and have clothed yourselves with the new self, which is being renewed in knowledge according to the image of its creator. [Colossians 3:9-10]

By the fourth century, orthodoxy had become a concern in the church; by the fifth century, it was a term some Christians used to identify themselves in their opposition to opinions they called heresy.* Along the way, the biblical focus on praxis was all but lost.

Today, Christianity is divided across denominational lines between conservatives who tend to emphasize orthodoxy and progressives* who stress orthopraxy. It is a question of which matters more: straightening out people's opinions about Jesus or straightening out their actions to conform with Jesus's life and teaching. Both may be important, but the emphasis on one or the other shapes the nature of a Christian community.

P

pagan, *noun* and *adjective*   Since the third century, when the African church theologian Tertullian introduced the practice, pagan has been the term favored by Christians for identifying people who do not accept their religion. Originally, a *paganus* was a villager—a country person, a rustic— but Roman soldiers called anyone not in military service a pagan. The Christians, understanding themselves to be enrolled in the army of God, picked up the practice from Roman military usage. Like many combatants who look on civilians with contempt, Christians often have had a low opinion of those who do not join their ranks.

In popular literature, some authors have put forth the idea that *paganus* became the equivalent of non-Christian because more ancient forms of worship continued in the countryside long after Christianity was established in the cities. This view, however, does not hold up under a study of early Christian documents. Christians were calling people pagans when the followers of Jesus constituted a tiny minority in the cities of the Roman empire.

In modern usage, pagan has almost the same meaning as heathen* but, according to modern English dictionaries, heathen is the more derisive term.

panentheism, *noun*   Although not a biblical word, panentheism has grown in popularity among Christian theologians such as Charles Hartshorne, John Cobb, Matthew Fox, and Marcus Borg. Karl C. F. Krause (1781–1832) may have been the first to use the term. He constructed it from *pan*, all + *en*, in + *theism*, confidence in God. In other words, panentheism is a philosophy founded on the notion that all things are in God.* Those who use the term to describe their approach to religion are usually doing so to repudiate theism, a doctrine which holds that God created the universe and intervenes in nature and in history.

Panentheism has appealed to many who identify with certain images of God found in the Bible. The first of these is the newer, more literal translation of the Bible's opening passage, which sug-

---

gests that God did not create* the world out of nothing but that God is the wind or spirit* within the creation that makes the chaos habitable.

> In the beginning when God created the heavens and the earth, the earth was a formless void and darkness covered the face of the deep, while a wind from God swept over the face of the waters. [Genesis 1:1-2]

> God is spirit, and those who worship him must worship in spirit and truth. [John 4:24]

> They would search for God and perhaps grope for him and find him—though indeed he is not far from each one of us. For "In him we live and move and have our being." [Acts 17:27-28]

Panentheism is not a peculiarly Christian approach to religion. One example of panentheism appeared in 1959 in the book *Judaism* by Isadore Epstein.[16] He defined his attitude with the words of Moses Cordovera (1522–76), "God is all reality, but not all reality *is* God." Those who find either such cryptic explanations or philosophical discourses on the subject difficult to grasp might get a clearer picture of panentheism from the 2003 novel, *Flying to Tombstone*, by Gordon McBride:

> "... her flying time was not taken up exclusively by practical thoughts. Even more important to her just then, Maddie could not get out of her mind something that Marcus Borg had written in the book the study group was reading. 'If God is not thought of,' he wrote, 'as a supernatural being separate from the universe, then the persuasive force of much of modern atheism vanishes.' His alternative is an idea called, and not originally by him, 'panentheism,' that God is present in all things, all times and all places, but is more than that. God is both 'right here' and more than 'right here.' That meant to Maddie that God, understood in the panentheistic way, was there in the plane with her on the way to San Diego, and yet was not held captive there by her. This God did not take charge of her being safe on that flight any more than Jerry would. Maddie's flight safety depended on her, but the sense that she was not alone in that plane or anywhere else she went, changed her outlook and opened a whole new way of looking at her life. She saw that her purported disbelief was actually a kind of feeble belief system, one that constantly failed her, as time after time she bargained with a God in whom she did not believe for something she wanted or wanted to have happen differently than the way it turned out. What was it that the Christian Bible said about putting God to the test? That was what her unsatisfying sort-of faith had been about—constantly testing God. Would he step in and give her what she wanted? Would he bring her father and mother back together again? Would he wipe away Art's cancer? The answer to all of those questions was 'no.' And in her disappointment, she realized, she had concluded that God simply did not exist. But now, armed with a new sense of what the word 'god' could mean, Maddie speculated about how such a changed idea of him might work. And then she asked herself, why 'him' or 'he' after all? It was another one of those tiny, rare insights that become life changing. Weaning herself away from the habitual use of the masculine pronoun for designating God, she decided, became an essential first step, a part of her rethinking the *being* of God. This was not about feminism or anti-patriarchy or any other correct or fashionable thinking; it was about moving on into another—a liberating—understanding of the sacred so that spiritual ideas might have credibility in her life."[17]

Although liberal and progressive* Christians are not likely to include the term panentheism in their worship or preaching, having a name for their understanding of God has been affirming. Their instincts feel more legitimate when they can identify them with the thoughts of serious philosophers and theologians. They also have found affirmation in the discovery that, although the term has been around only since the nineteenth century, panentheism is an ancient approach to religion. As Karen Armstrong pointed out in her book, *The History of God*, seeing God as an all-encompassing spirit runs through the long histories of Judaism, Christianity, and Islam.[18]

parable, *noun*   The English word parable comes directly from the Greek *parabole*, formed from *para*, alongside of + *ballo*, to throw. This formation is quite similar to the Greek for devil,* *diabolos*, from *dia*, across + *ballo*. The image of a parable is something thrown alongside rather than something thrown across the path that will cause a person to stumble. In other words, a parable gets at an idea indirectly. Instead of dealing with a concept head on, a speaker throws out a story that is somewhat parallel to the issue at hand. A parable is an extended metaphor and can be a fairly complex story or a simple statement.

> Jesus told them another **parable**: "The kingdom of heaven is like yeast that a woman took and mixed in with three measures of flour until all of it was leavened . . .
> "The kingdom of heaven is like treasure hidden in a field, which someone found and hid; then in his joy he goes and sells all that he has and buys that field.
> "Again, the kingdom of heaven is like a merchant in search of fine pearls; on finding one pearl of great value, he went and sold all that he had and bought it.
> "Again, the kingdom of heaven is like a net that was thrown into the sea and caught fish of every kind; when it was full, they drew it ashore, sat down, and put the good into baskets but threw out the bad." [Matthew 13:33, 44-48]

According to tradition, Jesus frequently employed parables in his teaching.

> Jesus told the crowds all these things in **parables**; without a **parable** he told them nothing. [Matthew 13:34]

In first-century Palestine, the parable was a familiar form of teaching, but as Christianity moved into the Greek and Roman world, the purpose of the parable was lost. Christians tried to turn them into allegories, in which every character in a story was assigned a place in real life. In more recent times, when Bible scholars realized that parables were not allegories, some thought that each parable had a single point, but even that approach has been challenged. Brandon Scott, author of *Re-Imagine the World: An Introduction to the Parables of Jesus*, has said, "Parables are not simple, and they don't make simple points." Scott has also said, "Parables don't have anything to do with religion. They're about life."[19]

Through parables, Jesus challenged conventional ways of thinking. Listening to a parable with an open mind, his hearers were often bewildered—an appropriate response for today as well. A memory of that bewilderment may well be represented in the gospels as we have received them.

> The reason I speak to them in **parables** is that "seeing they do not perceive, and hearing they do not listen, nor do they understand." With them indeed is fulfilled the prophecy of Isaiah that says: "You will indeed listen, but never understand, and you will indeed look, but never perceive." [Matthew 13:13-14]

Marks a word in the text that has its own entry   **207**

FROM LITERAL TO LITERARY

Although it seems improbable that Jesus told parables with the intention of proving that his hearers were dull witted so that he could fulfill a prophecy, the episode suggests that many of Jesus's hearers were confused by his parables. All anyone can honestly say on first hearing a parable is, "Huh?" or "What?" Within Jesus's original audiences, however, some people reacted with suspicion or anger. Jesus often told parables about the kingdom,* which made them think that he was trying to undermine the current regime. This was a dangerous business. Charles W. F. Smith began his book *The Jesus of the Parables* with the words, "Jesus used parables and Jesus was put to death. The two facts are related and it is necessary to understand the connection."[20]

Over the centuries, parables have acquired names, some of which are quite misleading. A serious student of the Bible should probably forget about the name in order to take on the challenge of a parable but, for purposes of identification, here are several with both the conventional names and suggested alternative titles.

The sower	The foolish farmer	Matthew 13:3-8, Mark 4:3-9, Luke 8:5-8
The wheat and the weeds	The patient farmer	Matthew 13:24-30
The unmerciful servant	The ruthless slave*	Matthew 18:23-38
Laborers in the vineyard	The arbitrary employer	Matthew 20:1-15
The wedding banquet	The royal reception	Matthew 22:1-13
The talents, or pounds	The investors	Matthew 25:14-30, Luke 19:12-27
The good Samaritan*	The compassionate foreigner	Luke 10:30-35
The friend at midnight	The obnoxious friend	Luke 11:5-8
The great banquet	The lavish dinner party	Luke 14:15-24
The prodigal son	The indulgent father*	Luke 15:11-32
The lost coin	The careless woman	Luke 15:8-9
The lost sheep	The careless shepherd*	Luke 15:4-6
The unjust steward*	The cunning manager	Luke 16:1-8
Dives and Lazarus	Rich man, poor man	Luke 17:19-31
The widow and the judge*	The corrupt magistrate	Luke 18:1-8
The Pharisee* and the publican	The self-righteous and the humble	Luke 18:10-14

DID YOU KNOW . . .

... that *parabole* is pronounced *pahr-ahb-ohl-ay*?
For more help with pronunciation, see "Pronouncing Transliterated Hebrew and Greek Words" on page 15.

---

paradise, *noun* The Greek word *paradeisos* and the Hebrew *pardec* are probably Persian in origin. They meant an enclosed park or garden. *Pardec* appears in its original sense three times in the Hebrew Scriptures.

Marks a word in the text that has its own entry

> I said to the king, "If it pleases the king, let letters be given me to the governors of the province Beyond the River, that they may grant me passage until I arrive in Judah; and a letter to Asaph, the keeper of the king's **forest**, directing him to give me timber to make beams for the gates of the temple fortress, and for the wall of the city, and for the house that I shall occupy." [Nehemiah 2:7-8]

> I made myself gardens and **parks**, and planted in them all kinds of fruit trees. [Ecclesiastes 2:5]

> A garden locked is my sister, my bride, a garden locked, a fountain sealed. Your channel is an **orchard** of pomegranates with all choicest fruits. [Song of Solomon 4:12-13]

In the Septuagent, the Greek version of the Hebrew Scriptures, the translators used *paradeisos* for the Hebrew *gan* where the word occurs in the second and third chapters of Genesis, beginning with:

> The LORD God planted a **garden** in Eden, in the east; and there he put the man whom he had formed. Out of the ground the LORD God made to grow every tree that is pleasant to the sight and good for food, the tree of life also in the midst of the **garden**, and the tree of the knowledge of good and evil. [Genesis 2:8-9]

In the later literature of Judaism, paradise came to stand for a future state of blessedness, either material or spiritual. The early Christian writers used *paradeisos* in this sense. The word appears three times in the specifically Christian portions of the Bible.

> One of the criminals said, "Jesus, remember me when you come into your kingdom." He replied, "Truly I tell you, today you will be with me in **Paradise**." [Luke 23:42-43]

> I know a person in Christ who fourteen years ago was caught up to the third heaven—whether in the body or out of the body I do not know; God knows. And I know that such a person—whether in the body or out of the body I do not know; God knows— was caught up into **Paradise** and heard things that are not to be told, that no mortal is permitted to repeat. [II Corinthians 12:2-4]

> Let anyone who has an ear listen to what the Spirit is saying to the churches. To everyone who conquers, I will give permission to eat from the tree of life that is in the **paradise** of God. [Revelation 2:7]

Over the ages, Christians have engaged in speculation about paradise, whether it is a holding area for the faithful who have died and are waiting for the general resurrection,* or a synonym for heaven.* In popular understanding, the second view usually triumphs; paradise has become a metaphor applied to a state of heavenly bliss. The metaphor also works as an identification of human longing for an existence free from hunger, ignorance, and all that is disgusting or ugly.

Paraclete—see **advocate**

partner—see **fellowship**

passion, *noun*   In Christian literature, the Passion became a shorthand reference to the suffering and death of Jesus commemorated on Good Friday and Easter.* This usage developed through a false etymology based on the Greek word for suffering, *pascho*. The commemoration took place at the time of the Passover,* in Greek *pascha*. By the Middle Ages, perhaps because of the annual references, the Passion had become a central element in Christian piety, one associated in people's

---

minds with sacrifice* and atonement.* Although suggestions of Jesus's suffering on behalf of others appear in the Bible, they are not connected to sacrifice and atonement in the way that they were in later theology.

> From that time on, Jesus began to show his disciples that he must go to Jerusalem and undergo great **suffering** at the hands of the elders and chief priests and scribes, and be killed, and on the third day be raised. [Matthew 16:21]

> For as the lightning flashes and lights up the sky from one side to the other, so will the Son of Man be in his day. But first he must endure much **suffering** and be rejected by this generation. [Luke 17:24-25]

> After Jesus's **suffering** he presented himself alive to them by many convincing proofs, appearing to them during forty days and speaking about the kingdom of God. [Acts 1:3]

> Although he was a Son, he learned obedience through what he **suffered**; and having been made perfect, he became the source of eternal salvation for all who obey him. [Hebrews 5:8-9]

> For Christ also **suffered** for sins once for all, the righteous for the unrighteous, in order to bring you to God. [I Peter 3:18]

Although the Greek word *pascho* is a verb, it often appears in the Bible in the form of a noun. Originally *pascho* meant to experience whatever befalls a person, good or bad but, in the Bible, it always means to endure ill treatment or ill fortune.

> When they came to the crowd, a man came to him, knelt before him, and said, "Lord, have mercy on my son, for he is an epileptic and he **suffers** terribly; he often falls into the fire and often into the water." [Matthew 17:14-15]

> Now there was a woman who had been suffering from hemorrhages for twelve years. She had **endured** much under many physicians, and had spent all that she had; and she was no better, but rather grew worse. [Mark 5:25-26]

> At that very time there were some present who told him about the Galileans whose blood Pilate had mingled with their sacrifices. He asked them, "Do you think that because these Galileans **suffered** in this way they were worse sinners than all other Galileans?" [Luke 13:1-2]

> God has so arranged the body, giving the greater honor to the inferior member, that there may be no dissension within the body, but the members may have the same care for one another. If one member **suffers**, all suffer together with it; if one member is honored, all rejoice together with it. [I Corinthians 12:24-26]

Perhaps because of Jesus's experience, for his followers *pascho* became something of a virtue. To suffer on behalf of faith was said to be ennobling.

> God has graciously granted you the privilege not only of believing in Christ, but of **suffering** for him as well—since you are having the same struggle that you saw I had and now hear that I still have. [Philippians 1:29-30]

> For it is a credit to you if, being aware of God, you endure pain while **suffering** unjustly. If you endure when you are beaten for doing wrong, what credit is that? But if you endure when you do right and **suffer** for it, you have God's approval. For to this you have been called, because Christ

also **suffered** for you, leaving you an example, so that you should follow in his steps.
[I Peter 2:19-21]

Using passion as a metaphor to identify what Jesus endured on the last days of his life may have been useful shorthand, but the practice has had negative consequences. The focus on Jesus's suffering has filled some Christians with a morbid fascination with violence that may have contributed to their own violent behavior toward those who hold different beliefs. Dramatizations of the Passion, which began in the seventeenth century, have often stirred up aggressive anti-Semitism. Even the dramatic Palm Sunday readings of the passion story have at times aroused Christians enough to burn Jewish homes and businesses. Another negative result of making a virtue of suffering has been that some devoted followers of Jesus have been almost suicidal in their desire for martyrdom.

The obsession with suffering has often obscured the central meaning of the Jesus story. According to the gospels, Jesus was so intent on presenting a vision of a domination-free society that he risked bringing down on his head the wrath of the Roman empire. The risk he took when "he set his face to go to Jerusalem" [Luke 9:51] was not motivated by a suicidal desire but by the love he had for the people he was trying to teach.

pastor—see **shepherd**

patience, *noun*   The Greek word translated patience or long suffering—*makrothumia*—has the same root as lust.* Both are based on *thuo*, the word that meant the fire* of sacrifice and that came to be a metaphor used commonly for passion or suffering.

In the case of patience, the prefix *makro* has become in English macro-, which means large or extensive, as in macro-economics, the study of the economy as a whole. *Makrothumia* can be thought of as burning for a long time or burning slowly. It is a colorful metaphor suggesting the virtue of keeping intense feelings under control. A fire raging unchecked destroys everything in its path, but a fire on the hearth provides light and warmth for the house.

For the early Christian writers, patience was a quality they associated with the divine presence and with those who were close to God.

Do you imagine, whoever you are, that when you judge those who do such things and yet do them yourself, you will escape the judgment of God? Or do you despise the riches of his kindness and forbearance and **patience**? [Romans 2:3-4]

I received mercy, so that in me, as the foremost, Jesus Christ might display the utmost **patience**, making me an example to those who would come to believe in him for eternal life.
[I Timothy 1:16]

As an example of suffering and **patience**, beloved, take the prophets who spoke in the name of the Lord. [James 5:10]

In these early Christian writings, the message to the followers of Jesus was fairly obvious. If they wanted to live their lives to the fullest possible extent, they would have to acquire patience along with the other virtues.

The fruit of the Spirit is love, joy, peace, **patience**, kindness, generosity, faithfulness, gentleness, and self-control. [Galatians 5:22-23]

> May you be made strong with all the strength that comes from his glorious power, and may you be prepared to endure everything with **patience**, while joyfully giving thanks to the Father, who has enabled you to share in the inheritance of the saints in the light. [Colossians 1:11-12]

> We want each one of you to show the same diligence so as to realize the full assurance of hope to the very end, so that you may not become sluggish, but imitators of those who through faith and **patience** inherit the promises. [Hebrews 6:11-12]

The slow burning fire metaphor makes sense in contemporary psychological terms. Denial or repression of intense feelings can lead to mental health problems. Allowing intense feelings to control behavior can lead to problems in relationships as well as with the law. The metaphor is a reminder that a person can both acknowledge and manage intense feelings.

peace, *noun*   The English word peace cannot adequately convey the full breadth of the biblical words it translates. The Hebrew *shalom* could mean safety, harmony, prosperity, health, well-being, or the absence of war. The Greek *eirene*, which in classical times meant the absence of war, took on all the connotations of *shalom* when it became the translation for that word in the Greek version of the Hebrew Scriptures. Here are some examples for each category of how *shalom* and *eirene* appear in English translation:

Safety

Gideon perceived that it was the angel of the Lord; and Gideon said, "Help me, Lord God! For I have seen the angel of the Lord face to face." But the Lord said to him, "**Peace** be to you; do not fear, you shall not die." [Judges 6:22-23]

When a strong man, fully armed, guards his castle, his property is **safe**. [Luke 11:21]

Harmony

Jonathan said to David, "Go in **peace**, since both of us have sworn in the name of the Lord, saying, 'The Lord shall be between me and you, and between my descendants and your descendants, forever.'" [I Samuel 20:42]

Meanwhile the church throughout Judea, Galilee, and Samaria had **peace** and was built up. Living in the fear of the Lord and in the comfort of the Holy Spirit, it increased in numbers. [Acts 9:31]

Prosperity

The meek shall inherit the land, and delight themselves in abundant **prosperity**. [Psalm 37:11]

There shall be a sowing of **peace**; the vine shall yield its fruit, the ground shall give its produce, and the skies shall give their dew; and I will cause the remnant of this people to possess all these things. [Zechariah 8:12]

Health

There is no soundness in my flesh because of your indignation; there is no **health** in my bones because of my sin. [Psalm 38:3]

Marks a word in the text that has its own entry

If a brother or sister is naked and lacks daily food, and one of you says to them, "Go in **peace**; keep warm and eat your fill," and yet you do not supply their bodily needs, what is the good of that? [James 2:15-16]

Well-being

Then the LORD said to Abram . . . "As for yourself, you shall go to your ancestors in **peace**; you shall be buried in a good old age." [Genesis 15:13, 15]

If Timothy comes, see that he has nothing to fear among you, for he is doing the work of the Lord just as I am; therefore let no one despise him. Send him on his way in **peace**, so that he may come to me; for I am expecting him with the brothers. [I Corinthians 16:10-11]

Absence of war

Solomon had dominion over all the region west of the Euphrates from Tiphsah to Gaza, over all the kings west of the Euphrates; and he had **peace** on all sides. [I Kings 4:24]

What king, going out to wage war against another king, will not sit down first and consider whether he is able with ten thousand to oppose the one who comes against him with twenty thousand? If he cannot, then, while the other is still far away, he sends a delegation and asks for the terms of **peace**. [Luke 14:31-32]

In the teachings of the prophets, *shalom* could either be a false promise or the vision of a better age to come.

For from the least to the greatest of them, everyone is greedy for unjust gain; and from prophet to priest, everyone deals falsely. They have treated the wound of my people carelessly, saying, "**Peace, peace**," when there is no peace. [Jeremiah 6:13-14]

They have misled my people, saying, "**Peace**," when there is no **peace**; and because, when the people build a wall, these prophets smear whitewash on it. [Ezekiel 13:10]

Thus says the LORD concerning the prophets who lead my people astray, who cry "**Peace**" when they have something to eat, but declare war against those who put nothing into their mouths. [Micah 3:5]

How beautiful upon the mountains are the feet of the messenger who announces **peace**, who brings good news, who announces salvation, who says to Zion, "Your God reigns." [Isaiah 52:7]

I will make a covenant of **peace** with them; it shall be an everlasting covenant with them; and I will bless them and multiply them, and will set my sanctuary among them forevermore. [Ezekiel 37:26]

Let me hear what God the LORD will speak, for he will speak **peace** to his people, to his faithful, to those who turn to him in their hearts. [Psalm 85:8]

The followers of Jesus associated him with both the warning against the false promises of peace and the vision of peace proclaimed by the prophets.

"Do not think that I have come to bring **peace** to the earth; I have not come to bring **peace**, but a sword. For I have come to set a man against his father, and a daughter against her mother, and a daughter-in-law against her mother-in-law; and one's foes will be members of one's own household." [Matthew 10:34-36]

Christ Jesus came and proclaimed **peace** to you who were far off and peace to those who were near. [Ephesians 2:17]

The **peace** of God, which surpasses all understanding, will guard your hearts and your minds in Christ Jesus. [Philippians 4:7]

Let the **peace** of Christ rule in your hearts, to which indeed you were called in the one body. And be thankful. [Colossians 3:15]

So central was the longing for peace that it was from earliest times a standard form of greeting and farewell in personal encounters and in correspondence.

Moses went back to his father-in-law Jethro and said to him, "Please let me go back to my kindred in Egypt and see whether they are still living." And Jethro said to Moses, "Go in **peace**." [Exodus 4:18]

The king sent an answer: "To Rehum the royal deputy and Shimshai the scribe and the rest of their associates who live in Samaria and in the rest of the province Beyond the River, **greeting**." [Ezra 4:17]

Then King Darius wrote to all peoples and nations of every language throughout the whole world: "May you have abundant **prosperity**!" [Daniel 6:25]

While they were talking about this, Jesus himself stood among them and said to them, "**Peace** be with you." [Luke 24:36]

To all God's beloved in Rome, who are called to be saints: Grace to you and **peace** from God our Father and the Lord Jesus Christ. [Romans 1:7]

Finally, brothers and sisters, farewell. Put things in order, listen to my appeal, agree with one another, live in peace; and the God of love and **peace** will be with you. [II Corinthians 13:11]

The biblical meaning of peace makes it a rich metaphor pointing to the most profound of human longings: the desire for safety, harmony, prosperity, health, well-being, and the absence of war. This one word points a vision of the way the world ought to be.

Pentecost, *noun*; **Pentecostal**, *adjective*   Following the ancient process of attaching new experiences to existing festivals, the original followers of Jesus celebrated the beginning of new life for their community on the day of the Jewish festival known in Hellenistic circles as Pentecost, so named because the holiday occurred fifty days after Passover. Also called the Feast of Weeks (a week of weeks plus one more Sabbath equals fifty days), it was originally a fertility rite held in conjunction with the wheat harvest. The people of Israel transformed the primitive festival into a celebration of their receiving the Torah through Moses. The early Christians continued the process when they not only adopted the name and date of the festival but also its traditional imagery of wind and fire* originally associated with Moses receiving the commandments on Mt. Sinai.

When the day of **Pentecost** had come, they were all together in one place. And suddenly from heaven there came a sound like the rush of a violent wind, and it filled the entire house where they were sitting. Divided tongues, as of fire, appeared among them, and a tongue rested on each of them. All of them were filled with the Holy Spirit and began to speak in other languages, as the Spirit gave them ability. Now there were devout Jews from every nation under heaven liv-

Marks a word in the text that has its own entry

ing in Jerusalem. And at this sound the crowd gathered and was bewildered, because each one heard them speaking in the native language of each. [Acts 2:1-6]

This legend my have grown out of the same experience that St. Paul refers to in I Corinthians 15:6, where he says that Jesus "appeared to more than five hundred brothers and sisters at one time." What seems indisputable is that, after a period of extreme stress, the community had an experience of hope and joy. The experience was of such importance that the Jesus followers wanted to remember it each year.

The person who wrote the Acts of Apostles might have mentioned *glossa*, translated as languages or tongues, after hearing about an early Christian practice but not knowing what *glossa* was like. St. Paul, writing long before the Acts, knew all about *glossa*, which he compared unfavorably with prophecy.

> Those who speak in a **tongue** do not speak to other people but to God; for nobody understands them, since they are speaking mysteries in the Spirit. On the other hand, those who prophesy speak to other people for their upbuilding and encouragement and consolation. Those who speak in a **tongue** build up themselves, but those who prophesy build up the church.
> [I Corinthians 14:2-4]

African Americans, mostly in the midwestern and southeastern parts of the United States, revived the practice of speaking in tongues, also known as glossolalia, in the early twentieth century. Christians of European descent at first joined them and later developed their own congregations. Apparently, many people find deeply satisfying the state of mind in which they utter unintelligible sounds.

Christopher Bryant, Anglican monk and psychologist, believed that some terrors of early childhood, those which occur before speech is possible, may never have been dealt with and need to find expression. These feelings, which Bryant called "a backlog of fear," find expression through speaking in tongues. This practice may be spiritually rewarding and similar to what went on in the early church, but it is the exact opposite of the experience described in the Pentecost legend. In the story about the first Christian Pentecost, the gift of the Spirit was the ability to speak in foreign languages so that people from other countries could understand what the Jesus followers had to say. Although no one can understand what a person speaking in tongues might be saying, those who encourage the practice call themselves Pentecostal.

perfect, *adjective*   The biblical words that appear in English as perfect had different origins and different connotations. The Hebrew *tamim* arose in the cult as a description of an appropriate sacrifice, that is, an animal that was without any obvious flaws or weaknesses. The word meant entire, whole, complete, or blameless. In the first Greek translation of the Hebrew Scriptures, *tamim* became *teleios*, which evolved from *telos*, the goal or end. *Teleios* could mean an action completed or, when attributed to a person, full grown or mature. The related verb form, *teleioo*, could mean either to bring to a conclusion or to make perfect.

> When anyone offers a sacrifice of well-being to the LORD, in fulfillment of a vow or as a freewill offering, from the herd or from the flock, to be acceptable it must be **perfect**; there shall be no blemish in it. [Leviticus 22:21]

> You must remain **completely loyal** to the LORD your God. [Deuteronomy 18:13]

> Now therefore revere the LORD, and serve him in **sincerity** and in faithfulness; put away the gods that your ancestors served beyond the River and in Egypt, and serve the LORD. [Joshua 24:14]

> I will study the way that is **blameless**. When shall I attain it? I will walk with integrity of heart within my house. [Psalm 101:2]

Above all, *tamim* was a characteristic attributed to God.*

> For I will proclaim the name of the LORD; ascribe greatness to our God! The Rock, his work is **perfect,** and all his ways are just. A faithful God, without deceit, just and upright is he. [Deuteronomy 32:3-4]

> This God—his way is **perfect**; the promise of the LORD proves true; he is a shield for all who take refuge in him. [II Samuel 22:31]

> Do you know the balancings of the clouds, the wondrous works of the one whose knowledge is **perfect,** you whose garments are hot when the earth is still because of the south wind? [Job 37:16-17]

> The law of the LORD is **perfect**, reviving the soul; the decrees of the LORD are sure, making wise the simple. [Psalm 19:7]

The early followers of Jesus used *teleios* and *teleioo* in reference to human beings becoming full grown, morally mature.

> Jesus said to him, "If you wish to be **perfect**, go, sell your possessions, and give the money to the poor, and you will have treasure in heaven; then come, follow me." [Matthew 19:21]

> Yet among the **mature** we do speak wisdom, though it is not a wisdom of this age or of the rulers of this age, who are doomed to perish. [I Corinthians 2:6]

> Let those of us then who are **mature** be of the same mind; and if you think differently about anything, this too God will reveal to you. [Philippians 3:15]

> My brothers and sisters, whenever you face trials of any kind, consider it nothing but joy, because you know that the testing of your faith produces endurance; and let endurance have its full effect, so that you may be **mature** and complete, lacking in nothing. [James 1:2-4]

> Whoever obeys his word, truly in this person the love of God has reached **perfection**. By this we may be sure that we are in him. [I John 2:5]

They also used *teleios* and *teleioo* as characteristic of experiences that they identified with God.

> Be **perfect**, therefore, as your heavenly Father is **perfect**. [Matthew 5:48]

> Do not be conformed to this world, but be transformed by the renewing of your minds, so that you may discern what is the will of God—what is good and acceptable and **perfect**. [Romans 12:2]

> Every generous act of giving, with every **perfect** gift, is from above, coming down from the Father of lights, with whom there is no variation or shadow due to change. [James 1:17]

Neither *tamim* nor *teleios* had quite the sense of the English perfect, which implies absolute conformity to an ideal or a state of excellence leaving no possibility for improvement.

Marks a word in the text that has its own entry

DID YOU KNOW ...

... that *teleioo* is pronounced *tayl-ih-oh-oh*?
For more help with pronunciation, see "Pronouncing
Transliterated Hebrew and Greek Words" on page 15.

Pharisee, *noun*   The Pharisees were the reforming party of first-century Judaism. The Greek word *Pharisaios* transcribed a Hebrew word *Perushim*, meaning the separated ones or the separatists. The Pharisees attempted to separate themselves from what they considered the corrupt practices of the temple authorities who collaborated with the Roman occupation and who had adopted Roman culture, including the wearing of the toga. They established centers of learning and worship for the purpose of adapting the wisdom of ancient Israel to the conditions of their own time. Their leaders were scribes, that is, scholars devoted to the study of the law* and commentaries on the texts of accepted Hebrew Scripture, which constituted their Bible.* The Pharisees would address an especially honored scholar as rabbi, which became a common title for teachers in the Pharisee tradition. A community of Pharisees would meet in a synagogue, in Greek *synagoge*, literally a place of getting together.

Jesus of Nazareth and his first followers may have been Pharisees. Certainly Jesus and his friends were in dialogue with the Pharisees and had much in common with them. St. Paul was proud to claim his heritage as a Pharisee.

> If anyone else has reason to be confident in the flesh, I have more: circumcised on the eighth day, a member of the people of Israel, of the tribe of Benjamin, a Hebrew born of Hebrews; as to the law, a **Pharisee**; as to zeal, a persecutor of the church; as to righteousness under the law, blameless. [Philippians 3:4-6]

Much of the teaching attributed to Jesus closely parallels what has been preserved from what the Pharisees taught. His major points of difference with them seem to have been his accepting attitude toward people who were not Jews and his rejection of some aspects of the purity* regulations. According to tradition, Jesus not only attended synagogue, but was a recognized teacher.

> Jesus went about all the cities and villages, teaching in their synagogues, and proclaiming the good news of the kingdom, and curing every disease and every sickness. [Matthew 9:35]

His visit to the synagogue in his home town may be an accurate description of what went on at a worship service in a synagogue.

> When Jesus came to Nazareth, where he had been brought up, he went to the synagogue on the sabbath day, as was his custom. He stood up to read, and the scroll of the prophet Isaiah was given to him. He unrolled the scroll and found the place where it was written: "The Spirit of the Lord is upon me, because he has anointed me to bring good news to the poor. He has sent me to proclaim release to the captives and recovery of sight to the blind, to let the oppressed go free, to proclaim the year of the Lord's favor." And he rolled up the scroll, gave it back to the attendant, and sat down. The eyes of all in the synagogue were fixed on him. Then he began to say to them, "Today this scripture has been fulfilled in your hearing." [Luke 4:16-21]

This pattern conforms to what is known of later synagogue practice. The teacher would stand to read from a sacred Hebrew text and then sit to interpret it. Many people present, whose language

---

Marks a word in the text that has its own entry

was Greek or Aramaic, probably could not understand the Hebrew, so the teacher's interpretation would include a translation.

From the accounts of the early Christians, modern scholarship has drawn the conclusion that both Judaism and Christianity have their roots in the first-century movement of the Pharisees. In the latter part of the first century, the two groups became competitors. (See the entry on **Jews** and Judeans.) The antagonism is reflected in what Christians call the New Testament.

> Woe to you, scribes and **Pharisees,** hypocrites! For you tithe mint, dill, and cummin, and have neglected the weightier matters of the law: justice and mercy and faith. It is these you ought to have practiced without neglecting the others. [Matthew 23:23]

> They sent to him some **Pharisees** and some Herodians to trap him in what he said. [Mark 12:13]

> By refusing to be baptized by John, the **Pharisees** and the lawyers rejected God's purpose for themselves. [Luke 7:30]

> Many, even of the authorities, believed in him. But because of the **Pharisees** they did not confess it, for fear that they would be put out of the synagogue; for they loved human glory more than the glory that comes from God. [John 12:42-43]

The second meaning of Pharisee in the Oxford English Dictionary is "a self-righteous person; a formalist; a hypocrite." This metaphorical use of the word evolved from the bias of the Christian gospels.

Philistine, *noun*   The Philistines were a tribe of people living on the Mediterranean coast in the southwest part of what is now Palestine before the arrival of the Israelites. Known in Hebrew as *Pelishti*, a Philistine was always an enemy, resisting the occupation of the land by the tribes of Israel.

> The **Philistines** came up and encamped in Judah, and made a raid on Lehi. The men of Judah said, "Why have you come up against us?" They said, "We have come up to bind Samson, to do to him as he did to us." [Judges 15:9-10]

> The word of Samuel came to all Israel. In those days the **Philistines** mustered for war against Israel, and Israel went out to battle against them; they encamped at Ebenezer, and the Philistines encamped at Aphek. The **Philistines** drew up in line against Israel, and when the battle was joined, Israel was defeated by the Philistines, who killed about four thousand men on the field of battle. [I Samuel 4:1-2]

> The **Philistines** stood on the mountain on the one side, and Israel stood on the mountain on the other side, with a valley between them. And there came out from the camp of the **Philistines** a champion named Goliath, of Gath, whose height was six cubits and a span. [I Samuel 17:3-4]

> Thus says the Lord GOD: Because with unending hostilities the **Philistines** acted in vengeance, and with malice of heart took revenge in destruction; therefore thus says the Lord GOD, I will stretch out my hand against the **Philistines,** cut off the Cherethites, and destroy the rest of the seacoast. [Ezekiel 25:15-16]

Since at least the sixteenth century, Philistine has served as a metaphor for any perceived enemy, especially an art or literary critic. From that evolved the use of the metaphor to identify anyone whose views are smugly conventional and whose taste is hopelessly common.

poor, *noun* and *adjective*   One consistent theme throughout the entire Bible is the obligation of the reader to emulate God's concern for the poor. The centrality of this theme to the message of the Hebrew Scriptures might be more obvious to those fortunate enough to read the texts in the original language. Hebrew has six words translated into English as poor in the sense of being economically impoverished. Although these words appear to have been used interchangeably, they have distinct connotations that evolved into metaphors for the poor.

ani, depressed or afflicted

If you lend money to my people, to the **poor** among you, you shall not deal with them as a creditor; you shall not exact interest from them. [Exodus 22:25]

You deliver a **humble** people, but your eyes are upon the haughty to bring them down. [II Samuel 22:28]

I am **lowly** and in pain; let your salvation, O God, protect me. [Psalm 69:29]

The LORD enters into judgment with the elders and princes of his people: It is you who have devoured the vineyard; the spoil of the **poor** is in your houses. What do you mean by crushing my people, by grinding the face of the **poor**? says the Lord GOD of hosts. [Isaiah 3:14-15]

anav, depressed
same root as *ani*

The **poor** shall eat and be satisfied; those who seek him shall praise the LORD. [Psalm 22:26]

The **meek** shall inherit the land, and delight themselves in abundant prosperity. [Psalm 37:11]

Seek the LORD, all you **humble** of the land, who do his commands; seek righteousness, seek humility; perhaps you may be hidden on the day of the Lord's wrath. [Zephaniah 2:3]

dal, weak or thin

They will give back the fruit of their toil, and will not swallow it down; from the profit of their trading they will get no enjoyment. For they have crushed and abandoned the **poor**, they have seized a house that they did not build. [Job 20:18-19]

Happy are those who consider the **poor**; the LORD delivers them in the day of trouble. [Psalm 41:1]

Because you trample on the **poor** and take from them levies of grain, you have built houses of hewn stone, but you shall not live in them; you have planted pleasant vineyards, but you shall not drink their wine. [Amos 5:11]

ebyon, destitute, a beggar

You shall not pervert the justice due to your **poor** in their lawsuits. [Exodus 23:6]

They should make … days of feasting and gladness, days for sending gifts of food to one another and presents to the **poor**. [Esther 9:22]

Did I not weep for those whose day was hard? Was not my soul grieved for the **poor**? [Job 30:25]

Marks a word in the text that has its own entry   **219**

micken, indigent

Better is a **poor** but wise youth than an old but foolish king, who will no longer take advice. [Ecclesiastes 4:13]

There was a little city with few people in it. A great king came against it and besieged it, building great siegeworks against it. Now there was found in it a **poor** wise man, and he by his wisdom delivered the city. Yet no one remembered that **poor** man. [Ecclesiastes 9:14-15]

rush, lacking necessities

The field of the **poor** may yield much food, but it is swept away through injustice. [Proverbs 13:23]

Whoever gives to the **poor** will lack nothing, but one who turns a blind eye will get many a curse. [Proverbs 28:27]

If you see in a province the oppression of the **poor** and the violation of justice and right, do not be amazed at the matter; for the high official is watched by a higher, and there are yet higher ones over them. [Ecclesiastes 5:8]

Often for emphasis a writer used two of these metaphors in combination. In these examples, *ani* is translated as poor and *ebyon* as needy.

You shall not withhold the wages of **poor** and **needy** laborers, whether other Israelites or aliens who reside in your land in one of your towns. [Deuteronomy 24:14]

The wicked draw the sword and bend their bows to bring down the **poor** and **needy**, to kill those who walk uprightly; their sword shall enter their own heart, and their bows shall be broken. [Psalm 37:14-15]

This was the guilt of your sister Sodom: she and her daughters had pride, excess of food, and prosperous ease, but did not aid the **poor** and **needy**. [Ezekiel 16:49]

In much the same way, *dal* and *ebyon* are paired, again with *ebyon* appearing as needy in English.

The LORD raises up the **poor** from the dust; he lifts the **needy** from the ash heap, to make them sit with princes and inherit a seat of honor. [I Samuel 2:8]

Those who oppress the **poor** insult their Maker, but those who are kind to the **needy** honor him. [Proverbs 14:31]

Hear this word, you cows of Bashan who are on Mount Samaria, who oppress the **poor**, who crush the **needy**, who say to their husbands, "Bring something to drink!" [Amos 4:1]

The translators' opinion that these words for poor have approximately the same meaning becomes even more obvious in the different ways they have handled the combination of *ani* and *dal*.

They caused the cry of the **poor** *(dal)* to come to him, and he heard the cry of the **afflicted** *(ani)*. [Job 34:28]

Ah, you who make iniquitous decrees, who write oppressive statutes, to turn aside the **needy** *(dal)* from justice and to rob the **poor** *(ani)* of my people of their right, that widows may be your spoil, and that you may make the orphans your prey! [Isaiah 10:1-2]

                                      Marks a word in the text that has its own entry

> I will leave in the midst of you a people **humble** *(ani)* and **lowly** *(dal)*. They shall seek refuge in the name of the Lord. [Zephaniah 3:12]

On at least one occasion, a poet used four of the metaphors in combination:

> Give justice to the **weak** *(dal)* and the orphan;
> maintain the right of the **lowly** *(ani)* and the **destitute** *(rush)*.
> Rescue the **weak** *(dal)* and the **needy** *(ebyon)*;
> deliver them from the hand of the wicked. [Psalm 82:3-4]

The early followers of Jesus, writing in Greek, did not have such a rich vocabulary to draw on. Although they echoed the teachings about the poor found in Hebrew Scripture, they had to express themselves primarily through forms of the word *ptochos,* which originally suggested the cringing posture of a beggar. The begging metaphor came to encompass all those who suffered from economic deprivation. An exploitive economic system that could cause such deprivation can be seen in the story of the widow's mite.*

> A **poor** widow came and put in two small copper coins, which are worth a penny. Then he called his disciples and said to them, "Truly I tell you, this **poor** widow has put in more than all those who are contributing to the treasury. For all of them have contributed out of their abundance; but she out of her poverty has put in everything she had, all she had to live on." [Mark 12:42-44]

> Jesus said to him, "If you wish to be perfect, go, sell your possessions, and give the money to the **poor,** and you will have treasure in heaven; then come, follow me." [Matthew 19:21]

> The Spirit of the Lord is upon me, because he has anointed me to bring good news to the **poor.** He has sent me to proclaim release to the captives and recovery of sight to the blind, to let the oppressed go free, to proclaim the year of the Lord's favor. [Luke 4:18-19]

> Judas Iscariot said, "Why was this perfume not sold for three hundred denarii and the money given to the **poor**?" (He said this not because he cared about the poor, but because he was a thief; he kept the common purse and used to steal what was put into it.) [John 12:5-6]

> You know the generous act of our Lord Jesus Christ, that though he was rich, yet for your sakes he became **poor,** so that by his **poverty** you might become rich. [II Corinthians 8:9]

> Listen, my beloved brothers and sisters. Has not God chosen the **poor** in the world to be rich in faith and to be heirs of the kingdom that he has promised to those who love him? But you have dishonored the **poor.** Is it not the rich who oppress you? Is it not they who drag you into court? [James 2:5-6]

Understanding *ptochos* to mean being a beggar instead of being merely indigent can help make sense of the aphorism that begins the section in Matthew's gospel known as the Beatitudes, an identification of the blessed*:

> Blessed are the **poor** in spirit, for theirs is the kingdom of heaven. [Matthew 5:3]

Poor in this passage might be taken as a metaphor from the Hebrew tradition of using *ani* or *anav* to mean lowly or humble. It is also possible that with this figure of speech Matthew is drawing on the Greek image of the beggar. Being humble in spirit* is much more passive than being beggars in spirit. The statement may claim that those who desire God's spirit with the desperation that a hungry beggar seeks food are indeed blessed or fortunate because they are more likely than others to become aware of God's realm or kingdom.* That is, those who beg for the spirit may become conscious of a dimension in human experience that is beyond what they can see, hear, taste, or touch.

Or it could be that Matthew was working with the same material that came to Luke's attention, but that Matthew decided to spiritualize the teaching in order to avoid offending what today we would call middle-class readers.

> Then Jesus looked up at his disciples and said: "Blessed are you who are **poor,** for yours is the kingdom of God." [Luke 6:20]

The idea that God prefers poor people to rich people, or even to economically comfortable people, has seldom been appealing to those who live above the poverty level. They tend to read Luke's version as simply a way of offering hope to the poor so that low-income workers will not quit trying to get ahead. If the rich and the moderately well off draw on the Bible to justify* their elevated economic status, they may prefer to put aside Luke and concentrate on the passages that take wealth to be a sign of God's favor.

> Isaac sowed seed in that land, and in the same year reaped a hundredfold. The LORD blessed him, and the man became rich; he prospered more and more until he became very wealthy. [Genesis 26:12-13]

> The blessing of the LORD makes rich, and he adds no sorrow with it. [Proverbs 10:22]

> The LORD blessed the latter days of Job more than his beginning; and he had fourteen thousand sheep, six thousand camels, a thousand yoke of oxen, and a thousand donkeys. [Job 42:12]

> Jesus said, "Truly I tell you, there is no one who has left house or brothers or sisters or mother or father or children or fields, for my sake and for the sake of the good news, who will not receive a hundredfold now in this age." [Mark 10:29-30]

The followers of Jesus in the present age have to decide how to live with the contradiction in the Bible's teachings about poverty and wealth. Even if they feel that their level of economic comfort is a sign of God's favor, however, they still must come to terms with the accumulated weight of the tradition that demands their concern for the poor. In today's complex economy such a concern may lead them beyond providing a free lunch for the homeless to challenging an oppressive political system.

power, *noun* The concept of power was so important to the people of Israel that they had numerous ways of expressing it, or perhaps the translators were not happy about the prospect of providing readers of the English Bible with such a variety of metaphors.

> Then the male goat grew exceedingly great; but at the height of its **power,** the great horn was broken, and in its place there came up four prominent horns toward the four winds of heaven.—*atsam*, to bind or break, from *etsem*, bone [Daniel 8:8]

> Reuben, you are my firstborn, my might and the first fruits of my vigor, excelling in rank and excelling in **power.**—*az*, strength [Genesis 49:3]

> Then when the copy of King Artaxerxes' letter was read before Rehum and the scribe Shimshai and their associates, they hurried to the Jews in Jerusalem and by force and **power** made them cease.—*chail*, military force [Ezra 4:23]

You, O king, the king of kings—to whom the God of heaven has given the kingdom, the **power**, the might, and the glory, into whose hand he has given human beings, wherever they live, the wild animals of the field, and the birds of the air, and whom he has established as ruler over them all—you are the head of gold.—*chesen*, Chaldean, from *chacam*, to occupy or possess [Daniel 2:37-38]

Now the rest of all the acts of Asa, all his **power**, all that he did, and the cities that he built, are they not written in the Book of the Annals of the Kings of Judah? But in his old age he was diseased in his feet.—*geburah*, force or valor [I Kings 15:23]

Let your work be manifest to your servants, and your glorious **power** to their children.—*hadar*, magnificence [Psalm 90:16]

When the troops came to the camp, the elders of Israel said, "Why has the LORD put us to rout today before the Philistines? Let us bring the ark of the covenant of the LORD here from Shiloh, so that he may come among us and save us from the **power** of our enemies."—*kaph*, an animal's paw [I Samuel 4:3]

Your right hand, O LORD, glorious in **power**—your right hand, O LORD, shattered the enemy.—*koach*, vigor [Exodus 15:6]

Look, the Sovereign, the LORD of hosts, will lop the boughs with terrifying **power**; the tallest trees will be cut down, and the lofty will be brought low.—*maaratsah*, violence, from *arats*, to dread or fear [Isaiah 10:33]

While still rising in **power**, his kingdom shall be broken and divided toward the four winds of heaven, but not to his posterity, nor according to the dominion with which he ruled; for his kingdom shall be uprooted and go to others besides these.—*malkuth*, same root as *melek*, king* [Daniel 11:4]

As soon as the royal **power** was firmly in his hand he killed his servants who had murdered his father the king.—*mamlakah*, same root as *melek*, king* [II Kings 14:5]

Here we are, slaves to this day—slaves in the land that you gave to our ancestors to enjoy its fruit and its good gifts. Its rich yield goes to the kings whom you have set over us because of our sins; they have **power** also over our bodies and over our livestock at their pleasure, and we are in great distress.—*mashal*, rule [Nehemiah 9:36-37]

Has any god ever attempted to go and take a nation for himself from the midst of another nation, by trials, by signs and wonders, by war, by a mighty hand and an outstretched arm, and by terrifying displays of **power**, as the LORD your God did for you in Egypt before your very eyes?—*mora*, from *yare*, fear* [Deuteronomy 4:34]

The loss of children and widowhood shall come upon you in full measure, in spite of your many sorceries and the great **power** of your enchantments.—*otsmah*, powerfulness or abundance [Isaiah 47:9]

Look at Behemoth, which I made just as I made you; it eats grass like an ox. Its strength is in its loins, and its **power** in the muscles of its belly.—*on*, ability [Job 40:15-16]

I was ashamed to ask the king for a band of soldiers and cavalry to protect us against the enemy on our way, since we had told the king that the hand of our God is gracious to all who seek him, but his **power** and his wrath are against all who forsake him.—*oz*, stout or bold [Ezra 8:22]

The LORD! His adversaries shall be shattered; the Most High will thunder in heaven. The LORD will judge the ends of the earth; he will give strength to his king, and exalt the **power** of his anointed.—*qeren*, horn [I Samuel 2:10]

Now in the twelfth month, which is the month of Adar, on the thirteenth day, when the king's command and edict were about to be executed, on the very day when the enemies of the Jews hoped to gain **power** over them, but which had been changed to a day when the Jews would gain **power** over their foes, the Jews gathered in their cities throughout all the provinces of King Ahasuerus to lay hands on those who had sought their ruin; and no one could withstand them, because the fear of them had fallen upon all peoples.—*shalat*, governance or authority* [Esther 9:1-2]

No one has **power** over the wind to restrain the wind, or **power** over the day of death; there is no discharge from the battle, nor does wickedness deliver those who practice it.—*shallit* and *shilton*, both from *shalat* [Ecclesiastes 8:8]

Awesome is God in his sanctuary, the God of Israel; he gives **power** and strength to his people. Blessed be God!—*taatsumah*, from *atsam*, to bind or break [Psalm 68:35]

They shall stumble over one another, as if to escape a sword, though no one pursues; and you shall have no **power** to stand against your enemies.—*tequomah*, from *qum*, to rise [Leviticus 26:37]

Abram said to Sarai, "Your slave-girl is in your **power**; do to her as you please." Then Sarai dealt harshly with her, and she ran away from her.—*yad*, hand or authority* [Genesis 16:6]

Balaam said to Balak, "I have come to you now, but do I have **power** to say just anything? The word God puts in my mouth, that is what I must say."—*yakol*, ability [Numbers 22:38]

May God be gracious to us and bless us and make his face to shine upon us, that your way may be known upon earth, your saving **power** among all nations.—*yeshuah*, deliverance, from *yasha*, to save [Psalm 67:1-2]

Let the groans of the prisoners come before you; according to your great **power** preserve those doomed to die.—*zeroa*, outstretched arm [Psalm 79:11]

The situation in Greek is less bewildering. Usually the word translated as power is *dynamis*, the source of such English words as dynamic, dynamo, and dynamite. *Dynamis* evolved from *dynamai*, a verb meaning be able or can. Although the Greek word that appears in English as power is most often *dynamis*, two other Greek words may be the source. Occasionally *basileia* becomes royal power instead of kingdom* and *exousia* becomes power instead of authority.*

Dynamis often stands for a deed of power, or miracle,* but it appears in other contexts as well.

Characteristic of God*

Jesus answered them, "You are wrong, because you know neither the scriptures nor the **power** of God." [Matthew 22:29]

Again the high priest asked him, "Are you the Messiah, the Son of the Blessed One?" Jesus said, "I am; and 'you will see the Son of Man seated at the right hand of the **Power**,' and 'coming with the clouds of heaven.'" [Mark 14:61-62]

For I am not ashamed of the gospel; it is the **power** of God for salvation to everyone who has faith, to the Jew first and also to the Greek. [Romans 1:16]

For the message about the cross is foolishness to those who are perishing, but to us who are being saved it is the **power** of God. [I Corinthians 1:18]

Possession of Christ*

When you are assembled, and my spirit is present with the **power** of our Lord Jesus, you are to hand this man over to Satan for the destruction of the flesh, so that his spirit may be saved in the day of the Lord. [I Corinthians 5:4-5]

God put this **power** to work in Christ when he raised him from the dead and seated him at his right hand in the heavenly places, far above all rule and authority and power and dominion, and above every name that is named, not only in this age but also in the age to come. [Ephesians 1:20-21]

May grace and peace be yours in abundance in the knowledge of God and of Jesus our Lord. His divine **power** has given us everything needed for life and godliness, through the knowledge of him who called us by his own glory and goodness. [II Peter 1:2-3]

Manifestation of the Holy Spirit*

Then Jesus, filled with the **power** of the Spirit, returned to Galilee, and a report about him spread through all the surrounding country. [Luke 4:14]

May the God of hope fill you with all joy and peace in believing, so that you may abound in hope by the **power** of the Holy Spirit. [Romans 15:13]

Equipment for the saints (see **holy**)

You will receive **power** when the Holy Spirit has come upon you; and you will be my witnesses in Jerusalem, in all Judea and Samaria, and to the ends of the earth. [Acts 1:8]

May you be made strong with all the strength that comes from his glorious **power**, and may you be prepared to endure everything with patience, while joyfully giving thanks to the Father, who has enabled you to share in the inheritance of the saints in the light. [Colossians 1:11-12]

I pray that, according to the riches of his glory, he may grant that you may be strengthened in your inner being with **power** through his Spirit, and that Christ may dwell in your hearts through faith, as you are being rooted and grounded in love. [Ephesians 3:16-17]

Ability

For it is as if a man, going on a journey, summoned his slaves and entrusted his property to them; to one he gave five talents, to another two, to another one, to each according to his **ability**. Then he went away. [Matthew 25:14-15]

As I can testify, they voluntarily gave according to their **means**, and even beyond their **means**. [II Corinthians 8:3]

Mythical spirits*

> For I am convinced that neither death, nor life, nor angels, nor rulers, nor things present, nor things to come, nor **powers**, nor height, nor depth, nor anything else in all creation, will be able to separate us from the love of God in Christ Jesus our Lord. [Romans 8:38-39]

> Each in his own order: Christ the first fruits, then at his coming those who belong to Christ. Then comes the end, when he hands over the kingdom to God the Father, after he has destroyed every ruler and every authority and **power**. [I Corinthians 15:23-24]

> Jesus Christ . . . has gone into heaven and is at the right hand of God, with angels, authorities, and **powers** made subject to him. [I Peter 3:21-22]

The rich variety of Hebrew metaphors translated as power have one thing in common with the Greek *dynamis*: the capacity to get something done. The early followers of Jesus seem to have an understanding of power that was similar to that found in the Hebrew Scriptures. For them, God meant enthusiasm, energy, strength, and determination. Their concern about mythical powers suggests that they often felt caught in an economic and political system that made them feel helpless and left them bogged down in discouragement and despair.* What they found in the life and teachings of Jesus empowered them to take action.

Today, the power metaphor stands not only for the capabilities received through faith* but also for the divine source of capacity for action.

pray, *verb;* **prayer**, *noun*   Today, most references to praying assume a spiritual or religious context, but that was not always the case. In earlier days, English-speaking people could refer to any petition or request made to a court or governing authority as a prayer. They could also use the word pray as a form of polite address when asking for a favor from any ordinary person. In the seventeenth century, when the King James Version of the Bible was produced, "I pray," and its contraction "prithee," were common forms of expression. They could be used by people in addressing each other as well as in approaching God. This practice helps explain the King James Version's frequent translation of the little Hebrew word *na*, which functioned much like words translated as behold.* In most places, the translators of the New Revised Standard Version have chosen to ignore *na*, but occasionally they have employed the old form of address. In other places, they have inserted please or oh.

na

> Moses said, "If now I have found favor in your sight, O Lord, I **pray**, let the Lord go with us. Although this is a stiff-necked people, pardon our iniquity and our sin, and take us for your inheritance." [Exodus 34:9]

> Saul said to Samuel, "I have sinned; for I have transgressed the commandment of the LORD and your words, because I feared the people and obeyed their voice. Now therefore, I **pray**, pardon my sin, and return with me, so that I may worship the LORD." [I Samuel 15:24-25]

> Then Abraham said, "**Oh** do not let the Lord be angry if I speak." [Genesis 18:30]

> Then Rachel said to Leah, "**Please** give me some of your son's mandrakes." [Genesis 30:14]

A number of other Hebrew words and several Greek words sometimes appear in English as pray or prayer, but these words tend to be translated in a variety of other ways depending on the context. The list below includes the meaning of the root that lies behind the metaphorical use of each word.

anna, perhaps a contraction of *aheb* (love*) and *na*

Then I called on the name of the LORD: "O LORD, I **pray**, save my life!" [Psalm 116:4]

Then they cried out to the LORD, "**Please**, O LORD, we **pray**, do not let us perish on account of this man's life." [Jonah 1:14]

"Remember now, O LORD, I **implore** you, how I have walked before you in faithfulness with a whole heart, and have done what is good in your sight." Hezekiah wept bitterly. [II Kings 20:3]

Save us, we **beseech** you, O LORD! O LORD, we **beseech** you, give us success! [Psalm 118:25]

palal, to judge*

Now then, return the man's wife; for he is a prophet, and he will **pray** for you and you shall live. [Genesis 20:7]

Hannah **prayed** and said, "My heart exults in the LORD; my strength is exalted in my God. My mouth derides my enemies, because I rejoice in my victory." [I Samuel 2:1]

Then Isaiah son of Amoz sent to Hezekiah, saying, "Thus says the LORD, the God of Israel: I have heard your **prayer** to me about King Sennacherib of Assyria." [II Kings 19:20]

The LORD was so angry with Aaron that he was ready to destroy him, but I **interceded** also on behalf of Aaron at that same time. [Deuteronomy 9:20]

Thus says the LORD: The wealth of Egypt and the merchandise of Ethiopia, and the Sabeans, tall of stature, shall come over to you and be yours, they shall follow you; they shall come over in chains and bow down to you. They will make **supplication** to you, saying, "God is with you alone, and there is no other; there is no god besides him." [Isaiah 45:14]

Bear your disgrace, you also, for you have brought about for your sisters a more favorable **judgment**; because of your sins in which you acted more abominably than they, they are more in the right than you. [Ezekiel 16:52]

tephillah, from *palal*

For you, O LORD of hosts, the God of Israel, have made this revelation to your servant, saying, "I will build you a house"; therefore your servant has found courage to pray *(palal)* this **prayer** to you. [II Samuel 7:27]

Regard your servant's **prayer** and his plea, O LORD my God, heeding the cry and the **prayer** that your servant prays *(palal)* to you today. [I Kings 8:28]

Let my **prayer** be counted as incense before you, and the lifting up of my hands as an evening sacrifice. [Psalm 141:2]

sha'al, to inquire

Pray for the peace of Jerusalem: "May they prosper who love you." [Psalm 122:6]

Then Jacob **asked** him, "Please tell me your name." But he said, "Why is it that you **ask** my name?" And there he blessed him. [Genesis 32:29]

Ask rain from the LORD in the season of the spring rain, from the LORD who makes the storm clouds, who gives showers of rain to you, the vegetation in the field to everyone.
[Zechariah 10:1]

Joshua shall stand before Eleazar the priest, who shall **inquire** for him by the decision of the Urim before the LORD. [Numbers 27:21]

Spend the money for whatever you wish—oxen, sheep, wine, strong drink, or whatever you **desire**. [Deuteronomy 14:26]

No one shall be found among you who makes a son or daughter pass through fire, or who practices divination, or is a soothsayer, or an augur, or a sorcerer, or one who casts spells, or who **consults** ghosts or spirits, or who seeks oracles from the dead. [Deuteronomy 18:10-11]

May his children wander about and **beg**; may they be driven out of the ruins they inhabit.
[Psalm 109:10]

athar, to burn incense

Isaac **prayed** to the LORD for his wife, because she was barren; and the LORD granted his **prayer**, and his wife Rebekah conceived. [Genesis 25:21]

Then Pharaoh called Moses and Aaron, and said, **"Pray** to the LORD to take away the frogs from me and my people, and I will let the people go to sacrifice to the LORD." [Exodus 8:8]

They buried the bones of Saul and of his son Jonathan in the land of Benjamin in Zela, in the tomb of his father Kish; they did all that the king commanded. After that, God heeded **supplications** for the land. [II Samuel 21:14]

Before them stood seventy of the elders of the house of Israel, with Jaazaniah son of Shaphan standing among them. Each had his censer in his hand, and the **fragrant** cloud of incense was ascending. [Ezekiel 8:11]

amar, to say or speak

King David went on to **pray** thus, "Blessed be the LORD, the God of Israel, who today has granted one of my offspring to sit on my throne and permitted me to witness it." [I Kings 1:48]

I **pray**, "Only do not let them rejoice over me, those who boast against me when my foot slips."
[Psalm 38:16]

Then God **said**, "Let there be light"; and there was light. [Genesis 1:3]

So I **intend** to build a house for the name of the LORD my God, as the LORD said to my father David, "Your son, whom I will set on your throne in your place, shall build the house for my name." [I Kings 5:5]

Benaiah son of Jehoiada answered the king, "Amen! May the LORD, the God of my lord the king, so **ordain**." [I Kings 1:36]

paga, to impinge, by accident or design

What is the Almighty, that we should serve him? And what profit do we get if we **pray** to him? [Job 21:15]

He poured out himself to death, and was numbered with the transgressors; yet he bore the sin of many, and made **intercession** for the transgressors. [Isaiah 53:12]

Even when Elnathan and Delaiah and Gemariah **urged** the king not to burn the scroll, he would not listen to them. [Jeremiah 36:25]

The LORD saw that there was no one, and was appalled that there was no one to **intervene**; so his own arm brought him victory, and his righteousness upheld him. [Isaiah 59:16]

Naomi said to Ruth, her daughter-in-law, "It is better, my daughter, that you go out with his young women, otherwise you might be **bothered** in another field." [Ruth 2:22]

Jacob went on his way and the angels of God **met** him. [Genesis 32:1]

Samson answered the Philistines, "Swear to me that you yourselves will not **attack** me." [Judges 15:12]

lachash, to whisper, mumble

LORD, in distress they sought you, they poured out a **prayer** when your chastening was on them. [Isaiah 26:16]

When David saw that his servants were **whispering** together, he perceived that the child was dead. [II Samuel 12:19]

The wicked have venom like the venom of a serpent, like the deaf adder that stops its ear, so that it does not hear the voice of **charmers** or of the cunning enchanter. [Psalm 58:4-5]

For now the Sovereign, the LORD of hosts, is taking away from Jerusalem and from Judah support and staff . . . warrior and soldier, judge and prophet, diviner and elder, captain of fifty and dignitary, counselor and skillful magician and expert **enchanter**. [Isaiah 3:1-3]

tsela (Aramaic), to bow

Whatever is needed—young bulls, rams, or sheep for burnt offerings to the God of heaven, wheat, salt, wine, or oil, as the priests in Jerusalem require—let that be given to them day by day without fail, so that they may offer pleasing sacrifices to the God of heaven, and **pray** for the life of the king and his children. [Ezra 6:9-10]

Although Daniel knew that the document had been signed, he continued to go to his house, which had windows in its upper room open toward Jerusalem, and to get down on his knees three times a day to **pray** to his God and praise him, just as he had done previously. [Daniel 6:10]

ba'u (Aramaic), a request or petition

All the presidents of the kingdom, the prefects and the satraps, the counselors and the governors are agreed that the king should establish an ordinance and enforce an interdict, that whoever **prays** to anyone, divine or human, for thirty days, except to you, O king, shall be thrown into a den of lions. [Daniel 6:7]

Marks a word in the text that has its own entry

Then they responded to the king, "Daniel, one of the exiles from Judah, pays no attention to you, O king, or to the interdict you have signed, but he is saying his **prayers** three times a day." [Daniel 6:13]

euchomai, wish

Paul replied, "Whether quickly or not, I **pray** to God that not only you but also all who are listening to me today might become such as I am—except for these chains." [Acts 26:29

For we rejoice when we are weak and you are strong. This is what we **pray** for, that you may become perfect. [II Corinthians 13:9]

For I could **wish** that I myself were accursed and cut off from Christ for the sake of my own people, my kindred according to the flesh. [Romans 9:3]

Beloved, I **pray** that all may go well with you and that you may be in good health, just as it is well with your soul. [III John 1:2]

proseuchomai, toward + wish

I say to you, Love your enemies and **pray** for those who persecute you. [Matthew 5:44]

In the morning, while it was still very dark, Jesus got up and went out to a deserted place, and there he **prayed**. [Mark 1:35]

Then Peter began to explain it to them, step by step, saying, "I was in the city of Joppa **praying**, and in a trance I saw a vision." [Acts 11:4-5]

Likewise the Spirit helps us in our weakness; for we do not know how to **pray** as we ought, but that very Spirit intercedes with sighs too deep for words. [Romans 8:26]

And this is my **prayer**, that your love may overflow more and more with knowledge and full insight. [Philippians 1:9]

Rejoice always, **pray** without ceasing, give thanks in all circumstances; for this is the will of God in Christ Jesus for you. [I Thessalonians 5:16-18]

deomai, to beg

Repent therefore of this wickedness of yours, and **pray** to the Lord that, if possible, the intent of your heart may be forgiven you. [Acts 8:22]

Night and day we **pray** most earnestly that we may see you face to face and restore whatever is lacking in your faith. [I Thessalonians 3:10]

Then Jesus said to his disciples, "The harvest is plentiful, but the laborers are few; therefore **ask** the Lord of the harvest to send out laborers into his harvest." [Matthew 9:37-38]

So we are ambassadors for Christ, since God is making his appeal through us; we **entreat** you on behalf of Christ, be reconciled to God. [II Corinthians 5:20]

Once, when Jesus was in one of the cities, there was a man covered with leprosy. When he saw Jesus, he bowed with his face to the ground and **begged** him, "Lord, if you choose, you can make me clean." [Luke 5:12]

Paul replied, "I am a Jew, from Tarsus in Cilicia, a citizen of an important city; I **beg** you, let me speak to the people." [Acts 21:39]

deesis, from *deomai*

The angel said to him, "Do not be afraid, Zechariah, for your **prayer** has been heard. Your wife Elizabeth will bear you a son, and you will name him John." [Luke 1:13]

Then they said to him, "John's disciples, like the disciples of the Pharisees, frequently fast and **pray**, but your disciples eat and drink." [Luke 5:33]

Brothers and sisters, my heart's desire and **prayer** to God for them is that they may be saved. [Romans 10:1]

Therefore confess your sins to one another, and pray *(euchomai)* for one another, so that you may be healed. The **prayer** of the righteous is powerful and effective. [James 5:16]

aiteo, to beg

I **pray** therefore that you may not lose heart over my sufferings for you; they are your glory. [Ephesians 3:13]

Give to everyone who **begs** from you, and do not refuse anyone who wants to borrow from you. [Matthew 5:42]

Until now you have not **asked** for anything in my name. **Ask** and you will receive, so that your joy may be complete. [John 16:24]

From everyone to whom much has been given, much will be required; and from the one to whom much has been entrusted, even more will be **demanded**. [Luke 12:48]

The jailer **called** for lights, and rushing in, he fell down trembling before Paul and Silas. [Acts 16:29]

erotao, to interrogate

There is sin that is mortal; I do not say that you should **pray** about that. [I John 5:16]

Jesus did not answer her at all. And his disciples came and **urged** him, saying, "Send her away, for she keeps shouting after us." [Matthew 15:23]

When Jesus was alone, those who were around him along with the twelve **asked** him about the parables. [Mark 4:10]

While Jesus was speaking, a Pharisee **invited** him to dine with him; so he went in and took his place at the table. [Luke 11:37]

They all alike began to make excuses. The first said to him, "I have bought a piece of land, and I must go out and see it; **please** accept my regrets." [Luke 14:18]

When he heard that Jesus had come from Judea to Galilee, he went and **begged** him to come down and heal his son, for he was at the point of death. [John 4:47]

We **appeal** to you, brothers and sisters, to respect those who labor among you, and have charge of you in the Lord and admonish you. [I Thessalonians 5:12]

A survey of the biblical words translated as pray or prayer reveals that, with the possible exceptions of *proseuchomai* and *deesis*, people in former times used the same language for their relationship with God as they used to describe certain interactions among themselves. For the most part, these words indicate an appeal from the weaker to the stronger of two parties. These forms of

---

entreaty may at times have been simply expressions of good manners. People today trying to be polite "beg" to differ in an argument and say "please" when giving orders to a subordinate. Yet, for the most part, the words for prayer and praying are requests that the petitioner earnestly desires to receive from someone with the power to bestow favors.

For people who believe that God responds to prayers, the biblical language of prayer is quite congenial. For those who are not convinced that God intervenes in nature or in human history, however, the language can be a barrier to the practice of religion.* For them, the idea that God grants and withholds favors, either arbitrarily or judgmentally, may be repugnant to the vision of a loving and merciful God. In reaction to the notion of an interventionist God, they tend to renounce prayer or God or both.

Other skeptics are not so easily put off. They find great value in a discipline of prayer that does not include the expectation that God will do anything at all in response to their wishing, asking, requesting, imploring, beseeching, appealing, whispering, urging, demanding or begging. Instead of an attempt to prompt God into taking action, prayer can be a way of enhancing the life of the one who prays.[21] Even without an expectation of external results, prayer can encourage perspective, reduce stress, strengthen bonds of affection, enhance enjoyment, free creativity, and nourish faith.*

presbyter—see priest

priest, *noun*   In the Hebrew Scriptures, *kohen* is the title for anyone who presides at a ritual sacrifice. The Greek word for a person who performs this function is *hiereus*. The Latin is *sacerdos*. Some confusion among Christians arose in the third or fourth century when they imitated their neighbors of other persuasions and began calling their ministers *sacerdos* or *hiereus*. As a result, they began to equate those titles with *presbyteros*, or elder, the title of leaders in the early church. As the English language evolved, *presbyteros* became priest. Priest then was used as the translation for *kohen, hiereus, sacerdos,* and *presbyteros*.

The term *kohen* applied to the person who presided at sacrifices to a god* in any tradition.

> After Abram's return from the defeat of Chedorlaomer and the kings who were with him, the king of Sodom went out to meet him at the Valley of Shaveh (that is, the King's Valley). And King Melchizedek of Salem brought out bread and wine; he was **priest** of God Most High. [Genesis 14:17-18]

> Pharaoh gave Joseph the name Zaphenath-paneah; and he gave him Asenath daughter of Potiphera, **priest** of On, as his wife. Thus Joseph gained authority over the land of Egypt. [Genesis 41:45]

> Moses was keeping the flock of his father-in-law Jethro, the **priest** of Midian; he led his flock beyond the wilderness, and came to Horeb, the mountain of God. [Exodus 3:1]

> If your gift for a burnt offering is from the flock, from the sheep or goats, your offering shall be a male without blemish. It shall be slaughtered on the north side of the altar before the LORD, and Aaron's sons the **priests** shall dash its blood against all sides of the altar. [Leviticus 1:10-11]

> When they rose early on the next morning, Dagon had fallen on his face to the ground before the ark of the LORD, and the head of Dagon and both his hands were lying cut off upon the threshold; only the trunk of Dagon was left to him. This is why the **priests** of Dagon and all who enter the house of Dagon do not step on the threshold of Dagon in Ashdod to this day. [I Samuel 5:4-5]

*Marks a word in the text that has its own entry

> Then all the people of the land went to the house of Baal, and tore it down; his altars and his images they broke in pieces, and they killed Mattan, the **priest** of Baal, before the altars. [II Kings 11:18]

The early Christians used *hiereus* mostly in reference to the temple in Jerusalem, but to them it was also a generic title for anyone who presided at a sacrifice. The title high priest in the Jerusalem temple was *archiereus, arche*, first in rank + *hiereus*. (The term hierarchy evolved from the same combination with the components reversed.)

> Jesus said to him, "See that you say nothing to anyone; but go, show yourself to the **priest**, and offer the gift that Moses commanded, as a testimony to them." [Matthew 8:4]

> They took Jesus to Annas, who was the father-in-law of Caiaphas, the **high priest** that year. [John 18:13]

> The **priest** of Zeus, whose temple was just outside the city, brought oxen and garlands to the gates; he and the crowds wanted to offer sacrifice. [Acts 14:13]

> So also Christ did not glorify himself in becoming a high priest, but was appointed by the one who said to him, "You are my Son, today I have begotten you"; as he says also in another place, "You are a **priest** forever, according to the order of Melchizedek." [Hebrews 5:5-6]

In only two of the works that made it into the Christian Bible,* we find followers of Jesus called priests; in both cases, the word is a metaphor indicating the entire community.

> You are a chosen race, a royal **priest**hood, a holy nation, God's own people, in order that you may proclaim the mighty acts of him who called you out of darkness into his marvelous light. [I Peter 2:9]

> To him who loves us and freed us from our sins by his blood, and made us to be a kingdom, **priests** serving his God and Father, to him be glory and dominion forever and ever. Amen. [Revelation 1:5-6]

> Blessed and holy are those who share in the first resurrection. Over these the second death has no power, but they will be **priests** of God and of Christ, and they will reign with him a thousand years. [Revelation 20:6]

Originally *presbyteros* had quite a different meaning from *hiereus*. Literally, a *presbyteros* was one of the old ones, an elder, but it came to be a popular metaphor identifying a person of any age who was respected for wisdom. Eventually, it became the title used for a member of a governing council in Judea, including the council in Jerusalem called the Sanhedrin.

> After Jesus had finished all his sayings in the hearing of the people, he entered Capernaum. A centurion there had a slave whom he valued highly, and who was ill and close to death. When he heard about Jesus, he sent some Jewish **elders** to him, asking him to come and heal his slave. [Luke 7:1-3]

> The chief priests and the **elders** of the people gathered in the palace of the high priest, who was called Caiaphas. [Matthew 26:3]

> Again they came to Jerusalem. As Jesus was walking in the temple, the chief priests, the scribes, and the **elders** came to him and said, "By what authority are you doing these things? Who gave you this authority to do them?" [Mark 11:27-28]

---

*Marks a word in the text that has its own entry

Although St. Paul did not use the term in any of his surviving correspondence, those who came after him did. As was probably the case with the title apostle,* the appearance of Christian elders in Acts may be an anachronism. The same is probably true for the use of the term in the letters written in Paul's name but by a later hand. When the early Christians called a leader *presbyteros*, they were probably following the Judean custom, but a reader can never be sure whether this was a metaphor of respect, a title for a recognized office in the church, or literally an old person.

> Certain individuals came down from Judea and were teaching the brothers, "Unless you are circumcised according to the custom of Moses, you cannot be saved." And after Paul and Barnabas had no small dissension and debate with them, Paul and Barnabas and some of the others were appointed to go up to Jerusalem to discuss this question with the apostles and the **elders**. [Acts 15:1-2]

> Do not neglect the gift that is in you, which was given to you through prophecy with the laying on of hands by the council of **elders**. [I Timothy 4:14]

> I left you behind in Crete for this reason, so that you should put in order what remained to be done, and should appoint **elders** in every town, as I directed you. [Titus 1:5]

> Are any among you sick? They should call for the **elders** of the church and have them pray over them, anointing them with oil in the name of the Lord. [James 5:14]

> The **elder** to the elect lady and her children, whom I love in the truth, and not only I but also all who know the truth. [II John 1:1]

The sixteenth-century reformers once again made a distinction between *hiereus* and *presbyteros*, between priest and elder, with many of them preferring presbyter as the title for Christian ministers. To them, priest was too closely associated with the discarded concept of the Eucharist* being offered as a sacrifice.* Anglicans, however, continued to use priest and presbyter interchangeably. The only general agreement about the use of priest in the reformed churches was the emphasis on the priesthood of all believers originally found in I Peter and Revelation.

The present followers of Jesus have inherited these two metaphors initially used to help understand the nature of Christian community: *presbyteros*, an old one, and *hiereus*, a priest. The Christians of the generations following St. Paul seemed to need some structure, so appointing councils of old ones, or at least wise ones, may have been important to them. At the same time, all the other religions around them had priests. Perhaps to feel legitimate, they needed priests as well.

As titles for leaders, priest and elder or presbyter—along with bishop* and deacon*—are used in different ways by the various Christian denominations. Once these terms lose their metaphorical sense and become levels of authority in a hierarchy, they have lost most of their connection with the Bible.

progressive, *adjective;* **progress**, *noun* The Greek word the followers of Jesus used for progress was *prokope*, which appears in two of the epistles.

> I know that I will remain and continue with all of you for your **progress** and joy in faith, so that I may share abundantly in your boasting in Christ Jesus when I come to you again. [Philippians 1:25-26]

Put these things into practice, devote yourself to them, so that all may see your **progress**.
[I Timothy 4:15]

Progress suggests movement and is closely related to the figure of speech found in the Greek word usually translated as follow, *akolutheo*, which literally meant to take the same road. Since the word does not suggest one behind another, it could as accurately be translated as accompany. The emphasis was on the common journey rather than the declared destination. In many instances, *akolutheo* can be taken both literally and figuratively, both as actually walking together and as accepting a student-teacher relationship.

> As Jesus passed along the Sea of Galilee, he saw Simon and his brother Andrew casting a net into the sea—for they were fishermen. And Jesus said to them, "Follow me and I will make you fish for people." And immediately they left their nets and **followed** him. [Mark 1:16-18]

> Jesus, looking at the man, loved him and said, "You lack one thing; go, sell what you own, and give the money to the poor, and you will have treasure in heaven; then come, **follow** me."
> [Mark 10:21]

> As they were going along the road, someone said to him, "I will **follow** you wherever you go." And Jesus said to him, "Foxes have holes, and birds of the air have nests; but the Son of Man has nowhere to lay his head." To another he said, "**Follow** me." But he said, "Lord, first let me go and bury my father." But Jesus said to him, "Let the dead bury their own dead; but as for you, go and proclaim the kingdom of God." Another said, "I will **follow** you, Lord; but let me first say farewell to those at my home." Jesus said to him, "No one who puts a hand to the plow and looks back is fit for the kingdom of God." [Luke 9:57-62]

> Whoever serves me must **follow** me, and where I am, there will my servant be also. Whoever serves me, the Father will honor. [John 12:26]

The adjective progressive, then, implies students who have agreed to accompany a teacher along a way* that the teacher has set for them. The term progressive is now used to identify an approach to Christianity that emphasizes an inclusive welcome, a critical study of the Bible and tradition, and a dedication to bringing social and environmental justice and peace to all people, especially those who have been oppressed and powerless.

DID YOU KNOW . . .

. . . that *prokope* is pronounced *prohk-ohp-ay*?
For more help with pronunciation, see "Pronouncing
Transliterated Hebrew and Greek Words" on page 15.

---

propitiation, *noun*   Although the word propitiation does not appear in the New Revised Standard Version of the Bible, it is familiar to many Christians through their worship and their reading of the King James Version. In the seventeenth century, the English translators chose propitiation to translate three Greek words that suggest appeasement because they are rooted in the Greek *hilaos,* as is *hilaros,* meaning cheerful. Recent translators, however, have preferred to use atone or atonement.* Their reasoning seems to be that when these three words occur in the early Greek version of the Hebrew Scriptures, they stand for Hebrew words related to *kaphar,* such as *kippur,* meaning to

---

cover. For example, the cover (that is, the lid) for the ark of the covenant is called the *kapporeth*. In most instances, however, *kaphar* and its derivatives appear in English as atone or atonement or other words suggesting pardon or forgiveness rather than propitiation.

hilasterion

Being justified freely by his grace through the redemption that is in Christ Jesus: Whom God hath set forth to be a **propitiation** through faith in his blood. [Romans 3:24-25, KING JAMES VERSION]

And thou shalt make a **mercy seat** of pure gold: two cubits and a half shall be the length thereof, and a cubit and a half the breadth thereof.—*kapporeth* [Exodus 25:17, KING JAMES VERSION]

hilaskomai

He is the **propitiation** for our sins: and not for ours only, but also for the sins of the whole world. [I John 2:2, KING JAMES VERSION]

Help us, O God of our salvation, for the glory of thy name: and deliver us, and **purge** away our sins, for thy name's sake.—*kaphar* [Psalm 79:9, KING JAMES VERSION]

hilasmos

Herein is love, not that we loved God, but that he loved us, and sent his Son to be the **propitiation** for our sins. [I John 4:10, KING JAMES VERSION]

Then shalt thou cause the trumpet of the jubilee to sound on the tenth day of the seventh month, in the day of **atonement** shall ye make the trumpet sound throughout all your land. —*kippur* [Leviticus 25:9, KJV]

Although modern translators have recoiled at the idea of God's being appeased by the death of Jesus, the question remains as to how well the early Greek-speaking Christians understood the Hebrew concept of covering sins.* If Paul and the author of the first letter attributed to John knew their scriptures only in Greek, they might well have been using a metaphor that suggested trying to put a grumpy God into a better mood. If they were familiar with the Hebrew Bible, however, they would have been using a metaphor that suggested putting a cover over anything ugly or disgusting in the past so that people could get on with their lives.

prostitute, prostitution—see know, Magdalene, sodomite

purity, *noun;* **pure**, *adjective*   The concept of purity was expressed in Hebrew primarily by *tahor*, clean, and by *tame*, unclean. The parallel words in Greek were *katharos* and *akathartos*, respectively, words related to the English catharsis and cathartic. These words went through a two-stage development as figures of speech. Their literal meanings had to do with things, which could be clean or dirty.

Their earliest use as metaphors arose in connection with what people thought was appropriate for contact with the divine. Only those who were pure according to the standards of the cult could present themselves to God. Anything that was strange, such as the animals sacrificed and eaten in other cultures, was unclean. So was anything that suggested the leaking away of power, such as the loss of menstrual blood or various other body fluids, physical deformities, birth, and death. Finally, as the ceremonial meaning faded, the metaphors took on a moral sense.

Literal (Hebrew)

You shall make a lampstand of **pure** gold. The base and the shaft of the lampstand shall be made of hammered work; its cups, its calyxes, and its petals shall be of one piece with it. [Exodus 25:31]

I will sprinkle **clean** water upon you, and you shall be clean from all your uncleannesses, and from all your idols I will cleanse you. [Ezekiel 36:25]

I said, "Let them put a **clean** turban on his head." So they put a **clean** turban on his head and clothed him with the apparel. [Zechariah 3:5]

Literal (Greek)

So Joseph took the body and wrapped it in a **clean** linen cloth. [Matthew 27:59]

Out of the temple came the seven angels with the seven plagues, robed in **pure** bright linen, with golden sashes across their chests. [Revelation 15:6]

Cultic (Hebrew)

Among those that chew the cud or have divided hoofs, you shall not eat the following: the camel, for even though it chews the cud, it does not have divided hoofs; it is **unclean** for you. The rock badger, for even though it chews the cud, it does not have divided hoofs; it is **unclean** for you. The hare, for even though it chews the cud, it does not have divided hoofs; it is **unclean** for you. The pig, for even though it has divided hoofs and is cleft-footed, it does not chew the cud; it is **unclean** for you. Of their flesh you shall not eat, and their carcasses you shall not touch; they are **unclean** for you. [Leviticus 11:4-8]

Speak to the people of Israel, saying: If a woman conceives and bears a male child, she shall be ceremonially **unclean** seven days; as at the time of her menstruation, she shall be **unclean** . . . If she bears a female child, she shall be **unclean** two weeks, as in her menstruation; her time of blood purification shall be sixty-six days. [Leviticus 12:2, 5]

Speak to the people of Israel and say to them: When any man has a discharge from his member, his discharge makes him ceremonially **unclean**. [Leviticus 15:2]

The priest shall make an examination, and if it appears deeper than the skin and its hair has turned white, the priest shall pronounce him **unclean**; this is a leprous disease, broken out in the boil . . . But if the spot remains in one place and does not spread, it is the scar of the boil; the priest shall pronounce him **clean**. [Leviticus 13:20, 23]

Cultic (Greek)

There was a leper who came to him and knelt before him, saying, "Lord, if you choose, you can make me **clean**." He stretched out his hand and touched him, saying, "I do choose. Be made clean!" Immediately his leprosy was cleansed. [Matthew 8:2-3]

Jesus said to them, "Then do you also fail to understand? Do you not see that whatever goes into a person from outside cannot defile, since it enters, not the heart but the stomach, and goes out into the sewer?" (Thus he declared all foods **clean**.) [Mark 7:18-19]

They had come to hear him and to be healed of their diseases; and those who were troubled with **unclean** spirits were cured. [Luke 6:18]

Marks a word in the text that has its own entry

For the unbelieving husband is made holy through his wife, and the unbelieving wife is made holy through her husband. Otherwise, your children would be **unclean**, but as it is, they are holy. [I Corinthians 7:14]

Moral (Hebrew)

Create in me a **clean** heart, O God, and put a new and right spirit within me. [Psalm 51:10]

You meet those who gladly do right, those who remember you in your ways. But you were angry, and we sinned; because you hid yourself we transgressed. We have all become like one who is **unclean**, and all our righteous deeds are like a filthy cloth. We all fade like a leaf, and our iniquities, like the wind, take us away. [Isaiah 64:5-6]

I have seen your abominations, your adulteries and neighings, your shameless prostitutions on the hills of the countryside. Woe to you, O Jerusalem! How long will it be before you are made **clean**? [Jeremiah 13:27]

Moral (Greek)

Blessed are the **pure** in heart, for they will see God. [Matthew 5:8]

When they opposed and reviled Paul, in protest he shook the dust from his clothes and said to them, "Your blood be on your own heads! I am **innocent**. From now on I will go to the Gentiles." [Acts 18:6]

Be sure of this, that no fornicator or **impure** person, or one who is greedy (that is, an idolater), has any inheritance in the kingdom of Christ and of God. [Ephesians 5:5]

Shun youthful passions and pursue righteousness, faith, love, and peace, along with those who call on the Lord from a **pure** heart. [II Timothy 2:22]

Religion that is **pure** and undefiled before God, the Father, is this: to care for orphans and widows in their distress, and to keep oneself unstained by the world. [James 1:27]

The purity metaphors have caused two kinds of problems for the followers of Jesus: how to decide which of the rules apply to them, and how to appreciate the teachings about purity attributed to Jesus without demeaning the Pharisees* and contributing to anti-Semitism.

Christians of every tradition have had to wrestle with the questions about how seriously to take certain parts of the Hebrew Scripture. The Anglicans in their Articles of Religion have stated the case this way:

> "Although the law given from God by Moses, as touching Ceremonies and Rites, do not bind Christian men, . . . yet not withstanding, no Christian man whatsoever is free from the obedience of the Commandments which are called Moral." (Article VII)

For centuries, Christian women who had given birth were forbidden access to the church until after a ritual of purification. This was thought to be one of the moral commandments. Although most Christians now have decided that the purity regulations regarding birth belong to the category of Rites and Ceremonies, they are still divided about into which category to place homosexual* behavior.

Even responsible scholars have difficulty discussing the purity rules in a way that is respectful of the Pharisees. They want to show how the followers of Jesus were free from a burden that many of them were unable to carry. For example, shepherds and farm laborers could not follow all the rules and still earn a living. Although many individuals by reason of their circumstances could not follow the purity regulations, the Purity Code was of extreme importance to the Jews* as a people. The Purity Code helped them establish and maintain their identity when they either had no ready access to the temple in Jerusalem or when they perceived the temple leadership to be corrupt. Of all the clans and ethnic groups that existed under Roman rule in the first century, the only people to survive with their identity and religion intact until the twenty-first century are the Judeans.

R

rabbi—see **teacher**

ransom—see **redeem**

realm—see **kingdom of God**

reconcile, *verb*; **reconciliation**, *noun*   The Greek root of the word translated reconcile is *allasso,* meaning to change. In the Greek Scriptures, the word on one occasion, when it appears in Matthew's gospel, is *diallasso,* literally to change through or to change thoroughly. Elsewhere, the word is *katallasso,* which means to change down. The noun form, reconciliation, is formed on the latter.

The concept of reconciliation is not difficult to grasp. Nearly everyone goes through the monthly struggle of trying to reconcile a check register with a bank statement. If the account has been active, the checkbook balance will never agree with the bank balance at the end of the month. The reconciliation is accomplished by changing the figures based on the outstanding checks and the uncredited deposits so that some sense can be made of the two ending balances.

Reconciliation at the temple in first-century Jerusalem was the business of changing various kinds of money down to base values so that people could exchange their coins for temple currency. When first-century writers used reconciliation in regard to human affairs, they did not mean that two people of differing opinions reached an agreement or that two people who had been fighting lived in harmony. The word reconciled—always used in the passive voice when the reference is to human beings—meant that people allowed themselves to be changed to the point where they could make sense out of their differences. This was the possibility Matthew was holding out when he attributed these words to Jesus:

> So when you are offering your gift at the altar, if you remember that your brother or sister has something against you, leave your gift there before the altar and go; first **be reconciled** to your brother or sister, and then come and offer your gift. [Matthew 5:23-24]

The same meaning is behind St. Paul's advice to married people who were part of the Christian community in Corinth.

> To the married I give this command—not I but the Lord—that the wife should not separate from her husband (but if she does separate, let her remain unmarried or else **be reconciled** to her husband), and that the husband should not divorce his wife. [I Corinthians 7:10-11]

No two people can work together as colleagues or live together as spouses without disagreeing as much as they agree. If neither of them is willing to submit to the tyranny of the other, they are going to argue. They can argue, even fight, constructively if they are not under the moral burden of having to always reach agreement or harmony. Reconciliation is a better goal, each person being changed so that together they can find a way to live with their differences.

For the ultimate reconciliation to take place, a finite person being reconciled to the infinite, a similar process of inward change is necessary. Paul uses the same *katallasso* metaphor in writing about a relationship with God* as he used in giving advice to estranged marriage partners.

> All this is from God, who **reconciled** us to himself through Christ, and has given us the ministry of **reconciliation**; that is, in Christ God was **reconciling** the world to himself, not counting their trespasses against them, and entrusting the message of **reconciliation** to us. [II Corinthians 5:18-19]

Whether talking about living with differences of other people or difficulties with whatever one imagines God to be, the reconcile metaphor can deepen the discussion. In either case, what is required is a willingness to give up being in complete control of the situation and to allow inward change to happen. Although this open attitude is best expressed in the passive voice, be reconciled, the action is not completely passive. Giving up control and allowing for change requires the courage to make a clear decision that the relationship is more important than being right.

redeem, *verb*; **redemption**, *noun*   The early followers of Jesus sometimes employed the metaphor redeem to describe what they felt about their relationship to him. Originally, the equivalent terms in both Hebrew and Greek referred to common legal and business transactions as well as to religious practice. The two basic words in Hebrew, *ga'al* and *padah*, meant to liberate, usually in exchange for money or something else of value, in English known as ransom. Two Greek words, *poieo* and *apolytrosis*, had similar meanings.

In Leviticus, *ga'al* is used in reference to both property and people.

> Throughout the land that you hold, you shall provide for the **redemption** of the land. If anyone of your kin falls into difficulty and sells a piece of property, then the next of kin shall come and **redeem** what the relative has sold. [Leviticus 25:24-25]

> If resident aliens among you prosper, and if any of your kin fall into difficulty with one of them and sell themselves to an alien, or to a branch of the alien's family, after they have sold themselves they shall have the right of **redemption**; one of their brothers may **redeem** them, or their uncle or their uncle's son may **redeem** them, or anyone of their family who is of their own flesh may **redeem** them; or if they prosper they may **redeem** themselves. [Leviticus 25:47-49]

Padah appears in passages with much the same meaning: to set free from slavery or to save from death.

> When a man sells his daughter as a slave, she shall not go out as the male slaves do. If she does not please her master, who designated her for himself, then he shall let her be **redeemed**; he shall have no right to sell her to a foreign people, since he has dealt unfairly with her. [Exodus 21:7-8]

> When Pharaoh stubbornly refused to let us go, the LORD killed all the firstborn in the land of Egypt, from human firstborn to the firstborn of animals. Therefore I sacrifice to the LORD every male that first opens the womb, but every firstborn of my sons I **redeem**. [Exodus 13:15]

From this historical distance, we cannot do more than speculate on the possibility that the sacrifice of the firstborn child was once a cult practice among the Hebrew-speaking people. We can say with assurance, however, that the theme of redemption became central to the telling of the story about their ancestors having been freed from slavery in Egypt. In retelling the story, they could use either of their words for redeem.

> It was because the LORD loved you and kept the oath that he swore to your ancestors, that the LORD has brought you out with a mighty hand, and **redeemed** you from the house of slavery, from the hand of Pharaoh king of Egypt.—*padah* [Deuteronomy 7:8]

> With your strong arm you **redeemed** your people, the descendants of Jacob and Joseph.—*ga'al* [Psalm 77:15]

In time, both words came to be used as metaphors for personal or communal deliverance from oppression. Occasionally, both words appear in the same sentence.

> Do not hide your face from your servant, for I am in distress—make haste to answer me. Draw near to me, **redeem** (*ga'al*) me, **set** me **free** (*padah*) because of my enemies. [Psalm 69:17-18]

> For the LORD has **ransomed** (*padah*) Jacob, and has **redeemed** (*ga'al*) him from hands too strong for him. [Jeremiah 31:11]

Followers of Jesus who felt that he had set them free from sin* and despair* naturally seized upon the popular metaphor. When a verb was called for, they used *poieo*:

> We had hoped that he was the one to **redeem** Israel. Yes, and besides all this, it is now the third day since these things took place. [Luke 24:21]

> When the fullness of time had come, God sent his Son, born of a woman, born under the law, in order to **redeem** those who were under the law, so that we might receive adoption as children. [Galatians 4:4-5]

> He it is who gave himself for us that he might **redeem** us from all iniquity and purify for himself a people of his own who are zealous for good deeds. [Titus 2:14]

When they wrote about the action of being redeemed or ransomed, as in the manumission of a slave, and needed a noun, they used the metaphor *apolytrosis*, formed from *apo*, away from + *lutron*, something that loosens.

> God is the source of your life in Christ Jesus, who became for us wisdom from God, and righteousness and sanctification and **redemption**, in order that, as it is written, "Let the one who boasts, boast in the Lord." [I Corinthians 1:30-31]

> In Jesus Christ we have **redemption** through his blood, the forgiveness of our trespasses, according to the riches of his grace that he lavished on us. [Ephesians 1:7-8]

> God has rescued us from the power of darkness and transferred us into the kingdom of his beloved Son, in whom we have **redemption**, the forgiveness of sins. [Colossians 1:13-14]

With kidnaping being a source of revenue for both revolutionaries and common criminals, the concept of ransom remains familiar in modern times; not so for its ancient equivalent redemption. All that most people know of redeeming in the basic sense is clipping manufacturers' coupons from the paper and turning them in at the supermarket for a slight reduction in price. They would also understand the metaphorical use of the word if told that a third-floor, walk-up apartment had redeeming features. Neither of the common uses of redeem come close to opening up the imagery implicit in the use of the metaphor in the Bible.

To make the best use of the redemption metaphor, people today must concentrate on the idea of liberation. The idea will come to make spiritual sense if they can identify those negative forces from which they want to be set free: unfounded anxiety, baseless fear, self-denigration, greed, or addiction.

DID YOU KNOW . . .

. . . that *poieo* is pronounced *poy-ay-oh*?
For more help with pronunciation, see "Pronouncing
Transliterated Hebrew and Greek Words" on page 15.

---

religion   The word religion carries many connotations, as can be seen from the variety of Greek words in the Bible that are translated religion.

> When the accusers stood up, they did not charge him with any of the crimes that I was expecting. Instead they had certain points of disagreement with him about their own **religion** and about a certain Jesus, who had died, but whom Paul asserted to be alive.—*deisidaimonia*, from *deilos* fearful + *daimonion,* deity or divinity = fear of the gods [Acts 25:18-19]

> Without any doubt, the mystery of our **religion** is great: He was revealed in flesh, vindicated in spirit, seen by angels, proclaimed among Gentiles, believed in throughout the world, taken up in glory.— *eusebeia*, piety, devotion [I Timothy 3:16]

> If any think they are religious, and do not bridle their tongues but deceive their hearts, their **religion** is worthless. **Religion** that is pure and undefiled before God, the Father, is this: to care for orphans and widows in their distress, and to keep oneself unstained by the world.— *threskeia*, cult, system of ceremonial observance [James 1:26-27]

These words suggest responses to the same human problem. From a rational point of view, human existence makes no sense at all. No one can provide a logical answer to such questions as: Why was I born? Why did the universe come into being? What is the meaning of it all? Although, at some level, many people always have suspected that the universe has no inherent meaning, in recent years science has made that suspicion difficult to avoid. Steven Weinberg, a Nobel Prize winner in particle physics, put the matter bluntly when he wrote that "the more the universe seems comprehensible, the more it seems pointless."[22]

In 1965, the Archbishop of Canterbury, William Temple, dealt directly with the pointless nature of human existence in a book with the title *What Christians Stand for in the Secular World.* He noted that, before Hitler became chancellor of the German Reich, theologians could undertake the task of showing that Christianity enables us to "make sense" of the world with the meaning "show that it *is* sense." He went on to say:

> "All that seems remote today. We must still claim that Christianity enables us to 'make sense' of the world, not meaning that we can show that it is sense, but with the more literal and radical meaning of making into sense what, till it is transformed, is largely non-

sense—a disordered chaos waiting to be reduced to order as the Spirit of God gives it shape."23

Generalizing from Archbishop Temple's comments about the task of Christianity, we could say that any religion is the business of trying to make sense of that which is, by nature, nonsense. Most people cannot carry on in a world perceived as chaos, so they will find or invent some way to create meaning and purpose in life. Some of these ways are clearly identified as religions. Other ways are masked as secular pursuits.

In the industrialized regions of the twenty-first century, much religion is highly individualistic with the practitioners being generally unaware that they have chosen to find meaning in the accumulation of wealth, or in the improvement of their status, or in sexual conquests, or in gaining media attention. Many people, especially in the United States, may publicly profess allegiance to one of the organized religions but make critical decisions based on the values that adhere to the materialistic religion they unconsciously may have chosen.

Organized religions remain attractive for some because they provide an experience of community as well as a system of symbols and rituals that give structure and meaning to life. Others may turn to formal religion when the materialistic, secular religions fail to satisfy their deepest longings or to uphold them in a crisis.

repent, *verb*; **repentance**, *noun*   Many children brought up with the King James Version of the Bible were puzzled by the passages that told about God repenting. From their Sunday school lessons, they had learned that to repent was to be sorry for your sins* and be determined to do better, but from what they had learned about God in other lessons, they found it hard to imagine God sinning and having to make amends. Few teachers knew that, whenever the Hebrew Scriptures said that God repented, the original word was *nacham*, which did not necessarily have to do with bad behavior but was a metaphor that could mean changing your mind.* The literal meaning of *nacham* may have been to sigh, which was often an expression of regret.

Perhaps for the benefit of all the confused children, the translators of the New Revised Standard Version decided never to say that God repented but instead say that God had a change of mind. Human beings could change their minds but they could also repent. Some examples of *nacham* that at times have been translated repent:

> The LORD was **sorry** that he had made humankind on the earth, and it grieved him to his heart. [Genesis 6:6]

> When Pharaoh let the people go, God did not lead them by way of the land of the Philistines, although that was nearer; for God thought, "If the people face war, they may **change their minds** and return to Egypt." [Exodus 13:17]

> I had heard of you by the hearing of the ear, but now my eye sees you; therefore I despise myself, and **repent** in dust and ashes. [Job 42:5-6]

> For their sake the LORD remembered his covenant, and **showed compassion** according to the abundance of his steadfast love. [Psalm 106:45]

> You have rejected me, says the LORD, you are going backward; so I have stretched out my hand against you and destroyed you—I am weary of **relenting**. [Jeremiah 15:6]

*Marks a word in the text that has its own entry

Another Hebrew word, *shub*—meaning literally to turn back—in some places has been interpreted as a metaphor and translated as repent.

> If they **repent** with all their heart and soul in the land of their enemies, who took them captive, and pray to you toward their land, which you gave to their ancestors, the city that you have chosen, and the house that I have built for your name; then hear in heaven your dwelling place their prayer and their plea, maintain their cause and forgive your people who have sinned against you. [I Kings 8:48-50]

> If one does not **repent**, God will whet his sword; he has bent and strung his bow; he has prepared his deadly weapons, making his arrows fiery shafts. [Psalm 7:12-13]

> Zion shall be redeemed by justice, and those in her who **repent**, by righteousness. [Isaiah 1:27]

> Therefore I will judge you, O house of Israel, all of you according to your ways, says the Lord GOD. **Repent** and turn from all your transgressions; otherwise iniquity will be your ruin. [Ezekiel 18:30]

Occasionally *nacham* and *shub* occur in parallel within the same sentence, indicating that they could be understood as having approximately the same meaning.

> **Turn** (*shub*), O LORD! How long? **Have compassion** (*nacham*) on your servants! [Psalm 90:13]

> Because of this the earth shall mourn, and the heavens above grow black; for I have spoken, I have purposed; I have not **relented** (*nacham*) nor will I **turn back** (*shub*). [Jeremiah 4:28]

> Who knows whether he will not **turn** (*shub*) and **relent** (*nacham*), and leave a blessing behind him, a grain offering and a drink offering for the LORD, your God? [Joel 2:14]

In the Greek parts of the Bible, two words that meant something like changing one's mind have been taken as metaphors and translated as repent. The more common verb is *metanoeo*, from *meta*, again + *noeo*, to think. *Noeo* is the verb derived from *nous*, mind. The noun translated as repentance is *metanoia*, from the same roots. The word with a similar meaning is *metamellomai*, from *meta*, again + *mello*, to intend, have in mind.

According to tradition, *metanoeo* and *metanoia* were central to the messages of both John the Baptist and Jesus.

> In those days John the Baptist appeared in the wilderness of Judea, proclaiming, "**Repent**, for the kingdom of heaven has come near." [Matthew 3:1-2]

> From that time Jesus began to proclaim, "**Repent**, for the kingdom of heaven has come near." [Matthew 4:17]

> So the twelve went out and proclaimed that all should **repent**. [Mark 6:12]

> Jesus answered, "Those who are well have no need of a physician, but those who are sick; I have come to call not the righteous but sinners to **repentance**." [Luke 5:31-32]

> Do you despise the riches of his kindness and forbearance and patience? Do you not realize that God's kindness is meant to lead you to **repentance**? [Romans 2:4]

> The Lord is not slow about his promise, as some think of slowness, but is patient with you, not wanting any to perish, but all to come to **repentance**. [II Peter 3:9]

Metamellomai occurs much less frequently. The translators in recent times have taken it to be the equivalent of the Hebrew *nacham* and, unlike the translators of the King James Version, have not suggested that either St. Paul or God needed to repent, but Judas did.

> When Judas, his betrayer, saw that Jesus was condemned, he **repented** and brought back the thirty pieces of silver to the chief priests and the elders. [Matthew 27:3]

> Even if I made you sorry with my letter, I do not **regret** it (though I did **regret** it, for I see that I grieved you with that letter, though only briefly). [II Corinthians 7:8]

> The Lord has sworn and will not **change his mind**, "You are a priest forever." [Hebrews 7:21]

Most people do not use the words repent and repentance in ordinary conversation. They have become totally associated with conservative and evangelical preaching. For those who have a negative reaction to such language, the original biblical metaphors may be much more useful in understanding the Bible's wisdom. To review:

nacham—to regret

shub—to turn back

metanoia and *metanoeo*—to think again

metamellomai—to change one's intentions

Many people with no connections to organized religious institutions are open to a challenge that calls them to think again about how their lives are going, to admit that they regret some of the choices they have made, and to consider a major change in what they intend for the future and for the direction their lives may take.

resurrection, *noun;* **raise**, *verb*   In the early Christian writings, two Greek nouns are translated resurrection. Each evolved from a verb rendered in English as raise. The first noun, *anastasis,* comes from the verb *anistemi,* which meant to stand up from a reclining or crouching position. The other noun, *egersis,* is from the verb *egeiro,* which originally had to do with collecting or gathering one's faculties, especially in the act of rousing one's self from rest or sleep. *Agora,* the public market and gathering place, comes from the same root.

> **Get up**, let us be going. See, my betrayer is at hand.—*egeiro* [Mark 14:42]

> She went back and called her sister Mary, and told her privately, "The Teacher is here and is calling for you." And when she heard it, she **got up** quickly and went to him.—*egeiro* [John 11:28-29]

> As Jesus was walking along, he saw a man called Matthew sitting at the tax booth; and he said to him, "Follow me." And he **got up** and followed him.—*anistemi* [Matthew 9:9]

> Peter **got up** and ran to the tomb; stooping and looking in, he saw the linen cloths by themselves; then he went home, amazed at what had happened.—*anistemi* [Luke 24:12]

These simple terms had became useful metaphors to Jews who had apparently adopted a vision of the future that dealt with a nagging question, "How could a just God allow his people to suffer endlessly at the hands* of their enemies and be scattered over the face of the earth?" An emotionally satisfying answer was found in a fantasy expressed in one of the visions attributed to the prophet Ezekiel.

---

*Marks a word in the text that has its own entry   **245**

Then he said to me, "Mortal, these bones are the whole house of Israel. They say, 'Our bones are dried up, and our hope is lost; we are cut off completely.' Therefore prophesy, and say to them, Thus says the Lord GOD: I am going to open your graves, and bring you up from your graves, O my people; and I will bring you back to the land of Israel." [Ezekiel 37:11-12]

The idea that God would one day raise up the dead was not particularly popular with the priestly party in Jerusalem, perhaps because they had come to terms with the occupation forces of Rome, but it appealed strongly to some Pharisees who insisted that God would see to it that ultimately justice would prevail.

One of the many indications that Jesus and his friends may have been of the Pharisee* persuasion appears in the way the gospels relate Jesus's response to questions about the resurrection. For example, each of the first three gospels tells a story about how members of the priestly party, known as Sadducees, came to Jesus with a trick question that was intended to show the absurdity of the resurrection, but Jesus cleverly extricated himself from their trap.

Some Sadducees, who say there is no **resurrection** (*anastasis*), came to him and asked him a question, saying, "Teacher, Moses wrote for us that 'if a man's brother dies, leaving a wife but no child, the man shall marry the widow and raise up children for his brother.' There were seven brothers; the first married and, when he died, left no children; and the second married her and died, leaving no children; and the third likewise; none of the seven left children. Last of all the woman herself died. In the **resurrection** (*anastasis*) whose wife will she be? For the seven had married her." Jesus said to them, "Is not this the reason you are wrong, that you know neither the scriptures nor the power of God? For when they **rise** (*anistemi*) from the dead, they neither marry nor are given in marriage, but are like angels in heaven. And as for the dead being **raised** (*egeiro*), have you not read in the book of Moses, in the story about the bush, how God said to him, 'I am the God of Abraham, the God of Isaac, and the God of Jacob'? He is God not of the dead, but of the living; you are quite wrong." [Mark 12:18-27]

The fact that the editors Matthew and Luke also chose to include the story suggests that, at least by the end of the first century, resurrection imagery was important to the followers of Jesus, but exactly what they made of the symbol is not clear.

When early Christian writers used such terms as metaphors, they may have been thinking like Pharisees and insisting that God would prove to be just, or they may have been using resurrection imagery to help them with their horror of physical death. They could die in peace with the confidence that they would someday get another life. Note, however, that for many of them, this view of another life may have been quite different from the Greek notion of immortality. Unlike resurrection, which will be the result of an arbitrary act of God, immortality means that life on the other side of the grave is assured by the persistence of personality, that is, the indestructibility of the soul.*

Sometimes the resurrection metaphor was used to identify present realities, such as the possibility of being restored to health after an illness:

The prayer of faith will save the sick, and the Lord will **raise** them up.—*egeiro* [James 5:15]

In writing to the Christian community in Rome, Paul uses the metaphor in talking about living up to the best that is within each person. Sometimes Paul wrote about the followers of Jesus being

*Marks a word in the text that has its own entry

raised to a new life in the here and now, a life free from the death-dealing tendency to avoid responsibility and accountability.

> Therefore we have been buried with him by baptism into death, so that, just as Christ was **raised** (*egeiro*) from the dead by the glory of the Father, so we too might walk in newness of life. For if we have been united with him in a death like his, we will certainly be united with him in a **resurrection** (*anastasis*) like his. We know that our old self was crucified with him so that the body of sin might be destroyed, and we might no longer be enslaved to sin. For whoever has died is freed from sin. But if we have died with Christ, we believe that we will also live with him. We know that Christ, being **raised** (*egeiro*) from the dead, will never die again; death no longer has dominion over him. The death he died, he died to sin, once for all; but the life he lives, he lives to God. So you also must consider yourselves dead to sin and alive to God in Christ Jesus. [Romans 6:4-11]

The mention of Christ being raised from death opens the question of what Paul and the other first-century followers of Jesus might have meant by that familiar phrase. Some suppose that they were referring to a fact of history, a resuscitation of Jesus's corpse. Others would say that God had intervened in history by giving the dead Jesus a new body that looked something like the old one but was not easily recognized even by his closest friends. This new body had peculiar powers. It could appear and disappear in a moment, could pass through locked doors, and could be in two different places at once.

Still others, those who read the final chapters of the gospels with a critical eye, have come to the conclusion that these stories about the risen Christ were originally understood as hymns of praise, poetic expressions of the faithful whose lives had been transformed by their encounter with the Jesus story. This latter view finds substantial support in the writings of Paul, who never mentions an empty tomb and who insists that his encounter with the risen Lord was no different from that of the first disciples.

> For I handed on to you as of first importance what I in turn had received: that Christ died for our sins in accordance with the scriptures, and that he was buried, and that he was **raised** on the third day in accordance with the scriptures, and that he appeared to Cephas, then to the twelve. Then he appeared to more than five hundred brothers and sisters at one time, most of whom are still alive, though some have died. Then he appeared to James, then to all the apostles. Last of all, as to one untimely born, he appeared also to me.—*egeiro* [I Corinthians 15:3-8]

Note that, in using the word appeared, Paul has employed the language of vision* and subjective experience rather than the language of objective reporting and facts. Still, if he had chosen to do so, he could have talked about his vision of Jesus without referring to any body being raised, but apparently that metaphor already had become a central part of the vocabulary that Jesus's followers used in describing their experiences. How they developed that vocabulary is largely a matter of conjecture, but the gospels and Paul's letters do contain some tantalizing hints.

First, look at the gospels with the original meaning of the raised and resurrection metaphors in mind. Who was lifted up from a crouching or cowering position and boldly proclaimed what they had learned from Jesus? Who finally got themselves together and got on with the business begun by Jesus? Then, think about the way the followers of Jesus talked about themselves.

> We who are many, are one body in Christ, and individually we are members one of another. [Romans 12:5]

> Now you are the body of Christ and individually members of it. [I Corinthians 12:27]

What we may have here is the merging of two powerful metaphors—raised up and body of Christ. When Christians talk about the resurrection of Christ, they may be proclaiming that death did not have the last word in the Jesus story because his followers were raised up to be his new body.* When they say that they believe in the resurrection of the dead,* they may be proclaiming that, no matter how much a person has given in to destructive tendencies, new life is always possible.

revelation—see apocalypse

righteous—see justification

rock, *noun*   Anyone who has visited Israel or Palestine will not be surprised to learn that rock is one of the most common metaphors in the Bible. Rock dominates the landscape. Hebrew has two words for rock: *tsur* and *cela*. They seem to be used interchangeably, but *cela* often carries a sense of loftiness as in a steep or rugged face of a cliff. More often than not, rock is a metaphor for God, frequently used in association with other figures of speech such as fortress, refuge, and salvation.*

tsur

> For I will proclaim the name of the LORD, ascribe greatness to our God! The **Rock**, his work is perfect, and all his ways are just. A faithful God, without deceit, just and upright is he. [Deuteronomy 32:3-4]

> The God of Israel has spoken, the **Rock** of Israel has said to me: One who rules over people justly, ruling in the fear of God, is like the light of morning, like the sun rising on a cloudless morning, gleaming from the rain on the grassy land. [II Samuel 23:3-4]

> Incline your ear to me; rescue me speedily. Be a **rock** of refuge for me, a strong fortress to save me. [Psalm 31:2]

> O come, let us sing to the LORD; let us make a joyful noise to the **rock** of our salvation! [Psalm 95:1]

cela

> You are indeed my **rock** and my fortress; for your name's sake lead me and guide me. [Psalm 31:3]

> I say to God, my **rock**, "Why have you forgotten me? Why must I walk about mournfully because the enemy oppresses me?" [Psalm 42:9]

Occasionally *tsur* and *cela* are used in parallel, which suggests that the two metaphors for God carried similar connotations.

> David said: The LORD is my **rock** *(cela)*, my fortress, and my deliverer, my God, my **rock** *(tsur)*, in whom I take refuge, my shield and the horn of my salvation, my stronghold and my refuge, my savior; you save me from violence. [II Samuel 22:2-3]

> The LORD is my **rock** *(cela)*, my fortress, and my deliverer, my God, my **rock** *(tsur)* in whom I take refuge, my shield, and the horn of my salvation, my stronghold. [Psalm 18:2]

Marks a word in the text that has its own entry

> Be to me a **rock** *(tsur)* of refuge, a strong fortress, to save me, for you are my **rock** *(cela)* and my fortress. [Psalm 71:3]

The rock had other religious associations in addition to being a God metaphor. A rock could be used as an altar for the offering of sacrifice.* A knife made of flint rock was used in circumcision.* From out of rock came life-sustaining water. Rock stood for a sense of steadiness and security or protection. Rock is the source of life itself.

> The angel of God said to Gideon, "Take the meat and the unleavened cakes, and put them on this **rock** *(cela)*, and pour out the broth." And he did so. Then the angel of the LORD reached out the tip of the staff that was in his hand, and touched the meat and the unleavened cakes; and fire sprang up from the **rock** *(tsur)* and consumed the meat and the unleavened cakes; and the angel of the LORD vanished from his sight. [Judges 6:20-21]

> At that time the LORD said to Joshua, "Make **flint** knives and circumcise the Israelites a second time." So Joshua made **flint** knives, and circumcised the Israelites at Gibeath-haaraloth.—*tsur* [Joshua 5:2-3]

> I waited patiently for the LORD; he inclined to me and heard my cry. He drew me up from the desolate pit, out of the miry bog, and set my feet upon a **rock**, making my steps secure.—*cela* [Psalm 40:1-2]

> See, a king will reign in righteousness, and princes will rule with justice. Each will be like a hiding place from the wind, a covert from the tempest, like streams of water in a dry place, like the shade of a great **rock** in a weary land.—*cela* [Isaiah 32:1-2]

> God split **rocks** *(tsur)* open in the wilderness, and gave them drink abundantly as from the deep. He made streams come out of the **rock** *(cela)*, and caused waters to flow down like rivers. [Psalm 78:15-16]

> Listen to me, you that pursue righteousness, you that seek the LORD. Look to the **rock** from which you were hewn, and to the quarry from which you were dug.—*tsur* [Isaiah 51:1]

Rock was also used figuratively to indicate hiding from God. This theme was picked up in the words of a gospel hymn: "Well, I run to the rock just to hide my face: And the rocks cried out, no hiding place: There's no hiding place down here."

> Enter into the **rock**, and hide in the dust from the terror of the LORD, and from the glory of his majesty.—*tsur* [Isaiah 2:10]

> On that day people will throw away to the moles and to the bats their idols of silver and their idols of gold, which they made for themselves to worship, to enter the caverns of the **rocks** *(tsur)* and the clefts in the **crags** *(cela)*, from the terror of the LORD, and from the glory of his majesty, when he rises to terrify the earth. [Isaiah 2:20-21]

> The terror you inspire and the pride of your heart have deceived you, you who live in the clefts of the **rock**, who hold the height of the hill. Although you make your nest as high as the eagle's, from there I will bring you down, says the LORD.—*cela* [Jeremiah 49:16]

One negative connotation of the rock metaphor was the picture of a dry and barren land, a scene of desolation and despair.* Another is God the Rock pictured not as a refuge but as a threat.

Leave the towns, and live on the **rock**, O inhabitants of Moab! Be like the dove that nests on the sides of the mouth of a gorge.—*cela* [Jeremiah 48:28]

Therefore, thus says the Lord GOD: See, I am against you, O Tyre! I will hurl many nations against you, as the sea hurls its waves. They shall destroy the walls of Tyre and break down its towers. I will scrape its soil from it and make it a bare **rock**.—*cela* [Ezekiel 26:3-4]

The LORD of hosts, him you shall regard as holy; let him be your fear, and let him be your dread. He will become a sanctuary, a stone one strikes against; for both houses of Israel he will become a **rock** one stumbles over—a trap and a snare for the inhabitants of Jerusalem.—*tsur* [Isaiah 8:13-14]

Are you not from of old, O LORD my God, my Holy One? You shall not die. O LORD, you have marked them for judgment; and you, O **Rock**, have established them for punishment.—*tsur* [Habakkuk 1:12]

Although Jesus and his followers did not call God a rock, they seem to have been influenced by the rock imagery. The word for rock in Greek is *petra*, the source of Jesus's name for Simon, *Petros* or in English, Peter. In the naming of Peter and in the assertion about the reliability of Jesus's words, the gospels appear to have been drawing on the Hebrew use of the rock metaphor suggesting steadiness and security.

And I tell you, you are Peter, and on this **rock** I will build my church, and the gates of Hades will not prevail against it. [Matthew 16:18]

Everyone then who hears these words of mine and acts on them will be like a wise man who built his house on **rock**. The rain fell, the floods came, and the winds blew and beat on that house, but it did not fall, because it had been founded on **rock**. [Matthew 7:24-25]

The parable of the foolish farmer may have been influenced by the Hebrew use of rock to indicate a barren, desolate land. A prophesy in the Bible's last book also seems to pick up on the tradition of using rocks to picture desolation. In addition, the prophecy echoes the theme of trying to hide from God in or among the rocks.

A sower went out to sow his seed; and as he sowed, some fell on the path and was trampled on, and the birds of the air ate it up. Some fell on the **rock**; and as it grew up, it withered for lack of moisture. [Luke 8:5-6]

Then the kings of the earth and the magnates and the generals and the rich and the powerful, and everyone, slave and free, hid in the caves and among the **rocks** of the mountains, calling to the mountains and **rocks**, "Fall on us and hide us from the face of the one seated on the throne and from the wrath of the Lamb." [Revelation 6:15-16]

St. Paul uses two rock metaphors from the Hebrew Scriptures to identify his understanding of Jesus as the Christ.* Like Paul's letter to the Romans, the first letter attributed to Peter uses the image of the rock that causes stumbling.

As it is written, "See, I am laying in Zion a stone that will make people stumble, a **rock** that will make them fall, and whoever believes in him will not be put to shame." [Romans 9:33]

All drank the same spiritual drink. For they drank from the spiritual **rock** that followed them, and the **rock** was Christ. [I Corinthians 10:4]

> To you then who believe, he is precious; but for those who do not believe, "The stone that the builders rejected has become the very head of the corner," and "A stone that makes them stumble, and a **rock** that makes them fall." They stumble because they disobey the word, as they were destined to do. [I Peter 2:7-8]

People who have spent their lives on the Great Plains of America may have trouble relating to God as the Rock. They may not react much at all to any metaphorical uses of rocks in the Bible. Those who have been fortunate enough to traverse rugged mountain terrain, however, can readily sense what the Hebrew-speaking people meant when they employed rock imagery. Jesus's early followers were as familiar with the outcropping of rocks and the craggy cliff faces of Palestine as were the people of ancient Israel. As they walked with Jesus from village to village, at times they must have been impressed with the immovability of the immense rocks in which they could find shelter as well as annoyed by the smaller rocks that could cause them to stumble. They not only understood the rock metaphors of the Hebrew Scriptures, but they also employed the same images to convey their convictions about Jesus.

S

sabbath, *noun*   The Hebrew word *shabbat* apparently came from a verb that meant to desist, but the idea is so old that true etymology may be lost. The idea of stopping all work on appointed days may even be older than the seven-day week. At least in some biblical passages, *shabbat* is related to lunar festivals. The seven-day cycle originally may have marked the phases of the moon.

> I am now about to build a house for the name of the LORD my God and dedicate it to him, for offering fragrant incense before him and for the regular offering of the rows of bread, and for burnt offerings morning and evening on the **sabbaths** and the new moons and the appointed festivals of the LORD our God as ordained forever for Israel. [II Chronicles 2:4]

> Hear this you that trample on the needy and bring to ruin the poor of the land saying, "When will the new moon be over so that we may sell grain; and the **sabbath** so that we may offer wheat for sale?" [Amos 8:4-5]

> I will put an end to all her mirth, her festivals, her new moons, her **sabbaths**, and all her appointed festivals. [Hosea 2:11]

From these and other passages, it is clear that *shabbat* was a time when all business was supposed to cease and when people were to relax and enjoy themselves. At some point, the seven-day week became standard and two myths* developed to explain the practice. One represents the rest God took after the work of creation* and the other indicates a remembrance of delivery from slavery.*

> The seventh day is a **sabbath** to the LORD your God; you shall not do any work—you, your son, or your daughter, your male or female slave, your livestock, or the alien resident in your towns. In six days the LORD made heaven and earth, the sea and all that is in them, but rested the seventh day; therefore the LORD blessed the **sabbath** day and consecrated it. [Exodus 20:10-11]

> Remember that you were a slave in the land of Egypt, and the LORD your God brought you out from there with a mighty hand and an outstretched arm; therefore the LORD your God commanded you to keep the **sabbath** day. [Deuteronomy 5:15]

Marks a word in the text that has its own entry

As different as these two reasons for sabbath may be, they agree on the central point that life works best if everybody gets one day out of seven to rest. The people of ancient Israel figured out that, in the long run, they got more work out of their slaves and animals if they gave them a day off after six days of labor. As time went on, the seven-day week became part of their identity. Under the pressure of conquest and the foreign occupation of their country, they became increasingly detailed in the rules about what could and could not be done on the sabbath. These rules became part of what is known as the Purity* Code. Public gatherings for worship were allowed and even mandated. These sabbath convocations required a doubling of the usual sacrifices.*

> Six days shall work be done; but the seventh day is a **sabbath** of complete rest, a holy convocation; you shall do no work: it is a **sabbath** to the LORD throughout your settlements. [Leviticus 23:3]

> On the **sabbath** day: two male lambs a year old without blemish, and two-tenths of an ephah of choice flour for a grain offering mixed with oil, and its drink offering—this is the burnt offering for every **sabbath**, in addition to the regular burnt offering and its drink offering. [Numbers 28:9-10]

Sabbath regulations, however, were not limited to the seven-day cycle. They also developed standards for the seven-year cycle.

> Six years you shall sow your field, and six years you shall prune your vineyard, and gather in their yield; but in the seventh year there shall be a **sabbath** of complete rest for the land, a sabbath for the LORD: you shall not sow your field or prune your vineyard. [Leviticus 25:3-4]

> Moses commanded them: "Every seventh year, in the scheduled year of remission, during the festival of booths, when all Israel comes to appear before the LORD your God at the place that he will choose, you shall read this law before all Israel in their hearing." [Deuteronomy 31:10-11]

The followers of Jesus were obviously ambivalent about the sabbath regulations. Except for academics, until the middle of the twentieth century, few Christians took seriously the sabbath year, and then only a few of the clergy and other professionals in addition to the professors adopted the idea. As for the sabbath day, although the earliest followers of Jesus being Gallileans and Judeans observed it, they preserved stories about Jesus flouting the sabbath regulations. It cannot be said with certainty whether these stories reflect Jesus's attitude or whether they come from a time when Christians were mostly Gentile.

> At that time Jesus went through the grainfields on the **sabbath**; his disciples were hungry, and they began to pluck heads of grain and to eat. When the Pharisees saw it, they said to him, "Look, your disciples are doing what is not lawful to do on the **sabbath**." He said to them, "Have you not read what David did when he and his companions were hungry? He entered the house of God and ate the bread of the Presence, which it was not lawful for him or his companions to eat, but only for the priests. Or have you not read in the law that on the **sabbath** the priests in the temple break the **sabbath** and yet are guiltless? I tell you, something greater than the temple is here. But if you had known what this means, 'I desire mercy and not sacrifice,' you would not have condemned the guiltless. For the Son of Man is lord of the **sabbath**." He left that place and entered their synagogue; a man was there with a withered hand, and they asked him, "Is it lawful to cure on the **sabbath**?" so that they might accuse him. He said to them, "Suppose one of you has only one sheep and it falls into a pit on the **sabbath**; will you not lay hold of it and lift it out? How much more valuable is a human being than a sheep! So it is lawful to do good on the

sabbath." Then he said to the man, "Stretch out your hand." He stretched it out, and it was restored, as sound as the other. [Matthew 12:1-13]

Jesus said to them "The **sabbath** was made for humankind, and not humankind for the **sabbath**; so the Son of Man is lord even of the **sabbath**." [Mark 2:27-28]

Now Jesus was teaching in one of the synagogues on the sabbath. And just then there appeared a woman with a spirit that had crippled her for eighteen years. She was bent over and was quite unable to stand up straight. When Jesus saw her, he called her over and said, "Woman, you are set free from your ailment." When he laid his hands on her, immediately she stood up straight and began praising God. But the leader of the synagogue, indignant because Jesus had cured on the **sabbath**, kept saying to the crowd, "There are six days on which work ought to be done; come on those days and be cured, and not on the **sabbath** day." [Luke 13:10-14]

The man who had been healed went away and told the Jews that it was Jesus who had made him well. Therefore the Jews started persecuting Jesus, because he was doing such things on the **sabbath**. But Jesus answered them, "My Father is still working, and I also am working." [John 5:15-17]

Although the earliest followers of Jesus observed the sabbath, they also gathered on the first day of the week to celebrate the resurrection.* When the church became primarily a Gentile phenomenon, they began to call the first day of the week, rather than the seventh, the sabbath and to adopt some of the sabbath regulations found in Hebrew Scripture. The first day of the week was to be for worship and the people were to desist from most forms of work. During this transition, sabbath also came to be used as a metaphor indicating a quality of existence promised for life after death.*

So then, a **sabbath** rest still remains for the people of God; for those who enter God's rest also cease from their labors as God did from his. [Hebrews 4:9-10]

The seven-day week was one of the gifts that the people of Israel offered to the world at large. The rhythm of working six days and resting the seventh has been so valuable that it has superceded all other arrangements, such as rest only on the tenth day or on the new moon, or no rest at all for slaves and other laborers. As a figure of speech, sabbath time now refers to rhythms of work and rest on a daily, annual, or seven-year basis in addition to the weekly routine.

sacrifice, *verb* and *noun*   Neither the Hebrew nor the Greek language can make a distinction between the ritual sacrifice of animals and the slaughter of animals for human consumption. In the general culture that persisted well into the early Christian era, many temples doubled as slaughterhouses. Most of the faithful in any religious cult under ordinary circumstances would not eat meat unless the animal had first been dedicated to their god* and part of the animal left at the temple as an offering. The Hebrew verbs *zabach* and *shachat* and the Greek *thuo* in their most basic sense could mean either to slaughter or to sacrifice.

zabach

Whenever you desire you may **slaughter** and eat meat within any of your towns, according to the blessing that the Lord your God has given you; the unclean and the clean may eat of it, as they would of gazelle or deer. [Deuteronomy 12:15]

You shall not make a covenant with the inhabitants of the land, for when they prostitute themselves to their gods and **sacrifice** to their gods, someone among them will invite you, and you
will eat of the **sacrifice**. [Exodus 34:15]

shachat

After they had struck down the Philistines that day from Michmash to Aijalon, the troops were
very faint; so the troops flew upon the spoil, and took sheep and oxen and calves, and **slaughtered** them on the ground. [I Samuel 14:31-32]

Aaron shall present the bull as a sin offering for himself, and shall make atonement for himself
and for his house; he shall **slaughter** the bull as a sin offering for himself. [Leviticus 16:11]

thuo

Again he sent other slaves, saying, "Tell those who have been invited: Look, I have prepared my
dinner, my oxen and my fat calves have been **slaughtered**, and everything is ready; come to the
wedding banquet." [Matthew 22:4]

Consider the people of Israel; are not those who eat the sacrifices partners in the altar? What do
I imply then? That food **sacrificed** to idols is anything, or that an idol is anything? No, I imply that
what pagans sacrifice, they **sacrifice** to demons and not to God. I do not want you to be partners
with demons. [I Corinthians 10:18-20]

The devout could also use the nouns derived from the verbs *zabach* and *thuo* as metaphors,
pointing to some other important aspect of their relationship with the divine.

zabach

The **sacrifice** acceptable to God is a broken spirit; a broken and contrite heart, O God, you will
not despise. [Psalm 51:17]

Let them thank the LORD for his steadfast love, for his wonderful works to humankind. And let
them offer thanksgiving **sacrifices**, and tell of his deeds with songs of joy. [Psalm 107:21-22]

thusia

I have been paid in full and have more than enough; I am fully satisfied, now that I have received
from Epaphroditus the gifts you sent, a fragrant offering, a **sacrifice** acceptable and pleasing to
God. [Philippians 4:18]

Like living stones, let yourselves be built into a spiritual house, to be a holy priesthood, to offer
spiritual **sacrifices** acceptable to God through Jesus Christ. [I Peter 2:5]

Apparently the first followers of Jesus extended the metaphorical use of sacrifice in attempting
to make sense out of Jesus's execution by the Roman authorities. No matter what their religion, the
people to whom the Jesus followers first presented their story would have had a context in which to
interpret Jesus's death as a kind of sacrifice. The understanding of sacrifice as practiced at the temple in Jerusalem, however, probably influenced the Christian use of the metaphor more than did
the practices of other cults.

It is impossible to state with any degree of accuracy what was the accepted view of sacrifice at any
given point in the history of Judaism, but scholars have identified in the texts certain practices by
reason of their similarity to the customs of other cultures. The two earliest forms appear to be the

offerings of the first fruits and the firstborn. The first-fruit offering survived in Judaism in the use of the unleavened bread in the spring, and the sacrifice of the firstborn in the Passover observance.

> The choicest of the **first fruits** of your ground you shall bring into the house of the LORD your God. [Exodus 23:19]

> You shall set apart to the LORD all that first opens the womb. All the firstborn of your livestock that are males shall be the Lord's. But every **firstborn** donkey you shall redeem with a sheep; if you do not redeem it, you must break its neck. Every **firstborn** male among your children you shall redeem. [Exodus 13:12-13]

Contrary to modern interpretation, the emphasis in these sacrificial offerings was not on suffering and death, nor were the offerings bribes to gain favor with a deity or to appease the deity's anger. Lacking our assurance that life will continue from year to year, the devotees of these cults apparently thought that the first grain of the harvest and the first animal born to a mother should have its breath or soul* (Hebrew *nephesh*) released and used to strengthen the life of its kind that would follow.

The same held true for mankind. In the early stages of religious development, parents probably sacrificed their firstborn son in order that his soul force could be made available to strengthen the lives of the rest of his generation. As they developed a more sophisticated culture, the people of Israel abolished child sacrifice, but the necessity to redeem* this sacrifice remained part of the law.

The renewal of life remained a basic element in Hebrew sacrifice in the time of Jesus. The emphasis was never on the death of the victim. The actual ceremony described in the book Leviticus makes the emphasis clear.

> If the offering is a **sacrifice** of well-being, if you offer an animal of the herd, whether male or female, you shall offer one without blemish before the LORD. You shall lay your hand on the head of the offering and slaughter it at the entrance of the tent of meeting; and Aaron's sons the priests shall dash the blood against all sides of the altar. [Leviticus 3:1-2]

The sprinkling of the blood dramatizes the release of the victim's *nephesh*, as the book later explains.

> For the **life** of every creature—its blood is its **life**; therefore I have said to the people of Israel: You shall not eat the blood of any creature, for the **life** of every creature is its blood. [Leviticus 17:14]

After the sprinkling of the blood, the priest burns part of the animal on the altar and the rest is consumed by the worshipers. In this act, a human being could share a meal with God, restoring peace and strengthening the bond between them. Human beings could weaken the bond by violating a cultic taboo or by committing a moral offense, that is, by sin.* According to this way of thinking, sin could damage the soul, making harmony with God an impossibility. The remedy for the damaged soul was a sacrifice to make atonement.* The life-giving energy released by the animal's death could cleanse and purify the sin-sick soul.

In writing about the death of Jesus, his early followers presumably had temple practice in mind when they used the sacrifice metaphor. Somehow, through Jesus, they felt that they had been healed and restored to a relationship with God.

> For our paschal lamb, Christ, has been **sacrificed**. Therefore, let us celebrate the festival, not with the old yeast, the yeast of malice and evil, but with the unleavened bread of sincerity and truth. [I Corinthians 5:7-8]

> Therefore be imitators of God, as beloved children, and live in love, as Christ loved us and gave himself up for us, a fragrant offering and **sacrifice** to God. [Ephesians 5:1-2]

Although the gospel writers did not use the sacrifice metaphor directly, the way they told the story of Jesus's death indicates that they were probably influenced by the use of the term already in circulation in the Christian communities. The writers quickly pass over the matter of the Romans scourging Jesus and executing him. They do not dwell on his physical suffering and violent death, but they each use a phrase indicating that what was once the life of Jesus was now available to his followers. Sometimes, in English translation, this connection with the once-commonly accepted understanding of sacrifice is not obvious.

> Then Jesus gave a loud cry and **breathed his last**. [Mark 15:37]

That phase "breathed his last," which also appears in Luke 23:46, is a translation of the Greek *ekpneo*, formed by *ek*, from or out of + *pneo*, to breathe. *Pneo* is the root of *pneuma*, or spirit,* the Greek equivalent of *nephesh*.

Matthew and John use *pneuma* itself. They both write that Jesus "gave up his *pneuma*," but the translators of the New Revised Standard Version chose to use a different English phrase for Matthew.

> When Jesus had received the wine, he said, "It is finished." Then he bowed his head and **gave up his spirit**. [John 19:30]

> Then Jesus cried again with a loud voice and **breathed his last**. [Matthew 27:50]

With their understanding of sacrifice, the early followers of Jesus found themselves using parallel metaphors when writing about him—the first fruits and the firstborn. The sacrifices of the first fruits and the firstborn, annually recalled to mind in the spring observances, enrich and strengthen those who follow.

> For as all die in Adam, so all will be made alive in Christ. But each in his own order: Christ the **first fruits,** then at his coming those who belong to Christ. [I Corinthians 15:22-23]

> For those whom he foreknew he also predestined to be conformed to the image of his Son, in order that he might be the **firstborn** within a large family. [Romans 8:29]

By the Middle Ages, when the sacrifice of animals was no longer common, the meaning of the metaphor slowly eroded, giving way to an emphasis on Jesus's suffering and pain. With this twist, the metaphor suggested that Jesus endured punishment that he did not deserve as a substitute for human beings who richly deserved punishment for their behavior.

The sacrifice metaphor went through other changes when it became associated with the memorial meal that Christians regularly celebrated. By the beginning of the second century, Christians were calling the memorial meal a Eucharist,* which took place at an altar. By the end of the second century, the one who presided at the meal was called a priest. Picking up on the ancient use of sacrifice as a metaphor indicating any kind of an offering, the bread and wine ceremony came to be understood as a sacrifice.

As the sacrifice metaphor among Christians has changed over the ages, so has the meaning of the English word. Originally, it meant to make sacred or to make holy*and was a reasonable translation for the biblical words *zabach* and *thuo*. In more recent times, sacrifice has come to mean any intentional loss for a long-term gain. We have sacrifice plays in bridge, chess, and baseball. When vendors cut prices, they say they are selling at a sacrifice.

To understand the death of Jesus through the modern usage of the sacrifice metaphor may trivialize the event. Employing the medieval emphasis on violent death, the passion* of Jesus, works for some people but may turn away others who have no stomach for violence in any form. For people of any persuasion, the metaphor could be illuminating if they would consider the meaning of sacrifice as the first followers of Jesus probably used the term. Like the firstborn whose life is released for the sake of those who follow, Jesus—by giving up his life—enhanced the lives of his followers.

saint—see **holy**

salvation, *noun*; **save**, *verb*   The Hebrew and Greek words for save and salvation had different origins, but in the Bible they are used in much the same way. The Hebrew words are *yasha* for save and *yesha* for salvation, which originally meant to be open or free from hindrance. The Greek words, *sozo* and *soteria*, meant rescue or keeping from harm. By the time the Greek translation of the Hebrew Scriptures became available, *yasha* had evolved from being primarily a military term for victory to a personal one for protection against any kind of threat.

> The LORD **saved** Israel that day from the Egyptians; and Israel saw the Egyptians dead on the seashore. [Exodus 14:30]

> When you go to war in your land against the adversary who oppresses you, you shall sound an alarm with the trumpets, so that you may be remembered before the LORD your God and be **saved** from your enemies. [Numbers 10:9]

> The people of Israel said to Samuel, "Do not cease to cry out to the LORD our God for us, and pray that he may **save** us from the hand of the Philistines." [I Samuel 7:8]

> Turn, O LORD, **save** my life; deliver me for the sake of your steadfast love. For in death there is no remembrance of you; in Sheol who can give you praise? [Psalm 6:4-5]

> Those who have clean hands and pure hearts, who do not lift up their souls to what is false, and do not swear deceitfully. They will receive blessing from the LORD, and vindication from the God of their **salvation**. [Psalm 24:4-5]

> From the heavens you uttered judgment; the earth feared and was still when God rose up to establish judgment, to **save** all the oppressed of the earth. [Psalm 76:8-9]

When Israel had suffered defeat after defeat, and no longer had confidence that their God* would give them military victory, they began to project an apocalyptic* end to history when Israel would be free at last.

> Then the Lord GOD will wipe away the tears from all faces, and the disgrace of his people he will take away from all the earth, for the LORD has spoken. It will be said on that day, Lo, this is our God; we have waited for him, so that he might **save** us. [Isaiah 25:8-9]

For I am with you, says the LORD, to **save** you; I will make an end of all the nations among which I scattered you, but of you I will not make an end. [Jeremiah 30:11]

The trees of the field shall yield their fruit, and the earth shall yield its increase. They shall be secure on their soil; and they shall know that I am the LORD, when I break the bars of their yoke, and **save** them from the hands of those who enslaved them. [Ezekiel 34:27]

Thus says the LORD of hosts: I will **save** my people from the east country and from the west country; and I will bring them to live in Jerusalem. They shall be my people and I will be their God, in faithfulness and in righteousness. [Zechariah 8:7-8]

The Greek *sozo* had many of the same connotations as the Hebrew *yasha*, but the early Christians used it more for natural disasters, such as drowning or disease, than for military threats.

A windstorm arose on the sea, so great that the boat was being swamped by the waves; but Jesus was asleep. And they went and woke him up, saying, "Lord, **save** us! We are perishing!" [Matthew 8:24-25]

Jesus said to him, "Receive your sight; your faith has **saved** you." [Luke 18:42]

A violent wind, called the northeaster, rushed down from Crete. Since the ship was caught and could not be turned head-on into the wind, we gave way to it and were driven . . . When neither sun nor stars appeared for many days, and no small tempest raged, all hope of our being **saved** was at last abandoned. [Acts 27:14-15, 20]

The prayer of faith will **save** the sick, and the Lord will raise them up; and anyone who has committed sins will be forgiven. [James 5:15]

The followers of Jesus also used *sozo* to write about an immediate rescue from an inclination toward self-destructive behavior, that is, salvation from sin.*

An angel of the Lord appeared to him in a dream and said, "Joseph, son of David, do not be afraid to take Mary as your wife, for the child conceived in her is from the Holy Spirit. She will bear a son, and you are to name him Jesus, for he will **save** his people from their sins." [Matthew 1:20-21]

A woman in the city, who was a sinner, having learned that Jesus was eating in the Pharisee's house, brought an alabaster jar of ointment. She stood behind him at his feet, weeping, and began to bathe his feet with her tears and to dry them with her hair . . . Then he said to her, "Your sins are forgiven." But those who were at the table with him began to say among themselves, "Who is this who even forgives sins?" And he said to the woman, "Your faith has **saved** you; go in peace." [Luke 7:37-38, 48-50]

Zacchaeus stood there and said to the Lord, "Look, half of my possessions, Lord, I will give to the poor; and if I have defrauded anyone of anything, I will pay back four times as much." Then Jesus said to him, "Today **salvation** has come to this house, because he too is a son of Abraham. For the Son of Man came to seek out and to **save** the lost." [Luke 19:8-10]

The saying is sure and worthy of full acceptance, that Christ Jesus came into the world to **save** sinners—of whom I am the foremost. [I Timothy 1:15]

For some, the interest in sin may have been the result of fears provoked by the possibility of judgment* and eternal punishment from which they hoped to be saved. For others, the desire for salvation was provoked by the terrors of the approaching last days.

> Brother will betray brother to death, and a father his child, and children will rise against parents and have them put to death; and you will be hated by all because of my name. But the one who endures to the end will be **saved**. [Matthew 10:21-22]

> In those days there will be suffering, such as has not been from the beginning of the creation that God created until now, no, and never will be. And if the Lord had not cut short those days, no one would be **saved**; but for the sake of the elect, whom he chose, he has cut short those days. [Mark 13:19-20]

> Someone asked him, "Lord, will only a few be **saved**?" He said to them, "Strive to enter through the narrow door; for many, I tell you, will try to enter and will not be able." [Luke 13:23-24]

> Much more surely then, now that we have been justified by his blood, will we be **saved** through him from the wrath of God. For if while we were enemies, we were reconciled to God through the death of his Son, much more surely, having been reconciled, will we be **saved** by his life. [Romans 5:9-10]

The metaphors save and salvation can refer to rescue from at least three conditions:

1. Some people live in terror of eternal punishment and long to be set free from their fear.

2. Others want to be saved from their compulsions and addictions and other self-destructive behavior.

3. Still others want to be rescued from emptiness, meaninglessness, and despair.

What makes use of the metaphors at times awkward is that people can be talking about #1, even be convinced that the issue is what happens after they die, when their real problem is #2 or #3.

Samaritan, *noun*   According to tradition, about 900 years before the time of Jesus, King Omri established Samaria (Hebrew *Shomeron*) as the capital of the northern tribes of Israel. Sixty years later, the Assyrians conquered Samaria and resettled it with people from various parts of the empire. The settlers picked up some aspects of the indigenous religion and eventually established a temple on Mt. Gerizim. At the time of Jesus, the Judeans believed that the Samaritans, their neighbors to the north with a similar religion, were the descendants of these settlers and not genuine Israelites.

> In the thirty-first year of King Asa of Judah, Omri began to reign over Israel; he reigned for twelve years, six of them in Tirzah. He bought the hill of **Samaria** from Shemer for two talents of silver; he fortified the hill, and called the city that he built, Samaria, after the name of Shemer, the owner of the hill. [I Kings 16:23-24]

> In the fourth year of King Hezekiah, which was the seventh year of King Hoshea son of Elah of Israel, King Shalmaneser of Assyria came up against **Samaria**, besieged it, and at the end of three years, took it. In the sixth year of Hezekiah, which was the ninth year of King Hoshea of Israel, **Samaria** was taken. The king of Assyria carried the Israelites away to Assyria, settled them in Halah, on the Habor, the river of Gozan, and in the cities of the Medes. [II Kings 18:9-11]

> The king of Assyria brought people from Babylon, Cuthah, Avva, Hamath, and Sepharvaim, and placed them in the cities of **Samaria** in place of the people of Israel; they took possession of **Samaria**, and settled in its cities. When they first settled there, they did not worship the LORD;

---

therefore the LORD sent lions among them, which killed some of them. So the king of Assyria was told, "The nations that you have carried away and placed in the cities of **Samaria** do not know the law of the god of the land; therefore he has sent lions among them; they are killing them, because they do not know the law of the god of the land." Then the king of Assyria commanded, "Send there one of the priests whom you carried away from there; let him go and live there, and teach them the law of the god of the land." So one of the priests whom they had carried away from **Samaria** came and lived in Bethel; he taught them how they should worship the LORD. [II Kings 17:24-28]

Reports of the hostility of the Judeans to the Samaritans show up in the Christian gospels but, according to tradition, Jesus was sympathetic to them, as were his disciples.

On the way to Jerusalem Jesus was going through the region between **Samaria** and Galilee. As he entered a village, ten lepers approached him. Keeping their distance, they called out, saying, "Jesus, Master, have mercy on us!" When he saw them, he said to them, "Go and show yourselves to the priests." And as they went, they were made clean. Then one of them, when he saw that he was healed, turned back, praising God with a loud voice. He prostrated himself at Jesus' feet and thanked him. And he was a **Samaritan**. Then Jesus asked, "Were not ten made clean? But the other nine, where are they? Was none of them found to return and give praise to God except this foreigner?" [Luke 17:11-18]

So he came to a **Samaritan** city called Sychar, near the plot of ground that Jacob had given to his son Joseph. Jacob's well was there, and Jesus, tired out by his journey, was sitting by the well. It was about noon. A **Samaritan** woman came to draw water, and Jesus said to her, "Give me a drink." (His disciples had gone to the city to buy food.) The **Samaritan** woman said to him, "How is it that you, a Jew, ask a drink of me, a woman of **Samaria**?" (Jews do not share things in common with **Samaritans**.) . . . Many **Samaritans** from that city believed in him because of the woman's testimony, "He told me everything I have ever done." So when the **Samaritans** came to him, they asked him to stay with them; and he stayed there two days. [John 4:5-9, 39-40]

Now after Peter and John had testified and spoken the word of the Lord, they returned to Jerusalem, proclaiming the good news to many villages of the **Samaritans**. [Acts 8:25]

A sympathetic view of Samaritans also is evident in one of the best-known parables* attributed to Jesus, the one known as the "Good Samaritan":

A man was going down from Jerusalem to Jericho, and fell into the hands of robbers, who stripped him, beat him, and went away, leaving him half dead. Now by chance a priest was going down that road; and when he saw him, he passed by on the other side. So likewise a Levite, when he came to the place and saw him, passed by on the other side. But a **Samaritan** while traveling came near him; and when he saw him, he was moved with pity. He went to him and bandaged his wounds, having poured oil and wine on them. Then he put him on his own animal, brought him to an inn, and took care of him. The next day he took out two denarii, gave them to the innkeeper, and said, "Take care of him; and when I come back, I will repay you whatever more you spend." [Luke 10:30-35]

In this odd twist of fate, the name of a despised race and culture became a Christian metaphor indicating people who take responsibility for acts of compassion and kindness. Numerous ministries, hospitals, and benevolent organizations have called themselves Samaritans. Individuals who reach out to help others without expecting anything in return are often called Good Samaritans.

Satan, *noun*   The early followers of Jesus had four names for the influences in their lives that opposed what they understood to be the will of God: Satan, the Devil, Beelzebul, and the Evil One. The reputation of Satan came to them through Hebrew folklore. The word *satan* originally meant an adversary or an accuser who could be an ordinary human being.

> The commanders of the Philistines said to Achish, "Send the man David back, so that he may return to the place that you have assigned to him; he shall not go down with us to battle, or else he may become an **adversary** to us in the battle." [I Samuel 29:4]

> Then the Lord raised up an **adversary** against Solomon, Hadad the Edomite; he was of the royal house in Edom. [I Kings 11:14]

In the Hebrew tradition, *satan* was also a position in the heavenly court, something like a prosecuting attorney, whose responsibility it was to identify those who were doing wrong and to present the evidence against them to God.

> He showed me the high priest Joshua standing before the angel of the Lord, and **Satan** standing at his right hand to accuse him. [Zechariah 3:1]

> One day the heavenly beings came to present themselves before the Lord, and **Satan** also came among them. The Lord said to **Satan**, "Where have you come from?" **Satan** answered the Lord, "From going to and fro on the earth, and from walking up and down on it." [Job 1:6-7]

As the tradition evolved, Satan became a corrupt prosecutor, falsely accusing innocent people. This change occurred as *satan* was becoming a proper name and was developing a reputation not only for bringing false accusations but also for luring people into actions that would provoke God's anger. If given a chance, Satan would tempt* people to deny their unique responsibilities as human beings.

> **Satan** stood up against Israel, and incited David to count the people of Israel. [I Chronicles 21:1]

> Then **Satan** entered into Judas called Iscariot, who was one of the twelve; he went away and conferred with the chief priests and officers of the temple police about how he might betray him to them. [Luke 22:3-4]

> "Ananias," Peter asked, "why has **Satan** filled your heart to lie to the Holy Spirit and to keep back part of the proceeds of the land? While it remained unsold, did it not remain your own? And after it was sold, were not the proceeds at your disposal? How is it that you have contrived this deed in your heart? You did not lie to us but to God!" Now when Ananias heard these words, he fell down and died. [Acts 5:3-5]

> Anyone whom you forgive, I also forgive. What I have forgiven, if I have forgiven anything, has been for your sake in the presence of Christ. And we do this so that we may not be outwitted by **Satan**; for we are not ignorant of his designs. [II Corinthians 2:10-11]

According to tradition, another function of Satan was to inflict innocent people with disease and disability.

> Just then there appeared a woman with a spirit that had crippled her for eighteen years. She was bent over and was quite unable to stand up straight. When Jesus saw her, he called her over and said, "Woman, you are set free from your ailment." When he laid his hands on her, immediately she stood up straight and began praising God. But the leader of the synagogue, indignant

> because Jesus had cured on the sabbath, kept saying to the crowd, "There are six days on which work ought to be done; come on those days and be cured, and not on the sabbath day." But the Lord answered him and said, "You hypocrites! Does not each of you on the sabbath untie his ox or his donkey from the manger, and lead it away to give it water? And ought not this woman, a daughter of Abraham whom **Satan** bound for eighteen long years, be set free from this bondage on the sabbath day?" [Luke 13:11-16]

> To keep me from being too elated, a thorn was given me in the flesh, a messenger of **Satan** to torment me, to keep me from being too elated. [II Corinthians 12:7]

For the Greek-speaking early followers of Jesus, the term *diabolos*, the slanderer, became synonymous with Satan. The origin of the term has something in common with the word parable,* both based on the verb *ballo*, to throw. In this case, the prefix is *dia*, which means across. The slanderer throws obstacles across the path, trying to make people stumble, just as the false accuser tries to make people misbehave. It is not hard to see how the Greek and Hebrew traditions merged.

> Again, the **devil** took him to a very high mountain and showed him all the kingdoms of the world and their splendor; and he said to him, "All these I will give you, if you will fall down and worship me." Jesus said to him, "Away with you, **Satan**! for it is written, 'Worship the Lord your God, and serve only him.'" [Matthew 4:8-10]

> The great dragon was thrown down, that ancient serpent, who is called the **Devil** and **Satan**, the deceiver of the whole world—he was thrown down to the earth, and his angels were thrown down with him. [Revelation 12:9]

Another title the early Christians used for the Devil—*Beelzebul*—like Satan came from the Hebrew tradition. Originally, the name was *Baal-zebub*: *ba'al*, lord + *zebub*, flies, suggesting filth. This was a twist on the name of a tribal God done deliberately to malign an enemy.

> Ahaziah had fallen through the lattice in his upper chamber in Samaria, and lay injured; so he sent messengers, telling them, "Go, inquire of **Baal-zebub**, the god of Ekron, whether I shall recover from this injury." [II Kings 1:2]

When the Lord of the Flies appears in a Christian story, the account is often about demon* possession.

> Now Jesus was casting out a demon that was mute; when the demon had gone out, the one who had been mute spoke, and the crowds were amazed. But some of them said, "He casts out demons by **Beelzebul**, the ruler of the demons." Others, to test him, kept demanding from him a sign from heaven. But he knew what they were thinking and said to them, "Every kingdom divided against itself becomes a desert, and house falls on house. If **Satan** also is divided against himself, how will his kingdom stand?—for you say that I cast out the demons by **Beelzebul**. Now if I cast out the demons by **Beelzebul**, by whom do your exorcists cast them out? Therefore they will be your judges." [Luke 11:14-19]

> A disciple is not above the teacher, nor a slave above the master; it is enough for the disciple to be like the teacher, and the slave like the master. If they have called the master of the house **Beelzebul**, how much more will they malign those of his household! [Matthew 10:24-25]

In recent times, scholars have concluded from their studies of early Christian literature that a fourth title for Satan was in use at the time. This title was *poneros*, the personification of evil.*

Let your word be "Yes, Yes" or "No, No"; anything more than this comes from **the evil one.** [Matthew 5:37]

I am not asking you to take them out of the world, but I ask you to protect them from **the evil one.** [John 17:15]

With all of these, take the shield of faith, with which you will be able to quench all the flaming arrows of **the evil one.** [Ephesians 6:16]

I am writing to you, fathers, because you know him who is from the beginning. I am writing to you, young people, because you have conquered **the evil one.** I write to you, children, because you know the Father. I write to you, fathers, because you know him who is from the beginning. I write to you, young people, because you are strong and the word of God abides in you, and you have overcome **the evil one.** [I John 2:13-14]

Through the ages, many of Jesus's followers have thought of Satan as a real being and have argued about the extent of his power. At one extreme, Satan was a power independent of God and in a constant battle with God over the control of the universe. At the other end of the spectrum, Satan was seen as being subordinate to God, a rebellious angel,* but only an angel who somehow fit into God's plan for the universe.

Other followers of Jesus have found Satan to be more useful as a metaphor than as the name of a real being. Satan as a metaphor can help people identify and cope with forces beyond their understanding.

save—see **salvation**

savior, *noun*   In Hebrew the word for savior, *yasha*, has the same root as the words for salvation* and save, sometimes translated as deliverance and deliver. In the Hebrew Scriptures, the savior referred to is usually God, but a savior could be a human leader whom God provided.

God

David said: The LORD is my rock, my fortress, and my deliverer, my God, my rock, in whom I take refuge, my shield and the horn of my salvation, my stronghold and my refuge, my **savior**; you save me from violence. [II Samuel 22:2-3]

They forgot God, their **Savior**, who had done great things in Egypt, wondrous works in the land of Ham, and awesome deeds by the Red Sea. [Psalm 106:21-22]

I will make your oppressors eat their own flesh, and they shall be drunk with their own blood as with wine. Then all flesh shall know that I am the LORD your **Savior**, and your Redeemer, the Mighty One of Jacob. [Isaiah 49:26]

Human

Then the LORD turned to Gideon and said, "Go in this might of yours and **deliver** Israel from the hand of Midian; I hereby commission you." [Judges 6:14]

It will be a sign and a witness to the LORD of hosts in the land of Egypt; when they cry to the LORD because of oppressors, he will send them a **savior**, and will defend and deliver them. [Isaiah 19:20]

Marks a word in the text that has its own entry

The Greek term for savior, *soter*, like its Hebrew equivalent, has the same root as the words for salvation and save. In common use, however, *soter* was the form of address used for many gods such as Serapis, Isis, and Heracles in addition to the God of Israel. *Soter* was also a term of respect for outstanding human beings. A government official, a physician, or a teacher might be called *soter*. For example, the students of the philosopher Epicurus called him their *soter*. Savior, like Son of God,* was one of the many titles claimed by Roman emperors. The early Christians followed Hebrew custom in referring to the God of Israel as their savior. They followed Greek custom in calling their teacher a savior. They may also have been following their own habit of conferring imperial titles on Jesus.

God

Mary said, "My soul magnifies the Lord, and my spirit rejoices in God my **Savior,** for he has looked with favor on the lowliness of his servant." [Luke 1:46-48]

For to this end we toil and struggle, because we have our hope set on the living God, who is the **Savior** of all people, especially of those who believe. [I Timothy 4:10]

When the goodness and loving kindness of God our **Savior** appeared, he saved us, not because of any works of righteousness that we had done, but according to his mercy, through the water of rebirth and renewal by the Holy Spirit. [Titus 3:4-5]

Now to him who is able to keep you from falling, and to make you stand without blemish in the presence of his glory with rejoicing, to the only God our **Savior,** through Jesus Christ our Lord, be glory, majesty, power, and authority, before all time and now and forever. [Jude 1:24-25]

Jesus

Blessed be the Lord God of Israel, for he has looked favorably on his people and redeemed them. He has raised up a mighty **savior** for us in the house of his servant David. [Luke 1:68-69]

The Samaritans said to the woman, "It is no longer because of what you said that we believe, for we have heard for ourselves, and we know that this is truly the **Savior** of the world." [John 4:42]

Our citizenship is in heaven, and it is from there that we are expecting a **Savior,** the Lord Jesus Christ. [Philippians 3:20]

Therefore, brothers and sisters, be all the more eager to confirm your call and election, for if you do this, you will never stumble. For in this way, entry into the eternal kingdom of our Lord and **Savior** Jesus Christ will be richly provided for you. [II Peter 1:10-11]

The savior metaphor is a reminder that, although many people might not use the term, they are likely to organize their lives around their dedication to a savior, who may appear as one of three types:

1. **A savior within history.** As in ancient times, a savior could be a political or religious leader, a healer, or a teacher. In more recent times, a savior also could be a movement or a cause. This sort of savior is what theologians may call pure immanence. A savior within history may provide meaning and direction for life, but this sort of savior has a built-in weakness. The leader or teacher may prove to be morally or intellectually flawed. The cause may come to an end through its own success or failure, or it may be taken over by adherents whose values differ from the vision of the founders. When a purely immanent savior fails, the followers are left without any purpose or meaning for their lives.

2. **A savior untouched by history.** People can find saviors in myths,* philosophies, and ideals that have no substantial connection with real life. These are the saviors sometimes known as pure transcendence. They serve as a distraction, lifting minds from the anxieties produced by the pressures of existence. The trouble is that sometimes existence intrudes on the imagination, and suddenly the savior from outside of history evaporates, having proved to be no more substantial than the morning dew on the grass when the sun comes up. In such cases, the devotees may have the sensation that they, too, are evaporating into nothing.

3. **A savior both within history and unlimited by history.** The genius of Jesus's early followers was to cast him in this dual role as one from heaven* who became a human being, a savior who is both immanent and transcendent. Jesus was an earth-bound teacher, whose story his followers wove into a myth that connected them with a sense of the ultimate. When they can maintain their balance between reliance on the Jesus of history and on the heavenly projection, they find they have the capacity to live enthusiastically in a world where meaning is never absolute and where any purpose may be subject to question.

scapegoat, *noun*   Scapegoat became a popular metaphor among the first English-speaking people who could read the Bible in their own language. The term was apparently invented by William Tyndale in 1530 to express what he mistakenly thought was the meaning of the Hebrew *azazel*. He combined goat with scape, as in escape, to leave. Today, people may search in vain to find the word scapegoat in a modern translation, but they can still find the ancient ritual described if they know where to look: Leviticus 16:7-10.

New Revised Standard Version	King James Version
Aaron shall take the two goats and set them before the LORD at the entrance of the tent of meeting; and Aaron shall cast lots on the two goats, one lot for the LORD and the other lot for **Azazel**. Aaron shall present the goat on which the lot fell for the LORD, and offer it as a sin offering; but the goat on which the lot fell for **Azazel** shall be presented alive before the LORD to make atonement over it, that it may be sent away into the wilderness to **Azazel**.	Aaron shall take the two goats, and present them before the LORD at the door of the tabernacle of the congregation. And Aaron shall cast lots upon the two goats; one lot for the LORD, and the other lot for the **scapegoat**. And Aaron shall bring the goat upon which the LORD's lot fell, and offer him for a sin offering. But the goat, on which the lot fell to be the **scapegoat**, shall be presented alive before the LORD, to make an atonement with him, and to let him go for a **scapegoat** into the wilderness.

This business of leaving the second goat without a name and sending it "to Azazel" is based on research that led to the discovery of the goat demons who were sometimes worshiped in ancient Israel. Azazel appears to have been the chief of the goat demons, known collectively as the *Serim*, who haunted the desert. Evidence exists to suggest that most Semitic tribes offered sacrifices to them. One king of Israel thought that the sacrifices were so important for the well-being of his people that he appointed priests to make sure that the worship of the *Serim* would continue at local cult sites.

The Levites had left their common lands and their holdings and had come to Judah and Jerusalem, because Jeroboam and his sons had prevented them from serving as priests of the LORD, and had appointed his own priests for the high places, and for the **goat-demons**, and for the calves that he had made. [II Chronicles 11:14-15]

When the priestly party in Jerusalem eventually got the upper hand, they did their best to put a stop to the practice of worshiping the *Serim*. As was the custom, they wrote the new rules back into history, as if they had received them from Moses.

The LORD spoke to Moses: Speak to Aaron and his sons and to all the people of Israel and say to them: This is what the LORD has commanded. If anyone of the house of Israel slaughters an ox or a lamb or a goat in the camp, or slaughters it outside the camp, and does not bring it to the entrance of the tent of meeting, to present it as an offering to the LORD before the tabernacle of the LORD, he shall be held guilty of bloodshed; he has shed blood, and he shall be cut off from the people. This is in order that the people of Israel may bring their sacrifices that they offer in the open field, that they may bring them to the LORD, to the priest at the entrance of the tent of meeting, and offer them as sacrifices of well-being to the LORD. The priest shall dash the blood against the altar of the LORD at the entrance of the tent of meeting, and turn the fat into smoke as a pleasing odor to the LORD, so that they may no longer offer their sacrifices for **goat-demons**, to whom they prostitute themselves. This shall be a statute forever to them throughout their generations. [Leviticus 17:1-7]

Although the practice of sacrificing to the *Serim* may have been suppressed, the ritual of sending a living goat to Azazel, chief of the *Serim,* may have continued. As the directions said, the priest was to take two goats to decide which would be sacrificed to the God* of Israel and which would be sent to Azazel. The idea seems to have been that the priest could use the second goat to make atonement,* that is, to carry away the sins of the people. The goat would then be impure, not a fit subject for sacrifice. The polluted goat was then driven out into the wilderness to live among the goat demons. With their sins sent off with the goat, the people were ready to worship their God.

So potent was this ritual for transferring sin onto the goat that apparently the person who took the goat out to the edge of town risked some of the sinful pollution rubbing off on himself or his clothing. He could not rejoin the worshiping community until he had taken a bath and had his clothes laundered.

The one who sets the goat free for **Azazel** shall wash his clothes and bathe his body in water, and afterward may come into the camp. [Leviticus 16:26]

The more people who know about the practice of loading sins onto a goat and driving it away, the more powerful the metaphor becomes in modern usage. When a corporation or government agency decides to load all the blame for a systemic problem onto one person, the designated "goat" is usually banished to a professional "wilderness." No one left in the organization wants to hear from such a person ever again. If the situation was sufficiently serious, anyone who had been at all close to the designated scapegoat may suffer from contamination that will require some effort to remove.

scripture—see **Bible**

sect—see **heresy**

self—see **soul**

servant—see **deacon**, **slave**

shame, *noun* and *verb;* **ashamed** and **shameful**, *adjectives*   A number of Hebrew words appear in English translations as shame. The great variety of images suggests how important the concept was to the development of religion and morality.

> "O my God, I am too **ashamed** and embarrassed to lift my face to you, my God, for our iniquities have risen higher than our heads, and our guilt has mounted up to the heavens."—*kalam*, originally to wound physically, but later used figuratively meaning to taunt or to insult [Ezra 9:6]

> How long, you people, shall my honor suffer **shame**? How long will you love vain words, and seek after lies?—*kelimmah*, same root as *kalam,* above [Psalm 4:2]

> Tamar answered Amnon, "No, my brother, do not force me; for such a thing is not done in Israel; do not do anything so vile! As for me, where could I carry my **shame**?"—*cherpah*, to expose by stripping [II Samuel 13:12-13]

> A child who gathers in summer is prudent, but a child who sleeps in harvest brings **shame**.—*bush*, to pale, to have color drain from the face [Proverbs 10:5]

> Therefore the protection of Pharaoh shall become your **shame**, and the shelter in the shadow of Egypt your humiliation.—*bosheth*, same root as *bush,* above [Isaiah 30:3]

A similar variety of Greek words in the Christian writings are translated shame.

> Their end is destruction; their god is the belly; and their glory is in their **shame**; their minds are set on earthly things.—*aischune*, disfigurement, an appearance that would cause others to avert their eyes [Philippians 3:19]

> Take no part in the unfruitful works of darkness, but instead expose them. For it is **shameful** even to mention what such people do secretly.—*aischron*, same root as *aischune,* above [Ephesians 5:11-12]

> I say this to your **shame**. Can it be that there is no one among you wise enough to decide between one sister or brother and another.—*entrope*, based on a verb meaning to turn or revolve, hence mixed-up, confused [I Corinthians 6:5]

> For you put up with it when someone makes slaves of you, or preys upon you, or takes advantage of you, or puts on airs, or gives you a slap in the face. To my **shame**, I must say, we were too weak for that!—*atimia*, the opposite of honor. The root of the word for honor* means to put a high price on something, so presumably adding the negative particle *a* would suggest something, or somebody, worth very little. [II Corinthians 11:20-21]

For many people, shame and guilt* are synonymous, but psychotherapists make a useful distinction between the two. Guilt is the existential condition of being in the wrong and the bad feelings that arise from having done something wrong or having failed to do what is right, while shame is feeling bad about what you are. The two sets of feelings get mixed up because they often occur simultaneously.

Parents use the language of shame to help their children develop a set of internal controls so that they can function acceptably with other people. Whenever the internal controls fail to operate, the parents let the children know that their performance was not acceptable. Shame is the feeling of being unacceptable. Shame functions effectively as an early warning device that helps people from getting into the kind of trouble that will cause them to be alienated from particular individuals or from society as a whole.

At the same time, shame can be overdone. Excessive shame can be debilitating. Shame can lead to feeling self-contempt and lashing out in destructive behavior. For the early followers of Jesus, his shameful death on the cross* provided them with a new understanding of their condition, an understanding that set them free from the burden of shame and let them claim their places as individuals of worth.

share—see **fellowship**

shepherd, *noun* and *verb*   The Bible has very little to say about real shepherds, but the Hebrew and Greek words for those who tend sheep appear frequently as figures of speech. Both as an analogy and a metaphor, the Hebrew *roeh* (from the verb *ra'ah*, to herd sheep) is used for God as well as for human leaders of various sorts—kings, priests, and teachers. Even death could be a shepherd. The same is true of the Greek *poimen*.

The God* of Israel as *roeh*

His bow remained taut, and his arms were made agile by the hands of the Mighty One of Jacob, by the name of the **Shepherd**, the Rock of Israel, by the God of your father, who will help you, by the Almighty who will bless you with blessings of heaven above, blessings of the deep that lies beneath, blessings of the breasts and of the womb. [Genesis 49:24-25]

The Lord is my **shepherd**, I shall not want. [Psalm 23:1]

Give ear, O **Shepherd** of Israel, you who lead Joseph like a flock! You who are enthroned upon the cherubim, shine forth before Ephraim and Benjamin and Manasseh. Stir up your might, and come to save us! [Psalm 80:1-2]

See, the Lord God comes with might, and his arm rules for him; his reward is with him, and his recompense before him. He will feed his flock like a **shepherd**; he will gather the lambs in his arms, and carry them in his bosom, and gently lead the mother sheep. [Isaiah 40:10-11]

Human leaders as *roeh* (Kings*)

Then all the tribes of Israel came to David at Hebron, and said, "Look, we are your bone and flesh. For some time, while Saul was king over us, it was you who led out Israel and brought it in. The Lord said to you: It is you who shall be **shepherd** of my people Israel, you who shall be ruler over Israel." [II Samuel 5:1-2]

The Lord chose his servant David, and took him from the sheepfolds; from tending the nursing ewes he brought him to be the **shepherd** of his people Jacob, of Israel, his inheritance. [Psalm 78:70-71]

The Lord says of Cyrus, "He is my **shepherd**, and he shall carry out all my purpose"; and who says of Jerusalem, "It shall be rebuilt," and of the temple, "Your foundation shall be laid." [Isaiah 44:28]

Human leaders as *roeh* (Priests*)

Mortal, prophesy against the **shepherds** of Israel: prophesy, and say to them—to the **shepherds**: Thus says the Lord God: Ah, you **shepherds** of Israel who have been feeding yourselves! Should not **shepherds** feed the sheep? You eat the fat, you clothe yourselves with the wool, you slaughter the fatlings; but you do not feed the sheep. [Ezekiel 34:2-3]

Human leaders as *roeh* (Teachers*)

The sayings of the wise are like goads, and like nails firmly fixed are the collected sayings that are given by one **shepherd**. Of anything beyond these, my child, beware. Of making many books there is no end, and much study is a weariness of the flesh. [Ecclesiastes 12:11-12]

Death* as *roeh*

Mortals cannot abide in their pomp; they are like the animals that perish. Such is the fate of the foolhardy, the end of those who are pleased with their lot. Like sheep they are appointed for Sheol; Death shall be their **shepherd**; straight to the grave they descend, and their form shall waste away; Sheol shall be their home. [Psalm 49:12-14]

By the time of Jesus, shepherds were highly regarded in figures of speech, but real, live shepherds suffered from disrespect. Because their occupations required them to live most of the time in open fields, they could not attend synagogue or the temple nor could they adhere to the purity* regulations. As representatives of a despised occupation, the shepherds in Luke's story of Jesus's birth show the author's concern for the outcasts of society.

In that region there were **shepherds** living in the fields, keeping watch over their flock by night. [Luke 2:8]

The early Christians mostly used the noun *poimen* and the related verb *poimaino* as figures of speech related to Jesus.

And you, Bethlehem, in the land of Judah, are by no means least among the rulers of Judah; for from you shall come a ruler who is to **shepherd** my people Israel. [Matthew 2:6]

When the Son of Man comes in his glory, and all the angels with him, then he will sit on the throne of his glory. All the nations will be gathered before him, and he will separate people one from another as a **shepherd** separates the sheep from the goats. [Matthew 25:31-32]

As Jesus went ashore, he saw a great crowd; and he had compassion for them, because they were like sheep without a **shepherd**; and he began to teach them many things. [Mark 6:34]

Now may the God of peace, who brought back from the dead our Lord Jesus, the great **shepherd** of the sheep, by the blood of the eternal covenant, make you complete in everything good so that you may do his will, working among us that which is pleasing in his sight, through Jesus Christ, to whom be the glory forever and ever. [Hebrews 13:20-21]

The Gospel of John makes the most of the shepherd metaphor attributing its use to Jesus himself. Although Jesus may not have spoken these words, they reflect the importance of the metaphor in the early church.

I am the good **shepherd**. The good **shepherd** lays down his life for the sheep. The hired hand, who is not the shepherd and does not own the sheep, sees the wolf coming and leaves the sheep and runs away—and the wolf snatches them and scatters them. The hired hand runs away because a hired hand does not care for the sheep. I am the good **shepherd**. I know my own and my own know me, just as the Father knows me and I know the Father. And I lay down my life for

---

Marks a word in the text that has its own entry   **269**

> the sheep. I have other sheep that do not belong to this fold. I must bring them also, and they will listen to my voice. So there will be one flock, one **shepherd**. [John 10:11-16]

Perhaps some of Jesus's early followers were not familiar with the teaching about the shepherd that John attributed to Jesus—at least they did not take seriously the part that there was to be just one shepherd, not a chief with assistant shepherds. Instead of referring to human church leaders as hired hands, they began calling them shepherds, too.

> Keep watch over yourselves and over all the flock, of which the Holy Spirit has made you overseers, to **shepherd** the church of God that he obtained with the blood of his own Son. [Acts 20:28]

> Now as an elder myself and a witness of the sufferings of Christ, as well as one who shares in the glory to be revealed, I exhort the elders among you to tend the flock of God that is in your charge, exercising the oversight, not under compulsion but willingly, as God would have you do it—not for sordid gain but eagerly. Do not lord it over those in your charge, but be examples to the flock. And when the chief **shepherd** appears, you will win the crown of glory that never fades away. [I Peter 5:1-4]

> The gifts he gave were that some would be apostles, some prophets, some evangelists, some **pastors** and teachers. [Ephesians 4:11]

In this last example, the translators have set aside the usual translation *poimen* in favor of a word with Latin instead of Old English roots. As soon as Christianity moved into Latin-speaking areas, the leaders of the church—especially the bishops*—were typically known as pastors and carried shepherds' crooks as a sign of their office.

Even for people who have never seen a real shepherd, the metaphor works for communicating something important about a direct relationship with God or a connection formed through Jesus. Regarding human leadership, however, the imagery of shepherd and sheep has problems. It suggests that members of congregations are to follow their leaders without question or protest. It assumes that ordinary people are to have no say in the direction the church is taking. John insisted there could only be one shepherd, Jesus. If the whole church is the risen body* of Jesus, then every member has a shepherding capacity and responsibility.

The shepherd metaphor also indicates leadership. Some church people, however, use the related term pastoral, primarily in reference to personal encounters such as visiting the sick, counseling troubled people, and comforting the bereaved.

sin, **original sin**, *nouns*   In both the Hebrew and Greek languages, the word translated sin is based on a metaphor taken from hunting. Both the Hebrew *chatah* and the Greek *hamartia* originally meant that the hunter missed what he was shooting at. The arrow fell short of the target.

> Haughty eyes and a proud heart—the lamp of the wicked—are **sin**. [Proverbs 21:4]

> If . . . you warn the righteous not to **sin**, and they do not **sin**, they shall surely live, because they took warning; and you will have saved your life. [Ezekiel 3:21]

> If another member of the church **sins** against you, go and point out the fault when the two of you are alone. If the member listens to you, you have regained that one. [Matthew 18:15]

So you also must consider yourselves dead to **sin** and alive to God in Christ Jesus. [Romans 6:11]

Thousands of years ago, human beings observed that their actions often fell short of their best intentions. Their behavior was frequently off the mark, a sidestepping or evasion of responsibility. The result of such behavior tends to be a kind of death,* the deadening of relationships and of self-esteem. Or, as St. Paul put it:

The wages of **sin** is death. [Romans 6:23]

The puzzle for the ancients was that in some ways human beings seem to be born with a desire for self-preservation but, at the same time, they seem to have a built-in tendency for behavior that is self-destructive and destructive to the community. Christians from an early date called this universal human tendency original sin. As with all their other observations of the mysterious, the ancients invented explanations for the unexplainable. Some of the Hebrew-speaking people attributed the problem to the presence in each person of an evil *yetser* and a good *yetser*. In English translations of the Bible, *yetser* appears as imagination, inclination, or purpose.

The LORD said in his heart, "I will never again curse the ground because of humankind, for the **inclination** of the human heart is evil from youth." [Genesis 8:21]

O LORD, the God of Abraham, Isaac, and Israel, our ancestors, keep forever such **purposes** and thoughts in the hearts of your people, and direct their hearts toward you. [I Chronicles 29:18]

We are no better off today, even with the help of modern psychology, to explain why people can be motivated by both a desire for self-preservation and for self-destruction, by both altruism and a total disregard for the well-being of other people. Christians in the fourth century came up with an explanation that has had tragic consequences. Augustine of Hippo decided that the tendency toward sin was passed from generation to generation through the generative act itself. Sex is sinful, so everyone is born sinful and has a capacity for doing good only through the grace* of God transmitted in baptism.* In spite of the protests by Britain's first theologian of note, a layman from Wales whose name was Pelagius, the views of Augustine prevailed.

The result in the western world has been a terrible preoccupation with sex and a disparagement of women. Even worse, the Augustinian view of sin reduces a sense of personal responsibility for one's behavior. As Peter Brown, one of his recent biographers, put it, to accept Augustine's view of sin is to drift into a kind of languid piety.

Far healthier than what has been the official Christian view of original sin is to follow Pelagius in recognizing that we have no satisfactory explanation for the tendency toward sin and that we are responsible for our choices. Although Pelagius has been called a heretic,* no council ever condemned him. His condemnation came through a Pope who was under pressure from the emperor, who was a supporter of Augustine.

The sin metaphor, understood as missing the mark, can be quite useful in helping troubled people figure out where they might have gone wrong. Instead of seeing themselves as hopelessly corrupt, they can learn to accept responsibility for those actions that did not deal directly with the issue at hand. They can make progress in recognizing their inclination to sidestep unpleasant situations, leaving them to develop into severe problems.

Marks a word in the text that has its own entry   **271**

DID YOU KNOW . . .

. . . that *hamartia* is pronounced *hahm-ahr-tee-ah*?
For more help with pronunciation, see "Pronouncing
Transliterated Hebrew and Greek Words" on page 15.

---

sisters and brothers, *noun phrase*   The most frequently used Greek metaphor indicating participation in the early communities of Jesus followers was *adelphoi*, the plural of *adelphos*, which comes from a Greek root meaning from the same womb. A teaching attributed to Jesus in the Gospel according to John may have emerged from this metaphor:

> No one can enter the kingdom of God without being born of water and Spirit. What is born of the flesh is flesh, and what is born of the Spirit is spirit. Do not be astonished that I said to you, "You must be born from above." [John 3:5-7]

In other words, with this metaphorical language, the Spirit is the womb that nurtures all the followers of Jesus so that they can be born with a new dimension to their lives. Since all are from the same spiritual womb, they are sisters and brothers. They are bound to treat each other with the love and respect that seem to come naturally to a healthy family.* According to one tradition recorded in the gospels, Jesus thought that the family born of the Spirit was more important than natural families.

> While he was still speaking to the crowds, his mother and his **brothers** were standing outside, wanting to speak to him. Someone told him, "Look, your mother and your **brothers** are standing outside, wanting to speak to you." But to the one who had told him this, Jesus replied, "Who is my mother, and who are my **brothers**?" And pointing to his disciples, he said, "Here are my mother and my **brothers**! For whoever does the will of my Father in heaven is my brother (*adelphos*) and sister (*adelphe*) and mother." [Matthew 12:46-50]

Until the publication of the New Revised Standard Version, *adelphoi* was nearly always translated into English as brethren or brothers. The editors of the New Revised Standard Version recognized that *adelphos* was a masculine form, like actor, which could include the feminine. Actress refers to women only, but in a reference to a group of both male and female players, the male plural form actors is appropriate. When either *adelphoi* or actors appears in a sentence, the context may or may not indicate whether only men or both women and men are included. Although the New Revised Standard Version more often than not translates *adelphoi* as brothers and sisters, in the foregoing passage the editors decided to use just brothers, even though other passages indicate that Jesus had sisters as well.

In a curious twist on the *adelphoi* metaphor, among the people who claim that the Bible is the literal word of God are those who hold that gospel references to Jesus having brothers and sisters must not be taken literally. Although the passage contrasts the normal meaning of *adelphoi* with the figurative usage, Christians who insist that the mother of Jesus was perpetually a virgin would have us think that, in the following passages, the brothers and sisters of Jesus were cousins or children of Joseph from a previous marriage.

> Is not this the carpenter's son? Is not his mother called Mary? And are not his **brothers** James and Joseph and Simon and Judas? And are not all his **sisters** with us? [Matthew 13:55-56; see also Mark 6:1-6]

> Then after three years I did go up to Jerusalem to visit Cephas and stayed with him fifteen days; but I did not see any other apostle except James the Lord's **brother**.
> [Paul writing to the Galatians 1:18-19]

Most objective readers can figure out for themselves when the brothers and sisters being written about are members of a natural family and when the words are being used metaphorically. They need sharp eyes, however, to spot the inconsistencies in the New Revised Standard Version translations of passages in which *adelphoi* is clearly being used in the figurative sense, even though they are flagged by footnotes. The real problem with these alternate forms is that they obscure the centrality of the sister and brother metaphor in early Christian tradition. The only virtue of the alternatives seems to be that they are gender inclusive.

> Why do you see the speck in your **neighbor's** eye, but do not notice the log in your own eye? [Matthew 7:3]

> If another **member of the church** sins against you, go and point out the fault when the two of you are alone. If the **member** listens to you, you have regained that one. [Matthew 18:15]

> You are not to be called rabbi, for you have one teacher, and you are all **students**. [Matthew 23:8]

> And the king will answer them, "Truly I tell you, just as you did it to one of the least of these who are **members of my family,** you did it to me." [Matthew 25:40]

> Be on your guard! If another **disciple** sins, you must rebuke the offender, and if there is repentance, you must forgive. [Luke 17:3]

> Therefore, **friends,** select from among yourselves seven men of good standing, full of the Spirit and of wisdom, whom we may appoint to this task. [Acts 6:3]

> Peter invited them in and gave them lodging. The next day he got up and went with them, and some of the **believers** from Joppa accompanied him. [Acts 10:23]

This last translation of *adelphoi*, used frequently in the Acts of the Apostles, is particularly unfortunate because it implies that what distinguished the followers of Jesus was their ability to believe* what they had been told about him rather than their willingness to participate in a community* attempting to live according to his teachings.

Although applying the sisters and brothers metaphor to a faith community can be abused by hypocrites, it continues to catch the vision of human relationships that the early followers of Jesus maintained. They were to treat each other with love and respect, wanting the best for each other and refusing to exploit each other. The brothers and sisters can function as a healthy family, especially for those whose natural families let them down.

slave, slavery, *nouns*   Slavery was an integral part of the social system in ancient Israel, in the time of Jesus, and in the Christian world until early in the nineteenth century. In ancient Israel, the Hebrew-speaking people had at least three terms for servants bound to their masters: *ebed* for a male slave, *amah* for a female slave, and *shiphchah* for a slave-girl or maid. The equivalents in Greek were *doulos* for a male slave, *doule* for a female slave, *pais* for a slave-boy, and *paidiske* for a slave-girl. The condition of slavery was *abodah* in Hebrew and *douleia* in Greek.

People could become slaves by losing a battle, by falling into debt, or by being born to a slave. Slaves held many positions in society, from being household servants to being powerful government officials, as revealed by the story of Sarah and Hagar and the Joseph legends in Genesis. Only in the Bible are the words for slave translated as servant.

> Sarah saw the son of Hagar the Egyptian, whom she had borne to Abraham, playing with her son Isaac. So she said to Abraham, "Cast out this **slave woman** with her son; for the son of this slave woman shall not inherit along with my son Isaac." [Genesis 21:9-10]

> When Joseph's master heard the words that his wife spoke to him, saying, "This is the way your **servant** treated me," he became enraged. And Joseph's master took him and put him into the prison, the place where the king's prisoners were confined; he remained there in prison. [Genesis 39:19-20]

> On the third day, which was Pharaoh's birthday, he made a feast for all his **servants**, and lifted up the head of the chief cupbearer and the head of the chief baker among his **servants**. [Genesis 40:20]

> The chief cupbearer said to Pharaoh, "I remember my faults today. Once Pharaoh was angry with his **servants**, and put me and the chief baker in custody in the house of the captain of the guard. We dreamed on the same night, he and I, each having a dream with its own meaning. A young Hebrew was there with us, a **servant** of the captain of the guard. When we told him, he interpreted our dreams to us, giving an interpretation to each according to his dream." . . . So Pharaoh said to Joseph, "Since God has shown you all this, there is no one so discerning and wise as you. You shall be over my house, and all my people shall order themselves as you command; only with regard to the throne will I be greater than you." [Genesis 41:9-12, 39-40]

The last passage reveals the fluid situation with ancient forms of slavery. A lowly house boy might gain a position with political power. That possibility lies behind this observation:

> Under three things the earth trembles; under four it cannot bear up: a **slave** when he becomes king, and a fool when glutted with food; an unloved woman when she gets a husband, and a **maid** when she succeeds her mistress. [Proverbs 30:21-23]

Because slavery was essential to the economic and social well-being of the Israelites, it was a highly regulated institution, as a sample of the rules suggest.

> When you buy a male Hebrew **slave**, he shall serve six years, but in the seventh he shall go out a free person, without debt. If he comes in single, he shall go out single; if he comes in married, then his wife shall go out with him. If his master gives him a wife and she bears him sons or daughters, the wife and her children shall be her master's and he shall go out alone. But if the **slave** declares, "I love my master, my wife, and my children; I will not go out a free person," then his master shall bring him before God. He shall be brought to the door or the doorpost; and his master shall pierce his ear with an awl; and he shall serve him for life. When a man sells his daughter as a **slave**, she shall not go out as the male **slaves** do. If she does not please her master, who designated her for himself, then he shall let her be redeemed; he shall have no right to sell her to a foreign people, since he has dealt unfairly with her. [Exodus 21:2-8]

> When a slaveowner strikes a **male** or **female slave** with a rod and the slave dies immediately, the owner shall be punished. But if the **slave** survives a day or two, there is no punishment; for the slave is the owner's property. [Exodus 21:20-21]

> When a slaveowner strikes the eye of a **male** or **female slave**, destroying it, the owner shall let the slave go, a free person, to compensate for the eye. If the owner knocks out a tooth of a **male** or **female slave**, the slave shall be let go, a free person, to compensate for the tooth. [Exodus 21:26-27]

The demand for compassionate treatment of slaves was reinforced by a reminder of the legends that told of the ancestors being slaves in Egypt.

> The seventh day is a sabbath to the LORD your God; you shall not do any work—you, or your son or your daughter, or your **male** or **female slave**, or your ox or your donkey, or any of your livestock, or the resident alien in your towns, so that your male and female slave may rest as well as you. Remember that you were a **slave** in the land of Egypt, and the LORD your God brought you out from there with a mighty hand and an outstretched arm; therefore the LORD your God commanded you to keep the sabbath day. [Deuteronomy 5:14-15]

> Thus says the LORD, the God of Israel: I myself made a covenant with your ancestors when I brought them out of the land of Egypt, out of the house of **slavery**, saying, "Every seventh year each of you must set free any Hebrews who have been sold to you and have served you six years; you must set them free from your service." But your ancestors did not listen to me or incline their ears to me. [Jeremiah 34:13-14]

By the time of Jesus, the institution of slavery had not changed much. Throughout the Roman empire, slavery continued to be an integral part of the social structure. As had been the case in more ancient times, slavery was somewhat fluid. A slave could hold a position at various levels in society. In the parables* attributed to Jesus, slaves appear in a variety of roles: field hands, household servants, government officials, farm agents, and business managers.

> He put before them another parable: "The kingdom of heaven may be compared to someone who sowed good seed in his field; but while everybody was asleep, an enemy came and sowed weeds among the wheat, and then went away. So when the plants came up and bore grain, then the weeds appeared as well. And the **slaves** of the householder came and said to him, 'Master, did you not sow good seed in your field? Where, then, did these weeds come from?'" [Matthew 13:24-27]

> Who among you would say to your **slave** who has just come in from plowing or tending sheep in the field, "Come here at once and take your place at the table"? Would you not rather say to him, "Prepare supper for me, put on your apron and serve me while I eat and drink; later you may eat and drink"? Do you thank the **slave** for doing what was commanded? [Luke 17:7-9]

> The kingdom of heaven may be compared to a king who wished to settle accounts with his **slaves**. When he began the reckoning, one who owed him ten thousand talents was brought to him; and, as he could not pay, his lord ordered him to be sold, together with his wife and children and all his possessions, and payment to be made. [Matthew 18:23-25]

> Listen to another parable. There was a landowner who planted a vineyard, put a fence around it, dug a wine press in it, and built a watchtower. Then he leased it to tenants and went to another

---

*Marks a word in the text that has its own entry   **275**

country. When the harvest time had come, he sent his **slaves** to the tenants to collect his produce. [Matthew 21:33-34]

For it is as if a man, going on a journey, summoned his **slaves** and entrusted his property to them; to one he gave five talents, to another two, to another one, to each according to his ability. Then he went away. [Matthew 25:14-15]

In the narratives, *pais* also occurs in identifying slaves or servants holding a variety of positions. *Pais* meant literally a child. The word was the equivalent of the English "boy," indicating a man of any age who performs the functions of a servant.

When Jesus entered Capernaum, a centurion came to him, appealing to him and saying, "Lord, my **servant** is lying at home paralyzed, in terrible distress." [Matthew 8:5-6]

At that time Herod the ruler heard reports about Jesus; and he said to his **servants**, "This is John the Baptist; he has been raised from the dead, and for this reason these powers are at work in him." [Matthew 14:1-2]

The followers of Jesus not only took slavery for granted, they encouraged the slaves in their communities to accept their lot.

Were you a **slave** when called? Do not be concerned about it. Even if you can gain your freedom, make use of your present condition now more than ever. For whoever was called in the Lord as a **slave** is a freed person belonging to the Lord. [I Corinthians 7:21-22]

Slaves, obey your earthly masters with fear and trembling, in singleness of heart, as you obey Christ; not only while being watched, and in order to please them, but as **slaves** of Christ, doing the will of God from the heart. Render service with enthusiasm, as to the Lord and not to men and women, knowing that whatever good we do, we will receive the same again from the Lord, whether we are **slaves** or free. [Ephesians 6:5-8]

Slaves, obey your earthly masters in everything, not only while being watched and in order to please them, but wholeheartedly, fearing the Lord. Whatever your task, put yourselves into it, as done for the Lord and not for your masters, since you know that from the Lord you will receive the inheritance as your reward; you serve the Lord Christ. [Colossians 3:22-24]

Because slavery was common and unquestioned, it is not surprising that *doulos* was a popular metaphor indicating a variety of human conditions. Jesus is supposed to have used slave as a figure of speech, and Paul used the metaphor to describe Jesus.

Jesus called the twelve to him and said, "You know that the rulers of the Gentiles lord it over them, and their great ones are tyrants over them. It will not be so among you; but whoever wishes to be great among you must be your servant, and whoever wishes to be first among you must be your **slave**; just as the Son of Man came not to be served but to serve, and to give his life a ransom for many." [Matthew 20:25-28]

Jesus answered them, "Very truly, I tell you, everyone who commits sin is a **slave** to sin. The **slave** does not have a permanent place in the household; the son has a place there forever. So if the Son makes you free, you will be free indeed." [John 8:34-36]

One day, as we were going to the place of prayer, we met a **slave-girl** who had a spirit of divination and brought her owners a great deal of money by fortune-telling. While she followed Paul and us, she would cry out, "These men are **slaves** of the Most High God, who proclaim to you a way of salvation." [Acts 16:16-17]

Do you not know that if you present yourselves to anyone as obedient **slaves**, you are **slaves** of the one whom you obey, either of sin, which leads to death, or of obedience, which leads to righteousness? But thanks be to God that you, having once been **slaves** of sin, have become obedient from the heart to the form of teaching to which you were entrusted, and that you, having been set free from sin, have **become slaves** (verb form, *douloo*) of righteousness. I am speaking in human terms because of your natural limitations. For just as you once presented your members as **slaves** to impurity and to greater and greater iniquity, so now present your members as **slaves** to righteousness for sanctification. When you were **slaves** of sin, you were free in regard to righteousness. [Romans 6:16-20]

Let the same mind be in you that was in Christ Jesus, who, though he was in the form of God, did not regard equality with God as something to be exploited, but emptied himself, taking the form of a **slave**, being born in human likeness. [Philippians 2:5-7]

Slave-boy, *pais*, also appears in the gospels and in the Acts of the Apostles as a metaphor indicating the relationship of both King David and Jesus to God.

Blessed be the Lord God of Israel, for he has looked favorably on his people and redeemed them. He has raised up a mighty savior for us in the house of his **servant** David. [Luke 1:68-69]

They raised their voices together to God and said, "Sovereign Lord, who made the heaven and the earth, the sea, and everything in them, it is you who said by the Holy Spirit through our ancestor David, your **servant**: 'Why did the Gentiles rage, and the peoples imagine vain things?'" [Acts 4:24-25]

Here is my **servant**, whom I have chosen, my beloved, with whom my soul is well pleased. I will put my Spirit upon him, and he will proclaim justice to the Gentiles. [Matthew 12:18]

The God of Abraham, the God of Isaac, and the God of Jacob, the God of our ancestors has glorified his **servant** Jesus, whom you handed over and rejected in the presence of Pilate, though he had decided to release him. [Acts 3:13]

The slave metaphor is used today to indicate the reality of certain forms of bondage that may not have existed in the ancient world. Women are bought and sold for the international sex industry. Some textile workers have no possibility of escape from their machines. Children are kidnapped and forced to work as field hands or household servants, any resistance being met with severe beatings.

Although the followers of Jesus have often failed to face the reality of slavery on a practical level, they have continued to make use of the slave metaphor. The metaphor suggests that people can seem bound to pursue certain forms of sin* or to attempt righteous conduct. People can feel bound to God or bound to resist even the notion of God.

Sodomite, *noun*   The word sodomite entered the English moral and legal lexicons through a misunderstanding of one Bible passage and the mistranslation of one word.

In English today, sodomy means anal or oral copulation, usually with a person of the same sex. A sodomite is obviously a person who engages in sodomy. The practice and the practitioners derived their labels from the story about the cities of Sodom and Gomorrah in the eighteenth and nineteenth chapters of Genesis. A person approaching the story for the first time, however, without any predisposition to find references to homosexual* behavior, might find none. The grave sin mentioned in 18:20 is not made explicit, nor is the offense of the men in the nineteenth chapter clear, although much has been made of their shouted conversation with Lot concerning two mysterious strangers he was harboring in his house.*

> The men of **Sodom,** both young and old, all the people to the last man, surrounded the house; and they called to Lot, "Where are the men who came to you tonight? Bring them out to us, so that we may know them." [Genesis 19:4-5]

The key word is know, a common Hebrew euphemism for sexual intercourse. With the possible exception of the horrifying and somewhat parallel story in Judges 19, when the verb to know is used in a sexual sense, it refers to heterosexual intercourse. That being the case, the key word can be taken in its more basic meaning. What the men of Sodom may have wanted was to interrogate the strangers who were being sheltered by Lot, an untrustworthy alien in their midst.

If the author or editor of the story had meant to imply that the offense committed by the men of Sodom was homosexual in nature, the prophets who frequently refer to their destruction apparently missed the point.

> Hear the word of the LORD, you rulers of **Sodom**! Listen to the teaching of our God, you people of Gomorrah! . . . When you stretch out your hands, I will hide my eyes from you; even though you make many prayers, I will not listen; your hands are full of blood. Wash yourselves; make yourselves clean; remove the evil of your doings from before my eyes; cease to do evil, learn to do good; seek justice, rescue the oppressed, defend the orphan, plead for the widow.
> [Isaiah 1:10, 15-17]

> This was the guilt of your sister **Sodom**: she and her daughters had pride, excess of food, and prosperous ease, but did not aid the poor and needy. They were haughty, and did abominable things before me; therefore I removed them when I saw it. [Ezekiel 16:49-50]

> But in the prophets of Jerusalem I have seen a more shocking thing: they commit adultery and walk in lies; they strengthen the hands of evildoers, so that no one turns from wickedness; all of them have become like **Sodom** to me, and its inhabitants like Gomorrah. [Jeremiah 23:14]

The references to Sodom in the Epistles are equally devoid of specific mention of homosexual practices. The lust* condemned in the Second Epistle of Peter and the Epistle of Jude was probably of a sexual nature but could easily have been heterosexual.

> If by turning the cities of **Sodom** and Gomorrah to ashes God condemned them to extinction and made them an example of what is coming to the ungodly, . . . then the Lord knows how to rescue the godly from trial, and to keep the unrighteous under punishment until the day of judgment—especially those who indulge their flesh in depraved lust, and who despise authority.
> [II Peter 2:6, 9-10]

> And the angels who did not keep their own position, but left their proper dwelling, he has kept in eternal chains in deepest darkness for the judgment of the great Day. Likewise, **Sodom** and Gomorrah and the surrounding cities, which, in the same manner as they, indulged in sexual immorality and pursued unnatural lust, serve as an example by undergoing a punishment of eternal fire. [Jude 1:6-7]

The Sodom and Gomorrah story, and the use made of it by other biblical authors, seem to indicate a sense in the tradition that God opposes many forms of corrupt behavior, but there is little indication that homosexual relationships as such offend God. Perhaps English-speaking people would not have stayed with their notions about Sodom if it had not been for the mistranslation of the Hebrew word *qadhesh*. The King James Version translates it sodomite, but the word had nothing to do with Sodom or with stable homosexual relationships. The word *qadhesh*, which literally means holy* one, appears in both masculine and feminine forms. The term identified men and women who served in fertility temples. Apparently, part of the ritual included having sexual intercourse with these holy ones. Modern English translations have come closer to the original meaning by substituting temple prostitutes for sodomites, but the King James Version had already made its mark on the culture and on the Anglo-Saxon legal system.

> There shall be no whore of the daughters of Israel, nor a **sodomite** of the sons of Israel.
> [Deuteronomy 23:17, KING JAMES VERSION]

> And there were also **sodomites** in the land: and they did according to all the abominations of the nations which the LORD cast out before the children of Israel. [I Kings 14:24, KING JAMES VERSION]

> Asa did that which was right in the eyes of the LORD, as did David his father. And he took away the **sodomites** out of the land, and removed all the idols that his fathers had made.
> [I Kings 15:11-12, KING JAMES VERSION]

Whether the male cult prostitutes were available to men or to women, or to both, remains a matter of conjecture, but the reason for denouncing them was clear: the fertility rites of the Canaanites were in competition with the worship of the LORD God of Israel. Even if the holy ones did participate in homosexual acts, that is not the point of the denunciations.

If not for the misreading of a story in Genesis and the early mistranslation of a key word, sodomite could have been a useful metaphor. It could have applied to people who violate basic precepts of hospitality and justice, whose lives are based on lying and greed.

Son of   In the languages of the Bible, expressions beginning with son of or sons of had the same sort of connotations that such words do in English. They can convey an accepted identity. For example, in the nineteenth century, boot and shoe makers were known as sons of wax and farmers as sons of the soil. They can express feelings that the beholden evokes in the beholder. The prime example of this second usage is the curse son of a bitch, which says as much about the speaker it does about the one being cursed.

In biblical times, tribal affiliation was often identified by son, *ben* in Hebrew and *huios* in Greek. Because *ben* could include both sexes, translators have sometimes translated it as children, especially in the case of *ben israel*. In many places *ben israel* has become simply Israelite.

> The fortress will disappear from Ephraim, and the kingdom from Damascus; and the remnant of Aram will be like the glory of the **children of Israel**, says the LORD of hosts. [Isaiah 17:3]

> The **Israelites** were fruitful and prolific; they multiplied and grew exceedingly strong, so that the land was filled with them. [Exodus 1:7]

> Every other grain offering, mixed with oil or dry, shall belong to all the **sons of Aaron** equally.
> [Leviticus 7:10]

> Then Jesus said to him, "Today salvation has come to this house, because he too is a **son of Abraham**." [Luke 19:9]

> An angel of the Lord appeared to him in a dream and said, "Joseph, **son of David**, do not be afraid to take Mary as your wife, for the child conceived in her is from the Holy Spirit." [Matthew 1:20]

Similarly, *ben* could connote membership in a professional guild. Several psalms are attributed to the sons of Korah, which could have been primarily a tribal association but also could have been a guild of temple functionaries. More clearly, a guild were the *bene nabiim*, the sons of the prophets.

> The **company of prophets** who were in Bethel came out to Elisha, and said to him, "Do you know that today the LORD will take your master away from you?" And he said, "Yes, I know; keep silent." [II Kings 2:3]

> Then Amos answered Amaziah, "I am no prophet, nor a **prophet's son**; but I am a herdsman, and a dresser of sycamore trees." [Amos 7:14]

In the early Christian writings, *huios* occurs frequently as a means of identifying certain perceived qualities in particular individuals, but from the English translations this is not always apparent.

> So Jesus appointed the twelve: Simon (to whom he gave the name Peter); James son of Zebedee and John the brother of James (to whom he gave the name Boanerges, that is, **Sons of Thunder**).—*huioi brontes* [Mark 3:16-17]

> Whatever house you enter, first say, "Peace to this house!" And if anyone is there **who shares in peace,** your peace will rest on that person; but if not, it will return to you.—*huios eirenes*, son of peace* [Luke 10:6]

> While I was with them, I protected them in your name that you have given me. I guarded them, and not one of them was lost except the **one destined to be lost.** —*huios tes apoleias*, son of perdition [John 17:12]

> There was a Levite, a native of Cyprus, Joseph, to whom the apostles gave the name Barnabas (which means **"son of encouragement"**).—*huios parakleseos*, see **advocate** [Acts 4:36]

With this background on the biblical metaphors employing son of, a student of the Bible is perhaps better equipped to appreciate the similar metaphors early Christian writers used to describe their thoughts and feelings about Jesus.

Son of David   If, during his lifetime, anyone had called Jesus the Son of David, that claim would go a long way toward explaining the Romans' determination to get rid of him. David was the revered tenth-century BCE king who united the Hebrew-speaking tribes. The Romans had their own puppet ruler sitting on the throne* of David. They would take anyone else with a claim to being King David's rightful heir as a threat to the peace and stability of that corner of the empire, yet all four gospels put forward that idea.

> "What do you think of the Messiah? Whose son is he?" They said to Jesus, "The **son of David**." [Matthew 22:42]

> As he and his disciples and a large crowd were leaving Jericho, Bartimaeus son of Timaeus, a blind beggar, was sitting by the roadside. When he heard that it was Jesus of Nazareth, he began to shout out and say, "Jesus, **Son of David**, have mercy on me!" [Mark 10:46-47; see also Luke 18:39]

Has not the scripture said that the Messiah is descended from **David** and comes from Bethlehem, the village where David lived? [John 7:42]

Although Jesus taught about a different kind of kingdom,* one not based on political or military power, the metaphor used by his followers may have cost him his life and certainly caused them trouble in the early years of the movement.

Son of God   In using the metaphor Son of God for Jesus, his followers were being as subversive as they were in calling him Son of David or Son of Man. The great conquerors who became emperors, such as Alexander the Great and Augustus Caesar, called themselves sons of God in order to encourage loyalty among their subjects. They encouraged stories of their virgin births* in order to back up their claims. Anybody calling Jesus Son of God, *huios tou theou* in Greek, would have been putting Jesus on a par with the Roman emperor. Even whispering such a title for Jesus was a subversive move, but the term appears in all four gospels and in many of the epistles.

> The tempter came and said to Jesus, "If you are the **Son of God,** command these stones to become loaves of bread." [Matthew 4:3]

> Whenever the unclean spirits saw Jesus, they fell down before him and shouted, "You are the **Son of God!**" [Mark 3:11]

> All of them asked, "Are you, then, the **Son of God**?" Jesus said to them, "You say that I am." [Luke 22:70]

> Martha said to Jesus, "Yes, Lord, I believe that you are the Messiah, the **Son of God,** the one coming into the world." [John 11:27]

> It is no longer I who live, but it is Christ who lives in me. And the life I now live in the flesh I live by faith in the **Son of God,** who loved me and gave himself for me. [Galatians 2:20]

Although the follows of Jesus in choosing the Son of God metaphor were probably influenced by the practice of applying the term to conquerors, it is not without precedence in the Hebrew Scriptures:

> When people began to multiply on the face of the ground, and daughters were born to them, the **sons of God** saw that they were fair; and they took wives for themselves of all that they chose . . . The Nephilim were on the earth in those days—and also afterward—when the **sons of God** went in to the daughters of humans, who bore children to them. These were the heroes that were of old, warriors of renown. [Genesis 6:1-2, 4]

In this story, the sons of God may have been angels.* In other stories, angels appear in human form. Perhaps some of Jesus's followers thought he was like an angel.

Of the three "Son of" metaphors, only Son of God has ever been taken literally. Nobody has ever claimed that King David or Adam was actually Jesus's father but, by the fourth century, many Christians were attempting to explain how God was in reality the father of Jesus in a way that was different from God's being the father of everyone. In some of their explanations, Jesus appears to be like the sons of God in the Genesis story, the Nephilim, half human and half God. Trying to come up with a logical explanation of how Jesus could have been both a human being and God caused great controversy among the church leaders, ultimately leading to a major split in the church.

The church is similarly divided today over the question: Is calling Jesus the Son of God stating a presumed fact or employing a useful metaphor? For those in the first camp, being a Christian is a matter of believing. For those in the second, being a follower of Jesus is more a matter of experience. In their experience, coming into contact with Jesus—through the stories about him, his teachings, and the communities that are dedicated to following him—produces the sensation that they are in the presence of God. Using the metaphor Son of God helps them to express the depth of their experience, which they cannot describe adequately using ordinary language in ordinary ways.

Son of Man   Son of Man, in Hebrew *ben adam*, was a fairly common expression. The son of adam* metaphor may be fairly translated as mortal, but this practice has obscured the frequent use of the term. Although the Greek equivalent, *huios tou anthropou*, occurs infrequently, referring to human beings in general, it gets the same treatment.

> The LORD came down to see the city and the tower, which **mortals** had built. [Genesis 11:5]

> I searched with my mind how to cheer my body with wine—my mind still guiding me with wisdom—and how to lay hold on folly, until I might see what was good for **mortals** to do under heaven during the few days of their life. [Ecclesiastes 2:3]

> He said to me: O **mortal**, stand up on your feet, and I will speak with you. And when he spoke to me, a spirit entered into me and set me on my feet; and I heard him speaking to me. He said to me, **Mortal**, I am sending you to the people of Israel, to a nation of rebels who have rebelled against me; they and their ancestors have transgressed against me to this very day. [Ezekiel 2:1-3]

> But someone has testified somewhere, "What are human beings that you are mindful of them, or **mortals**, that you care for them?" [Hebrews 2:6, quoting Psalm 8:4]

Although the prophet Daniel, like Ezekiel, is addressed as *ben adam*, the term appears in one other place in the book attributed to him, a vision in which the metaphor seems to have a meaning related to a dream described earlier in the Aramaic portion of the document.

> Then one in **human form** touched my lips, and I opened my mouth to speak, and said to the one who stood before me, "My lord, because of the vision such pains have come upon me that I retain no strength. How can my lord's servant talk with my lord? For I am shaking, no strength remains in me, and no breath is left in me." [Daniel 10:16-17]

The Aramaic equivalent of *ben adam* was *bar enash*, the phrase used in a dream sequence that pictures the great empires as beasts, which are to be destroyed and replaced by one like a *bar enash*.

> As I watched in the night visions, I saw one like a **human being** coming with the clouds of heaven. And he came to the Ancient One and was presented before him. To him was given dominion and glory and kingship, that all peoples, nations, and languages should serve him. His dominion is an everlasting dominion that shall not pass away, and his kingship is one that shall never be destroyed. [Daniel 7:13-14]

The early Christians writing in Greek used the similar metaphor, *huios tou anthropou*, in reference to Jesus. How much they were influenced by the connotations attached to the Hebrew and Aramaic equivalents is impossible to say. At times, they may have been thinking about Jesus as a representative of humankind; at other times, they may have seen him as the mysterious figure in

*Marks a word in the text that has its own entry

Daniel's visions, the one who was ushering in a new age. Two examples that seem to stress the humanity of Jesus:

> And Jesus said to him, "Foxes have holes, and birds of the air have nests; but the **Son of Man** has nowhere to lay his head." [Matthew 8:20]

> For John came neither eating nor drinking, and they say, "He has a demon"; the **Son of Man** came eating and drinking, and they say, "Look, a glutton and a drunkard, a friend of tax collectors and sinners!" Yet wisdom is vindicated by her deeds. [Matthew 11:18-19]

Many of the *huios tou anthropou* occurrences suggest the influence of Daniel's dream. Whether Jesus ever used the title in reference to himself, or if he ever used the metaphor at all, is a matter of dispute. If even his disciples used the metaphor in public, however, the Romans who knew the story about Daniel's dream would have assumed that Jesus was a threat. They would have considered subversive any talk about one like a son of man replacing the empire. Son of Man was as dangerous a title as Son of David, or indeed, Son of God. Here is a sampling from the many references to *huios tou anthropou* in the gospels and the Revelation to John:

> When they persecute you in one town, flee to the next; for truly I tell you, you will not have gone through all the towns of Israel before the **Son of Man** comes. [Matthew 10:23]

> Then he began to teach them that the **Son of Man** must undergo great suffering, and be rejected by the elders, the chief priests, and the scribes, and be killed, and after three days rise again. [Mark 8:31]

> People will faint from fear and foreboding of what is coming upon the world, for the powers of the heavens will be shaken. Then they will see "the **Son of Man** coming in a cloud" with power and great glory. [Luke 21:26-27]

> So Jesus said, "When you have lifted up the **Son of Man**, then you will realize that I am he, and that I do nothing on my own, but I speak these things as the Father instructed me." [John 8:28]

> Then I turned to see whose voice it was that spoke to me, and on turning I saw seven golden lampstands, and in the midst of the lampstands I saw one like the **Son of Man**, clothed with a long robe and with a golden sash across his chest. [Revelation 1:12-13]

The fact that the metaphor does not appear in the earlier Christian writings, the genuine letters of Paul, suggests that it might represent a later tradition written back into the Jesus story. When the Son of Man metaphor was first applied to Jesus will never be known with certainty, but it is clear that, at a relatively early date, the followers of Jesus had seized upon the phrase to express their thoughts and feelings about him. The metaphor was ideally suited to their convictions that he was a human being like them but, at the same time, instilled in them hope and confidence that they had not known before.

soul, *noun*   In the Bible, the Greek word for soul is *psyche*, from which the English word psyche evolved. When the word soul appears in English translations of the Greek portions of the Bible, the word was always *psyche* in the original, but *psyche* is often translated as life, obscuring what the early Christians thought Jesus had taught about the soul. For example, if the translators had been consistent, the following passages would read:

> Therefore I tell you, do not worry about your **soul,** what you will eat or what you will drink, or about your body, what you will wear. [Matthew 6:25]

> Whoever comes to me and does not hate father and mother, wife and children, brothers and sisters, yes, and even his own **soul,** cannot be my disciple. [Luke 14:26]

When *psyche* appears in the form of an adjective, *psychikos,* the translators use different English words, all of which present a contrast with the spiritual.*

> It is sown a **natural** body; it is raised a spiritual body. There is a **natural** body, and there is a spiritual body. [I Corinthians 15:44, KING JAMES VERSION]

> But it is not the spiritual that is first, but the **physical,** and then the spiritual.
> [I Corinthians 15:46]

> If you have bitter envy and selfish ambition in your hearts, do not be boastful and false to the truth. Such wisdom does not come down from above, but is earthly, **unspiritual,** devilish.
> [James 3:14-15]

This distinction between soul and spirit,* *psyche* and *pneuma,* appears to be quite consistent in the early Christian writings.

> May the God of peace himself sanctify you entirely; and may your spirit and **soul** and body be kept sound and blameless at the coming of our Lord Jesus Christ. [I Thessalonians 5:23]

> Indeed, the word of God is living and active, sharper than any two-edged sword, piercing until it divides **soul** from spirit, joints from marrow; it is able to judge the thoughts and intentions of the heart. [Hebrews 4:12]

Seeing how the Greek Scriptures use the *psyche* metaphor, readers of English translations must wonder what connotations the first readers of these works associated with the word. They probably knew that *psyche,* like *pneuma,* once meant breath. In common usage, it seems to have meant the quality of being able to breathe, that is, being alive as opposed to being dead or being an inanimate object. The early Christians apparently did not think of *psyche* as an inextinguishable something that survives death. The Greek idea of souls separating from bodies did not become the dominant Christian view until much later.

In some cases, *psyche* seems to imply more than simply being alive. It seems to stand for the particular quality of a particular living being, the essence of a person. Perhaps the word in English that comes as close as any to what *psyche* meant is self. A person has a self that is different from every other person. Discovery of one's self is a dynamic realization. Some have made this discovery through a popular meditation technique that involves sitting quietly, observing one's thoughts. On reflection, questions arise: What is the self? The one having the thoughts? The observer? The one noticing the observer? The one asking the questions? The dynamic within each person's *psyche* seems to be suggested in many places where the word appears.

> Mary said, "My **soul** magnifies the Lord, and my spirit rejoices in God my Savior." [Luke 1:46-47]

> Then he said, "I will do this: I will pull down my barns and build larger ones, and there I will store all my grain and my goods. And I will say to my **soul,** 'Soul, you have ample goods laid up for many years; relax, eat, drink, be merry.'" [Luke 12:18-19]

> Now my **soul** is troubled. And what should I say—"Father, save me from this hour"? No, it is for this reason that I have come to this hour. [John 12:27]

When the soul metaphor is understood as referring to the self, some familiar passages take on new meaning. All four gospels have some version of the following teaching attributed to Jesus. Again, for the sake of consistency, *psyche* here appears as soul rather than life, which is used in the New Revised Standard Version.

> Jesus called the crowd with his disciples, and said to them, "If any want to become my followers, let them deny themselves and take up their cross and follow me. For those who want to save their **souls** will lose them, and those who lose their **souls** for my sake, and for the sake of the gospel, will save them. [Mark 8:34-35]

A person always lives in some danger of losing an aspect of self, especially self-respect. A person centered on self to the point of disregard for other people eventually loses respect for his or her own self. A yes person or a buck passer can lose a sense of self. A person who seeks safety by living in the shadow of the company, the church, or the spouse can likewise lose a sense of self.

The Hebrew equivalent of *psyche* is *nephesh*, also derived from a verb that means breathing. To get a sense of how often soul appears in the Hebrew Scriptures, a reader in English must turn to the King James Version. For the New Revised Standard Version, the translators have used a great variety of English words: one, anyone, person, individual, item, life, strength, I, we, you, and—following the basic meaning of the metaphor—himself, herself, and yourselves.

> When a man makes a vow to the LORD, or swears an oath to bind **himself** by a pledge, he shall not break his word; he shall do according to all that proceeds out of his mouth. [Numbers 30:2]

> When a woman makes a vow to the LORD, or binds **herself** by a pledge, while within her father's house, in her youth, and her father hears of her vow or her pledge by which she has bound **herself**, and says nothing to her; then all her vows shall stand, and any pledge by which she has bound **herself** shall stand. [Numbers 30:3-4]

> Take care and watch **yourselves** closely, so as neither to forget the things that your eyes have seen nor to let them slip from your mind all the days of your life; make them known to your children and your children's children. [Deuteronomy 4:9]

Although the Hebrew writers and editors do not seem to make a clear distinction between *nephesh* and *ruach*, soul and spirit,* their use of *nephesh* can expand a person's appreciation for the soul metaphor. Soul can stand for the whole person, the self in all its dimensions.

spirit, noun; **spiritual**, adjective   Both the Hebrew *ruach* and the Greek *pneuma* had a variety of meanings. In their most primitive sense, they stood for air. When air is moving, English-speaking people call it wind. When inhaled, it becomes breath. In each of the biblical languages, people used one word for air in all its forms. When their language was incapable of describing what they experienced as the power of a creator,* they sometimes described the creator's actions as being like the force of the wind and the life-sustaining quality of the air they breathed.

> In the beginning when God created the heavens and the earth, the earth was a formless void and darkness covered the face of the deep, while a **wind** from God swept over the face of the waters. [Genesis 1:1-2]

Marks a word in the text that has its own entry

> For my part, I am going to bring a flood of waters on the earth, to destroy from under heaven all flesh in which is the **breath** of life; everything that is on the earth shall die. [Genesis 6:17]

> Then the LORD said, "My **spirit** shall not abide in mortals forever, for they are flesh; their days shall be one hundred twenty years." [Genesis 6:3]

The reader has to understand the multiple meanings of the Greek *pneuma* to appreciate the word play in John's gospel. In the first example, *pneuma* is first translated spirit and then wind. In the second, a Greek-speaking person could easily understand the connection between breathed and *pneuma*, which meant breath as well as spirit.

> Jesus answered, "Very truly, I tell you, no one can enter the kingdom of God without being born of water and **Spirit**. What is born of the flesh is flesh, and what is born of the **Spirit** is **spirit**. Do not be astonished that I said to you, 'You must be born from above.' The **wind** blows where it chooses, and you hear the sound of it, but you do not know where it comes from or where it goes. So it is with everyone who is born of the **Spirit**." [John 3:5-8]

> When he Jesus had said this, he breathed on them and said to them, "Receive the Holy **Spirit**." [John 20:22]

The Latin *spiritus* and the English *gast* or ghost once had these multiple meanings as well. When the word spirit entered the English language, however, the word had lost its original meanings. What had once been a useful metaphor came to have a meaning restricted to what is supernatural, incorporeal, separated from the material world. Part of the reason for this narrow use of the term may be the way St. Paul used the adjective *pneumatikos*. He seemed to posit the notion that we live our lives as creatures of two overlapping realms, the realm of the spirit and the realm of the flesh.* The spiritual realm appears to be similar to what the gospels call the kingdom of heaven or kingdom* of God.

> For we know that the law is **spiritual**; but I am of the flesh, sold into slavery under sin. [Romans 7:14]

> And so, brothers and sisters, I could not speak to you as **spiritual** people, but rather as people of the flesh, as infants in Christ. [I Corinthians 3:1]

Today, when people talk about spiritual things, they often speak as if the two realms had no connection. Spiritual describes matters that are far removed from the hard realities of everyday life. The spiritual life often seems to be the life of contemplation, shut off from the pressures of family, community, and business. When people refer to the spiritual, they often appear to be talking about something that defies reason, logic, or good sense. The meaning of spiritual has become so fuzzy that one congregation came to the realization that, when the word came up in conversation, nobody knew what anyone else was talking about. Their solution was to declare a moratorium on the use of the word.

If congregations could use spirit in the sense of the original metaphor—the life-sustaining breath of God—they might be able to appreciate how the Bible people understood the internal force that called them to lives of service and that kept them going.

> Here is my servant, whom I uphold, my chosen, in whom my soul delights; I have put my **spirit** upon him; he will bring forth justice to the nations. [Isaiah 42:1]

Then afterward I will pour out my **spirit** on all flesh; your sons and your daughters shall prophesy, your old men shall dream dreams, and your young men shall see visions. [Joel 2:28]

Here is my servant, whom I have chosen, my beloved, with whom my soul is well pleased. I will put my **Spirit** upon him, and he will proclaim justice to the Gentiles. [Matthew 12:18]

To each is given the manifestation of the **Spirit** for the common good. [I Corinthians 12:7]

In the Bible, the word *ruach* or *pneuma,* standing alone without a modifier, is often the equivalent of Holy Spirit* or spirit of God, but a spirit is not always of God. Individual human beings have spirits . . .

Pharaoh awoke, and it was a dream. In the morning his **spirit** was troubled; so he sent and called for all the magicians of Egypt and all its wise men. Pharaoh told them his dreams, but there was no one who could interpret them to Pharaoh. [Genesis 41:7-8]

When the company of prophets who were at Jericho saw him at a distance, they declared, "The **spirit** of Elijah rests on Elisha." They came to meet him and bowed to the ground before him. [II Kings 2:15]

They were all weeping and wailing for her; but he Jesus said, "Do not weep; for she is not dead but sleeping." And they laughed at him, knowing that she was dead. But he took her by the hand and called out, "Child, get up!" Her **spirit** returned, and she got up at once. [Luke 8:52-55]

. . . and so do communities.

The **spirit** of the Egyptians within them will be emptied out, and I will confound their plans; they will consult the idols and the spirits of the dead and the ghosts and the familiar spirits. [Isaiah 19:3]

Sharpen the arrows! Fill the quivers! The LORD has stirred up the **spirit** of the kings of the Medes, because his purpose concerning Babylon is to destroy it, for that is the vengeance of the LORD, vengeance for his temple. [Jeremiah 51:11]

May the grace of our Lord Jesus Christ be with your **spirit**, brothers and sisters. [Galatians 6:18]

Moreover, a *ruach* or *pneuma* can also be experienced as a negative force.

Pride goes before destruction, and a haughty **spirit** before a fall. [Proverbs 16:18]

On that day, says the LORD of hosts, I will cut off the names of the idols from the land, so that they shall be remembered no more; and also I will remove from the land the prophets and the unclean **spirit**. [Zechariah 13:2]

Someone from the crowd answered him, "Teacher, I brought you my son; he has a **spirit** that makes him unable to speak; and whenever it seizes him, it dashes him down; and he foams and grinds his teeth and becomes rigid; and I asked your disciples to cast it out, but they could not do so." [Mark 9:17-18]

Then the man with the evil **spirit** leaped on them, mastered them all, and so overpowered them that they fled out of the house naked and wounded. [Acts 19:16]

Because the spirit metaphor can easily be misunderstood, those who use it must be careful to clarify what they have in mind. In the first place, they need to be clear within themselves what they mean, and then make sure that their intended meaning is clear to their audience. The congregation

---

that banned the use of the word for a time might have been overreacting, but at least they had identified the problem. The English language does not provide a recognizable substitute for either spirit or spiritual, so both forms of the metaphor must continue in use, but with reasonable caution.

star, *noun*   Stars are mentioned frequently in the Bible— *kokab* in Hebrew and *aster* in Greek— but the most famous star for Christians is the one in Matthew's gospel.

> In the time of King Herod, after Jesus was born in Bethlehem of Judea, wise men from the East came to Jerusalem, asking, "Where is the child who has been born king of the Jews? For we observed his **star** at its rising, and have come to pay him homage." When King Herod heard this, he was frightened, and all Jerusalem with him; and calling together all the chief priests and scribes of the people, he inquired of them where the Messiah was to be born. They told him, "In Bethlehem of Judea; for so it has been written by the prophet: 'And you, Bethlehem, in the land of Judah, are by no means least among the rulers of Judah; for from you shall come a ruler who is to shepherd my people Israel.'"
>
> Then Herod secretly called for the wise men and learned from them the exact time when the **star** had appeared. Then he sent them to Bethlehem, saying, "Go and search diligently for the child; and when you have found him, bring me word so that I may also go and pay him homage." When they had heard the king, they set out; and there, ahead of them, went the **star** that they had seen at its rising, until it stopped over the place where the child was. When they saw that the **star** had stopped, they were overwhelmed with joy. [Matthew 2:1-10]

This star behaves as no other star ever has or could. Not only did it move through the sky, but the wise men—the Magi, *magoi* in Greek—could tell what town the star was over. If that is not sufficient nonsense, the reader is supposed to believe that observers could tell which house* in the town the star was over. If any people in New England looked up into the night sky, they could not tell if a star was over New York City or Cambridge, Massachusetts. If any star, planet, or comet ever came close enough for anyone to know what northeastern seaboard town it was over, the northeastern seaboard would have been incinerated along with the rest of the world. Even if the author of the story did not have a twenty-first century first grader's knowledge of astronomy, the author must have looked up occasionally into the night sky and must have known that stars do not behave like the one in the story. Either the author was a very silly person, or the story is not about what we normally think of as a star.

The most plausible explanation for Matthew's star appeared in the December 1993 issue of the *Bible Review*. Written by Dale C. Allison, Jr., the piece was called, "What was the Star that Guided the Magi?" He points out that, in ancient times, the stars were thought to be living beings. He quotes Philo, the first-century Jewish philosopher, who wrote that the stars "are living creatures, but of a kind composed entirely of mind." Allison goes on to examine the understanding of stars revealed in the Hebrew Scriptures.[24] The book of Job speaks of a time . . .

> when the morning **stars** sang together and all the heavenly beings shouted for joy? [Job 38:7]

These heavenly beings had other functions in addition to singing and shouting. God could send them to support God's people in battle.

> The **stars** fought from heaven, from their courses they fought against Sisera. [Judges 5:20]

A star, which could be sent down from the sky to do God's bidding, was sometimes called an angel*—*malak* in Hebrew. Perhaps most revealing is the story of Jacob when he was alone in the desert with only a rock* for a pillow.

> "And he dreamed that there was a ladder set up on the earth, the top of it reaching to heaven; and the **angels** of God were ascending and descending on it." [Genesis 28:12]

The heavenly beings could come down out of the sky when God had a job for them. As Allison wrote, the "angels commonly served as guides in ancient literature." Probably the best known example of a guiding angel is the one that led the children of Israel out of bondage in Egypt to the promised land.

> God said, "I am going to send an **angel** in front of you, to guard you on the way and to bring you to the place that I have prepared." [Exodus 23:20]

Near the conclusion of his article, Dale Allison points out that thinking of heavenly bodies as angels was "an option for Christian theology" until the sixth century. (It was not until the Second Council of Constantinople in 553 that church leaders decided that the stars were not reasonable beings and did not have souls.) For example, in the Revelation to John, a star and an angel—*angelos* in Greek—appear to be one and the same.

> As for the mystery of the seven **stars** that you saw in my right hand, and the seven golden lamp-stands: the seven **stars** are the **angels** of the seven churches, and the seven lampstands are the seven churches. [Revelation 1:20]

If Matthew had an angel in mind in writing the story about the star, the account makes sense in the context of the time. Today, people who believe that the lights in the night sky are angels can accept the second chapter of the gospel as a report of an historical event. Those of a more skeptical nature may see the angel/star as a literary device used to push the point of view that Gentiles, represented in the story by the Magi, were destined to replace the Jews* as God's favored people.

steward, *noun*   Although the English word steward has been used to translate several Hebrew and Greek words, its use as a popular Christian metaphor is based primarily on the Greek *oikonomos*, a house* manager. The other words that appear as steward include:

> When Joseph saw Benjamin with his brothers, he said to the **steward** of his house, "Bring the men into the house, and slaughter an animal and make ready, for the men are to dine with me at noon."—*asher*, the one [Genesis 43:16]

> So they went up to the **steward** of Joseph's house and spoke with him at the entrance to the house.—*ish*, the man [Genesis 43:19]

> David assembled at Jerusalem all the officials of Israel, the officials of the tribes, the officers of the divisions that served the king, the commanders of the thousands, the commanders of the hundreds, the **stewards** of all the property and cattle of the king and his sons, together with the palace officials, the mighty warriors, and all the warriors.—*sar*, head man [I Chronicles 28:1]

> Thus says the Lord GOD of hosts: Come, go to this **steward**, to Shebna, who is master of the household, and say to him: What right do you have here? Who are your relatives here, that you have cut out a tomb here for yourself, cutting a tomb on the height, and carving a habitation for yourself in the rock?—*soken*, one who serves [Isaiah 22:15-16]

> Soon afterwards he went on through cities and villages, proclaiming and bringing the good news
> of the kingdom of God. The twelve were with him, as well as some women who had been cured
> of evil spirits and infirmities: Mary, called Magdalene, from whom seven demons had gone out,
> and Joanna, the wife of Herod's **steward** Chuza, and Susanna, and many others, who provided
> for them out of their resources.—*epitropos*, administrator [Luke 8:1-3]

> Jesus said to the servants, "Fill the jars with water." And they filled them up to the brim. He said
> to them, "Now draw some out, and take it to the **chief steward**." So they took it.—*architriklinos*,
> head waiter [John 2:7-8]

The Christian tradition of using steward as a metaphor began with the use of another word,
oikonomos, a house manager.

> Think of us in this way, as servants of Christ and **stewards** of God's mysteries. Moreover, it is
> required of **stewards** that they be found trustworthy. [I Corinthians 4:1-2]

> For a bishop, as God's **steward,** must be blameless; he must not be arrogant or quick-tempered
> or addicted to wine or violent or greedy for gain; but he must be hospitable, a lover of goodness,
> prudent, upright, devout, and self-controlled. He must have a firm grasp of the word that is trust-
> worthy in accordance with the teaching, so that he may be able both to preach with sound doc-
> trine and to refute those who contradict it. [Titus 1:7-9]

> Like good **stewards** of the manifold grace of God, serve one another with whatever gift each of
> you has received. [I Peter 4:10]

Perhaps because Christians have traditionally given a positive spin to the position of *oikonomos*, the
unjust steward who appeared in the King James Version of a parable* has now become a dishonest
manager.

> Then Jesus said to the disciples, "There was a rich man who had a **manager,** and charges were
> brought to him that this man was squandering his property. So he summoned him and said to
> him, 'What is this that I hear about you? Give me an accounting of your management, because
> you cannot be my **manager** any longer.' Then the manager said to himself, 'What will I do, now
> that my master is taking the position away from me? I am not strong enough to dig, and I am
> ashamed to beg. I have decided what to do so that, when I am dismissed as **manager,** people
> may welcome me into their homes.' So, summoning his master's debtors one by one, he asked
> the first, 'How much do you owe my master?' He answered, 'A hundred jugs of olive oil.' He said
> to him, 'Take your bill, sit down quickly, and make it fifty.' Then he asked another, 'And how
> much do you owe?' He replied, 'A hundred containers of wheat.' He said to him, 'Take your bill
> and make it eighty.' And his master commended the dishonest **manager** because he had acted
> shrewdly; for the children of this age are more shrewd in dealing with their own generation than
> are the children of light." [Luke 16:1-8]

Although the steward metaphor originally had to do with the stewardship of God's mysteries*
and grace,* church leaders have used it primarily in fundraising. The metaphor suggests that
church people do not own anything but are managers of God's property. They are supposed to figure how much of a return God has a right to expect from the property entrusted to them.

suffer—see **passion**

synagogue—see **Pharisee**

T

teacher, *noun*   According to the gospels, teacher was the term of respect the first followers of Jesus used most often in addressing him or talking about him. The respect for teachers has its roots in the Hebrew Scriptures, where four different words convey the idea of teacher.

> They cast lots for their duties, small and great, **teacher** and pupil alike.—*bin*, see **wisdom**
> [I Chronicles 25:8]
>
> See, God is exalted in his power; who is a **teacher** like him?—*yarah*, see **law, instruction**
> [Job 36:22]
>
> The words of the **Teacher**, the son of David, king in Jerusalem. Vanity of vanities, says the **Teacher**, vanity of vanities! All is vanity.—*qoheleth*, schoolmaster, from *qahal*, see **church**
> [Ecclesiastes 1:1-2]
>
> The Lord GOD has given me the tongue of a **teacher**, that I may know how to sustain the weary with a word. Morning by morning he wakens—wakens my ear to listen as those who are taught.—*limmud*, see **disciple** [Isaiah 50:4]

Although the Greek language has other words that mean teacher, by far the most common in the early Christian literature is *didaskolos*, from *didasko*, meaning to teach or instruct.* In the gospels, *didaskolos* appears most of the time in reference to Jesus.

> Now when Jesus saw great crowds around him, he gave orders to go over to the other side. A scribe then approached and said, "**Teacher**, I will follow you wherever you go." [Matthew 8:18-19]
>
> As Jesus sat at dinner in the house, many tax collectors and sinners came and were sitting with him and his disciples. When the Pharisees saw this, they said to his disciples, "Why does your **teacher** eat with tax collectors and sinners?" [Matthew 9:10-11]
>
> Jesus was in the stern, asleep on the cushion; and they woke him up and said to him, "**Teacher**, do you not care that we are perishing?" [Mark 4:38]
>
> Jesus spoke up and said to him, "Simon, I have something to say to you." "**Teacher**," he replied, "Speak." [Luke 7:40]
>
> Martha went back and called her sister Mary, and told her privately, "The **Teacher** is here and is calling for you." [John 11:28]

The gospels aside, in the Bible *didaskolos* never refers to Jesus. In the Acts of the Apostles and in the epistles, the people most frequently referred to as teachers are respected members of a Christian community.

> Now in the church at Antioch there were prophets and **teachers**: Barnabas, Simeon who was called Niger, Lucius of Cyrene, Manaen a member of the court of Herod the ruler, and Saul.
> [Acts 13:1]
>
> God has appointed in the church first apostles, second prophets, third **teachers**; then deeds of power, then gifts of healing, forms of assistance, forms of leadership, various kinds of tongues. Are all apostles? Are all prophets? Are all **teachers**? Do all work miracles? [I Corinthians 12:28-29]

Marks a word in the text that has its own entry

> Not many of you should become **teachers**, my brothers and sisters, for you know that we who teach will be judged with greater strictness. [James 3:1]

Paul, in his letter to the Galatians, used another word translated as teacher, *katecheo*, actually a verb meaning to make a sound down into the ears, that is, to instruct.* Like *didaskolos,* this word for teacher refers not to Jesus but to members of the community.

> Those who are taught the word must share in all good things with their **teacher**. [Galatians 6:6]

According to the gospels, some people used other respectful words for teacher in addressing Jesus or talking about him. One was *kathegetes*, formed from *kata*, concerning + *hegeomai*, to lead or to guide, the source of the English word hegemony.

> You are not to be called rabbi, for you have one **teacher**, and you are all students.
> [Matthew 23:8]

More frequently, the word is *rabbi*, from the Hebrew *rab*, which meant lord or master. In the gospels, *rabbi* as a form of address is used only for Jesus, except for one time when the disciples of John the Baptist call him *rabbi*. Less frequently, the disciples of Jesus call him *rabbouni*, a heightened form of *rabbi.*

> Now the betrayer had given them a sign, saying, "The one I will kiss is the man; arrest him." At once he came up to Jesus and said, "Greetings, **Rabbi**!" and kissed him. [Matthew 26:48-49]

> Then Peter said to Jesus, "**Rabbi**, it is good for us to be here; let us make three dwellings, one for you, one for Moses, and one for Elijah." [Mark 9:5]

> When Jesus turned and saw them following, he said to them, "What are you looking for?" They said to him, "**Rabbi**" (which, translated, means Teacher), "where are you staying?" [John 1:38]

> Now a discussion about purification arose between John's disciples and a Jew. They came to John and said to him, "**Rabbi**, the one who was with you across the Jordan, to whom you testified, here he is baptizing, and all are going to him." [John 3:25-26]

> Then Jesus said to him, "What do you want me to do for you?" The blind man said to him, "My **teacher**, let me see again."—*rabbouni* [Mark 10:51]

> Jesus said to her, "Mary!" She turned and said to him in Hebrew, "**Rabbouni**!" (which means Teacher). [John 20:16]

Apparently, for the writers and editors of the gospels, addressing Jesus as teacher indicated something more than respect. Jesus was the one to whom they turned for wisdom and for guidance. When the first communities of Jesus's followers were forming, one of the most important functions a member could provide appears to have been teaching. Teachers within Christian communities continue to play a key role in keeping alive and relevant what their predecessors learned from the one they called "Teacher."

tempt, *verb*; **temptation**, *noun*   Long ago, when the English word tempt was first used to translate the Greek verb *peirazo*, both words had the same double meaning. On the one hand, they could mean to test, try, examine, or prove; on the other hand, to entice. In recent memory, the English concept of temptation has lost its primary meaning and has become associated almost exclusively with enticement.

The basic meaning of the word has survived only with a prefix: ad + tempt = attempt. The shift in common usage explains why modern translations of the Bible use tempt and temptation far less frequently than the King James Version, but those places where the old language has held can be challenged. Take, for example, Luke's version of the dream-like account that introduces Jesus's public ministry. The translators of the New Revised Standard Version begin the story with tempt for the verb but, in the conclusion, they use test for the noun *peirasmos*. The reader of this English version, like the first readers of the Greek, must decide if the author intended an enticement or a trial.

> Jesus, full of the Holy Spirit, returned from the Jordan and was led by the Spirit in the wilderness, where for forty days he was **tempted** by the devil. He ate nothing at all during those days, and when they were over, he was famished . . . When the devil had finished every **test,** he departed from him until an opportune time. [Luke 4:1-2, 13]

According to tradition, Jesus faced many tests in his life and described his experience to his followers in those terms. The gospels use the same language in describing Jesus's encounters with his adversaries.

> "You are those who have stood by me in my **trials.**" [Luke 22:28]

> The Pharisees and Sadducees came, and to **test** Jesus they asked him to show them a sign from heaven. [Matthew 16:1]

Paul suggested that the followers of Jesus should expect the same sort of trials. He also wanted his readers to understand that the one overseeing the tests is God. In this teaching, Paul may have been influenced by the prayer attributed to Jesus, commonly called the Lord's Prayer.

> No **testing** has overtaken you that is not common to everyone. God is faithful, and he will not let you be **tested** beyond your strength, but with the **testing** he will also provide the way out so that you may be able to endure it. [I Corinthians 10:13]

> **Examine** yourselves to see whether you are living in the faith. [II Corinthians 13:5]

> Do not bring us to the time of **trial,** but rescue us from the evil one. [Matthew 6:13]

Apparently, the early Christian writers thought a certain amount of testing was necessary for both Jesus and his followers, but they did not think that reciprocity was in order.

> Peter said to Sapphira, "How is it that you have agreed together to put the Spirit of the Lord to the **test**? Look, the feet of those who have buried your husband are at the door, and they will carry you out." [Acts 5:9]

> Now therefore why are you putting God to the **test** by placing on the neck of the disciples a yoke that neither our ancestors nor we have been able to bear? [Acts 15:10]

The word temptation for *peirasmos* appears in the English text when the experiences being identified appear to be enticement with no redeeming qualities. In such cases, the verb *peirazo* used in the same context becomes tempt.

> Those who want to be rich fall into **temptation** and are trapped by many senseless and harmful desires that plunge people into ruin and destruction. [I Timothy 6:9]

Marks a word in the text that has its own entry   **293**

> Blessed is anyone who endures **temptation.** Such a one has stood the test (*dokimos*) and will receive the crown of life that the Lord has promised to those who love him. No one, when **tempted,** should say, "I am being **tempted** by God"; for God cannot be **tempted** by evil and he himself **tempts** no one. But one is **tempted** by one's own desire, being lured and enticed by it. [James 1:12-14]

Anyone attempting to use the test metaphor today is likely to uncover some personal ambivalence about the subject. Even as young children, most people want to be tested so that they can prove growth in skills and knowledge. As they grow older, some want to be tested on the athletic field or in the gymnasium, while some prefer the more intellectual competitions such as writing essays or entering spelling contests. At the same time, the fear of failing tests is so great that dreams of arriving for a test unprepared continue through old age. An exploration of these conflicting desires of wanting and fearing the test that will prove or disprove a person's value may raise the questions "Before whom am I taking the test?" and "Who will determine my grade?"

Following St. Paul's thinking on the subject of testing may be something of a threat, but his advice may also be comforting. The grades on one's performance that parents and peers hand out, and even the grades people give themselves, need not determine their worth as human beings. If they can imagine God being with them in their tests, they can probably endure the low marks of human graders and keep in perspective any high marks that come their way.

The enticement side of the metaphor also reveals some truths about human experience. Enticements often feel as if they have power over a person. They can disable the capacity for rational thought and sensible decision making. They can seem terribly unfair. If God is, then God either sends the temptations or allows them the power of enticement. This was the complaint of Eliza Doolittle's father in the Lerner and Loewe musical, *My Fair Lady*:

> The Lord above made liquor for temptation
> To see if man could turn away from sin
> The Lord above made liquor for temptation—but
> With a little bit of luck
> When temptation comes you'll give right in.

In this delightful, silly song, the enticement and the testing aspects of the temptation metaphor are merged. Some people have developed remarkable strength of character by overcoming addictions to substances or to behavior patterns that constantly tempt them. Many recovering from addiction have learned both to imagine God as the source of temptation and the one who enables them to resist and to pass the test. Others have taken the route of Alfred P. Doolittle and shown their contempt for God by giving right in.

test—see **temptation**

testament—see **covenant**

thank—see **grace**

throne, *noun*   Although a throne is a piece of furniture, namely a chair, the word even in ancient times was used as a metaphor indicating the authority of the one who sat in it. Although thrones are not popular in democratic societies, the equivalent type of metaphor continues in the use of the words chair and bench in the legislative and judicial branches of government, respectively. What was once true of throne is currently the case with chair and bench. In the Bible "the throne represents the continuity of power which may be assumed by a series of incumbents but transcends each individual personality."[25] It is the continuity of power that gives particular meaning to the metaphor as it came to be used in poetry and in visions of a divine realm.

The Hebrew word translated throne is *kisse,* which can also mean simply a seat—a chair or stool.

kisse as something to sit on

After they had eaten and drunk at Shiloh, Hannah rose and presented herself before the Lord. Now Eli the priest was sitting on the **seat** beside the doorpost of the temple of the Lord. [I Samuel 1:9]

The foolish woman is loud; she is ignorant and knows nothing. She sits at the door of her house, on a **seat** at the high places of the town. [Proverbs 9:13-14]

In those days when King Ahasuerus sat on his royal **throne** in the citadel of Susa, in the third year of his reign, he gave a banquet for all his officials and ministers. [Esther 1:2-3]

When the news reached the king of Nineveh, he rose from his **throne**, removed his robe, covered himself with sackcloth, and sat in ashes. [Jonah 3:6]

kisse as continuity of power

My lord the king—the eyes of all Israel are on you to tell them who shall sit on the **throne** of my lord the king after him. [I Kings 1:20]

Once and for all I have sworn by my holiness; I will not lie to David. His line shall continue forever, and his **throne** endure before me like the sun. [Psalm 89:35-36]

If a king judges the poor with equity, his **throne** will be established forever. [Proverbs 29:14]

His authority shall grow continually, and there shall be endless peace for the **throne** of David and his kingdom. He will establish and uphold it with justice and with righteousness from this time onward and forevermore. [Isaiah 9:7]

kisse as God's place

The Lord sits enthroned forever, he has established his **throne** for judgment. [Psalm 9:7]

The Lord is in his holy temple; the Lord's **throne** is in heaven. His eyes behold, his gaze examines humankind. [Psalm 11:4]

Glorious **throne**, exalted from the beginning, shrine of our sanctuary! O hope of Israel! O Lord! [Jeremiah 17:12-13]

You, O Lord, reign forever; your **throne** endures to all generations. [Lamentations 5:19]

kisse as opposition to God

For now I am calling all the tribes of the kingdoms of the north, says the Lord; and they shall come and all of them shall set their **thrones** at the entrance of the gates of Jerusalem, against all its surrounding walls and against all the cities of Judah. And I will utter my judgments against them, for all their wickedness in forsaking me. [Jeremiah 1:15-16]

Then all the princes of the sea shall step down from their **thrones**; they shall remove their robes and strip off their embroidered garments. They shall clothe themselves with trembling, and shall sit on the ground; they shall tremble every moment, and be appalled at you. [Ezekiel 26:16]

Speak to Zerubbabel, governor of Judah, saying, I am about to shake the heavens and the earth, and to overthrow the **throne** of kingdoms; I am about to destroy the strength of the kingdoms of the nations. [Haggai 2:21-22]

kisse in the heavenly court

Then Micaiah said, "Therefore hear the word of the LORD: I saw the LORD sitting on his **throne**, with all the host of heaven standing beside him to the right and to the left of him." [I Kings 22:19]

In the year that King Uzziah died, I saw the Lord sitting on a **throne**, high and lofty; and the hem of his robe filled the temple. Seraphs were in attendance above him. [Isaiah 6:1-2]

Over the heads of the living creatures there was something like a dome, shining like crystal, spread out above their heads. . . . Above the dome over their heads there was something like a **throne**, in appearance like sapphire; and seated above the likeness of a **throne** was something that seemed like a human form. [Ezekiel 1:22, 26]

As I watched, **thrones** were set in place, and an Ancient One took his **throne**, his clothing was white as snow, and the hair of his head like pure wool; his throne was fiery flames, and its wheels were burning fire. [Daniel 7:9]

In the heavenly court passages, the writers and editors of the Hebrew Scriptures pictured the divine judge surrounded by attendants. In some of these visions, the attendants appear to be associate justices participating in the cases brought before the divine tribunal. In the passage from Daniel quoted above, each associate had a throne. These visions of the heavenly court had a considerable impact on the imagery used by the early followers of Jesus. Although they used the Greek word *thronos,* they seem to have had in mind all the characteristics of the Hebrew *kisse.*

thronos in the heavenly court

Jesus said to them, "Truly I tell you, at the renewal of all things, when the Son of Man is seated on the **throne** of his glory, you who have followed me will also sit on twelve **thrones**, judging the twelve tribes of Israel." [Matthew 19:28]

Jesus said, "You are those who have stood by me in my trials; and I confer on you, just as my Father has conferred on me, a kingdom, so that you may eat and drink at my table in my kingdom, and you will sit on **thrones** judging the twelve tribes of Israel." [Luke 22:28-30]

At once I was in the spirit, and there in heaven stood a **throne**, with one seated on the throne! And the one seated there looks like jasper and carnelian, and around the throne is a rainbow that looks like an emerald. Around the throne are twenty-four **thrones**, and seated on the **thrones** are twenty-four elders, dressed in white robes, with golden crowns on their heads. [Revelation 4:2-4]

In the visions of the divine tribunal that appear in the gospels, the disciples of Jesus have apparently replaced the heavenly beings of the Hebrew Scriptures. Who the twenty-four elders in Revelation might be has been the subject of much debate. The author might have had in mind angels,* priests,* elders of the early church, or the holy* ones found in ancient Israel or among the followers of Jesus. Whoever the twenty-four elders might be, they seem to function as associate justices in the same way as the heavenly beings in Hebrew Scriptures and the disciples in the gospel vision of the heavenly court. For the Christian imagery to be consistent, of course, Jesus had to preside as chief justice, as he does in his role as Son of Man* in the Matthew passage. Elsewhere in the specifically Christian portions of the Bible, the *thronos* of Jesus represents continuity with the *kisse* of David.

Jesus enthroned

When the Son of Man comes in his glory, and all the angels with him, then he will sit on the **throne** of his glory. All the nations will be gathered before him, and he will separate people one from another as a shepherd separates the sheep from the goats. [Matthew 25:31-32]

The angel said to her, "Do not be afraid, Mary, for you have found favor with God. And now, you will conceive in your womb and bear a son, and you will name him Jesus. He will be great, and will be called the Son of the Most High, and the Lord God will give to him the **throne** of his ancestor David." [Luke 1:30-32]

Fellow Israelites, I may say to you confidently of our ancestor David that he both died and was buried, and his tomb is with us to this day. Since he was a prophet, he knew that God had sworn with an oath to him that he would put one of his descendants on his **throne**. [Acts 2:29-30]

Of the Son he says, "Your **throne**, O God, is forever and ever, and the righteous scepter is the scepter of your kingdom." [Hebrews 1:8]

One reason to identify the throne of Jesus with that of David is to avoid any confusion with the throne of God. If the Son occupies the throne, as the Letter to the Hebrews states, either the Father and the Son are totally fused or God has nowhere to sit. Other passages are quite clear that the throne belongs to God alone. The Letter to the Hebrews solves the dilemma by later stating that that Son has his own seat at the right hand of God.

thronos as God's place

I say to you, Do not swear at all, either by heaven, for it is the **throne** of God, or by the earth, for it is his footstool, or by Jerusalem, for it is the city of the great King. [Matthew 5:34-35]

Heaven is my **throne**, and the earth is my footstool. What kind of house will you build for me, says the Lord, or what is the place of my rest? [Acts 7:49]

Now the main point in what we are saying is this: we have such a high priest, one who is seated at the right hand of the **throne** of the Majesty in the heavens. [Hebrews 8:1]

John to the seven churches that are in Asia: Grace to you and peace from him who is and who was and who is to come, and from the seven spirits who are before his **throne**, and from Jesus Christ, the faithful witness, the firstborn of the dead, and the ruler of the kings of the earth. [Revelation 1:4-5]

The followers of Jesus also followed the Hebrew tradition in using the throne metaphor to identify opposition or potential opposition to divine authority. In these examples, *thronos* may refer to rulers on earth or to heavenly beings or perhaps to both. The author of Revelation may have located Satan's throne in Pergamum because it was an imperial city with temples and altars dedicated to

---

Greek gods so his emphasis could have been either on Satan* or on the cult leaders or on secular rulers.

thronos as opposition to God

He has brought down the powerful from their **thrones,** and lifted up the lowly. [Luke 1:52]

He is the image of the invisible God, the firstborn of all creation; for in him all things in heaven and on earth were created, things visible and invisible, whether **thrones** or dominions or rulers or powers. [Colossians 1:15-16]

And to the angel of the church in Pergamum write: These are the words of him who has the sharp two-edged sword: "I know where you are living, where Satan's **throne** is." [Revelation 2:12-13]

For the followers of Jesus, the throne imagery may be a helpful reminder of the secular powers that are determined to dominate society and of their own power to resist. By picturing Jesus as their judge,* his followers not only align their standards with his teaching, they also understand themselves to be participating in the exercise of his power over corruption. The throne metaphor can promote both realism and optimism—realism because it draws attention to the political and economic forces that oppress ordinary people and optimism because it pictures a world in which oppressive powers can be called to account.

DID YOU KNOW . . .

. . . that *kisse* is pronounced *kis-say*?
For more help with pronunciation, see "Pronouncing Transliterated Hebrew and Greek Words" on page 15.

---

tithe, *noun* and *verb*   A tithe—*ma'aser* in Hebrew and *dekate* in Greek—is literally one-tenth of something. The earliest mention of tithing in the Hebrew Scriptures appears in the Abraham legends. After winning an important military battle, Abraham is returning home with the booty when he encounters Melchizedek, the priest and king of Salem.

And King Melchizedek of Salem brought out bread and wine; he was priest of God Most High. He blessed him and said, "Blessed be Abram by God Most High, maker of heaven and earth; and blessed be God Most High, who has delivered your enemies into your hand!" And Abram gave him **one tenth** of everything. [Genesis 14:19-20]

This legend may have provided the rationale for the system that developed for the support of the landless Levites who managed the local rituals for the people of Israel and Judah.

I have given to the Levites as their portion the **tithe** of the Israelites, which they set apart as an offering to the LORD. Therefore I have said of them that they shall have no allotment among the Israelites. [Numbers 18:24]

The rules stated further that the Levites at each cult site should send "a tithe of the tithe" to Jerusalem for the support of the temple.

Then the LORD spoke to Moses, saying: You shall speak to the Levites, saying: When you receive from the Israelites the **tithe** that I have given you from them for your portion, you shall set apart an offering from it to the LORD, a **tithe** of the **tithe**. It shall be reckoned to you as your gift, the same as the grain of the threshing floor and the fullness of the wine press. Thus you also shall set apart an offering to the LORD from all the **tithes** that you receive from the Israelites; and from them you shall give the Lord's offering to the priest Aaron. [Numbers 18:25-28]

Outside of the figurative use of the term in the Epistle to the Hebrews, the only mention of tithing in the specifically Christian portion of the Bible is a scathing comment attributed to Jesus. In this verse, tithe appears in the verb form *apodekatoo*.

Woe to you, scribes and Pharisees, hypocrites! For you **tithe** mint, dill, and cummin, and have neglected the weightier matters of the law: justice and mercy and faith. [Matthew 23:23]

What supporting landless, religious functionaries and temple priests in Jerusalem have to do with a standard for offerings to support a church is open to question. With nothing in the teachings attributed to Jesus and nothing in the writings of St. Paul to back them up, church leaders who promote tithing may be more interested in separating the gullible from their money than they are in taking the Bible seriously.

DID YOU KNOW . . .

. . . that *apodekatoo* was pronounced *ah-po-dayk-aht-oh-oh*?
For more help with pronunciation, see "Pronouncing
Transliterated Hebrew and Greek Words" on page 15.

---

tongues—see **Pentecost**

transfiguration—see **vision**

tree—see **cross**

trespass, *noun* and *verb*   Most English-speaking people think of trespassing as wrongfully entering the property of someone else. Historically, the word included a much broader range of offenses, much like the biblical words it sometimes translates. One of the Hebrew words is *maal*, whose original meaning may have been to commit an act of treachery.

When any of you commit a **trespass** and sin unintentionally in any of the holy things of the LORD, you shall bring, as your guilt offering to the LORD, a ram without blemish from the flock, convertible into silver by the sanctuary shekel; it is a guilt offering. [Leviticus 5:15]

When any of you sin and commit a **trespass** against the LORD by deceiving a neighbor in a matter of a deposit or a pledge, or by robbery, or if you have defrauded a neighbor, or have found something lost and lied about it—if you swear falsely regarding any of the various things that one may do and sin thereby—when you have sinned and realize your guilt, and would restore what you took by robbery or by fraud or the deposit that was committed to you, or the lost thing that you found, or anything else about which you have sworn falsely, you shall repay the principal amount and shall add one-fifth to it. You shall pay it to its owner when you realize your guilt. [Leviticus 6:2-5]

Marks a word in the text that has its own entry   **299**

> Then Ezra the priest stood up and said to them, "You have **trespassed** and married foreign women, and so increased the guilt of Israel." [Ezra 10:10]

The other Hebrew word sometimes translated trespass is *pesha*, which most frequently is rendered transgress or transgression. Many other English words, however, have been used for *pesha*.

> When Abigail saw David, she hurried and alighted from the donkey, fell before David on her face, bowing to the ground. She fell at his feet and said, "Upon me alone, my lord, be the guilt; please let your servant speak in your ears, and hear the words of your servant . . . Please forgive the **trespass** of your servant; for the LORD will certainly make my lord a sure house, because my lord is fighting the battles of the LORD; and evil shall not be found in you so long as you live. [I Samuel 25:23-24, 28]

> I am going to send an angel in front of you, to guard you on the way and to bring you to the place that I have prepared. Be attentive to him and listen to his voice; do not rebel against him, for he will not pardon your **transgression**; for my name is in him. [Exodus 23:20-21]

> Then Jacob became angry, and upbraided Laban. Jacob said to Laban, "What is my **offense**? What is my sin, that you have hotly pursued me?" [Genesis 31:36]

> So the brothers approached Joseph, saying, "Your father gave this instruction before he died, 'Say to Joseph: I beg you, forgive the **crime** of your brothers and the wrong they did in harming you.' Now therefore please forgive the **crime** of the servants of the God of your father." [Genesis 50:16-17]

> In any case of **disputed ownership** involving ox, donkey, sheep, clothing, or any other loss, of which one party says, "This is mine," the case of both parties shall come before God; the one whom God condemns shall pay double to the other. [Exodus 22:9]

> See, my father, see the corner of your cloak in my hand; for by the fact that I cut off the corner of your cloak, and did not kill you, you may know for certain that there is no wrong or **treason** in my hands. I have not sinned against you, though you are hunting me to take my life. [I Samuel 24:11]

> Would that Job were tried to the limit, because his answers are those of the wicked. For he adds **rebellion** to his sin; he claps his hands among us, and multiplies his words against God. [Job 34:36-37]

> Some were sick through their **sinful ways**, and because of their iniquities endured affliction. [Psalm 107:17]

> One who forgives an **affront** fosters friendship, but one who dwells on disputes will alienate a friend. [Proverbs 17:9]

The Greek noun usually translated trespass is *paraptoma* from the verb *parapipto—para*, alongside + *pipto*, to fall. In other words, trespassing is stumbling off the public way* onto private property. In the Christian portion of the Bible, the verb only occurs once but the noun several times. In every case, the words are used in a figurative sense and were not to be taken literally.

> It is impossible to restore again to repentance those who have once been enlightened, and have tasted the heavenly gift, and have shared in the Holy Spirit, and have tasted the goodness of the word of God and the powers of the age to come, and then **have fallen away**, since on their own they are crucifying again the Son of God and are holding him up to contempt. [Hebrews 6:4-6]

If you forgive others their **trespasses**, your heavenly Father will also forgive you; but if you do not forgive others, neither will your Father forgive your **trespasses**. [Matthew 6:14-15]

The free gift is not like the **trespass**. For if the many died through the one man's **trespass**, much more surely have the grace of God and the free gift in the grace of the one man, Jesus Christ, abounded for the many. [Romans 5:15]

In Christ God was reconciling the world to himself, not counting their **trespasses** against them, and entrusting the message of reconciliation to us. [II Corinthians 5:19]

My friends, if anyone is detected in a **transgression**, you who have received the Spirit should restore such a one in a spirit of gentleness. Take care that you yourselves are not tempted. [Galatians 6:1]

Confess your **sins** to one another, and pray for one another, so that you may be healed. The prayer of the righteous is powerful and effective. [James 5:16]

Trespass can mean any of the things suggested by the Hebrew word *pesha*: transgression, crime, dispute, treason, rebellion, sinfulness, or affront. The Greek metaphor *paraptoma*, however, offers particular insight into the nature of wrongdoing. Not all objectionable behavior involves the intentionality inherent in sin.* As *paraptoma* suggests, people lose their moral balance. They fall into bad habits. They stumble and lose their way. They hurt other people without meaning to.

Trinity—see **Holy Spirit**

truth, *noun*   The original Hebrew and Greek metaphors that appear in English Bibles as the word truth have almost contradictory origins.

The root of the Hebrew word truth, *emeth*, is *aman*, usually translated faith.* In the dialects of Jesus's time, *aman* came to be pronounced, *amen*. It meant to build up or to support, to nurture as a parent or, consequently, to be firm, faithful, or trustworthy. When the English translations of the gospels report that Jesus began a pronouncement by saying, "Verily, verily" or "Truly, truly," the original Greek text employed a transliteration of the Hebrew, *Amen, amen*. That is another way of saying, "You can depend upon what I am about to tell you." The metaphor *emeth*, in the sense of being caring and dependable, was a favorite of the psalmists when addressing their prayers to God.

Lead me in your **truth**, and teach me, for you are the God of my salvation; for you I wait all day long. [Psalm 25:5]

Teach me your way, O LORD, that I may walk in your **truth**; give me an undivided heart to revere your name. [Psalm 86:11]

In contrast with the Hebrew, the Greek word for truth, *aletheia*, is a negative word formed by attaching the negative particle *a* to the root *lethe*, which meant forgetfulness or oblivion. In Greek mythology, those who drank from the waters of the river Lethe on their way into Hades would forget the past. In its ancient origins, *aletheia* meant that which is not forgotten. By the time of Jesus, Greek speakers might not have been conscious of using a negative term. Still, when they employed the word, they probably did not have in mind the certainty of being factually correct, the primary English connotation of truth. Equating factuality with truth did not become common practice until the seventeenth century. Until then, people who heard the word *aletheia*, attributed to Jesus in

John's gospel, most likely associated the word with the connotations of dependability and fidelity, which were similar to the Hebrew *emeth*.

> "If you continue in my word, you are truly my disciples; and you will know the **truth,** and the **truth** will make you free." [John 8:31-32]

> "When the Advocate comes, whom I will send to you from the Father, the Spirit of **truth** who comes from the Father, he will testify on my behalf." [John 15:26]

> "For this I was born, and for this I came into the world, to testify to the **truth.** Everyone who belongs to the **truth** listens to my voice." [John 18:37]

When a reader of the English translation of the Bible realizes that truth has little to do with facts or with absolutes, many passages have a more appealing ring, especially these pronouncements that the Gospel according to John attributes to Jesus. Thinking about truth as that which is not forgotten can also be a helpful reminder that both individuals and communities can lose sight of what were, in moments of crisis, profound understandings about the nature of their lives and relationships.

U

unclean—see **purity**

usury, *noun*   In the early translations of the Bible into English, the Hebrew word *neshek* became usury, but the New Revised Standard Version in all cases translates the term as charging interest. What the Hebrew-speaking people thought about charging interest on loans can be seen from the metaphor they chose. The root of *neshek* is a verb that meant to strike like a serpent. By contrast, the Greeks indicated a more favorable view by their metaphor, *tokos*, which came from a verb meaning to produce from seed. The negative attitude about charging interest is fairly consistent throughout the Hebrew Scriptures.

> If you lend money to my people, to the poor among you, you shall not deal with them as a creditor; you shall not **exact interest** from them. [Exodus 22:25]

> If any of your kin fall into difficulty and become dependent on you, you shall support them; they shall live with you as though resident aliens. Do not **take interest** in advance or otherwise make a profit from them, but fear your God; let them live with you. You shall not lend them your money at **interest** taken in advance, or provide them food at a profit. [Leviticus 25:35-37]

> On loans to a foreigner you may **charge interest,** but on loans to another Israelite you may not **charge interest,** so that the LORD your God may bless you in all your undertakings in the land that you are about to enter and possess. [Deuteronomy 23:20]

> He who "takes advance or accrued **interest;** shall he then live? He shall not. He has done all these abominable things; he shall surely die; his blood shall be upon himself." [Ezekiel 18:13]

The neutral or even positive attitude expressed by the Greek term toward the charging of interest shows up in a parable about investments attributed to Jesus in the gospels of Matthew and Luke.

> You ought to have invested my money with the bankers, and on my return I would have received what was my own with **interest.** [Matthew 25:27]

> Why then did you not put my money into the bank? Then when I returned, I could have collected it with **interest**. [Luke 19:23]

Even when interest charges appear in a positive sense, the early English translations of the Bible used the word usury. Until the seventeenth century, apparently usury did not convey a value judgment. Usury, charging interest to foreigners or receiving interest, was a good thing. Usury, charging interest to your own people, was a bad thing.

At some point after Christianity became fused with the Roman legal system, the church decided that Christians were bound to follow the moral, but not the ceremonial, laws of the Hebrew Scriptures, especially those laws that had explicit support in the gospels and the letters that came to be accepted as holy writ. According to Luke, Jesus had affirmed the laws against usury.

> "Do good and lend, expecting nothing in return." [Luke 6:35]

The Christian interpretation of the usury laws was that Christians could not charge other Christians interest on loans. Although Jews could not charge interest to each other, they could lend money at interest to Christians. Consequently, the Jews became the bankers of Europe. This system was accepted without question by the church for at least 1,400 years. Records exist of "the innumerable fables of the usurer who was prematurely carried to hell, or whose money turned to withered leaves in his strong box," wrote R. H. Tawney in *Religion and the Rise of Capitalism*. "Florence was the financial capital of medieval Europe; but even at Florence the secular authorities fined bankers right and left for usury in the middle of the fourteenth century, and, fifty years later, first prohibited credit transactions altogether, and then imported Jews to conduct a business forbidden to Christians."[26]

In the sixteenth century, John Calvin decided that only excessive interest was prohibited by the usury laws of the Bible. He thought that the development of the economy was being unnecessarily restricted and objected to the favorable position held by the Jewish bankers. Not all Christians agreed with this sudden attack on the authority of the Bible. In 1540, the Archbishop of Canterbury Thomas Cranmer protested against the embarrassment caused to reformers in England by the moral laxity allowed in economic transactions by the reformers on the continent. By the seventeenth century, however, both Anglicans and Roman Catholics had stopped preaching about the sin of usury. As time went on, Calvin's definition of usury became the accepted meaning of the word. Usury came to mean only excessive interest.

V

vine, *noun*   In ancient Israel, the vine was included in images of peace and contentment. The vine, Hebrew *gephen*, later became a metaphor identifying the people of Israel.

Gephen is used as part of the imagery associated with peace and contentment.

> Do not listen to Hezekiah; for thus says the king of Assyria: "Make your peace with me and come out to me; then every one of you will eat from your own **vine** and your own fig tree, and drink water from your own cistern." [II Kings 18:31]

> On that day, says the LORD of hosts, you shall invite each other to come under your **vine** and fig tree. [Zechariah 3:10]

---

*Marks a word in the text that has its own entry

> I will rebuke the locust for you, so that it will not destroy the produce of your soil; and your **vine** in the field shall not be barren, says the LORD of hosts. Then all nations will count you happy, for you will be a land of delight, says the LORD of hosts. [Malachi 3:11-12]

Gephen was also used to indicate the people of Israel in their relationship to God.

> Restore us, O God of hosts; let your face shine, that we may be saved. You brought a **vine** out of Egypt; you drove out the nations and planted it. You cleared the ground for it; it took deep root and filled the land. [Psalm 80:7-9]

> I planted you as a choice **vine,** from the purest stock. How then did you turn degenerate and become a wild vine? [Jeremiah 2:21]

> Thus says the LORD of hosts: Glean thoroughly as a **vine** the remnant of Israel; like a grape-gatherer, pass your hand again over its branches. [Jeremiah 6:9]

> Israel is a luxuriant **vine** that yields its fruit. The more his fruit increased the more altars he built; as his country improved, he improved his pillars. [Hosea 10:1]

The early followers of Jesus used the Greek word for vine, *ampelos*, in describing their relationship to him. They may well have associated the image with what came to them from the Hebrew tradition. They also probably made a connection with the imagery of the Eucharist, which included references to the fruit of the vine. The Gospel according to John makes elaborate use of the *ampelos* metaphor in words attributed to Jesus.

> I am the true **vine,** and my Father is the vinegrower. He removes every branch in me that bears no fruit. Every branch that bears fruit he prunes to make it bear more fruit. You have already been cleansed by the word that I have spoken to you. Abide in me as I abide in you. Just as the branch cannot bear fruit by itself unless it abides in the **vine,** neither can you unless you abide in me. I am the **vine,** you are the branches. Those who abide in me and I in them bear much fruit, because apart from me you can do nothing. Whoever does not abide in me is thrown away like a branch and withers; such branches are gathered, thrown into the fire, and burned. If you abide in me, and my words abide in you, ask for whatever you wish, and it will be done for you. My Father is glorified by this, that you bear much fruit and become my disciples. [John 15:1-8]

The vine became an important motif in Christian decorative art, but part of the reason may be that the vine has been a universal symbol for fertility and joy. Ecclesiasticus, a book in the apocrypha section of the Bible, represents wisdom* by a vine. Devotees of the god Bacchus used grape vines in their devotions. The Green Man with vines emerging from his mouth, found in the stone carvings of many medieval churches, is pre-Christian in origin.

The vine as a metaphor for Jesus, apart from its other associations, conveys the sense of the church as an organic whole, alive and growing, with each part drawing sustenance from the same source.

virgin birth, *noun*   Of all the early Christian writings that were included in the Bible, only two have anything to say about the birth of Jesus: Matthew and Luke. Although Luke tells the story from the mother's point of view and Matthew from her husband's, both indicate that they had not had sexual intercourse before Jesus was conceived. Both say that Mary was a virgin, in Greek, *parthenos*.

Marks a word in the text that has its own entry

In the sixth month the angel Gabriel was sent by God to a town in Galilee called Nazareth, to a **virgin** engaged to a man whose name was Joseph, of the house of David. The **virgin's** name was Mary. And he came to her and said, "Greetings, favored one! The Lord is with you." But she was much perplexed by his words and pondered what sort of greeting this might be. The angel said to her, "Do not be afraid, Mary, for you have found favor with God. And now, you will conceive in your womb and bear a son, and you will name him Jesus. He will be great, and will be called the Son of the Most High, and the Lord God will give to him the throne of his ancestor David. He will reign over the house of Jacob forever, and of his kingdom there will be no end." Mary said to the angel, "How can this be, since I am a **virgin**?" The angel said to her, "The Holy Spirit will come upon you, and the power of the Most High will overshadow you; therefore the child to be born will be holy; he will be called Son of God." [Luke 1:26-35]

Now the birth of Jesus the Messiah took place in this way. When his mother Mary had been engaged to Joseph, but before they lived together, she was found to be with child from the Holy Spirit. Her husband Joseph, being a righteous man and unwilling to expose her to public disgrace, planned to dismiss her quietly. But just when he had resolved to do this, an angel of the Lord appeared to him in a dream and said, "Joseph, son of David, do not be afraid to take Mary as your wife, for the child conceived in her is from the Holy Spirit. She will bear a son, and you are to name him Jesus, for he will save his people from their sins." All this took place to fulfill what had been spoken by the Lord through the prophet: "Look, the **virgin** shall conceive and bear a son, and they shall name him Emmanuel," which means, "God is with us." [Matthew 1:18-23]

In the Greek translation of the Hebrew Scriptures, *parthenos* stood for *bethulah*, the customary word for virgin, but it was also used for *almah*, which meant a young woman, a girl, or a maid. In Matthew's quote, which is Isaiah 14:7, the word in Hebrew was *almah*. The prophet was denouncing King Ahaz (about 735–15 BCE) and claiming that his replacement was on the way. The young woman who would give birth to his successor either was already pregnant or was about to be. This was not a prophecy about a virgin birth that would occur 700 years later, but the mistranslation into Greek created an appealing reference for the followers of Jesus. Although the quote from Isaiah fit into the scheme of Matthew's narrative, the passage was probably not his primary inspiration for the story.

In ancient times, after the death of a particularly noteworthy person, stories were told about the peculiar circumstances of his birth. Robert J. Miller has collected a number of these stories and included them in a book, *Born Divine—The Births of Jesus and Other Sons of God.*[27] Two of them might have had a particularly profound influence on the way that followers of Jesus told the story of his birth. These are the stories about Alexander the Great and Caesar Augustus. Like Jesus, each was honored for establishing a great kingdom.*

Miller took the first of these stories from Plutarch's *Life of Alexander*. The story describes the experience of his parents, Olympias and Philip of Macedonia in the days prior to Alexander's before Alexander's birth.

"Now prior to the night they were to be united as husband and wife in the bridal suite, the bride had a dream. There was a peal of thunder and a bolt of lightning struck her womb. The lightning touch off a big fire, which broke into flames that danced about until they died out. Some time later, after they were married, Philip dreamed that he put a seal on his wife's womb, a seal that he thought bore the image of a lion. Some seers became suspicious as a result of this dream and thought Philip should keep a closer watch on his wife. Another seer, Aristander of Telmessus, said that Olympias was pregnant, since no one puts a seal on something that is empty, and that the son to be born would be courageous and lion-like."[28]

The other story, one that appeared in the *History of Rome* by Dio Cassius, describes the divine origins of Augustus Caesar.

> "Attia (the mother of Augustus) emphatically asserted that her child had been fathered by Apollo. She said that once, while she was sleeping in his temple, she thought she had intercourse with a snake, and that because of this she had given birth at the end of her term. Before her child came to the light of day, she dreamed that her womb was lifted to the heavens and spread out over all the earth. That same night her husband Octavius thought that the sun rose from her thighs."[29]

Each of these successful conquerors was known in his lifetime as a son of God.* The birth stories came later. The same sequence might well have been true of Jesus. He was probably known as a son of God for some period of time before the birth stories emerged. Whether Matthew and Luke made up the stories they told, or whether they elaborated on tales they had heard, is open to question. The genealogies that they include (Matthew 1:2-16 and Luke 3:23-38), however, suggest that they might not have taken them literally. Both genealogies of Jesus trace his royal ancestry through Joseph. That others of the time did take the virgin birth story literally can be inferred from the efforts made by Jesus's detractors to raise questions about his paternity. The most notorious of these rumors was the tale that Jesus was the illegitimate son of a Roman soldier.

vision, *noun*   Visions play an important part in the unfolding drama of the Bible. The English word vision may represent either the Hebrew word *mareh* or one of the many variations based on the root *chazah*, the most important of which is *chazon*.

mareh

The LORD said to Samuel, "See, I am about to do something in Israel that will make both ears of anyone who hears of it tingle . . ." Samuel lay there until morning; then he opened the doors of the house of the LORD. Samuel was afraid to tell the **vision** to Eli. [I Samuel 3:11, 15]

The spirit lifted me up and brought me in a **vision** by the spirit of God into Chaldea, to the exiles. Then the **vision** that I had seen left me. [Ezekiel 11:24]

When I, Daniel, had seen the **vision**, I tried to understand it. Then someone appeared standing before me, having the appearance of a man, and I heard a human voice by the Ulai, calling, "Gabriel, help this man understand the **vision**." [Daniel 8:15-16]

Variations on the root *chazah*

The **vision** of Isaiah son of Amoz, which he saw concerning Judah and Jerusalem in the days of Uzziah, Jotham, Ahaz, and Hezekiah, kings of Judah.—*chazon* [Isaiah 1:1]

The **vision** of Obadiah. Thus says the Lord GOD concerning Edom: We have heard a report from the LORD, and a messenger has been sent among the nations: "Rise up! Let us rise against it for battle!"—*chazon* [Obadiah 1:1]

> After these things the word of the LORD came to Abram in a **vision,** "Do not be afraid, Abram, I am your shield; your reward shall be very great."—*machazeh* [Genesis 15:1]

> The godless will fly away like a dream, and not be found; they will be chased away like a **vision** of the night.—*chizzayon* [Job 20:8]

> Then the mystery was revealed to Daniel in a **vision** of the night, and Daniel blessed the God of heaven.—*chezev* [Daniel 2:19]

Two Greek words translated in English as vision, *horama* and *optasia*, come from the same verb, *horao*, which meant to glimpse or catch sight of.

> When Zechariah did come out, he could not speak to them, and they realized that he had seen a **vision** in the sanctuary. He kept motioning to them and remained unable to speak.—*optasia* [Luke 1:22]

> Now there was a disciple in Damascus named Ananias. The Lord said to him in a **vision,** "Ananias." He answered, "Here I am, Lord."—*horama* [Acts 9:10]

> One night the Lord said to Paul in a **vision,** "Do not be afraid, but speak and do not be silent; for I am with you, and no one will lay a hand on you to harm you, for there are many in this city who are my people."—*horama* [Acts 18:9-10]

> It is necessary to boast; nothing is to be gained by it, but I will go on to **visions** and revelations of the Lord.—*optasia* [II Corinthians 12:1]

To communicate the essence of a vision, sometimes the early followers of Jesus used *optanomai*, a passive verb form of *horao*. Although a literal translation of *optanomai* would read that a specific person was glimpsed by someone in a vision, the translators usually simplify the structure of the sentence to read that the person appeared to someone.

> The eleven were saying, "The Lord has risen indeed, and he has **appeared** to Simon!" [Luke 24:34]

> After his suffering Jesus presented himself alive to them by many convincing proofs, **appearing** to them during forty days and speaking about the kingdom of God. [Acts 1:3]

> For I handed on to you as of first importance what I in turn had received: that Christ died for our sins in accordance with the scriptures, and that he was buried, and that he was raised on the third day in accordance with the scriptures, and that he **appeared** to Cephas, then to the twelve. Then he **appeared** to more than five hundred brothers and sisters at one time, most of whom are still alive, though some have died. Then he **appeared** to James, then to all the apostles. Last of all, as to one untimely born, he **appeared** also to me. [I Corinthians 15:3-8]

The close connection between vision and appear comes through explicitly in Matthew's account of an event commonly called the Transfiguration (although metamorphosis would be a more literal translation of the Greek). The author uses first *optanomai* and then *horama*.

> Six days later, Jesus took with him Peter and James and his brother John and led them up a high mountain, by themselves. And he was transfigured before them, and his face shone like the sun, and his clothes became dazzling white. Suddenly there **appeared** to them Moses and Elijah, talking with him. Then Peter said to Jesus, "Lord, it is good for us to be here; if you wish, I will make three dwellings here, one for you, one for Moses, and one for Elijah." While he was still

---

Marks a word in the text that has its own entry

speaking, suddenly a bright cloud overshadowed them, and from the cloud a voice said, "This is my Son, the Beloved; with him I am well pleased; listen to him!" When the disciples heard this, they fell to the ground and were overcome by fear. But Jesus came and touched them, saying, "Get up and do not be afraid." And when they looked up, they saw no one except Jesus himself alone. As they were coming down the mountain, Jesus ordered them, "Tell no one about the **vision** until after the Son of Man has been raised from the dead." [Matthew 17:1-9]

In modern English usage, beyond seeing with the eyes, vision has three distinct but related meanings:

1. **Vision can mean anticipating and planning for the future.** Every not-for-profit organization is now supposed to have a vision statement.

2. **Vision can mean extraordinary insight and wisdom.** People express admiration for a leader who possesses such vision.

3. **Vision can mean an ecstatic or dream-like experience.** Such events are often associated with a divine presence.

In a narrative, #3 can be a literary device used to dramatize #1 or #2. In earlier times, that is, before the seventeenth century, most readers of the Bible would not wonder if a reported vision was a literary device or an event that took place in real time and physical space, nor would they have made a sharp distinction between a vision, which is essentially an internal experience, and an observation, seeing actual figures in front of their eyes. They knew that people had dreams at night and dream-like experiences while wide awake. These visions may have been just as real to them as seeing their families and neighbors.

With the limited evidence available, no one can be sure what a biblical author had in mind when reporting a vision or an appearing. Was this a device for moving the story along—a dramatization of someone's anticipating the future or developing extraordinary insight? Did the author think that a character in the story really had an ecstatic or dream-like experience? If it were the latter, did the author think that the figures appearing in the vision were external to the people having the vision? Followers of Jesus today are divided in their answers to these questions.

W

water—see **baptism**

way, *noun*   The Hebrew word *derek* meant literally a road or a journey, but in the Bible it appears more frequently as a metaphor indicating the course taken by a person's life. *Derek* is quite similar to the Greek word *hodos*, which also meant literally a road or highway but was often used figuratively for a way of life or a point of view. Finding this metaphorical use of the term particularly attractive, some of Jesus's early followers called themselves the Way.

Literal

Laban removed the male goats that were striped and spotted, and all the female goats that were speckled and spotted, every one that had white on it, and every lamb that was black, and put them in charge of his sons; and he set a distance of three days' **journey** between himself and Jacob, while Jacob was pasturing the rest of Laban's flock. [Genesis 30:35-36]

Gideon went up by the caravan **route** east of Nobah and Jogbehah, and attacked the army; for the army was off its guard. [Judges 8:11]

So Ruth set out from the place where she had been living, she and her two daughters-in-law, and they went on their **way** to go back to the land of Judah. [Ruth 1:7]

Figurative

The LORD said, "Shall I hide from Abraham what I am about to do, seeing that Abraham shall become a great and mighty nation, and all the nations of the earth shall be blessed in him? No, for I have chosen him, that he may charge his children and his household after him to keep the **way** of the LORD by doing righteousness and justice; so that the LORD may bring about for Abraham what he has promised him." [Genesis 18:17-19]

They did not listen even to their judges; for they lusted after other gods and bowed down to them. They soon turned aside from the **way** in which their ancestors had walked, who had obeyed the commandments of the LORD; they did not follow their example. [Judges 2:17]

Truly, O people in Zion, inhabitants of Jerusalem, you shall weep no more. He will surely be gracious to you at the sound of your cry; when he hears it, he will answer you. Though the Lord may give you the bread of adversity and the water of affliction, yet your Teacher will not hide himself any more, but your eyes shall see your Teacher. And when you turn to the right or when you turn to the left, your ears shall hear a word behind you, saying, "This is the **way**; walk in it." [Isaiah 30:19-20]

The imagery employed in the Isaiah example may have had an impact on the way Jesus's followers understood *hodos*.

Literal

Having been warned in a dream not to return to Herod, they left for their own country by another **road**. [Matthew 2:12]

Many people spread their cloaks on the **road**, and others spread leafy branches that they had cut in the fields. [Mark 11:8]

Then the master said to the slave, "Go out into the **roads** and lanes, and compel people to come in, so that my house may be filled." [Luke 14:23]

Then an angel of the Lord said to Philip, "Get up and go toward the south to the **road** that goes down from Jerusalem to Gaza." [Acts 8:26]

Figurative

For the gate is narrow and the **road** is hard that leads to life, and there are few who find it. [Matthew 7:14]

They came and said to him, "Teacher, we know that you are sincere, and show deference to no one; for you do not regard people with partiality, but teach the **way** of God in accordance with truth." [Mark 12:14]

In past generations God allowed all the nations to follow their own **ways**. [Acts 14:16]

Their mouths are full of cursing and bitterness. Their feet are swift to shed blood; ruin and misery are in their **paths**, and the **way** of peace they have not known. [Romans 3:14-17]

Figurative: following Jesus

Jesus said to him, "I am the **way,** and the truth, and the life. No one comes to the Father except through me." [John 14:6]

Meanwhile Saul, still breathing threats and murder against the disciples of the Lord, went to the high priest and asked him for letters to the synagogues at Damascus, so that if he found any who belonged to the **Way,** men or women, he might bring them bound to Jerusalem. [Acts 9:1-2]

Now there came to Ephesus a Jew named Apollos, a native of Alexandria. He was an eloquent man, well-versed in the scriptures. He had been instructed in the **Way** of the Lord; and he spoke with burning enthusiasm and taught accurately the things concerning Jesus, though he knew only the baptism of John. [Acts 18:24-25]

For this reason I sent you Timothy, who is my beloved and faithful child in the Lord, to remind you of my **ways** in Christ Jesus, as I teach them everywhere in every church. [I Corinthians 4:17]

Many will follow their licentious ways, and because of these teachers the **way** of truth will be maligned. [II Peter 2:2]

As metaphors *derek* and *hodos* indicate movement or progress* as opposed to a static condition. The English equivalent, the way, has the same characteristics.

widow's mite, *noun*   In a popular Bible story about a widow's gift of two mites to the temple, the King James Version of Mark and Luke used mite to translate the Greek *lepton*. The mite was originally a small Flemish coin of little value and was the equivalent of the little Roman coin whose name was derived from the adjective *leptos*, which meant small, thin, or light. When Mark used the term, he went on to explain that two *lepta* were equal to a *kodrantes*, which was worth one fourth of the basic copper coin. In seventeenth-century England, a fourth of a penny was called a farthing, so farthing was a suitable translation for *kodrantes*. With inflation, however, the mite and the farthing disappeared, so more modern English translations have had to use other terms to get across the idea of these small coins.

Although the mite fell out of circulation long ago, the widow's mite has remained in the vocabulary of English-speaking Christians as a metaphor indicating extreme generosity. Unfortunately, the use of the metaphor has blinded generations of Jesus's followers to what some scholars believe is the real point of the story, which is indicated by the context where Mark and Luke placed it.

As Jesus taught, he said, "Beware of the scribes, who like to walk around in long robes, and to be greeted with respect in the marketplaces, and to have the best seats in the synagogues and places of honor at banquets! They devour widows' houses and for the sake of appearance say long prayers. They will receive the greater condemnation." He sat down opposite the treasury, and watched the crowd putting money into the treasury. Many rich people put in large sums. A poor widow came and put in two **small copper coins,** which are worth a penny. Then he called his disciples and said to them, "Truly I tell you, this poor widow has put in more than all those who are contributing to the treasury. For all of them have contributed out of their abundance; but she out of her poverty has put in everything she had, all she had to live on." [Mark 12:38-44]

According to the gospels, Jesus was talking about the grave inequities in the economic and social system of the time when he observed the poor widow putting her two mites into the treasury. He pointed out that she had just given away all she had to live on. Anyone in the first century hearing this story could have pictured the widow's fate. With no welfare program, no social security, and no soup kitchens, her future held only starvation and death. Hers was not an act of generosity but of resignation and despair. A person familiar with the Hebrew Scriptures would have thought immediately of the response made by the widow of Zarephath to Elijah when he asked her for a morsel of bread.

> She said, "As the LORD your God lives, I have nothing baked, only a handful of meal in a jar, and a little oil in a jug; I am now gathering a couple of sticks, so that I may go home and prepare it for myself and my son, that we may eat it, and die." [I Kings 17:12]

Until fairly recent times, poor widows had little value to society. Even if their husbands had left them money or a house,* as Jesus was said to have pointed out, they were frequently victimized by unscrupulous businessmen. Without a man to protect them, many were reduced to begging or prostitution to stay alive. For others, like the widows in the stories, death by starvation was preferable.

The story of the widow's mite, placed back in the context of the gospels, can work as a metaphor suggesting injustice, especially injustice toward those people who have no means of making a contribution to the economy.

wife—see **marriage**

wine and **cup**, *nouns*   The people of ancient Israel seem to have had mixed feelings about wine. They see wine as a gift of God to be enjoyed, a suitable offering to give God as an expression of gratitude, and yet the Hebrew Scriptures post many warnings about drinking wine. They used wine as a metaphor suggesting what is most desired and what can be expected in God's realm, but they also used wine as a metaphor indicating God's anger and punishment.

The Hebrew-speaking people had several words for wine when they were writing about the drink in a positive sense.

> May God give you of the dew of heaven, and of the fatness of the earth, and plenty of grain and wine.—*tirosh*, suggesting the juice squeezed from grapes [Genesis 27:28]

> I would lead you and bring you into the house of my mother, and into the chamber of the one who bore me. I would give you spiced **wine** to drink, the juice of my pomegranates.—*asis*, suggesting the juice produced by treading [Song of Solomon 8:2]

> You cause the grass to grow for the cattle, and plants for people to use, to bring forth food from the earth, and **wine** to gladden the human heart, oil to make the face shine, and bread to strengthen the human heart.—*yayin*, suggesting the effervescence of fermentation
> [Psalm 104:14-15]

> On the day when you raise the sheaf, you shall offer a lamb a year old, without blemish, as a burnt offering to the LORD. And the grain offering with it shall be two-tenths of an ephah of choice flour mixed with oil, an offering by fire of pleasing odor to the LORD; and the drink offering with it shall be of **wine**, one-fourth of a hin.—*yayin* [Leviticus 23:12-13]

The Hebrew ambivalence about wine shows up in their concern for the purity of individuals set apart for the service of God, such as the temple priests, the Nazirites, and the prophet Daniel. In these cases, and in the warnings about the possible misuse of wine, the word *yayin* is nearly always included.

> And the LORD spoke to Aaron: Drink no **wine** or strong drink, neither you nor your sons, when you enter the tent of meeting, that you may not die; it is a statute forever throughout your generations. [Leviticus 10:8-9]

> Speak to the Israelites and say to them: When either men or women make a special vow, the vow of a nazirite, to separate themselves to the LORD, they shall separate themselves from **wine** and strong drink. [Numbers 6:2-3]

> Daniel resolved that he would not defile himself with the royal rations of food and **wine**; so he asked the palace master to allow him not to defile himself. [Daniel 1:8]

> If someone were to go about uttering empty falsehoods, saying, "I will preach to you of **wine** and strong drink," such a one would be the preacher for this people! [Micah 2:11]

> Wake up, you drunkards, and weep; and wail, all you **wine**-drinkers, over the **sweet wine** (*asis*), for it is cut off from your mouth. [Joel 1:5]

> They shall eat, but not be satisfied; they shall play the whore, but not multiply; because they have forsaken the LORD to devote themselves to whoredom. **Wine** and **new wine** (*tirosh*) take away the understanding. [Hosea 4:10-11]

In some places in the Hebrew Scripture, wine is the metaphor for what is most desired in this life, a symbol of God's wisdom and of God's coming reign. Some of these images feature the wine cup, in Hebrew *kos*, in place of a word for wine or in conjunction with one of the wine words.

> The LORD is my chosen portion and my **cup**; you hold my lot. [Psalm 16:5]

> Wisdom has built her house, she has hewn her seven pillars. She has slaughtered her animals, she has mixed her **wine**, she has also set her table. She has sent out her servant-girls, she calls from the highest places in the town, "You that are simple, turn in here!" To those without sense she says, "Come, eat of my bread and drink of the **wine** I have mixed."—*yayin* [Proverbs 9:1-5]

> On this mountain the LORD of hosts will make for all peoples a feast of rich food, a feast of **well-aged wines**, of rich food filled with marrow, of **well-aged wines** strained clear.—*shemer*, suggesting something preserved [Isaiah 25:6]

> Ho, everyone who thirsts, come to the waters; and you that have no money, come, buy and eat! Come, buy **wine** and milk without money and without price.—*yayin* [Isaiah 55:1]

> The time is surely coming, says the LORD, when the one who plows shall overtake the one who reaps, and the treader of grapes the one who sows the seed; the mountains shall drip **sweet wine**, and all the hills shall flow with it.—*asis* [Amos 9:13]

In other places in the Hebrew Scriptures, the wine and wine cup metaphors stand for God's anger and intention to punish offenders. As with the positive metaphors the wine cup, *kos*, appears in place of a word for wine or in conjunction with one of the wine words.

> You have made your people suffer hard things; you have given us **wine** to drink that made us reel.—*yayin* [Psalm 60:3]

> For in the hand of the LORD there is a **cup** with foaming **wine**, well mixed; he will pour a draught from it, and all the wicked of the earth shall drain it down to the dregs.—*yayin* [Psalm 75:8]

> I will make your oppressors eat their own flesh, and they shall be drunk with their own blood as with **wine**. Then all flesh shall know that I am the LORD your Savior, and your Redeemer, the Mighty One of Jacob.—*asis* [Isaiah 49:26]

> Rouse yourself, rouse yourself! Stand up, O Jerusalem, you who have drunk at the hand of the LORD the **cup** of his wrath, who have drunk to the dregs the bowl of staggering. [Isaiah 51:17]

> Thus the LORD, the God of Israel, said to me: Take from my hand this **cup** of the **wine** of wrath, and make all the nations to whom I send you drink it. They shall drink and stagger and go out of their minds because of the sword that I am sending among them.—*yayin* [Jeremiah 25:15-16]

In their writings, the early followers of Jesus betray the same ambivalence about wine as did the Israelites before them. In what they say about the actual drinking of wine and in their use of the wine and cup metaphors, they demonstrate positive and negative attitudes about the subject. In Greek, the word for wine is *oinos*, the root of our word oenology, the knowledge or study of wine.

Signs of the positive attitudes toward the drinking of wine are abundant. The most notable example is the story in John's gospel about Jesus turning water into wine. Whether this story describes an historical incident or whether it is was composed by an imaginative writer late in the first century is beside the point here. Without doubt, the story illustrates at least one Christian community's claim that Jesus had replaced Bacchus as the lord of wine.

> On the third day there was a wedding in Cana of Galilee, and the mother of Jesus was there. Jesus and his disciples had also been invited to the wedding. When the **wine** gave out, the mother of Jesus said to him, "They have no wine." And Jesus said to her, "Woman, what concern is that to you and to me? My hour has not yet come." His mother said to the servants, "Do whatever he tells you." Now standing there were six stone water jars for the Jewish rites of purification, each holding twenty or thirty gallons. Jesus said to them, "Fill the jars with water." And they filled them up to the brim. He said to them, "Now draw some out, and take it to the chief steward." So they took it. When the steward tasted the water that had become **wine**, and did not know where it came from (though the servants who had drawn the water knew), the steward called the bridegroom and said to him, "Everyone serves the good **wine** first, and then the inferior wine after the guests have become drunk. But you have kept the good **wine** until now."
> [John 2:1-10]

The positive appreciation of wine also shows up in the contrast between Jesus and John the Baptist, who is said to have lived like a Nazirite. A similar appreciation for the gift of wine is expressed in other ways as well. One of these positive comments, the example from I Timothy, some scholars think may have been a deliberate attempt to counter a tendency toward asceticism that was appearing in the church.

> John the Baptist has come eating no bread and drinking no **wine**, and you say, "He has a demon"; the Son of Man has come eating and drinking, and you say, "Look, a glutton and a drunkard, a friend of tax collectors and sinners!" [Luke 7:33-34]

> Jesus replied, "A man was going down from Jerusalem to Jericho, and fell into the hands of robbers, who stripped him, beat him, and went away, leaving him half dead . . . a Samaritan while traveling came near him; and when he saw him, he was moved with pity. He went to him and bandaged his wounds, having poured oil and **wine** on them. [Luke 10:30, 33-34]

Marks a word in the text that has its own entry

> No longer drink only water, but take a little **wine** for the sake of your stomach and your frequent ailments. [I Timothy 5:23]

One source of the early Christian appreciation of wine was no doubt its use in the ritual that came to be known as the Eucharist.* As was the case with bread,* for the followers of Jesus the sharing of wine in the ritual meal took on aspects of the temple sacrifices. The sharing of the cup took the place of the offerings of wine and the sprinkling of blood. Curiously, however, in the accounts of this practice found in the Bible, not one mentions wine by name. Instead, they all refer to the cup, in Greek *poterion*.

> In the same way he took the cup also, after supper, saying, "This **cup** is the new covenant in my blood. Do this, as often as you drink it, in remembrance of me." For as often as you eat this bread and drink the **cup**, you proclaim the Lord's death until he comes. [I Corinthians 11:25-26]

> Then he took a **cup**, and after giving thanks he gave it to them, and all of them drank from it. He said to them, "This is my blood of the covenant, which is poured out for many. Truly I tell you, I will never again drink of the fruit of the vine until that day when I drink it new in the kingdom of God." [Mark 14:23-25]

Because wine is not mentioned directly in connection with the ritual meal, some have concluded that the disciples drank something else, something not intoxicating. As evidence, they point to several warnings against the misuse of wine found in Christian writings as well as in the Hebrew Scriptures. One of the warnings, however, came from Paul as he reminded the Corinthians about the meaning of the tradition.

> When you come together, it is not really to eat the Lord's supper. For when the time comes to eat, each of you goes ahead with your own supper, and one goes hungry and another becomes drunk. [I Corinthians 11:20-21]

> Do not, for the sake of food, destroy the work of God. Everything is indeed clean, but it is wrong for you to make others fall by what you eat; it is good not to eat meat or drink **wine** or do anything that makes your brother or sister stumble. [Romans 14:20-21]

> Do not get drunk with **wine**, for that is debauchery; but be filled with the Spirit, as you sing psalms and hymns and spiritual songs among yourselves, singing and making melody to the Lord in your hearts. [Ephesians 5:18-19]

> Deacons likewise must be serious, not double-tongued, not indulging in much **wine**, not greedy for money. [I Timothy 3:8]

Oinos and *poterion* as metaphors, unlike their Hebrew equivalents, almost always convey negative connotations. They suggest either a terrible fate or the anger of God.

> Jesus answered, "You do not know what you are asking. Are you able to drink the **cup** that I am about to drink?" They said to him, "We are able." He said to them, "You will indeed drink my **cup**, but to sit at my right hand and at my left, this is not mine to grant, but it is for those for whom it has been prepared by my Father." [Matthew 20:22-23]

> Jesus said, "Abba, Father, for you all things are possible; remove this **cup** from me; yet, not what I want, but what you want." [Mark 14:36]

> Jesus said to Peter, "Put your sword back into its sheath. Am I not to drink the **cup** that the Father has given me?" [John 18:11]

> Then another angel, a second, followed, saying, "Fallen, fallen is Babylon the great! She has made all nations drink of the **wine** of the wrath of her fornication." Then another angel, a third, followed them, crying with a loud voice, "Those who worship the beast and its image, and receive a mark on their foreheads or on their hands, they will also drink the **wine** of God's wrath, poured unmixed into the **cup** of his anger, and they will be tormented with fire and sulfur in the presence of the holy angels and in the presence of the Lamb." [Revelation 14:8-10]

In the gospels, the only use of the wine metaphor that might be positive occurs in a saying attributed to Jesus. If this is one of the kingdom parables,* it might have had a negative shock value similar to that of yeast.* Perhaps the metaphor here is similar to the Hebrew wine metaphors that stand for all that is desirable in the reign of God.

> No one sews a piece of unshrunk cloth on an old cloak; otherwise, the patch pulls away from it, the new from the old, and a worse tear is made. And no one puts new **wine** into old wineskins; otherwise, the **wine** will burst the skins, and the **wine** is lost, and so are the skins; but one puts new **wine** into fresh wineskins. [Mark 2:21-22]

The Bible's mixed message on the desirability of drinking wine and on the contradictory uses of wine and cup as figures of speech are confusing at best. Then, too, the ritual identification of wine with blood has been a problem for the people who are put off by the sacrifice,* atonement,* and passion* metaphors. For these reasons, the wine and cup metaphors must be used with care to assure clear communication.

wisdom, *noun*   Although many passages of the Hebrew Scriptures emphasize the importance of wisdom, the book of Proverbs has the most to say on the subject. In this one collection, the editor needed four different Hebrew words to express what is meant by wisdom in the English language. The most frequently used word for wisdom is *chokmah*, which was the ability to translate thought into action. This is the word that Proverbs uses for the lengthy essay on wisdom in chapter eight.

> **Wisdom** cries out in the street; in the squares she raises her voice. At the busiest corner she cries out; at the entrance of the city gates she speaks: "How long, O simple ones, will you love being simple? How long will scoffers delight in their scoffing and fools hate knowledge?" [Proverbs 1:20-22]

> My child, be attentive to my **wisdom**; incline your ear to my understanding, so that you may hold on to prudence, and your lips may guard knowledge. [Proverbs 5:1-2]

> Does not **wisdom** call, and does not understanding raise her voice? . . . Take my instruction instead of silver, and knowledge rather than choice gold; for **wisdom** is better than jewels, and all that you may desire cannot compare with her. I, **wisdom**, live with prudence, and I attain knowledge and discretion . . . The LORD created me at the beginning of his work, the first of his acts of long ago. Ages ago I was set up, at the first, before the beginning of the earth. [Proverbs 8:1, 10-12, 22-23]

> A capable wife who can find? She is far more precious than jewels . . . She opens her mouth with **wisdom**, and the teaching of kindness is on her tongue. [Proverbs 31:10, 26]

Marks a word in the text that has its own entry

The other three words appear less often and are not always translated wisdom.

> The LORD stores up sound **wisdom** for the upright; he is a shield to those who walk blamelessly, guarding the paths of justice and preserving the way of his faithful ones.—*tushiah*, intellectual ability [Proverbs 2:7-8]

> **Wisdom** is a fountain of life to one who has it, but folly is the punishment of fools.—*sekel*, intelligence [Proverbs 16:22]

> To get **wisdom** is to love oneself; to keep understanding is to prosper.—*leb*, heart or mind* [Proverbs 19:8]

The early Christians had one Greek word, *sophia*, to convey the various aspects of wisdom found in the Hebrew Scriptures. They could personify wisdom in much the same way as Proverbs.

> For John the Baptist has come eating no bread and drinking no wine, and you say, "He has a demon"; the Son of Man has come eating and drinking, and you say, "Look, a glutton and a drunkard, a friend of tax collectors and sinners!" Nevertheless, **wisdom** is vindicated by all her children. [Luke 7:33-35]

> Also the **Wisdom** of God said, "I will send them prophets and apostles, some of whom they will kill and persecute." [Luke 11:49]

They understood wisdom to be a characteristic of Jesus and often identified Jesus with the personification of wisdom.

> The child grew and became strong, filled with **wisdom**; and the favor of God was upon him. [Luke 2:40]

> On the sabbath Jesus began to teach in the synagogue, and many who heard him were astounded. They said, "Where did this man get all this? What is this **wisdom** that has been given to him? What deeds of power are being done by his hands!" [Mark 6:2]

> God is the source of your life in Christ Jesus, who became for us **wisdom** from God, and righteousness and sanctification and redemption. [I Corinthians 1:30]

> I want their hearts to be encouraged and united in love, so that they may have all the riches of assured understanding and have the knowledge of God's mystery, that is, Christ himself, in whom are hidden all the treasures of **wisdom** and knowledge. [Colossians 2:2-3]

The early followers of Jesus also understood *sophia* to be one of the gifts that God imparts to the faithful.

> So make up your minds not to prepare your defense in advance; for I will give you words and a **wisdom** that none of your opponents will be able to withstand or contradict. [Luke 21:14-15]

> Then some of those who belonged to the synagogue of the Freedmen (as it was called), Cyrenians, Alexandrians, and others of those from Cilicia and Asia, stood up and argued with Stephen. But they could not withstand the **wisdom** and the Spirit with which he spoke. [Acts 6:9-10]

> To one is given through the Spirit the utterance of **wisdom**, and to another the utterance of knowledge according to the same Spirit. [I Corinthians 12:8]

At a slightly later period, some Christians equated *sophia* with the *logos*, or divine word,* found at the beginning of the Gospel according to John. In this development, *sophia* became something more than an emanation of God or a gift from God. Wisdom became a metaphor used to identify and to address the divine presence. Both the Hebrew and Greek words for wisdom are feminine. Wisdom personified is female. The practice of approaching God as Wisdom gives the followers of Jesus an additional opportunity for imagining God in female form, the other being Mary pictured as the mother* of God.

Using the metaphor wisdom, or Holy Wisdom, also appeals to many Christians who have problems using metaphors that imply an interventionist understanding of God. As wisdom functioned in and through Jesus, so wisdom can operate in and through those who follow him.

woe, *interjection* or *verb*   The Hebrew *oy* and the Greek *ouai* are similar in origin to the English woe. All three originated as an involuntary sound of dismay, something between a sigh and a groan. All three developed two uses: an expression of despair* in the face of calamity or a warning of calamity that is to come. In the latter sense, woe can take on the characteristics of a denunciation or a curse.*

Hebrew developed several variations of *oy—oya, iy, hoy,* and *hi*—but they all have the same meaning. Biblical Greek has only *ouai*.

Expression of despair

When they learned that the ark of the LORD had come to the camp, the Philistines were afraid; for they said, "Gods have come into the camp." They also said, "**Woe** to us! For nothing like this has happened before. **Woe** to us! Who can deliver us from the power of these mighty gods? These are the gods who struck the Egyptians with every sort of plague in the wilderness."—*oy* [I Samuel 4:6-8]

Woe is me, that I am an alien in Meshech, that I must live among the tents of Kedar.—*oya* [Psalm 120:5]

Who has **woe**? Who has sorrow? Who has strife? Who has complaining? Who has wounds without cause? Who has redness of eyes? Those who linger late over wine, those who keep trying mixed wines.—*oy* [Proverbs 23:29-30]

I said: "**Woe** is me! I am lost, for I am a man of unclean lips, and I live among a people of unclean lips; yet my eyes have seen the King, the LORD of hosts!"—*oy* [Isaiah 6:5]

Sympathetic warnings

Two are better than one, because they have a good reward for their toil. For if they fall, one will lift up the other; but **woe** to one who is alone and falls and does not have another to help.—*iy* [Ecclesiastes 4:9-10]

I looked, and a hand was stretched out to me, and a written scroll was in it. He spread it before me; it had writing on the front and on the back, and written on it were words of lamentation and mourning and **woe**.—*hi* [Ezekiel 2:9-10]

So when you see the desolating sacrilege standing in the holy place, as was spoken of by the prophet Daniel (let the reader understand), then those in Judea must flee to the mountains; . . .

Woe to those who are pregnant and to those who are nursing infants in those days! Pray that your flight may not be in winter or on a sabbath.—*ouai* [Matthew 24:15-16, 19-20]

If I proclaim the gospel, this gives me no ground for boasting, for an obligation is laid on me, and **woe** to me if I do not proclaim the gospel!—*ouai* [I Corinthians 9:16]

Denunciations and curses

For Jerusalem has stumbled and Judah has fallen, because their speech and their deeds are against the LORD, defying his glorious presence. The look on their faces bears witness against them; they proclaim their sin like Sodom, they do not hide it. **Woe** to them! For they have brought evil on themselves.—*oy* [Isaiah 3:8-9]

Woe to you who strive with your Maker, earthen vessels with the potter! Does the clay say to the one who fashions it, "What are you making?" or "Your work has no handles?" **Woe** to anyone who says to a father, "What are you begetting?" or to a woman, "With what are you in labor?"— *hoy* [Isaiah 45:9-10]

Woe to you, Chorazin! Woe to you, Bethsaida! For if the deeds of power done in you had been done in Tyre and Sidon, they would have repented long ago in sackcloth and ashes.—*ouai* [Matthew 11:21]

Woe to the world because of stumbling blocks! Occasions for stumbling are bound to come, but woe to the one by whom the stumbling block comes!—*ouai* [Matthew 18:7]

For the Son of Man goes as it is written of him, but **woe** to that one by whom the Son of Man is betrayed! It would have been better for that one not to have been born.—*ouai* [Mark 14:21]

Woe to you who are rich, for you have received your consolation. **Woe** to you who are full now, for you will be hungry. **Woe** to you who are laughing now, for you will mourn and weep. **Woe** to you when all speak well of you, for that is what their ancestors did to the false prophets.—*ouai* [Luke 6:24-26]

Sometimes the line between a sympathetic warning and a curse is not altogether clear, which is a problem for anyone using the woe metaphor in predicting a future calamity. Followers of Jesus have a problem in trying to decide if Jesus indulged in denunciations and curses or if he was always issuing friendly warnings. Some deal with the problem by deciding that Jesus could not have been cursing, so readers must be misinterpreting his words if they sound like curses to them. Others have decided if the words attributed to him were curses, they must have been made up by his followers because it would have been completely out of character for Jesus to talk like that. Still others rather like the picture of an angry Jesus denouncing the rich and powerful who oppress the poor and the weak.

woman—see **adam**

word, *noun*   Since the earliest days, the followers of Jesus have used word as a metaphor identifying both Jesus and the Bible.* To understand the nuances of the metaphor, it is necessary to appreciate the Hebrew *dabar*, which could mean either to speak or that which was spoken. It could also mean the result of what was spoken, that is, an event or a thing. To the ancients, words once uttered had inherent power,* as can be seen from their understanding of blessings* and of curses.* They

Marks a word in the text that has its own entry

understood all knowledge, insight, and wisdom* to have their source in the word of God that came to the chosen in dreams, visions,* and perceptions.

dabar, as to say or speak

Then God **said** to Noah, "Go out of the ark, you and your wife, and your sons and your sons' wives with you." [Genesis 8:15-16]

Ruth **said,** "May I continue to find favor in your sight, my lord, for you have comforted me and spoken kindly to your servant, even though I am not one of your servants." [Ruth 2:13]

Who is wise enough to understand this? To whom has the mouth of the LORD **spoken,** so that they may declare it? Why is the land ruined and laid waste like a wilderness, so that no one passes through? [Jeremiah 9:12]

At the end of the time that the king had set for them to be brought in, the palace master brought them into the presence of Nebuchadnezzar, and the king **spoke** with them. And among them all, no one was found to compare with Daniel, Hananiah, Mishael, and Azariah; therefore they were stationed in the king's court. [Daniel 1:18-19]

dabar, as that which was spoken

After these things the **word** of the LORD came to Abram in a vision, "Do not be afraid, Abram, I am your shield; your reward shall be very great." [Genesis 15:1]

When Ehud had finished presenting the tribute, he sent the people who carried the tribute on their way. But he himself turned back at the sculptured stones near Gilgal, and said, "I have a secret **message** for you, O king." So the king said, "Silence!" and all his attendants went out from his presence. [Judges 3:18-19]

Every **word** of God proves true; he is a shield to those who take refuge in him. Do not add to his **words,** or else he will rebuke you, and you will be found a liar. [Proverbs 30:5-6]

For as the rain and the snow come down from heaven, and do not return there until they have watered the earth, making it bring forth and sprout, giving seed to the sower and bread to the eater, so shall my **word** be that goes out from my mouth; it shall not return to me empty, but it shall accomplish that which I purpose, and succeed in the thing for which I sent it. [Isaiah 55:10-11]

The **words** of Amos, who was among the shepherds of Tekoa, which he saw concerning Israel in the days of King Uzziah of Judah and in the days of King Jeroboam son of Joash of Israel, two years before the earthquake. [Amos 1:1]

They made their hearts adamant in order not to hear the law and the **words** that the LORD of hosts had sent by his spirit through the former prophets. Therefore great wrath came from the LORD of hosts. [Zechariah 7:12]

dabar, as event or thing

The LORD said to Abraham, "Why did Sarah laugh, and say, 'Shall I indeed bear a child, now that I am old?' Is **anything** too wonderful for the LORD? At the set time I will return to you, in due season, and Sarah shall have a son." [Genesis 18:13-14]

The men said to Rahab, "Our life for yours! If you do not tell this **business** of ours, then we will deal kindly and faithfully with you when the LORD gives us the land." [Joshua 2:14]

When the townspeople rose early in the morning, the altar of Baal was broken down, and the sacred pole beside it was cut down, and the second bull was offered on the altar that had been built. So they said to one another, "Who has done **this**?" After searching and inquiring, they were told, "Gideon son of Joash did **it**." [Judges 6:28-29]

I persistently sent to you all my servants the prophets, saying, "I beg you not to do this abominable **thing** that I hate!" [Jeremiah 44:4]

The early followers of Jesus had two Greek words from which to choose in conveying the sense of *dabar* as a noun from the Hebrew tradition. One of the was *rema* and the other was *logos*. *Logos*, however, had an additional usage that was closer to the Hebrew *chokmah*, or wisdom.*

rema, as that which was spoken

Jesus answered, "It is written, 'One does not live by bread alone, but by every **word** that comes from the mouth of God.'" [Matthew 4:4]

If you are not listened to, take one or two others along with you, so that every **word** may be confirmed by the evidence of two or three witnesses. [Matthew 18:16]

He whom God has sent speaks the **words** of God, for he gives the Spirit without measure. [John 3:34]

Go, stand in the temple and tell the people the whole **message** about this life. [Acts 5:20]

So faith comes from what is heard, and what is heard comes through the **word** of Christ. But I ask, have they not heard? Indeed they have; for "Their voice has gone out to all the earth, and their **words** to the ends of the world." [Romans 10:17-18]

rema, as event or thing

Now, your relative Elizabeth in her old age has also conceived a son; and this is the sixth month for her who was said to be barren. For **nothing** will be impossible with God. [Luke 1:36-37]

When the angels had left them and gone into heaven, the shepherds said to one another, "Let us go now to Bethlehem and see this **thing** that has taken place, which the Lord has made known to us." [Luke 2:15]

We are witnesses to these **things**, and so is the Holy Spirit whom God has given to those who obey him. [Acts 5:32]

I know that such a person—whether in the body or out of the body I do not know; God knows— was caught up into Paradise and heard **things** that are not to be told, that no mortal is permitted to repeat. [II Corinthians 12:3-4]

logos, as that which was spoken

Everyone then who hears these **words** of mine and acts on them will be like a wise man who built his house on rock. [Matthew 7:24]

Those who are ashamed of me and of my **words** in this adulterous and sinful generation, of them the Son of Man will also be ashamed when he comes in the glory of his Father with the holy angels. [Mark 8:38]

Once while Jesus was standing beside the lake of Gennesaret, and the crowd was pressing in on him to hear the **word** of God, he saw two boats there at the shore of the lake; the fishermen had gone out of them and were washing their nets. [Luke 5:1-2]

The **message** about the cross is foolishness to those who are perishing, but to us who are being saved it is the power of God. [I Corinthians 1:18]

We have renounced the shameful things that one hides; we refuse to practice cunning or to falsify God's **word**; but by the open statement of the truth we commend ourselves to the conscience of everyone in the sight of God. [II Corinthians 4:2]

logos, as event or thing

I say to you that anyone who divorces his wife, except on the **ground** of unchastity, causes her to commit adultery; and whoever marries a divorced woman commits adultery. [Matthew 5:32]

They kept the **matter** to themselves, questioning what this rising from the dead could mean. [Mark 9:10]

I too decided, after investigating everything carefully from the very first, to write an orderly account for you, most excellent Theophilus, so that you may know the truth concerning the **things** about which you have been instructed. [Luke 1:3-4]

logos, as wisdom

In the beginning was the **Word**, and the **Word** was with God, and the **Word** was God. He was in the beginning with God. All things came into being through him, and without him not one thing came into being ... And the **Word** became flesh and lived among us, and we have seen his glory, the glory as of a father's only son, full of grace and truth. [John 1:1-3, 14]

We declare to you what was from the beginning, what we have heard, what we have seen with our eyes, what we have looked at and touched with our hands, concerning the **word** of life. [I John 1:1]

Then I saw heaven opened, and there was a white horse! Its rider is called Faithful and True, and in righteousness he judges and makes war. His eyes are like a flame of fire, and on his head are many diadems; and he has a name inscribed that no one knows but himself. He is clothed in a robe dipped in blood, and his name is called The **Word** of God. [Revelation 19:11-13]

Not everyone agrees that the authors of these last two passages were using *logos* to mean what it does in the first chapter of John's gospel, but Christians have employed the passages as part of a long-standing tradition relating Jesus to wisdom personified in Proverbs chapter 8 and to the writings of philosophers who expanded on the idea of wisdom being the divine pattern and power present in the material world.

For present-day followers of Jesus to evaluate the word metaphor, they first must make a distinction between word as a figure of speech identifying Jesus and as a figure of speech gathering up knowledge and insight associated with God.

Logos can be a useful metaphor in regard to Jesus if those who use the term keep in mind that it says more about them than about Jesus. Trying to be logical about the identification of Jesus with the preexistent Word of God has led to trouble in the past. Such philosophizing produced bloodshed in the fourth century when "there was a time when he was not" became a battle cry for those who opposed the idea. As a subjective image, however, *logos* can allow a person to articulate how

Jesus, through his life and teachings, helps to make sense of existence, which is perceived through history and science as well as through immediate experience.

People who regularly attend Christian worship services are familiar with the phrases the Word of God and the Word of the Lord used in association with readings from the Bible. For some, the word metaphor used in this context is simply a reminder of a long tradition associating knowledge and insight with openness to divine wisdom. The metaphor calls worshipers to pay attention and to ponder the readings found in the ancient texts. The repeated use of the phrases the Word of God and the Word of the Lord, however, have reinforced the idea in some Christians that the words being read in worship are to be taken literally as if dictated by God directly into the ears of the authors and editors whose works constitute the Bible. Although many of them find the idea of the Bible as the literal word of God to be quite attractive, others find that this position creates a barrier to their appreciation of what the ancient texts might have to say that would be relevant to the twenty-first-century mind.

worship, *noun* and *verb*   In addition to words for sacrifice,* Hebrew and Greek use a number of words translated as worship.

Hebrew

Then Abraham said to his young men, "Stay here with the donkey; the boy and I will go over there; we will **worship**, and then we will come back to you."—*shachah*, to prostrate oneself [Genesis 22:5]

God said, "I will be with you; and this shall be the sign for you that it is I who sent you: when you have brought the people out of Egypt, you shall **worship** God on this mountain."—*abad*, to work for [Exodus 3:12]

For the LORD has made the Jordan a boundary between us and you, you Reubenites and Gadites; you have no portion in the LORD. So your children might make our children cease to **worship** the LORD.—*yare*, to fear* [Joshua 22:25]

When the adversaries of Judah and Benjamin heard that the returned exiles were building a temple to the LORD, the God of Israel, they approached Zerubbabel and the heads of families and said to them, "Let us build with you, for we **worship** your God as you do, and we have been sacrificing to him ever since the days of King Esar-haddon of Assyria who brought us here."—*darash*, to follow [Ezra 4:1-2]

The Lord said: Because these people draw near with their mouths and honor me with their lips, while their hearts are far from me, and their **worship** of me is a human commandment learned by rote.—*yirah*, fear, noun form of the verb *yare* [Isaiah 29:13]

What is in your mind shall never happen—the thought, "Let us be like the nations, like the tribes of the countries, and **worship** wood and stone."—*sharath*, to serve [Ezekiel 20:32]

Then King Nebuchadnezzar fell on his face, **worshiped** Daniel, and commanded that a grain offering and incense be offered to him.—*segid*, to prostrate oneself [Daniel 2:46]

Those who **worship** vain idols forsake their true loyalty.—*shamar*, to guard [Jonah 2:8]

Greek

Suddenly Jesus met them and said, "Greetings!" And they came to him, took hold of his feet, and **worshiped** him.—*proskyneo*, to crouch like a dog, from *kyon*, dog [Matthew 28:9]

There was also a prophet, Anna the daughter of Phanuel, of the tribe of Asher. She was of a great age, having lived with her husband seven years after her marriage, then as a widow to the age of eighty-four. She never left the temple but **worshiped** there with fasting and prayer night and day.—*latreuo*, to serve [Luke 2:36-37]

They will put you out of the synagogues. Indeed, an hour is coming when those who kill you will think that by doing so they are offering **worship** to God.—*latreia*, service, noun form of *latreuo* [John 16:2]

Now in the church at Antioch there were prophets and teachers: Barnabas, Simeon who was called Niger, Lucius of Cyrene, Manaen a member of the court of Herod the ruler, and Saul. While they were **worshiping** the Lord and fasting, the Holy Spirit said, "Set apart for me Barnabas and Saul for the work to which I have called them."—*leitourgeo*, to render public service (see **liturgy**) [Acts 13:1-2]

This people honors me with their lips, but their hearts are far from me; in vain do they **worship** me, teaching human precepts as doctrines.—*sebomai*, to revere [Matthew 15:8-9]

For as I went through the city and looked carefully at the objects of your **worship**, I found among them an altar with the inscription, "To an unknown god." What therefore you **worship** as unknown, this I proclaim to you.—*sebasma*, something adored, and *eusebeo*, to be pious (see **religion**), both from the same root as *sebomai* [Acts 17:23]

They exchanged the truth about God for a lie and **worshiped** and served the creature rather than the Creator, who is blessed forever! Amen.—*sebazomai*, to venerate [Romans 1:25]

Do not let anyone disqualify you, insisting on self-abasement and **worship** of angels, dwelling on visions, puffed up without cause by a human way of thinking.—*threskeia*, religious cult (see **religion**) [Colossians 2:18]

From these examples, it appears that the ancients would recognize little of what most Christians do on Sunday mornings as worship.* Most Christians do not fall on their faces, unless overcome by emotion. They do not prostrate themselves, except as a prelude to ordination. They do not crouch like dogs, licking the master's hands or feet. They do not exhibit fear. Unless you count hymn singing as an expenditure of energy, they do no work, nor do they serve God in any visible way.

Worship in English has a different meaning from most of the biblical metaphors. The word was formed from worth + ship. Worship acknowledges a condition of being worthy. Traditionally, worship meant treating another with respect and honor. The other could be a human being or a god. The Greek words *sebomai* and *sebazomai*, both derived from *sebo*, are the only biblical words at all close to the English understanding of worship. The other metaphors are useful primarily as an indication of an attitude toward a relationship with God.

---

*Marks a word in the text that has its own entry

Y

Yahweh—see lord

yeast, *noun*   Among the first organisms domesticated by human beings were several forms of fungus known collectively in English as yeast or leaven. Evidence suggests that by 6000 BCE, people in Sumeria, Babylonia, and Egypt were using yeast in the brewing of beer, the making of wine,* and the baking of bread.* Although the baking of leavened bread had been known among the ancient Israelites for centuries before any of the Hebrew Scriptures began to take shape, some of the rituals described in Exodus and Leviticus may hearken back to a time when their primary diet consisted of unleavened bread. In such rituals, the presence of yeast was taboo. In all probability, these primitive customs became entangled with the later traditions of the unleavened bread being a symbol of the hurried escape from Egypt. Hebrew had two words for yeast and leaven: *se'or* and *chametz*.

> No grain offering that you bring to the LORD shall be made with **leaven** (*chametz*), for you must not turn any **leaven** (*se'or*) or honey into smoke as an offering by fire to the LORD. You may bring them to the LORD as an offering of choice products, but they shall not be offered on the altar for a pleasing odor. [Leviticus 2:11-12]

> Seven days you shall eat unleavened bread; on the first day you shall remove **leaven** (*se'or*) from your houses, for whoever eats **leavened** (*chametz*) bread from the first day until the seventh day shall be cut off from Israel . . . You shall observe the festival of unleavened bread, for on this very day I brought your companies out of the land of Egypt: you shall observe this day throughout your generations as a perpetual ordinance. [Exodus 12:15, 17]

In spite of leavened bread's popularity, yeast as a figure of speech had negative connotations. For example, in rabbinic writings, leaven in the dough was a metaphor for the human inclination toward evil.* Perhaps the negative attitudes toward leaven were the result of the mysterious, therefore frightening, nature of fermentation. Perhaps the reason was the association they made between fermentation and putrefaction. Christians generally followed this line of thought in their use of the Greek *zyme*, the root of our English word enzyme. Paul used yeast as a negative metaphor, and the gospels attribute to Jesus its use in casting aspersions on the Pharisees.*

> Let us celebrate the festival, not with the old **yeast**, the **yeast** of malice and evil, but with the unleavened bread of sincerity and truth. [I Corinthians 5:8]

> You were running well; who prevented you from obeying the truth? Such persuasion does not come from the one who calls you. A little **yeast** leavens the whole batch of dough. I am confident about you in the Lord that you will not think otherwise. But whoever it is that is confusing you will pay the penalty. [Galatians 5:7-10]

> Jesus cautioned them, saying, "Watch out—beware of the **yeast** of the Pharisees and the yeast of Herod." [Mark 8:15]

Given the consistently negative connotations of the yeast metaphor, Jesus would have shocked any audience by using it in a one-line parable* describing the kingdom* of heaven. To associate the realm of God with a verbal image of malice and evil would have been little short of blasphemy,* but it would have been in keeping with the tradition that Jesus told parables to shock people into new ways of thinking.

                                            *Marks a word in the text that has its own entry

Jesus told them another parable: "The kingdom of heaven is like **yeast** that a woman took and mixed in with three measures of flour until all of it was leavened." [Matthew 13:33]

Perhaps because of the gospels' influence on western thought, yeast has in recent times generally appeared as a positive metaphor suggesting that a large group can be energized by the enthusiasm of a few people. Christians who use the metaphor today, however, need to be sure that their context makes clear whether they are using yeast in a positive or negative sense.

DID YOU KNOW . . .

. . . that *zyme* is pronounced *zoo-may*?
For more help with pronunciation, see "Pronouncing
Transliterated Hebrew and Greek Words" on page 15.

---

yoke, *noun* and *verb*   The English word yoke has two distinct meanings, each with its own imagery for metaphors.

A yoke can be a bar, usually made of wood, fitted on the necks of two animals and attached to a farm implement or conveyance. The yoke makes possible the use of the combined strength of two animals—usually oxen, or horses, or mules. As metaphor, yoke can be used to identify two animals that have been paired for work, even if they are not physically linked at the moment. The same metaphor, either as a noun or a verb, can be used of human beings who have been linked for a specific task.

A yoke can also be frame fitted to the neck and shoulders of a single human being. Pails or baskets are suspended from the frame, which extends slightly beyond the shoulders. This device can enable an individual to carry loads far in excess of what is possible to carry by hand. The individual sort of yoke can be used as a metaphor indicating responsibility, obligation, servitude, or slavery.*

Hebrew has three words that are translated yoke. In both its literal and figurative sense, *ol* is used much like its English equivalent; it can mean the bar linking two animals or the bar worn by an individual human being. The bar itself, exclusive of its fittings, is called *motah,* which is the word for any wooden pole. The third word, *tsemed,* literally means paired or coupled. Because *tsemed* does not appear as a metaphor in the Hebrew Scriptures, we will concentrate on the other two Hebrew words for yoke.

ol in the literal sense

Now then, get ready a new cart and two milch cows that have never borne a **yoke,** and **yoke** the cows to the cart, but take their calves home, away from them. [I Samuel 6:7]

This is a statute of the law that the LORD has commanded: Tell the Israelites to bring you a red heifer without defect, in which there is no blemish and on which no **yoke** has been laid. [Numbers 19:2]

ol as metaphor

By your sword you shall live, and you shall serve your brother; but when you break loose, you shall break his **yoke** from your neck. [Genesis 27:40]

---

*Marks a word in the text that has its own entry

I am the LORD your God who brought you out of the land of Egypt, to be their slaves no more; I have broken the bars *(motah)* of your **yoke** and made you walk erect. [Leviticus 26:13]

Jeroboam and all the assembly of Israel came and said to Rehoboam, "Your father made our **yoke** heavy. Now therefore lighten the hard service of your father and his heavy **yoke** that he placed on us, and we will serve you." [I Kings 12:3-4]

I will break the Assyrian in my land, and on my mountains trample him under foot; his **yoke** shall be removed from them, and his burden from their shoulders. [Isaiah 14:25]

motah in the literal sense

The Levites carried the ark of God on their shoulders with the **poles**, as Moses had commanded according to the word of the LORD. [I Chronicles 15:15]

Thus the LORD said to me: Make yourself a **yoke** of straps and bars, and put them on your neck . . . Then the prophet Hananiah took the **yoke** from the neck of the prophet Jeremiah, and broke it. [Jeremiah 27:2, 28:10]

motah as metaphor

Is not this the fast that I choose: to loose the bonds of injustice, to undo the thongs of the **yoke**, to let the oppressed go free, and to break every **yoke**? [Isaiah 58:6]

Go, tell Hananiah, Thus says the LORD: You have broken wooden **bars** only to forge iron **bars** in place of them! [Jeremiah 28:13]

The trees of the field shall yield their fruit, and the earth shall yield its increase. They shall be secure on their soil; and they shall know that I am the LORD, when I break the **bars** of their yoke *(ol)*, and save them from the hands of those who enslaved them. [Ezekiel 34:27]

If you look at the excerpts from the Jeremiah story quoted above, you will see how a metaphor could become a concrete symbol. In trying to get the attention of the people, Jeremiah engages in what is sometimes called guerilla theater. He makes a common figure of speech into a prop for his performance. In all probability, the Jeremiah story influenced the use of the yoke metaphor among the followers of Jesus.

The Greek word for yoke used by the early Christians is *zygos,* which literally meant a coupling. (*Zygos* is the root of the English word zygote, the union of a sperm and an egg.) Like the words yoke and *ol,* in the literal sense *zygos* could mean either the device for linking two draft animals or the one borne on the neck and shoulders of a human being.

zygos as metaphor

Take my **yoke** upon you, and learn from me; for I am gentle and humble in heart, and you will find rest for your souls. For my **yoke** is easy, and my burden is light. [Matthew 11:29-30]

Now therefore why are you putting God to the test by placing on the neck of the disciples a **yoke** that neither our ancestors nor we have been able to bear? [Acts 15:10]

For freedom Christ has set us free. Stand firm, therefore, and do not submit again to a **yoke** of slavery. [Galatians 5:1]

Let all who are under the **yoke** of slavery regard their masters as worthy of all honor, so that the name of God and the teaching may not be blasphemed. [I Timothy 6:1]

Most people in the industrial world have never seen either kind of a yoke in use. They may have seen a yoke in a museum or hanging on the wall for decoration in a rustic bar or restaurant, but the yoke metaphor is not likely to carry with it the emotional content that it would have had for the people Jeremiah and Jesus were teaching. Metaphors related to weight, however, are still used and understood: load, baggage, burden, and freight. Note that in the Matthew passage quoted above, yoke is paired with burden. This metaphor, in Greek *phortion,* seems to have about the same meaning as *zygos.*

phortion as a metaphor similar to *zygos*

They tie up heavy **burdens,** hard to bear, and lay them on the shoulders of others; but they themselves are unwilling to lift a finger to move them. [Matthew 23:4]

Jesus said, "Woe also to you lawyers! For you load people with **burdens** hard to bear, and you yourselves do not lift a finger to ease them." [Luke 11:46]

All must test their own work; then that work, rather than their neighbor's work, will become a cause for pride. For all must carry their own **loads.** [Galatians 6:4-5]

Although yoke and burden can be understood as parallel metaphors in the teaching that Matthew attributes to Jesus, the modifying adjectives that accompany them in Greek have quite different connotations. The modifier for burden is *elaphros,* which in this context can only mean light, but the yoke of Jesus is said to be *chrestos,* which means useful, suitable, worthy, or good. This description is a complete reversal of every other figurative use of yoke in the Bible. The yoke from Jesus is not to be resented, broken, or laid aside but happily accepted. To live well, every person needs a sense of obligation and a willingness to serve but not such as will become a crushing burden of compulsive behavior or of guilt.* The yoke from Jesus is useful, and the load attached is not too heavy to carry.

Z

zeal—see **jealous**

Zion—see **Jerusalem**

INDEX TO THE HEBREW AND GREEK WORDS

Note: This is not a quick reference dictionary.
The English words may not be the equivalents of the
Hebrew and Greek words to which they are linked in the text.

HEBREW

INDEX TO OTHER FOREIGN WORDS

ENDNOTES

1.   William Safire, "On Language," *New York Times Magazine*, February 27, 2005, p. 38. [**Dedication**]

2.   John Brehm, "Sea of Faith," in David Lehman, ed., *The Best American Poetry 1999* (New York: Scribner, 1999), p. 45. [**Introduction**]

3.   James Strong (1822-1894) was a Methodist minister and professor of exegetical theology at Drew Theological Seminary. Strong spent more than 35 years directing the preparation of the landmark concordance that bears his name. First published in 1890, *Strong's Concordance of the Bible* remains the most widely used concordance and dictionary of Bible words from the King James Version of the Bible. [**Using This Book**]

4.   Thomas Henry Huxley, "Agnosticism" (1889), Collected Essays V, *The Huxley File* (Internet site created by Charles Blinderman and David Joyce, Clark University, 1998). [**agnostic**]

5.   Martyn Percy, *Power and the Church* (London: Cassell, 1998), p. 47. [**ambassador**]

6.   David Rosenberg and Harold Bloom, *The Book of J* (New York: Vintage, 1991), p. 3. [**Bible**]

7.   Robert F. Funk, Roy W. Hoover, and the Jesus Seminar, *The Five Gospels* (New York: Macmillan, 1993), pp. 471-532. [**Bible**]

8.   Clifton Fadiman, introduction to Stanislaw Jerzy Lec, *Unkempt Thoughts* (London: Minerva Press, 1962). [**blessed**]

9.   Bruno Bettelheim, *Symbolic Wounds—Puberty Rites and the Envious Male* (Glencoe, IL: Free Press, 1954). [**circumcise**]

10. From a letter by Charles Darwin to Asa Gray, quoted by Janet Browne, *Charles Darwin—The Power or Place, Volume II of a Biography* (New York: Alfred Knopf, 2002), p. 176. [**create**]

11. Michael Dirda, "Readings," *The Washington Post*, Book World, January 21, 1996. [**death**]

12. Rudolph Otto, translated by John W. Havery, *The Idea of the Holy* (New York: A Galaxy Book, 1958), pp. 12-30 (first published, 1923). [**holy**]

13. Sandy Havens, Emeritus Professor of Theatre at Rice University. [**house**]

14. Frank McCourt, *Angela's Ashes* (New York: Scribner, 1996), p. 128. [**Jew**]

15. C. S. Lewis, *The Lion, the Witch and the Wardrobe* (London: Geoffrey Bles, 1950). [**lion**]

16. Moses Cordovera (1522-76), quoted by Isidore Epstein, *Judaism* (Baltimore: Penguin Books, 1959), p. 244. [**panentheism**]

17. Gordon McBride, *Flying to Tombstone* (Baltimore: Publish America, 2002), pp. 130-131. [**panentheism**]

18. Karen Armstrong, *A History of God* (New York: Alfred A. Knopf, 1993), see especially pp. 352-353. [**panentheism**]

19. Bernard Brandon Scott, from a lecture reported in *AXIAL*, the journal of the SnowStar Institute of Religion, Winter 2004, p. 5. Bernard Brandon Scott, *Re-Imagine the World: An Introduction to the Parables of Jesus* (Santa Rosa, CA: Polebridge Press, 2001). [**parable**]

20. Charles W. F. Smith, *The Jesus of the Parables* (Philadelphia: Westminster Press, 1948), p. 17. [**parable**]

21. For more on skeptics at prayer, see James R. Adams, *So You Think You're Not Religious?* (Cambridge, MA: Cowley Publications, 1989), pp. 80-106. [**pray**]

22. Steven Weinberg, quoted by William J. Broad and James Glanz, "Does Science Matter?" *The New York Times, Science Times*, November 11, 2003. [religion]

23. William Temple, *What Christians Stand For in the Secular World* (Minneapolis: Fortress Press, 1963), p. 6. [religion]

24. Dale C. Allison, Jr., "What was the Star that Guided the Magi? *Bible Review*, December 1993, pp. 21-24, 63. [star]

25. Walter Wink, *Naming the Powers* (Philadelphia: Fortress Press, 1984), p. 20. [throne]

26. R. H. Tawney, *Religion and the Rise of Capitalism* (New York: Mentor Books, 1947), p. 39 (first published by Harcourt, Brace and Company, 1926). [usury]

27. Robert J. Miller, *Born Divine—The Births of Jesus and Other Sons of God* (Santa Rosa, CA: Polebridge Press, 2003). [virgin birth]

28. Plutarch, "Life of Alexander," *Born Divine*, p. 138. [virgin birth]

29. Dio Cassius, "History of Rome," *Born Divine*, pp. 140-141. [virgin birth]